To: Brother Erwin

May each day of this year and every year be blessed, knowing that their is a loving Savior in Heaven who gave all for you.

Day by day, Keep your eyes on Jesus and He will strengthen you to overcome anything and make it through anything.

from your brother in Christ,

-Bro. Murice

LIFT HIM UP

To order additional copies of *Lift Him Up,* or other books by Ellen G. White, call 1-800-765-6955.

Visit us at **www.reviewandherald.com** for information on other **Review and Herald® products.**

Fresh reasons to praise our Savior every day of the year

LIFT HIM UP

Ellen G. White

REVIEW AND HERALD® PUBLISHING ASSOCIATION
Since 1861 | www.reviewandherald.com

Cover designed by Haley Trimmer
Cover art by istockphoto.com
Typeset: Bembo 11.5/13

PRINTED IN U.S.A.

15 14 13 12 11 5 4 3 2 1

Library of Congress Cataloging-in-Publication Data
White, Ellen Gould Harmon, 1827-1915.
Lift Him up / Ellen G. White.
p. cm.
1. Devotional calendars—Seventh-Day Adventists. 2. Seventh-Day Adventist—Prayers and devotions. I. Title.
BV4811.W485 2011
242'.2—dc22

2011011761

ISBN 978-0-8280-2579-9

Foreword

Where can we find a more descriptive and appealing picture of the character of God as seen through Jesus Christ than that painted by Ellen White? Her inspired pen, dipped continually in the bottomless well of the love of God, portrays the goodness, kindness, and interest of the family of heaven in us. As we read these descriptions, our hearts cannot help responding enthusiastically to our God who loves us so. We feel constrained to echo the message sounded frequently by Ellen White: "Lift up Jesus, the Man of Calvary. Lift Him up in prayer, lift Him up in song." "Lift Him up, the Man of Calvary, higher and still higher, and let your message be, 'Behold the Lamb of God, which taketh away the sin of the world'" (manuscript 27, 1891; letter 174, 1896).

In this collection of Ellen White's pen pictures of our loving Savior and what He means to us, we are drawn to Him in a special way. You will want to read these devotional readings thoughtfully, and review them often, fixing them firmly in the halls of memory.

Ellen White tells us in these pages that "it is impossible for finite minds to make a just estimate of the love of God toward His fallen creatures. We are ever in danger of forgetting this great love, because we fail to meditate upon it, and allow ourselves to become absorbed in the things of this world. . . . Christ should be the theme of our thoughts, the object of our tenderest affection. We should let our minds dwell upon the precious characteristics of our Lord; we should contemplate the rich promises of His Word; we should meditate upon the glories of heaven" (*Signs of the Times*, Dec. 8, 1890).

Jesus was born in a manger that we might be born to life eternal. He became part of the human family that we might become part of the heavenly family. He lived in the midst of dust and poverty that we might live amid riches beyond description. He spent long nights in prayer that we might spend eternal ages in the presence of God. He went homeless that we might live in mansions He is preparing for us. Our precious Savior trod wearily the sandy trails of old Palestine that we might walk with tireless feet on the golden streets of the New Jerusalem. He accepted in our behalf the crown of thorns that He might be able to place on our heads the crowns of victory. He died the death that was ours that we might live forever the glorious life that is His.

This volume is about Jesus Christ. It exalts Him as our divine Savior and Redeemer, the source of our every blessing, and our only hope. That it may lift up Christ so effectively that every reader will have a closer, more rewarding walk with Him is the earnest prayer of

—*The Trustees of the Ellen G. White Estate, Silver Spring, Maryland*

The Author*

Ellen Gould (Harmon) White, cofounder of the Seventh-day Adventist Church, writer, lecturer, and counselor, and one upon whom Seventh-day Adventists believe the gift of prophecy was bestowed, was born in Gorham, Maine, November 26, 1827, one of eight children of Robert and Eunice Harmon.

During her 70 years of active service to the church, she found time to write voluminously. She is credited with having written 100,000 manuscript pages. This remarkable legacy to the church could alone have occupied Ellen White's entire life, had she dedicated her time to little else but writing.

However, her service for the church embraces much more than writing. Her diaries tell of her public work, her travels, her personal labor, hostessing, contacts with neighbors, as well as of her being a mother and housewife. God blessed her abundantly in these activities. Her ambitions and concerns, her satisfactions and joys, her sorrows—her whole life—were for the advancement of the cause she loved.

Ellen G. White is reputed to be the most translated woman author and the most translated author in American history. For example, her little book *Steps to Christ* is available in more than 100 languages.

After a full life dedicated to the service of God and others, she died on July 16, 1915, confidently trusting in Him whom she had believed.

---

* This page and the biographical notes on the following pages have been reproduced from *The Upward Look* (1982), pp. 7-13.

Biographical Notes

Ellen G. White, 1827-1915

The Early Years, 1827-1860

Born on a late fall day in a farmhouse near Gorham, Maine, Ellen Harmon spent her childhood and youth in nearby Portland. She married James White in 1846, and the struggling young couple lived in a variety of New England locations as they sought to encourage and instruct fellow Advent believers by their preaching, visiting, and publishing. After 11 irregular issues of *The Present Truth,* they launched the *Second Advent Review and Sabbath Herald** in Paris, Maine, in 1850. Thereafter they followed a steadily westward course—to Saratoga Springs, New York, and then Rochester, New York, in the early 1850s, and finally, in 1855, to Battle Creek, Michigan, where they resided for the next 20 years.

1827, November 26	Born at Gorham, Maine.
1836 (c.)	Broken nose and concussion at Portland, Maine.
1840, March	First heard William Miller present the Advent message.
1842, June 26	Baptized and accepted into Methodist Church.
1844, October 22	Disappointed when Christ did not come.
1844, December	First vision.
1845, Spring	Trip to eastern Maine to visit believers; met James White.
1846, August 30	Married James White.
1846, Autumn	Accepted seventh-day Sabbath.
1847-1848	Set up housekeeping at Topsham, Maine.
1847, August 26	Birth of first son, Henry Nichols.
1848, April 20-24	Attended first conference of Sabbathkeeping Adventists at Rocky Hill, Connecticut.
1848, November 18	Vision to begin publishing work—"Streams of Light."
1849, July	First of 11 numbers of *The Present Truth,* published as a result of the vision of November 1848.
1849, July 28	Birth of James Edson, second son.
1849-1852	Moved from place to place with her publisher-husband.
1851, July	First book published, A *Sketch of Experience and Views.*
1852-1855	In Rochester, New York, where husband published *Review and Herald* and *Youth's Instructor.*
1854, August 29	Third son, William Clarence, born.
1855, November	Moved with the publishing plant to Battle Creek, Michigan.
1855, December	"Testimony for the Church," number 1, a 16-page pamphlet, published.

1856, Spring	Moved into their own cottage on Wood Street.
1858, March 14	"Great Controversy" vision at Lovett's Grove, Ohio.
1860, September 20	Fourth son, John Herbert, born.
1860, December 14	Death of John Herbert at three months.

Years of Church Development, 1860-1868

The 1860s saw Ellen White and her husband in the forefront of the struggle to organize the Seventh-day Adventist Church into a stable institution. The decade was also crucial in that it encompassed the beginnings of Adventist health emphasis. Responding to Mrs. White's appeal, the church as a body began to see the importance of healthful living in the Christian life. In response to her "Christmas Vision" of 1865, our first health institution, the Western Health Reform Institute, was opened in 1866. The institute later grew into the Battle Creek Sanitarium.

1860, September 29	Name Seventh-day Adventist chosen.
1861, October 8	Michigan Conference organized.
1863, May	Organization of General Conference of Seventh-day Adventists.
1863, June 6	Health reform vision at Otsego, Michigan.
1863, December 8	Death of eldest son, Henry Nichols, at Topsham, Maine.
1864, Summer	Publication of *Spiritual Gifts,* volume 4, with 30-page article on health.
1864, August-September	Visit to James C. Jackson's medical institution, Our Home on the Hillside, Dansville, New York, en route to Boston, Massachusetts.
1865	Publication of six pamphlets, *Health: or How to Live.*
1865, August 16	James White stricken with paralysis.
1865, December 25	Vision calling for a medical institution.
1865, December	Mrs. White takes James White to northern Michigan as an aid to his recovery.
1866, September 5	Opening of Western Health Reform Institute, forerunner of Battle Creek Sanitarium.
1867	Purchased a farm at Greenville, Michigan, and built a home and engaged in farming and writing.

The Camp Meeting Years, 1868-1881

Residing at Greenville and Battle Creek, Michigan, respectively, until late 1872, and then dividing her time between Michigan and California, Ellen White spent her winters writing and publishing. During the summer she attended camp meetings, some years as many as 28! *Testimonies,* numbers 14-30, now found in *Testimonies,* volumes 2-4, were published during these years.

1868, September 1-7	Attended first SDA camp meeting, held in Brother Root's maple grove at Wright, Michigan.
1870, July 28	Second son, James Edson, married on his twenty-first birthday.
1870	*The Spirit of Prophecy,* volume 1, published; forerunner of *Patriarchs and Prophets.*
1872, July-September	In Rocky Mountains resting and writing en route to California.
1873-1874	Divided time between Battle Creek and California, attended camp meetings, and spent some months in 1873 in Colorado resting and writing.
1874, April 1	Comprehensive vision of the advance of the cause in California, Oregon, and overseas.
1874, June	With James White in Oakland, California, as he founded the Pacific Press Publishing Association and the *Signs of the Times.*
1875, January 3	At Battle Creek for dedication of Battle Creek College. Vision of publishing houses in other countries.
1876, February 11	William Clarence, third son and manager of the Pacific Press, married at the age of 21.
1876, August	Spoke to 20,000 at Groveland, Massachusetts, camp meeting.
1877	*The Spirit of Prophecy*, volume 2, published; forerunner of *The Desire of Ages*.
1877, July 1	Spoke to 5,000 at Battle Creek on temperance.
1878	*The Spirit of Prophecy,* volume 3, published; forerunner of last part of *The Desire of Ages,* and *The Acts of the Apostles.*
1878, November	Spent the winter in Texas.
1879, April	Left Texas to engage in the summer camp meeting work.
1881, August 1	With husband in Battle Creek when he was taken ill.
1881, August 6	Death of James White.
1881, August 13	Spoke for 10 minutes at James White's funeral at Battle Creek.

The 1880s, 1881-1891

Following James White's death in August 1881, Ellen White resided in California, at times in Healdsburg and at times in Oakland. She labored there, writing and speaking, until she left for Europe in August 1885, in response to the call of the General Conference. During the two years in Europe she resided in Basel, Switzerland, except for three extended visits to the Scandinavian countries, England, and Italy. Returning to the United States in August 1887, she soon made her way west to her Healdsburg home. She attended the 1888 General Conference session at Minneapolis in October and November; following the conference, while residing in Battle Creek, she worked among the churches in the Midwest and the East. After a year in the East she returned to California, but was called back to attend the General Conference session at Battle Creek in October 1889. She remained in the vicinity of Battle Creek until she left for Australia in September 1891.

1881, November	Attended the California camp meeting at Sacramento and participated in planning for a college in the West, which opened in 1882 at Healdsburg.
1882	*Early Writings* published, incorporating three of her early books.
1884	Last recorded public vision, at Portland, Oregon, camp meeting.
1884	*The Spirit of Prophecy,* volume 4, published; forerunner of *The Great Controversy.*
1885, Summer	Left California for trip to Europe.
1887, Summer	*The Great Controversy* published.
1888, October-November	Attended Minneapolis General Conference session.
1889	*Testimonies,* volume 5, published, embodying *Testimonies,* numbers 31-33—746 pages.
1890	*Patriarchs and Prophets* published.
1891, September 12	Sailed to Australia via Honolulu.

The Australian Years, 1891-1900

Responding to the call of the General Conference to visit Australia to aid in establishing an educational work, Ellen White arrived in Sydney, December 8, 1891. She accepted the invitation somewhat reluctantly, for she had wanted to get on with her writing of a larger book on the life of Christ. Soon after her arrival she was stricken with inflammatory rheumatism, which confined her to her bed for some eight months. Although suffering intensely, she persisted in writing. In early 1893 she went to New Zealand, where she worked until the end of the year. Returning to Australia in late December, she attended the first Australian camp meeting. At this camp meeting, plans for a rural school were developed that resulted in the establishment of what became Avondale College at Cooranbong, 90 miles north of Sydney. Ellen White purchased land nearby and built her Sunnyside home late in 1895. Here she resided, giving her attention to her writing and traveling among the churches until she returned to the United States in August 1900.

1892, June	Spoke at opening of Australian Bible School in two rented buildings in Melbourne.
1892	*Steps to Christ* and *Gospel Workers* published.
1894, January	Joined in planning for a permanent school in Australia.
1894, May 23	Visited the Cooranbong site.
1895, December	Moved to her Sunnyside home at Cooranbong, where much of *The Desire of Ages* was written.
1896	*Thoughts From the Mount of Blessing* published.
1898	*The Desire of Ages* published.
1899-1900	Encouraged the establishment of Sydney Sanitarium.
1900	*Christ's Object Lessons* published.
1900, August	Left Australia and returned to United States.

The Elmshaven Years, 1900-1915

When Ellen White settled at Elmshaven, her new home near St. Helena in northern California, she hoped to give most of her time to writing her books. She was 72 and still had a number of volumes that she wished to complete. She little realized how much traveling, counseling, and speaking she would also be called upon to do. The crisis created by the controversies in Battle Creek would also make heavy demands on her time and strength. Even so, by writing early in the morning, she was able to produce nine books during her Elmshaven years.

1900, October	Settled at Elmshaven.
1901, April	Attended the General Conference session at Battle Creek.
1902, February 18	Battle Creek Sanitarium fire.
1902, December 30	Review and Herald fire.
1903, October	Met the pantheism crisis.
1904, April-September	Journeyed east to assist in the beginning of the work in Washington, D.C., to visit her son Edson in Nashville, and to attend important meetings.
1904, November-December	Involved in securing and establishing Paradise Valley Sanitarium.
1905, May	Attended General Conference session in Washington, D.C.
1905	*The Ministry of Healing* published.
1905, June-December	Involved in securing and starting Loma Linda Sanitarium.
1906-1908	Busy at Elmshaven with literary work.
1909, April-September	At the age of 81 traveled to Washington, D.C., to attend the General Conference session. This was her last trip east.
1910, January	Took a prominent part in the establishment of the College

	of Medical Evangelists at Loma Linda.
1910	Gave attention to finishing *The Acts of the Apostles* and the reissuance of *The Great Controversy,* a work extending into 1911.
1911-1915	With advancing age, made only a few trips to southern California. At Elmshaven engaged in her book work, finishing *Prophets and Kings* and *Counsels to Parents and Teachers.*
1915, February 13	Fell in her Elmshaven home and broke her hip.
1915, July 16	Closed her fruitful life at the age of 87. Her last words were "I know in whom I have believed." *Testimonies,* volumes 6-9, were also published in the Elmshaven years.

---

* Now known as the *Adventist Review,* it is one of the oldest continuously published religious journals in the United States.

Topics

January	Lift Him Up as the Son of God
February	Lift Him Up as the Creator
March	Lift Him Up as the Son of Man
April	Lift Him Up as the Bread of Life
May	Lift Him Up as the Divine Lawgiver
June	Lift Him Up as the Master Teacher
July	Lift Him Up as the Chief Shepherd
August	Lift Him Up as the Crucified One
September	Lift Him Up as the Healer of Body and Soul
October	Lift Him Up as the Head of the Church
November	Lift Him Up as Our Advocate and Infallible Judge
December	Lift Him Up as the Coming King

Lift Him Up as the Son of God During the New Year

Whatsoever things are true, whatsoever things are honest, whatsoever things are just, whatsoever things are pure, whatsoever things are lovely, whatsoever things are of good report; if there be any virtue, and if there be any praise, think on these things. Philippians 4:8.

Already has the new year been ushered in; yet before we greet its coming, we pause to ask, What has been the history of the year that with its burden of records has now passed into eternity? The admonition of the apostle comes down the lines to every one of us, "Examine yourselves, whether ye be in the faith; prove your own selves." God forbid that at this important hour we should be so engrossed with other matters as to give no time to serious, candid, critical self-examination! Let things of minor consequence be put in the background, and let us now bring to the front the things which concern our eternal interests. . . .

No one of us can in our own strength represent the character of Christ; but if Jesus lives in the heart, the spirit dwelling in Him will be revealed in us; all our lack will be supplied. Who will seek at the beginning of this new year to obtain a new and genuine experience in the things of God? Make your wrongs right as far as possible. Confess your errors and sins one to another. Let all bitterness and wrath and malice be put away; let patience, long-suffering, kindness, and love become a part of your very being; then whatsoever things are pure and lovely and of good report will mature in your experience. . . .

What fruit have we borne during the year that is now past? What has been our influence upon others? Whom have we gathered to the fold of Christ? The eyes of the world are upon us. Are we living epistles of Christ, known and read of all men? Do we follow the example of Jesus in self-denial, in meekness, in humility, in forbearance, in cross-bearing, in devotion? Will the world be compelled to acknowledge us to be the servants of Christ? . . .

Shall we not in this new year seek to correct the errors of the past? It behooves us individually to cultivate the grace of Christ, to be meek and lowly of heart, to be firm, unwavering, steadfast in the truth; for thus only can we advance in holiness, and be made fit for the inheritance of the saints in light. Let us begin the year with an entire renunciation of self; let us pray for clear discernment, that we may understand our Savior's claims upon us, and that we may always and everywhere be witnesses for Christ (*Signs of the Times*, Jan. 4, 1883).

Lift up Jesus, you that teach the people. Lift Him up in exhortations, in sermons, in songs, in prayer. Let all your efforts be directed to pointing souls, confused, bewildered, and lost, to "the Lamb of God, which taketh away the sin of the world." Bid them look and live (*Review and Herald*, Apr. 12, 1892).

The Preexistence of the Son of God

And now, Father, glorify thou me in thy own presence with the glory which I had with thee before the world was made. John 17:5, RSV.

While God's Word speaks of the humanity of Christ when upon this earth, it also speaks decidedly regarding His preexistence. The Word existed as a divine being, even as the eternal Son of God, in union and oneness with His Father. From everlasting He was the Mediator of the covenant, the one in whom all nations of the earth, both Jews and Gentiles, if they accepted Him, were to be blessed. "The Word was with God, and the Word was God" (John 1:1). Before men or angels were created, the Word was with God, and was God.

The world was made by Him, "and without Him was not any thing made that was made" (verse 3). If Christ made all things, He existed before all things. The words spoken in regard to this are so decisive that no one need be left in doubt. Christ was God essentially, and in the highest sense. He was with God from all eternity, God over all, blessed forevermore.

The Lord Jesus Christ, the divine Son of God, existed from eternity, a distinct person, yet one with the Father. He was the surpassing glory of heaven. He was the commander of the heavenly intelligences, and the adoring homage of the angels was received by Him as His right. This was no robbery of God. "The Lord possessed me in the beginning of his way," He declares, "before his works of old. I was set up from everlasting, from the beginning, or ever the earth was. When there were no depths, I was brought forth; when there were no fountains abounding with water. Before the mountains were settled, before the hills was I brought forth: while as yet he had not made the earth, nor the fields, nor the highest part of the dust of the world. When he prepared the heavens, I was there: when he set a compass upon the face of the depths" (Proverbs 8:22-27).

There are light and glory in the truth that Christ was one with the Father before the foundation of the world was laid. This is the light shining in a dark place, making it resplendent with divine, original glory. This truth, infinitely mysterious in itself, explains other mysterious and otherwise unexplainable truths, while it is enshrined in light, unapproachable and incomprehensible. . . .

"The people which sat in darkness saw great light; and to them which sat in the region and shadow of death light is sprung up" (Matthew 4:16). Here the preexistence of Christ and the purpose of His manifestation to our world are presented as living beams of light from the eternal throne (*Selected Messages*, book 1, pp. 247, 248).

[Christ] says, and let My glory shine forth—the glory which I had with Thee before the world was (*Signs of the Times*, May 10, 1899).

The Self-existent Son of God

Jesus said unto them, Verily, verily, I say unto you, Before Abraham was, I am. John 8:58.

"Your father Abraham rejoiced to see my day: and he saw it, and was glad. Then said the Jews unto him, Thou art not yet fifty years old, and hast thou seen Abraham? Jesus said unto them, Verily, verily, I say unto you, Before Abraham was, I am."

Here Christ shows them that, although they might reckon His life to be less than fifty years, yet His divine life could not be reckoned by human computation. The existence of Christ before His incarnation is not measured by figures (*Signs of the Times*, May 3, 1899).

"Beforc Abraham was, I am." Christ is the preexistent, self-existent Son of God. The message He gave to Moses to give to the children of Israel was, "Thus shalt thou say unto the children of Israel, I AM hath sent me unto you."

The prophet Micah writes of Him, "But thou, Bethlehem Ephratah, though thou be little among the thousands of Judah, yet out of thee shall he come forth unto me that is to be ruler in Israel; whose goings forth have been from of old, from everlasting."

Through Solomon Christ declared: "The Lord possessed me in the beginning of his way, before his works of old. . . . When he gave to the sea his decree, that the waters should not pass his commandment: when he appointed the foundations of the earth: then I was by him, as one brought up with him: and I was daily his delight, rejoicing always before him."

In speaking of His preexistence, Christ carries the mind back through dateless ages. He assures us that there never was a time when He was not in close fellowship with the eternal God. He to whose voice the Jews were then listening had been with God as one brought up with Him.

Christ's words were spoken with a quiet dignity and with an assurance and power that sent conviction to the hearts of the scribes and Pharisees. They felt the power of the message sent from heaven. God was knocking at the door of their hearts, entreating entrance (*Signs of the Times*, Aug. 29, 1900).

He was equal with God, infinite and omnipotent. . . . He is the eternal, self-existent Son (manuscript 101, 1897).

In Christ is life, original, unborrowed, underived. "He that hath the Son hath life" (1 John 5:12). The divinity of Christ is the believer's assurance of eternal life. "He that believeth in me," said Jesus, "though he were dead, yet shall he live: and whosoever liveth and believeth in me shall never die." . . . Christ here looks forward to the time of His second coming (*The Desire of Ages*, p. 530).

Equal With the Father

Let this mind be in you, which was also in Christ Jesus: who, being in the form of God, thought it not robbery to be equal with God. Philippians 2:5, 6.

Lucifer in heaven, before his rebellion, was a high and exalted angel, next in honor to God's dear Son. His countenance, like those of the other angels, was mild and expressive of happiness. His forehead was high and broad, showing a powerful intellect. His form was perfect; his bearing noble and majestic. A special light beamed in his countenance and shone around him brighter and more beautiful than around the other angels; yet Christ, God's dear Son, had the preeminence over all the angelic host. He was one with the Father before the angels were created. Lucifer was envious of Christ, and gradually assumed command which devolved on Christ alone.

The great Creator assembled the heavenly host, that He might in the presence of all the angels confer special honor upon His Son. The Son was seated on the throne with the Father, and the heavenly throng of holy angels was gathered around them. The Father then made known that it was ordained by Himself that Christ, His Son, should be equal with Himself; so that wherever was the presence of His Son, it was as His own presence. The word of the Son was to be obeyed as readily as the word of the Father. His Son He had invested with authority to command the heavenly host. Especially was His Son to work in union with Himself in the anticipated creation of the earth and every living thing that should exist upon the earth. His Son would carry out His will and His purposes but would do nothing of Himself alone. The Father's will would be fulfilled in Him.

Lucifer was envious and jealous of Jesus Christ. Yet when all the angels bowed to Jesus to acknowledge His supremacy and high authority and rightful rule, he bowed with them; but his heart was filled with envy and hatred. . . .

Angels that were loyal and true sought to reconcile this mighty, rebellious angel to the will of his Creator. They justified the act of God in conferring honor upon Christ, and with forcible reasoning sought to convince Lucifer that no less honor was his now than before the Father had proclaimed the honor which He had conferred upon His Son. They clearly set forth that Christ was the Son of God, existing with Him before the angels were created; and that He had ever stood at the right hand of God, and His mild, loving authority had not heretofore been questioned; and that He had given no commands but what it was joy for the heavenly host to execute. They urged that Christ's receiving special honor from the Father, in the presence of the angels, did not detract from the honor that Lucifer had heretofore received. The angels wept. They anxiously sought to move him to renounce his wicked design and yield submission to their Creator; for all had heretofore been peace and harmony. . . . Lucifer refused to listen (*The Story of Redemption*, pp. 13-16).

Treason in Heaven

Where were you when I laid the foundation of the earth? . . . or who laid its cornerstone, when the morning stars sang together, and all the sons of God shouted for joy?
Job 38:4-7, RSV.

Many of Lucifer's sympathizers were inclined to heed the counsel of the loyal angels and repent of their dissatisfaction and be again received to the confidence of the Father and His dear Son. The mighty revolter then declared that he was acquainted with God's law, and if he should submit to servile obedience, his honor would be taken from him. No more would he be entrusted with his exalted mission. He told them that himself and they also had now gone too far to go back, and he would brave the consequences, for to bow in servile worship to the Son of God he never would; that God would not forgive, and now they must assert their liberty and gain by force the position and authority which was not willingly accorded to them.

The loyal angels hastened speedily to the Son of God and acquainted Him with what was taking place among the angels. They found the Father in conference with His beloved Son, to determine the means by which, for the best good of the loyal angels, the assumed authority of Satan could be forever put down. The great God could at once have hurled this archdeceiver from heaven; but this was not His purpose. He would give the rebellious an equal chance to measure strength and might with His own Son and His loyal angels. In this battle every angel would choose his own side and be manifested to all. It would not have been safe to suffer any who united with Satan in his rebellion to continue to occupy heaven. They had learned the lesson of genuine rebellion against the unchangeable law of God, and this is incurable. . . .

Then there was war in heaven. The Son of God, the Prince of heaven, and His loyal angels engaged in conflict with the archrebel and those who united with him. The Son of God and true, loyal angels prevailed; and Satan and his sympathizers were expelled from heaven. All the heavenly host acknowledged and adored the God of justice. Not a taint of rebellion was left in heaven. All was again peaceful and harmonious as before. . . .

The Father consulted His Son in regard to at once carrying out their purpose to make man to inhabit the earth (*The Story of Redemption*, pp. 16-19).

Satan's rebellion was to be a lesson to the universe through all coming ages—a perpetual testimony to the nature of sin and its terrible results. The working out of Satan's rule, its effects upon both men and angels, would show what must be the fruit of setting aside the divine authority. It would testify that with the existence of God's government is bound up the well-being of all the creatures He has made (*Patriarchs and Prophets*, pp. 42, 43).

Jesus Adored by Adam and Eve

And out of the ground made the Lord God to grow every tree. Genesis 2:9.

In the midst of the garden, near the tree of life, stood the tree of knowledge of good and evil. This tree was especially designed of God to be the pledge of their obedience, faith, and love to Him. Of this tree the Lord commanded our first parents not to eat, neither to touch it, lest they die. . . .

When Adam and Eve were placed in the beautiful garden they had everything for their happiness which they could desire. But God chose, in His all-wise arrangements, to test their loyalty before they could be rendered eternally secure. They were to have His favor, and He was to converse with them and they with Him. Yet He did not place evil out of their reach. Satan was permitted to tempt them. If they endured the trial they were to be in perpetual favor with God and the heavenly angels. . . .

It was decided in heaven's council for angels to visit Eden and warn Adam that he was in danger from the foe. Two angels sped on their way to visit our first parents. . . .

They told Adam and Eve that God would not compel them to obey—that He had not removed from them power to go contrary to His will; that they were moral agents, free to obey or disobey. . . .

They told them that Satan purposed to do them harm, and it was necessary for them to be guarded, for they might come in contact with the fallen foe; but he could not harm them while they yielded obedience to God's command, for, if necessary, every angel from heaven would come to their help rather than that he should in any way do them harm. . . .

The angels charged them to closely follow the instructions God had given them in reference to the tree of knowledge, for in perfect obedience they were safe, and this fallen foe could then have no power to deceive them. God would not permit Satan to follow the holy pair with continual temptations. He could have access to them only at the tree of knowledge of good and evil.

Adam and Eve assured the angels that they should never transgress the express command of God, for it was their highest pleasure to do His will. The angels united with Adam and Eve in holy strains of harmonious music, and as their songs pealed forth from blissful Eden, Satan heard the sound of their strains of joyful adoration to the Father and Son. And as Satan heard it his envy, hatred, and malignity increased, and he expressed his anxiety to his followers to incite them (Adam and Eve) to disobedience and at once bring down the wrath of God upon them and change their songs of praise to hatred and curses to their Maker (*The Story of Redemption*, pp. 24-31).

The Freedom of Choice

Eve was deceived by the serpent's cunning. 2 Corinthians 11:3, NIV.

Satan entered into the serpent and took his position in the tree of knowledge and commenced leisurely eating of the fruit.

Eve, unconsciously at first, separated from her husband in her employment. When she became aware of the fact she felt that there might be danger, but again she thought herself secure, even if she did not remain close by the side of her husband. She had wisdom and strength to know if evil came, and to meet it. This the angels had cautioned her not to do. . . .

Satan would convey the idea that by eating of the forbidden tree they would receive a new and more noble kind of knowledge than they had hitherto attained. This has been his special work, with great success, ever since his fall—to lead men to pry into the secrets of the Almighty and not be satisfied with what God has revealed, and not careful to obey that which He has commanded. He would lead them to disobey God's commands, and then make them believe that they are entering a wonderful field of knowledge. This is purely supposition, and a miserable deception. They fail to understand what God has revealed, and disregard His explicit commandments and aspire after wisdom, independent of God, and seek to understand that which He has been pleased to withhold from mortals. They are elated with their ideas of progression and charmed with their own vain philosophy, but grope in midnight darkness relative to true knowledge. They are ever learning and never able to come to the knowledge of the truth.

It was not the will of God that this sinless pair should have any knowledge of evil. He had freely given them the good but withheld the evil. . . .

Eve had thought herself capable of deciding between right and wrong. The flattering hope of entering a higher state of knowledge had led her to think that the serpent was her especial friend, possessing a great interest in her welfare. Had she sought her husband, and they had related to their Maker the words of the serpent, they would have been delivered at once from his artful temptation (*The Story of Redemption*, pp. 32-37).

Rebellion and apostasy are in the very air we breathe. We shall be affected by them unless we by faith hang our helpless souls upon Christ. If men are so easily misled now, how will they stand when Satan shall personate Christ, and work miracles? Who will be unmoved by his misrepresentations then—professing to be Christ when it is only Satan assuming the person of Christ, and apparently working the works of Christ? What will hold God's people from giving their allegiance to false christs? "Go not after them" (Luke 17:23) (*Selected Messages*, book 2, pp. 394, 395).

The Way to Salvation

I am the way, the truth, and the life: no man cometh unto the Father but by me. John 14:6.

Sorrow filled heaven, as it was realized that man was lost. . . . The whole family of Adam must die. I saw the lovely Jesus and beheld an expression of sympathy and sorrow upon His countenance. Soon I saw Him approach the exceeding bright light which enshrouded the Father. Said my accompanying angel, He is in close converse with His Father. The anxiety of the angels seemed to be intense while Jesus was communing with His Father. Three times He was shut in by the glorious light about the Father, and the third time He came out from the Father, His person could be seen. His countenance was calm, free from all perplexity and doubt, and shone with benevolence and loveliness, such as words cannot express.

He then made known to the angelic host that a way of escape had been made for lost man. He told them that He had been pleading with His Father, and had offered to give His life a ransom, to take the sentence of death upon Himself, that through Him man might find pardon; that through the merits of His blood, and obedience to the law of God, they could have the favor of God and be brought into the beautiful garden and eat of the fruit of the tree of life.

At first the angels could not rejoice, for their Commander concealed nothing from them, but opened to them the plan of salvation. Jesus told them that He would stand between the wrath of His Father and guilty man, that He would bear iniquity and scorn, and but few would receive Him as the Son of God. Nearly all would hate and reject Him. He would leave all His glory in heaven, appear upon earth as a man, humble Himself as a man, become acquainted by His own experience with the various temptations with which man would be beset, that He might know how to succor [help] those who should be tempted. . . . The weight of the sins of the whole world would be upon Him. He told them He would die and rise again the third day, and would ascend to His Father to intercede for wayward, guilty man (*The Story of Redemption*, pp. 42, 43).

Obedience through Jesus Christ gives to man perfection of character and a right to that tree of life. The conditions of again partaking of the fruit of the tree are plainly stated in the testimony of Jesus Christ to John: "Blessed are they that do his commandments, that they may have right to the tree of life, and may enter in through the gates into the city" (*The SDA Bible Commentary*, Ellen G. White Comments, vol. 1, p. 1086).

A Door of Hope for Sinners

We have seen and do testify that the Father sent the Son to be Saviour of the world. 1 John 4:14.

The angels of God were commissioned to visit the fallen pair and inform them that although they could no longer retain possession of their holy estate, their Eden home, because of their transgression of the law of God, yet their case was not altogether hopeless. They were then informed that the Son of God, who had conversed with them in Eden, had been moved with pity as He viewed their hopeless condition, and had volunteered to take upon Himself the punishment due to them, and die for them that man might yet live, through faith in the atonement Christ proposed to make for him.

Through Christ a door of hope was opened that man, notwithstanding his great sin, should not be under the absolute control of Satan. Faith in the merits of the Son of God would so elevate man that he could resist the devices of Satan. Probation would be granted him in which, through a life of repentance and faith in the atonement of the Son of God, he might be redeemed from his transgression of the Father's law, and thus be elevated to a position where his efforts to keep His law could be accepted.

The angels related to them the grief that was felt in heaven as it was announced that they had transgressed the law of God, which had made it expedient for Christ to make the great sacrifice of His own precious life.

When Adam and Eve realized how exalted and sacred was the law of God, the transgression of which made so costly a sacrifice necessary to save them and their posterity from utter ruin, they pleaded to die themselves, or to let them and their posterity endure the penalty of their transgression, rather than that the beloved Son of God should make this great sacrifice. The anguish of Adam was increased. He saw that his sins were of so great magnitude as to involve fearful consequences. And must it be that heaven's honored Commander, who had walked with him and talked with him while in his holy innocence, whom angels honored and worshiped, must be brought down from His exalted position to die because of his transgression?

Adam was informed that an angel's life could not pay the debt. . . . But the Son of God, who had in unison with the Father created man, could make an atonement for man acceptable to God, by giving His life a sacrifice and bearing the wrath of His Father. Angels informed Adam that, as his transgression had brought death and wretchedness, life and immortality would be brought to light through the sacrifice of Jesus Christ (*The Story of Redemption*, pp. 46-48).

Christ Alone Satisfies the Claims of God's Law

"For there is one God, and one mediator between God and men, the man Jesus Christ; who gave himself a ransom for all." 1 Timothy 2:5, 6.

The Son of God was next in authority to the great Lawgiver. He knew that His life alone could be sufficient to ransom fallen man. He was of as much more value than man as His noble, spotless character, and exalted office as commander of all the heavenly host were above the work of man. He was in the express image of His Father, not in features alone, but in perfection of character.

The blood of beasts could not satisfy the demands of God as an atoning sacrifice for the transgression of His law. The life of a beast was of less value than the life of the offending sinner, therefore could not be a ransom for sin. It could only be acceptable with God as a figure of the offering of His Son.

Man could not atone for man. His sinful, fallen condition would constitute him an imperfect offering, and atoning sacrifice of less value than Adam before his fall. God made man perfect and upright, and after his transgression there could be no sacrifice acceptable to God for him, unless the offering made should in value be superior to man as he was in his state of perfection and innocency.

The divine Son of God was the only sacrifice of sufficient value to fully satisfy the claims of God's perfect law. . . . Upon Christ no requirements were laid. He had power to lay down His life, and to take it again. No obligation was laid upon Him to undertake the work of atonement. It was a voluntary sacrifice that He made. His life was of sufficient value to rescue man from his fallen condition.

The Son of God was in the form of God, and He thought it not robbery to be equal with God. He was the only one, who as a man walked the earth, who could say to all men, Who of you convinceth me of sin? He had united with the Father in the creation of man, and He had power through His own divine perfection of character to atone for man's sin, and to elevate him, and bring him back to his first estate.

The sacrificial offerings, and the priesthood of the Jewish system, were instituted to represent the death and mediatorial work of Christ. All those ceremonies had no meaning, and no virtue, only as they related to Christ, who was Himself the foundation of, and who brought into existence the entire system. The Lord had made known to Adam, Abel, Seth, Enoch, Noah, Abraham, and the ancient worthies, especially Moses, that the ceremonial system of sacrifices and the priesthood, of themselves, were not sufficient to secure the salvation of one soul. . . .

The infinite sacrifice that Christ voluntarily made for man remains a mystery that angels cannot fully fathom (*Review and Herald*, Dec. 17, 1872).

A Perfect Sacrifice

An altar of earth you shall make for me and sacrifice on it your burnt offerings and your peace offerings, your sheep and your oxen; in every place where I cause my name to be remembered I will come to you and bless you. Exodus 20:24, RSV.

When Adam, according to God's special directions, made an offering for sin, it was to him a most painful ceremony. His hand must be raised to take life, which God alone could give, and make an offering for sin. It was the first time he had witnessed death. As he looked upon the bleeding victim, writhing in the agonies of death, he was to look forward by faith to the Son of God, whom the victim prefigured, who was to die man's sacrifice.

This ceremonial offering, ordained of God, was to be a perpetual reminder to Adam of his guilt, and also a penitential acknowledgment of his sin. This act of taking life gave Adam a deeper and more perfect sense of his transgression, which nothing less than the death of God's dear Son could expiate. He marveled at the infinite goodness and matchless love which would give such a ransom to save the guilty.

As Adam was slaying the innocent victim, it seemed to him that he was shedding the blood of the Son of God by his own hand. He knew that if he had remained steadfast to God, and true to His holy law, there would have been no death of beast or of man. Yet in the sacrificial offerings, pointing to the great and perfect offering of God's dear Son, there appeared a star of hope to illuminate the dark and terrible future, and relieve it of its utter hopelessness and ruin.

In the beginning the head of each family was considered ruler and priest of his own household. Afterward, as the race multiplied upon the earth, men of divine appointment performed this solemn worship of sacrifice for the people. The blood of beasts was to be associated in the minds of sinners with the blood of the Son of God. The death of the victim was to evidence to all that the penalty of sin was death. By the act of sacrifice the sinner acknowledged his guilt and manifested his faith, looking forward to the great and perfect sacrifice of the Son of God, which the offering of beasts prefigured.

Without the atonement of the Son of God there could be no communication of blessing or salvation from God to man. God was jealous for the honor of His law. The transgression of that law caused a fearful separation between God and man. To Adam in his innocency was granted communion, direct, free, and happy, with his Maker. After his transgression God would communicate to man through Christ and angels (*The Story of Redemption*, pp. 50, 51).

Such a sacrifice was of sufficient value to save the whole world. . . . This sacrifice was of such infinite value as to make a man who should avail himself of it more precious than fine gold, even a man than the golden wedge of Ophir (*ibid.*, pp. 48, 49).

Sacrifices and Ordinances Revealed God's Divine Love

Every priest stands daily at his service, offering repeatedly the same sacrifices, which can never take away sins. But when Christ had offered for all time a single sacrifice for sins, he sat down at the right hand of God. Hebrews 10:11, 12, RSV.

In patriarchal times the sacrificial offerings connected with divine worship constituted a perpetual reminder of the coming of a Savior, and thus it was with the entire ritual of the sanctuary services throughout Israel's history. In the ministration of the tabernacle, and of the Temple that afterward took its place, the people were taught each day, by means of types and shadows, the great truths relative to the advent of Christ as Redeemer, Priest, and King; and once each year their minds were carried forward to the closing events of the great controversy between Christ and Satan, the final purification of the universe from sin and sinners.

The sacrifices and offerings of the Mosaic ritual were ever pointing toward a better service, even a heavenly. The earthly sanctuary was "a figure for the time then present," in which were offered both gifts and sacrifices; its two holy places were "patterns of things in the heavens"; for Christ, our great High Priest, is today "a minister of the sanctuary, and of the true tabernacle, which the Lord pitched, and not man" (Hebrews 9:9, 23; 8:2).

From the day the Lord declared to the serpent in Eden, "I will put enmity between thee and the woman, and between thy seed and her seed" (Genesis 3:15), Satan has known that he can never hold absolute sway over the inhabitants of this world. When Adam and his sons began to offer the ceremonial sacrifices ordained by God as a type of the coming Redeemer, Satan discerned in these a symbol of communion between earth and heaven. During the long centuries that have followed, it has been his constant effort to intercept this communion. Untiringly has he sought to misrepresent God and to misinterpret the rites pointing to the Savior. . . .

While God has desired to teach men that from His own love comes the Gift which reconciles them to Himself, the archenemy of mankind has endeavored to represent God as one who delights in their destruction. Thus the sacrifices and ordinances designed of Heaven to reveal divine love have been perverted (*Prophets and Kings*, pp. 684-686).

In word and in deed the Messiah, during His earthly ministry, was to reveal to mankind the glory of God the Father. Every act of His life, every word spoken, every miracle wrought, was to make known to fallen humanity the infinite love of God. . . .

Thus, through patriarchs and prophets, as well as through types and symbols, God spoke to the world concerning the coming of a Deliverer from sin (*ibid.*, pp. 696, 697).

The Hope of the Ages

And hope maketh not ashamed; because the love of God is shed abroad in our hearts by the Holy Ghost which is given unto us. For when we were yet without strength, in due time Christ died for the ungodly. Romans 5:5, 6.

Through the long centuries of "trouble and darkness" and "dimness of anguish" (Isaiah 8:22) marking the history of mankind from the day our first parents lost their Eden home, to the time the Son of God appeared as the Savior of sinners, the hope of the fallen race was centered in the coming of a Deliverer to free men and women from the bondage of sin and the grave.

The first intimation of such a hope was given to Adam and Eve in the sentence pronounced upon the serpent in Eden when the Lord declared to Satan in their hearing, "I will put enmity between thee and the woman, and between thy seed and her seed; it shall bruise thy head, and thou shalt bruise his heel" (Genesis 3:15).

As the guilty pair listened to these words, they were inspired with hope; for in the prophecy concerning the breaking of Satan's power they discerned a promise of deliverance from the ruin wrought through transgression. Though they must suffer from the power of their adversary because they had fallen under his seductive influence and had chosen to disobey the plain command of Jehovah, yet they need not yield to utter despair. The Son of God was offering to atone with His own lifeblood for their transgression. To them was to be granted a period of probation, during which, through faith in the power of Christ to save, they might become once more the children of God.

Satan, by means of his success in turning man aside from the path of obedience, became "the god of this world" (2 Corinthians 4:4). The dominion that once was Adam's passed to the usurper. But the Son of God proposed to come to this earth to pay the penalty of sin, and thus not only redeem man, but recover the dominion forfeited. It is of this restoration that Micah prophesied when he said, "O Tower of the flock, the strong hold of the daughter of Zion, unto thee shall it come, even the first dominion" (Micah 4:8). . . .

This hope of redemption through the advent of the Son of God as Savior and King has never become extinct in the hearts of men. From the beginning there have been some whose faith has reached out beyond the shadows of the present to the realities of the future. Adam, Seth, Enoch, Methuselah, Noah, Shem, Abraham, Isaac, and Jacob—through these and other worthies the Lord has preserved the precious revealings of His will. And it was thus that to the children of Israel . . . God imparted a knowledge of the requirements of His law, and of the salvation to be accomplished through the atoning sacrifice of His beloved Son (*Prophets and Kings*, pp. 681-683).

The True Character of God in Christ

I will put enmity between you and the woman, and between your seed and her seed; he shall bruise your head, and you shall bruise his heel. Genesis 3:15, RSV.

The enmity referred to in the prophecy in Eden was not to be confined merely to Satan and the Prince of life. It was to be universal. Satan and his angels were to feel the enmity of all mankind. "I will put enmity," said God, "between thee and the woman, and between thy seed and her seed."

The enmity put between the seed of the serpent and the seed of the woman was supernatural. With Christ the enmity was in one sense natural; in another sense it was supernatural, as humanity and divinity were combined. And never was the enmity developed to such a marked degree as when Christ became an inhabitant of this earth. Never before had there been a being upon the earth who hated sin with so perfect a hatred as did Christ. He had seen its deceiving, infatuating power upon the holy angels, and all His powers were enlisted against it.

The purity and holiness of Christ, the spotless righteousness of Him who did no sin, was a perpetual reproach upon all sin in a world of sensuality and sin. In His life the light of truth was flashed amid the moral darkness with which Satan had enshrouded the world. Christ exposed Satan's falsehoods and deceiving character, and in many hearts destroyed his corrupting influence. It was this that stirred Satan with such intense hatred. With his hosts of fallen beings he determined to urge the warfare most vigorously; for there stood in the world One who was a perfect representative of the Father, One whose character and practices refuted Satan's misrepresentation of God. Satan had charged upon God the attribute he himself possessed. Now in Christ he saw God revealed in His true character—a compassionate, merciful Father, not willing that any should perish, but that all should come to Him in repentance, and have eternal life.

Intense worldliness has been one of Satan's most successful temptations. He designs to keep the hearts and minds of men so engrossed with worldly attractions that there will be no room for heavenly things. He controls their minds in their love of the world. Earthly things eclipse the heavenly, and put the Lord out of their sight and understanding. . . .

Satan reached only the heel; he could not touch the head. At the death of Christ, Satan saw that he was defeated. He saw that his true character was clearly revealed before all heaven, and that the heavenly beings and the worlds that God had created would be wholly on the side of God. . . . Christ's humanity would demonstrate for eternal ages the question which settled the controversy (*Selected Messages*, book 1, pp. 254, 255).

January
15

To Be a Prophet

The Lord thy God will raise up unto thee a Prophet from the midst of thee, of thy brethren, like unto me; unto him ye shall hearken. Deuteronomy 18:15.

The hope of Israel was embodied in the promise made at the time of the call of Abraham, and afterward repeated again and again to his posterity, "In thee shall all families of the earth be blessed" (Genesis 12:3). As the purpose of God for the redemption of the race was unfolded to Abraham, the Sun of Righteousness shone upon his heart, and his darkness was scattered. And when, at last, the Savior Himself walked and talked among the sons of men, He bore witness to the Jews of the patriarch's bright hope of deliverance through the coming of a Redeemer. "Your father Abraham rejoiced to see my day," Christ declared; "and he saw it, and was glad" (John 8:56).

The same blessed hope was foreshadowed in the benediction pronounced by the dying patriarch Jacob upon his son Judah. . . .

Through Moses, God's purpose to send His Son as the Redeemer of the fallen race was kept before Israel. On one occasion, shortly before his death, Moses declared, "The Lord thy God will raise up unto thee a Prophet from the midst of thee, of thy brethren, like unto me; unto him ye shall hearken." Plainly had Moses been instructed for Israel concerning the work of the Messiah to come. "I will raise them up a Prophet from among their brethren, like unto thee," was the word of Jehovah to His servant; "and will put my words in his mouth; and he shall speak unto them all that I shall command him" (Deuteronomy 18:15, 18) (*Prophets and Kings*, pp. 683, 684).

About 40 days after the birth of Christ, Joseph and Mary took Him to Jerusalem, to present Him to the Lord, and to offer sacrifice. . . .

The priest went through the ceremony of his official work. He took the child in his arms, and held it up before the altar. After handing it back to its mother, he inscribed the name "Jesus" on the roll of the firstborn. Little did he think, as the babe lay in his arms, that it was the Majesty of heaven, the King of glory. The priest did not think that this babe was the One of whom Moses had written, "A Prophet shall the Lord your God raise up unto you of your brethren, like unto me; him shall ye hear in all things whatsoever he shall say unto you" (Acts 3:22). He did not think that this babe was He whose glory Moses had asked to see. But One greater than Moses lay in the priest's arms; and when he enrolled the child's name, he was enrolling the name of One who was the foundation of the whole Jewish economy (*The Desire of Ages*, pp. 50-52).

The Wise Men Welcome Him

When Jesus was born in Bethlehem of Judea in the days of Herod the king, behold, there came wise men from the east to Jerusalem, saying, Where is he that is born King of the Jews? Matthew 2:1, 2.

The King of glory stooped low to take humanity; and angels, who had witnessed His splendor in the heavenly courts, as He was worshiped by all the heavenly hosts, were disappointed to find their divine Commander in a position of so great humiliation.

The Jews had separated themselves so far from God . . . that angels could not communicate to them the tidings of the advent of the infant Redeemer. God chooses the Wise Men of the East to do His will. . . .

"There came wise men from the east to Jerusalem, saying, Where is he that is born King of the Jews? for we have seen his star in the east, and are come to worship him." These men were not Jews; but they had been waiting for the predicted Messiah. They had studied prophecy, and knew the time was at hand when Christ would come; and they were anxiously watching for some sign of this great event, that they might be among the first to welcome the infant heavenly King, and worship Him.

These Wise Men were philosophers, and had studied the works of God in nature. In the wonders of the heavens, in the glories of the sun, moon, and stars, they traced the finger of God. They were not idolaters. They lived up to the dim light which shone upon them. . . . These Wise Men had seen the heavens illuminated with light, which enshrouded the heavenly host who heralded the advent of Christ to the humble shepherds. And after the angels returned to heaven, a luminous star appeared, and lingered in the heavens.

This light was a distant cluster of flaming angels, which appeared like a luminous star. The unusual appearance of the large, bright star which they had never seen before, hanging as a sign in the heavens, attracted their attention. They were not privileged to hear the proclamation of the angels to the shepherds. But the Spirit of God moved them out to seek this heavenly Visitor to a fallen world. The Wise Men directed their course where the star seemed to lead them. And as they drew nigh to the city of Jerusalem, the star was enshrouded in darkness, and no longer guided them. . . .

The Wise Men are surprised to see no unusual interest upon the subject of the coming of the Messiah. . . . The Wise Men plainly stated their errand. They were in search of Jesus, the King of the Jews, for they had seen His star in the east and had come to worship Him. . . .

The advent of Christ was the greatest event which had taken place since the creation of the world. . . . The eye of God was upon His Son every moment. . . . The gifts brought to them [Joseph and Mary] by the Wise Men sustained them while in the land of [Egypt] (*Review and Herald*, Dec. 24, 1872).

Jesus Keeps His First Passover

Now his parents went to Jerusalem every year at the feast of the passover. And when he was twelve years old, they went up to Jerusalem after the custom of the feast. Luke 2:41, 42.

Joseph and Mary went up to Jerusalem every year to the feast of the Passover, according to the requirements of the Jewish law. Christ's childhood days were ended. He had entered upon the period of youth. Joseph and Mary, as was their custom, prepared to take their long journey to Jerusalem. They took Jesus with them. They went in company with many others who were on their way to Jerusalem to observe this solemn festival.

It is impossible for human minds to understand the meditations of the Son of God as He looked with interest upon the Temple for the first time. As He walked its courts, and His eye discerned the work of the ministering priest, the altar with its bleeding victim, the holy incense arising to God, and the mysteries of the Holy of Holies behind the veil, and comprehended the reality which these ceremonies prefigured, what thoughts were awakened within His breast we cannot conjecture. Christ Himself was the key to unlock all these sacred mysteries which were indefinitely understood by Joseph and Mary. These were all instituted to represent Christ, and were fulfilled in His death.

The Passover was a name given to this ceremony in commemoration of the wonderful event of the Hebrews' leaving Egypt. The night they left Egypt, the destroying angel entered every house and slew from the firstborn of the king upon his throne down to the firstborn of the lowest slave. . . .

The Lord gave special directions to the Hebrews, for each family to slay a lamb and sprinkle the blood upon their doorposts, that when the destroying angel should go forth upon his errand of death, the blood upon the post of the door should be to them a sign that those who were within the house were the worshipers of the true God. The angel of death passed over the houses thus designated. Upon that eventful night the Hebrews were directed to be prepared for their journey. . . .

According to the directions given them of God, they were all prepared for their journey, ready for the word of command to go forth from Egypt. . . .

While the institution of the Passover was pointing backward to the miraculous deliverance of the Hebrews, it likewise pointed forward, showing the death of the Son of God before it transpired. In the last Passover our Lord observed with His disciples, He instituted the Lord's Supper in place of the Passover, to be observed in memory of His death. No longer had they need of the Passover, for He, the great antitypical Lamb, was ready to be sacrificed for the sins of the world. Type met antitype in the death of Christ (*Youth's Instructor,* May 1873).

January
18

An Obedient Son to Earthly Parents

And being found in fashion as a man, he humbled himself. Philippians 2:8.

How great must be the humiliation of the Son of God, that He should live in the despised and wicked town of Nazareth. The most holy place upon earth would have been greatly honored by the presence of the world's Redeemer a single year. The palaces of kings would have been exalted to receive Christ as a guest. But the Redeemer of the world passed by the courts of royalty and made His home in a humble mountain village for 30 years, thus conferring distinction upon despised Nazareth.

The Redeemer of the world passed up and down the hills and mountains, from the great plain to the mountain valley. He enjoyed nature's beautiful scenery. He was delighted with the fields glowing with the beautiful flowers, and in listening to the birds of the air, and uniting His voice with them in their happy songs of praise. The groves and mountains were His places of retreat for prayer, and frequently whole nights were spent in communion with His Father..

Notwithstanding the sacred mission of Christ, His exalted relationship with God, of which He was fully aware, He was not above performing the practical duties of life. He was the Creator of the world, and yet He acknowledged His obligation to His earthly parents, and at the call of duty, in compliance with the wishes of His parents, He returned with them from Jerusalem after the Passover, and was subject unto them.

He submitted to restraints of parental authority, and acknowledged the obligations of a son, a brother, friend, and citizen. He discharged His duties to His earthly parents with respectful courtesy. He was the Majesty of heaven. He had been the great commander in heaven. Angels loved to do His bidding. And now He was a willing servant, a cheerful, obedient son.

Jesus was not turned aside by any influence from the faithful service expected of a son. He did not aim to do anything remarkable to distinguish Himself from other youth, or to proclaim His heavenly birth. Even His friends and relatives, in all the years that Christ's life was passed among them, saw no special marks of His divinity. Christ was sedate, self-denying, gentle, cheerful, kind, and ever obedient. He avoided display, but was firm as a rock to principle.

In the little notice given of His childhood and youthful life is an example for parents as well as children, that the more quiet and unnoticed the period of childhood and youth is passed, and the more natural and free from artificial excitement, the more safe will it be for the children, and the more favorable for the formation of a character of purity, natural simplicity, and true moral worth (*Youth's Instructor*, February 1873).

A Spotless Example

For we have not an high priest which cannot be touched with the feeling of our infirmities; but was in all points tempted like as we are, yet without sin. Hebrews 4:15.

The life of Christ had been so secluded at Nazareth that the world did not know Him as the Son of God—their Redeemer. He was regarded as nothing more than the son of Joseph and Mary. His life in childhood and youth was remarkable. His silence in regard to His exalted character and mission contains an instructive lesson to all youth. His faithful obedience to His parents until He was thirty years of age is a pattern for youth to imitate more than the Jesus in Gethsemane and upon Calvary.

We shall never be required to endure the agony of the Son of God which He bore for a guilty world; but His life of submission and faithful obedience to His parents is the pattern for all children and youth. Although they may never experience, as did the Redeemer, the agony of Gethsemane or Calvary, they are required to imitate the life of Christ in humility, self-denial, self-sacrifice, and in filial, respectful obedience to their parents. . . .

The Lord had revealed to John that Jesus would be among the candidates who were to receive baptism at his hands, and that He would give him a special token whereby he might know the Lamb of God, and call the attention of the people to Him as the long-expected Messiah.

John had heard of the sinless character and spotless purity of the life of Christ, and that He claimed to be the Son of God. He had been informed of His wise questions and answers in the Temple, which astonished the grave doctors. He had listened to the recital of the Galilean youth silencing the doctors by His deep reasoning. He thought this must be the Son of God, the promised Messiah. . . .

As soon as the discerning eye of John rested upon Jesus, his spirit was stirred with the deepest emotion. He knew that He was not like any other man that had received the ordinance at his hand. He had strong convictions that this was the Christ of whom Moses and the prophets had written. His heart went out to Christ with intense love and reverence that he had never felt before. The very atmosphere of His presence was holy and awe-inspiring. . . . His heart had never been stirred with such emotions as when in the presence of Christ. . . .

Christ came to receive baptism, not with confession of sins to repentance, for He was without the taint of sin. . . . Through the perfection of His character He was accepted of the Father as a mediator for sinful man. . . . The Captain of our salvation was made perfect through suffering, and thus qualified to help fallen man just where he needed help (*Youth's Instructor*, January 1874).

One Superior to Angels

Being made so much better than the angels, as he hath by inheritance obtained a more excellent name than they. For unto which of the angels said he at any time, Thou art my Son, this day have I begotten thee? And again, I will be to him a Father, and he shall be to me a Son? And again, when he bringeth in the first begotten into the world, he saith, And let all the angels of God worship him. Hebrews 1:4-6.

Should the angel Gabriel be sent to this world to take upon himself human nature, and to teach the knowledge of God, how eagerly men would listen to his instruction. Supposing that he were able to set us a perfect example of purity and holiness, sympathizing with us in all our sorrows, bereavements, and afflictions, and suffering the punishment of our sins, how eagerly we would follow him. What exaltation he would receive. Men would desire to place him on the throne of David, and to gather the nations of earth under his banner.

If, when this heavenly being returned to his home, he should leave behind him a book containing the history of his mission, with revelations regarding the history of the world, how eagerly would its seal be broken! How anxiously men and women would seek to obtain a copy! Thinking people would store up the precious instruction for the benefit of future generations. Thousands from all parts of the world would copy the words of this book. With intense interest they would read and reread its pages. For a time all other interests would be subordinated to a study of its contents.

But One surpassing all that imagination can present came from heaven to this world. Nearly two thousand years ago a voice of strange and mysterious import was heard from the throne of God, "Sacrifice and offering thou wouldest not, but a body hast thou prepared me. . . . Lo, I come . . . to do thy will, O God."

A prophet said: "For unto us a child is born, unto us a son is given: and the government shall be upon his shoulder; and his name shall be called Wonderful, Counsellor, The mighty God, The everlasting Father, The Prince of Peace." . . .

As Paul beheld Christ in His power, he broke out into exclamations of admiration and amazement: "Without controversy great is the mystery of godliness: God was manifest in the flesh, justified in the Spirit, seen of angels, preached unto the Gentiles, believed on in the world, received up into glory." "By him were all things created, that are in heaven, and that are in earth, visible and invisible, whether they be thrones, or dominions, or principalities, or powers; all things were created by him, and for him. And he is before all things, and by him all things consist" . . . (*Signs of the Times*, Apr. 4, 1906).

To Seek and Save the Lost

For the Son of man is come to seek and to save that which was lost. Luke 19:10.

The heaven-appointed Teacher appears, and He is no less a personage than the Son of the Infinite God. Unroll the scroll, and read of Him. Moses declared to the children of Israel: "The Lord said unto me, They have well spoken that which they have spoken. I will raise them up a Prophet from among their brethren, like unto thee, and will put my words in his mouth; and he shall speak unto them all that I shall command him. And it shall come to pass, that whosoever will not hearken unto my words which he shall speak in my name, I will require it of him." Here is the prediction announcing the distinguished arrival. His words were not to be disregarded; for His authority was supreme, and His power invincible.

Unroll the scroll still further, and read what Isaiah says of His work: "The Spirit of the Lord God is upon me; because the Lord hath anointed me to preach good tidings unto the meek; he hath sent me to bind up the brokenhearted, to proclaim liberty to the captives, and the opening of the prison to them that are bound; to proclaim the acceptable year of the Lord, and the day of vengeance of our God; to comfort all that mourn; to appoint unto them that mourn in Zion, to give unto them beauty for ashes, the oil of joy for mourning, the garment of praise for the spirit of heaviness; that they might be called trees of righteousness, the planting of the Lord, that he might be glorified." . . .

Again we read of Christ as the messenger of the covenant yet to come, and as the Sun of Righteousness yet to arise. The prophets made Him their earliest and their latest theme. . . .

At His coming [the Jews] did not receive Him, because they had gathered a false idea as to the manner of His coming. This Jesus, a peasant and a carpenter, of obscure origin, the Son of God, the Messiah? It could not be.

But the peculiarity separating the Jews from other nations disappeared in Christ. He placed Himself where He could give instruction to all classes of people. Often He told them that He was related to the whole human family, Jew and Gentile. "I am not come to call the [self] righteous, but sinners to repentance," He declared. He came to seek and to save that which was lost. For this He left the ninety and nine; for this He laid off His royal robes, and veiled His divinity with humanity. The whole world is Christ's field of labor. A sphere narrower than this does not enter His thoughts (*Signs of the Times*, June 24, 1897).

January
22

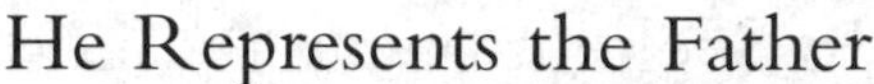

He Represents the Father

O righteous Father, the world hath not known thee: but I have known thee, and these have known that thou hast sent me. And I have declared unto them thy name, and will declare it: that the love wherewith thou has loved me may be in them, and I in them. John 17:25, 26.

Christ came into the world to represent the Father to man; for Satan had presented Him before the world in a false light. Because God is a God of justice, of terrible majesty, who has power to destroy as well as to preserve man, Satan caused men to regard Him with fear, to look upon Him as a tyrant. Jesus had been with the Father from the everlasting ages, before the creation of man, and He came to reveal the Father, declaring, "God is love." Jesus represented God as a kind Father, who careth for the subjects of His kingdom. He declared that not a sparrow falls to the ground without the notice of the Father, and that the children of men are of more value in His sight than many sparrows, that the very hairs of their head are all numbered.

The Lord is represented in the Old Testament as well as in the New Testament not only as a God of justice but as a Father of infinite love. The psalmist says: "The Lord executeth righteousness and judgment for all that are oppressed. . . . The Lord is merciful and gracious, slow to anger, and plenteous in mercy. . . . He hath not dealt with us after our sins; nor rewarded us according to our iniquities. For as the heaven is high above the earth, so great is his mercy toward them that fear him." . . .

Satan had clothed the Father in his own attributes, but Christ represented Him in His true character of benevolence and love. In the character in which Christ presented Him to the world it was as if He gave a new gift to man. . . .

The Son of God declared in positive terms that the world was destitute of the knowledge of God; but this knowledge was of the highest value, and it was His own peculiar gift, the inestimable treasure which He brought into the world. In the exercise of His sovereign prerogative He imparted to His disciples the knowledge of the character of God, in order that they might communicate it to the world. . . . Everyone who believes the message of God should lift up Jesus, point men to Christ, and say, "Behold the Lamb of God, which taketh away the sin of the world." . . .

The soul imbued with the love of Christ is one with Him; he communes with Christ, Christ is formed within, the hope of glory, and the Christian goes forth to represent the Father and the Son to the world (*Signs of the Times*, June 27, 1892).

A Restorer

Thou shalt be called, The repairer of the breach, The restorer of paths to dwell in.
Isaiah 58:12.

The Son of God came to the world as a restorer. He was the Way, the Truth, and the Life. Every word He uttered was spirit and life. He spoke with authority, conscious of His power to bless humanity, and deliver the captives bound by Satan; conscious also that by His presence He could bring to the world fullness of joy. He longed to help every oppressed and suffering member of the human family, and show that it was His prerogative to bless, not to condemn.

It was no robbery for Christ to do the works of God; for this was the purpose He came from heaven to fulfill, and for this the treasures of eternity were at His command. In the disposal of His gifts He was to know no control. He passed by the self-exalted, the honored, and the rich, and mingled with the poor and oppressed, bringing into their lives a brightness, a hope, and an aspiration they had never before known. He pronounced a blessing on all who should suffer for His sake, declaring: "Blessed are ye, when men shall revile you, and persecute you, and shall say all manner of evil against you falsely, for my sake." . . .

Christ distinctly appropriated to Himself the right to authority and allegiance. "Ye call me Master and Lord," He said, "and ye say well; for so I am." "One is your Master, even Christ." Thus He maintained the dignity that belonged to His name, and the authority and power He possessed in heaven.

There were occasions when He spoke with the dignity of His own true greatness. "He that hath ears to hear," He said, "let him hear." In these words He was only repeating the command of God, when from His excellent glory the Infinite One had declared, "This is my beloved Son, in whom I am well pleased; hear ye him." Standing amid the frowning Pharisees, who sought to make their own importance felt, Christ did not hesitate to compare Himself with the most distinguished representative men who had walked the earth, and to claim preeminence above them all.

Jonah was one of these men, held in high estimation by the Jewish nation. . . . As Christ recalled to the minds of His hearers, Jonah's message and his instrumentality in saving that people, He said: "The men of Nineveh shall rise in judgment with this generation, and shall condemn it: because they repented at the preaching of Jonas; and, behold, a greater than Jonas is here."

Christ knew that the Israelites regarded Solomon as the greatest king that ever wielded a scepter over an earthly kingdom. . . . Yet Christ declared: . . . "Behold, a greater than Solomon is here" (*Youth's Instructor*, Sept. 23, 1897).

Our Defender

For ye know the grace of our Lord Jesus Christ, that, though he was rich, yet for your sakes he became poor, that ye through his poverty might be rich. 2 Corinthians 8:9.

If there are those who think that they are making large sacrifices for the work, let them consider the sacrifice that Christ made in their behalf. The human race was under sentence of death, but the Son of God clothed His divinity with humanity, and came to this world to live and die in our behalf. He came to stand against the host of fallen angels. We must have a Defender, and when our Defender came, He was clothed with humanity; for He must be subject to all the temptations wherewith man is beset, that He might understand how to deliver the godly out of temptation. He took His stand at the head of the fallen race, that men and women might be enabled to stand on vantage ground.

Christ did not come to this world with a legion of angels. Laying aside His royal robe and kingly crown, He stepped down from His high command, and for our sake became poor, that we through His poverty might be made rich. This was the plan laid in the heavenly courts. The Redeemer of mankind was to be born in poverty, and He was to be a worker with His hands. He labored with His father at the carpenter's trade, and into all that He did He brought perfection. His companions sometimes found fault with Him because He was so thorough. What is the use of being so particular? they said. But He would work until He had brought what He was doing as near to perfection as He could, and then He would look up with the light of heaven shining from His face, and those who had criticized Him would turn away ashamed of themselves. Instead of retaliating when found fault with, He would begin to sing one of the psalms, and before those who had found fault with Him realized it, they, too, were singing.

Never should botch work of any kind be allowed in our institutions. Every student should be taught that in order to attain to perfection in character building, he must be faithful in the smallest duties appointed him. "Ye are God's husbandry, ye are God's building," and your work is to be done as in the sight of a holy God. Do your best, and heavenly angels will help you to carry the work on to perfection. . . . Christ left the heavenly courts, and came to this world to make an atonement for us. All who come to Him in living faith will be enabled to stand on vantage ground. . . .

Let us have characters so pure and holy that Christ can with joy present us to the Father. Let us be filled with the living principles of the truth for this time. Let us live lives that will lead sinners to the Saviour. . . . We may be made complete in Him. How? By becoming partakers of the divine nature (*Review and Herald*, June 1, 1905).

Assailed With the Fiercest Temptations

Because he himself has suffered and been tempted, he is able to help those who are tempted. Hebrews 2:18, RSV.

If, under trying circumstances, men of spiritual power, pressed beyond measure, become discouraged and desponding, if at times they see nothing desirable in life, that they should choose it, this is nothing strange or new. Let all such remember that one of the mightiest of the prophets fled for his life before the rage of an infuriated woman. A fugitive, weary and travel-worn, bitter disappointment crushing his spirits, he asked that he might die. But it was when hope was gone and his lifework seemed threatened with defeat, that he learned one of the most precious lessons of his life. In the hour of his greatest weakness he learned the need and the possibility of trusting God under circumstances the most forbidding.

Those who, while spending their life energies in self-sacrificing labor, are tempted to give way to despondency and distrust may gather courage from the experience of Elijah. God's watchful care, His love, His power, are especially manifest in behalf of His servants whose zeal is misunderstood or unappreciated, whose counsels and reproofs are slighted, and whose efforts toward reform are repaid with hatred and opposition.

It is at the time of greatest weakness that Satan assails the soul with the fiercest temptations. It was thus that he hoped to prevail over the Son of God; for by this policy he had gained many victories over man. When the willpower weakened and faith failed, then those who had stood long and valiantly for the right yielded to temptation. Moses, wearied with 40 years of wandering and unbelief, lost for a moment his hold on Infinite Power. He failed just on the borders of the Promised Land. So with Elijah. He who had maintained his trust in Jehovah during the years of drought and famine, he who had stood undaunted before Ahab, he who throughout that trying day on Carmel had stood before the whole nation of Israel the sole witness to the true God, in a moment of weariness allowed the fear of death to overcome his faith in God. And so it is today. . . .

Those who, standing in the forefront of the conflict, are impelled by the Holy Spirit to do a special work will frequently feel a reaction when the pressure is removed. Despondency may shake the most heroic faith and weaken the most steadfast will. But God understands, and He still pities and loves. He reads the motives and the purposes of the heart. . . . Heaven will not fail them in their day of adversity. Nothing is apparently more helpless, yet really more invincible, than the soul that feels its nothingness and relies wholly on God (*Prophets and Kings*, pp. 173-175).

Clothed in Christ's Righteousness

Offer the sacrifices of righteousness, and put your trust in the Lord. Psalm 4:5.

Paul realized his weakness, and well he might distrust his own strength. Referring to the law, he says, "The commandment, which was ordained to life, I found to be unto death." He had trusted in the deeds of the law. He says, concerning his own outward life, that as "touching the law" he was "blameless"; and he put his trust in his own righteousness. But when the mirror of the law was held up before him, and he saw himself as God saw him, full of mistakes, stained with sin, he cried out, "O wretched man that I am! who shall deliver me from the body of this death?"

Paul beheld the Lamb of God that taketh away the sin of the world. He heard the voice of Christ saying, "I am the way, the truth, and the life; no man cometh unto the Father, but by me." He determined to avail himself of the benefits of saving grace, to become dead to trespasses and sins, to have his guilt washed away in the blood of Christ, to be clothed with Christ's righteousness, to become a branch of the Living Vine. He walked with Christ, and Jesus became to him—not a part of salvation, while his own good deeds were another part, but—his all in all, the first and last and best in everything. He had the faith that draws life from Christ, that enabled him to conform his life to that of the divine example. This faith claims nothing for its possessor because of his righteousness, but claims everything because of the righteousness of Christ.

In the gospel the character of Christ is portrayed. As He descended step by step from His throne, His divinity was veiled in humanity; but in His miracles, His doctrines, His sufferings, His betrayal, His mockery, His trial, His death by crucifixion, His grave among the rich, His resurrection, His 40 days upon earth, His ascension, His triumph, His priesthood, are inexhaustible treasures of wisdom, recorded for us by inspiration in the Word of God. The waters of life still flow in abundant streams of salvation. The mysteries of redemption, the blending of the divine and the human in Christ, His incarnation, sacrifice, mediation will be sufficient to supply minds, hearts, tongues, and pens with themes for thought and expression for all time; and time will not be sufficient to exhaust the wonders of salvation, but through everlasting ages, Christ will be the science and the song of the redeemed soul. New developments of the perfection and glory of God in the face of Jesus Christ will be forever unfolding. And now there must be perfect reliance upon His merit and grace; there must be distrust of self, and living faith in Him (*Signs of the Times*, Nov. 24, 1890).

Only One Unerring Pattern

Christ also suffered for us, leaving us an example, that ye should follow his steps.
1 Peter 2:21.

Christ demands all. If He required less, His sacrifice was too dear, too great to make to bring us up to such a level. . . . "Be ye transformed by the renewing of your mind." This is a self-denying way. And when you think that the way is too strait, that there is too much self-denial in this narrow path; when you say, How hard to give up all, ask yourselves the question, What did Christ give up for me? This question puts anything that we may call self-denial in the shade.

Behold Him in the garden sweating great drops of blood. A solitary angel is sent from heaven to strengthen the Son of God. Follow Him on His way to the judgment hall, while He is derided, mocked, and insulted by that infuriated mob. Behold Him clothed in that old purple kingly robe. Hear the coarse jest and cruel mocking. See them place upon that noble brow the crown of thorns, and then smite Him with a reed, causing the thorns to penetrate His temples, and the blood to flow from that holy brow. Hear that murderous throng eagerly crying for the blood of the Son of God. He is delivered into their hands, and they lead the noble sufferer away, pale, weak, and fainting, to His crucifixion. He is stretched upon the wooden cross, and the nails are driven through His tender hands and feet.

Behold Him hanging upon the cross those dreadful hours of agony until the angels veil their faces from the horrid scene, and the sun hides its light, refusing to behold. Think of these things, and then ask, Is the way too strait? . . .

It is a blessed privilege to give up all for Christ. Look not at the lives of others and imitate them and rise no higher. You have only one true, unerring Pattern. It is safe to follow Jesus only. . . .

The oftener and more diligently you peruse the Scriptures, the more beautiful will they appear, and the less relish you will have for light reading. The daily study of the Scriptures will have a sanctifying influence upon the mind. You will breathe a heavenly atmosphere. Bind this precious volume to your hearts. It will prove to you a friend and guide in perplexity.

You have had objects in view in your life, and how steadily and perseveringly have you labored to attain those objects! You have calculated and planned until your anticipations were realized. There is an object before you now worthy of a persevering, untiring, lifelong effort. It is the salvation of your soul—everlasting life. And this demands self-denial, sacrifice, and close study. . . .

It is a great thing to be a child of God, and a joint heir with Christ (*Testimonies*, vol. 1, pp. 240-243).

Nature Sympathized With His Suffering

And it was about the sixth hour, and there was a darkness over all the earth until the ninth hour. And the sun was darkened, and the veil of the temple was rent in the midst. Luke 23:44, 45.

Faith and hope trembled in the expiring agonies of Christ because God had removed the assurance He had heretofore given His beloved Son of His approbation and acceptance. The Redeemer of the world then relied upon the evidences which had hitherto strengthened Him, that His Father accepted His labors and was pleased with His work. In His dying agony, as He yields up His precious life, He has by faith alone to trust in Him whom it has ever been His joy to obey. He is not cheered with clear, bright rays of hope on the right hand nor on the left. All is enshrouded in oppressive gloom.

Amid the awful darkness which is felt by sympathizing nature, the Redeemer drains the mysterious cup even to its dregs. Denied even bright hope and confidence in the triumph which will be His in the future, He cries with a loud voice: "Father, into thy hands I commend my spirit." He is acquainted with the character of His Father, with His justice, His mercy, and His great love, and in submission He drops into His hands. Amid the convulsions of nature are heard by the amazed spectators the dying words of the Man of Calvary.

Nature sympathized with the suffering of its Author. The heaving earth, the rent rocks, proclaimed that it was the Son of God who died. There was a mighty earthquake. The veil of the Temple was rent in twain. Terror seized the executioners and spectators as they beheld the sun veiled in darkness, and felt the earth shake beneath them, and saw and heard the rending of the rocks. The mocking and jeering of the chief priests and elders were hushed as Christ commended His spirit into the hands of His Father. The astonished throng began to withdraw and grope their way in the darkness to the city. They smote upon their breasts as they went and in terror, speaking scarcely above a whisper, said among themselves: "It is an innocent person that has been murdered. What if, indeed, He is, as He asserted, the Son of God?"

Jesus did not yield up His life till He had accomplished the work which He came to do, and exclaimed with His departing breath: "It is finished." Satan was then defeated. He knew that his kingdom was lost. Angels rejoiced as the words were uttered: "It is finished." The great plan of redemption, which was dependent on the death of Christ, had been thus far carried out. And there was joy in heaven that the sons of Adam could, through a life of obedience, be finally exalted to the throne of God. Oh, what love! What amazing love! that brought the Son of God to earth to be made sin for us, that we might be reconciled to God, and elevated to a life with Him in His mansions in glory (*Testimonies*, vol. 2, pp. 210-212).

The Magnitude of His Sacrifice

*And about the ninth hour Jesus cried with a loud voice, . . .
My God, my God, why hast thou forsaken me? Matthew 27:46.*

When men and women can more fully comprehend the magnitude of the great sacrifice which was made by the Majesty of heaven in dying in man's stead, then will the plan of salvation be magnified, and reflections of Calvary will awaken tender, sacred, and lively emotions in the Christian's heart. Praises to God and the Lamb will be in their hearts and upon their lips. Pride and self-esteem cannot flourish in the hearts that keep fresh in memory the scenes of Calvary. This world will appear of but little value to those who appreciate the great price of man's redemption, the precious blood of God's dear Son. All the riches of the world are not of sufficient value to redeem one perishing soul. Who can measure the love Christ felt for a lost world as He hung upon the cross, suffering for the sins of guilty men? This love was immeasurable, infinite.

Christ has shown that His love was stronger than death. He was accomplishing man's salvation; and although He had the most fearful conflict with the powers of darkness, yet, amid it all, His love grew stronger and stronger. He endured the hiding of His Father's countenance, until He was led to exclaim in the bitterness of His soul: "My God, my God, why hast thou forsaken me?" His arm brought salvation. The price was paid to purchase the redemption of man, when, in the last soul struggle, the blessed words were uttered which seemed to resound through creation: "It is finished." . . .

The length, the breadth, the height, the depth, of such amazing love we cannot fathom. The contemplation of the matchless depths of a Savior's love should fill the mind, touch and melt the soul, refine and elevate the affections, and completely transform the whole character. . . .

Christ yielded not in the least degree to the torturing foe, even in His bitterest anguish. Legions of evil angels were all about the Son of God, yet the holy angels were bidden not to break their ranks and engage in conflict with the taunting, reviling foe. Heavenly angels were not permitted to minister unto the anguished spirit of the Son of God. It was in this terrible hour of darkness, the face of His Father hidden, legions of evil angels enshrouding Him, the sins of the world upon Him, that the words were wrenched from His lips: "My God, my God, why hast thou forsaken me?" . . .

We should take broader and deeper views of the life, sufferings, and death of God's dear Son. When the atonement is viewed correctly, the salvation of souls will be felt to be of infinite value. In comparison with the enterprise of everlasting life, every other sinks into insignificance (*Testimonies*, vol. 2, pp. 212-215).

A New and Living Way for All

When he had received the drink, Jesus said, "It is finished." With that, he bowed his head and gave up his spirit. John 19:30, NIV.

Never before had the earth witnessed such a scene. The multitude stood paralyzed, and with bated breath gazed upon the Savior. Again darkness settled upon the earth, and a hoarse rumbling, like heavy thunder, was heard. There was a violent earthquake. The people were shaken together in heaps. The wildest confusion and consternation ensued. In the surrounding mountains, rocks were rent asunder, and went crashing down into the plains. Sepulchers were broken open, and the dead were cast out of their tombs. Creation seemed to be shivering to atoms. Priests, rulers, soldiers, executioners, and people, mute with terror, lay prostrate upon the ground.

When the loud cry, "It is finished," came from the lips of Christ the priests were officiating in the Temple. It was the hour of the evening sacrifice. The lamb representing Christ had been brought to be slain. Clothed in his significant and beautiful dress, the priest stood with lifted knife, as did Abraham when he was about to slay his son. With intense interest the people were looking on. But the earth trembles and quakes; for the Lord Himself draws near. With a rending noise the inner veil of the Temple is torn from top to bottom by an unseen hand, throwing open to the gaze of the multitude a place once filled with the presence of God. In this place the Shekinah had dwelt. Here God had manifested His glory above the mercy seat. No one but the high priest ever lifted the veil separating this apartment from the rest of the Temple. He entered in once a year to make an atonement for the sins of the people. But lo, this veil is rent in twain. The Most Holy Place of the earthly sanctuary is no longer sacred.

All is terror and confusion. The priest is about to slay the victim, but the knife drops from his nerveless hand and the lamb escapes. Type has met antitype in the death of God's Son. The great sacrifice has been made. The way into the holiest is laid open. A new and living way is prepared for all. No longer need sinful, sorrowing humanity await the coming of the high priest. Henceforth the Savior was to officiate as priest and advocate in the heaven of heavens. It was as if a living voice had spoken to the worshipers: There is now an end to all sacrifices and offerings for sin. The Son of God is come according to His word, "Lo, I come (in the volume of the book it is written of me,) to do thy will, O God." "By his own blood" He entereth "in once into the holy place, having obtained eternal redemption for us" (Hebrews 10:7; 9:12) (*The Desire of Ages*, pp. 756, 757).

Encircled With His Love

And walk in love, as Christ loved us and gave himself up for us, a fragrant offering and sacrifice to God. Ephesians 5:2, RSV.

The world that Satan has claimed and has ruled over with cruel tyranny, the Son of God has, by one vast achievement, encircled in His love and connected again with the throne of Jehovah. Cherubim and seraphim, and the unnumbered hosts of all the unfallen worlds, sang anthems of praise to God and the Lamb when this triumph was assured. They rejoiced that the way of salvation had been opened to the fallen race and that the earth would be redeemed from the curse of sin. How much more should those rejoice who are the objects of such amazing love!

How can we ever be in doubt and uncertainty, and feel that we are orphans? It was in behalf of those who had transgressed the law that Jesus took upon Him human nature; He became like unto us, that we might have everlasting peace and assurance. . . .

The very first step in approaching God is to know and believe the love that He has to us (1 John 4:16); for it is through the drawing of His love that we are led to come to Him.

The perception of God's love works the renunciation of selfishness. In calling God our Father, we recognize all His children as our brethren. We are all a part of the great web of humanity, all members of one family. In our petitions we are to include our neighbors as well as ourselves. No one prays aright who seeks a blessing for himself alone.

The infinite God, said Jesus, makes it your privilege to approach Him by the name of Father. Understand all that this implies. No earthly parents ever pleaded so earnestly with an erring child as He who made you pleads with the transgressor. No human, loving interest ever followed the impenitent with such tender invitations. God dwells in every abode; He hears every word that is spoken, listens to every prayer that is offered, tastes the sorrows and disappointments of every soul, regards the treatment that is given to father, mother, sister, friend, and neighbor. He cares for our necessities, and His love and mercy and grace are continually flowing to satisfy our need.

But if you call God your Father you acknowledge yourselves His children, to be guided by His wisdom and to be obedient in all things, knowing that His love is changeless. You will accept His plan for your life. As children of God, you will hold His honor, His character, His family, His work, as the objects of your highest interest. It will be your joy to recognize and honor your relation to your Father and to every member of His family. You will rejoice to do any act, however humble, that will tend to His glory or to the well-being of your kindred (*Thoughts From the Mount of Blessing*, pp. 104-106).

The Law of Life for the Universe

In the beginning you laid the foundations of the earth, and the heavens are the work of your hands. Psalm 102:25, NIV.

In the beginning, God was revealed in all the works of creation. It was Christ that spread the heavens, and laid the foundations of the earth. It was His hand that hung the worlds in space, and fashioned the flowers of the field. "His strength setteth fast the mountains." "The sea is his, and he made it" (Psalm 65:6; 95:5). It was He that filled the earth with beauty, and the air with song. And upon all things in earth, and air, and sky, He wrote the messages of the Father's love.

Now sin has marred God's perfect work, yet that handwriting remains. Even now all created things declare the glory of His excellence. There is nothing, save the selfish heart of man, that lives unto itself. No bird that cleaves the air, no animal that moves upon the ground, but ministers to some other life. There is no leaf of the forest, or lowly blade of grass, but has its ministry. Every tree and shrub and leaf pours forth that element of life without which neither man nor animal could live; and man and animal, in turn, minister to the life of tree and shrub and leaf. The flowers breathe fragrance and unfold their beauty in blessing to the world. The sun sheds its light to gladden a thousand worlds. The ocean, itself the source of all our springs and fountains, receives the streams from every land, but takes to give. The mists ascending from its bosom fall in showers to water the earth, that it may bring forth and bud.

The angels of glory find their joy in giving—giving love and tireless watchcare to souls that are fallen and unholy. Heavenly beings woo the hearts of men; they bring to this dark world light from the courts above; by gentle and patient ministry they move upon the human spirit, to bring the lost into a fellowship with Christ which is even closer than they themselves can know.

But turning from all lesser representations, we behold God in Jesus. Looking unto Jesus we see that it is the glory of our God to give. "I do nothing of myself," said Christ; "the living Father hath sent me, and I live by the Father." "I seek not mine own glory," but the glory of Him that sent Me. In these words is set forth the great principle which is the law of life for the universe. All things Christ received from God, but He took to give. So in the heavenly courts, in His ministry for all created beings: through the beloved Son, the Father's life flows out to all; through the Son it returns, in praise and joyous service, a tide of love, to the great Source of all. And thus through Christ the circuit of beneficence is complete, representing the character of the great Giver, the law of life (*The Desire of Ages*, pp. 20, 21).

The Creation of the World

In the beginning God created the heaven and the earth. Genesis 1:1.

The Father and the Son engaged in the mighty, wondrous work they had contemplated—of creating the world. The earth came forth from the hand of the Creator exceedingly beautiful. There were mountains and hills and plains; and interspersed among them were rivers and bodies of water. The earth was not one extensive plain, but the monotony of the scenery was broken by hills and mountains, not high and ragged as they now are, but regular and beautiful in shape. The bare, high rocks were never seen upon them, but lay beneath the surface, answering as bones to the earth. The waters were regularly dispersed. The hills, mountains, and very beautiful plains were adorned with plants and flowers, and tall, majestic trees of every description, which were many times larger and much more beautiful than trees now are. The air was pure and healthful, and the earth seemed like a noble palace. Angels beheld and rejoiced at the wonderful and beautiful works of God.

After the earth was created, and the beasts upon it, the Father and Son carried out their purpose, which was designed before the fall of Satan, to make man in their own image. They had wrought together in the creation of the earth and every living thing upon it. And now God said to His Son, "Let us make man in our image." As Adam came forth from the hand of his Creator he was of noble height and of beautiful symmetry. He was more than twice as tall as men now living upon the earth, and was well proportioned. His features were perfect and beautiful. . . . Eve was not quite as tall as Adam. Her head reached a little above his shoulders. She, too, was noble, perfect in symmetry, and very beautiful.

This sinless pair wore no artificial garments. They were clothed with a covering of light and glory, such as the angels wear. While they lived in obedience to God, this circle of light enshrouded them. Although everything God had made was in the perfection of beauty, and there seemed nothing wanting upon the earth which God had created to make Adam and Eve happy, yet He manifested His great love to them by planting a garden especially for them. A portion of their time was to be occupied in the happy employment of dressing the garden, and a portion in receiving the visits of angels, listening to their instruction, and in happy mediation (*The Story of Redemption*, pp. 20, 21).

Man came from the hand of God perfect in every faculty of mind and body; in perfect soundness, therefore in perfect health (*My Life Today*, p. 126).

Created in God's Image

And God said, Let us make man in our image, after our likeness. Genesis 1:26.

The life of Christ is to be revealed in humanity. Man was the crowning act of the creation of God, made in the image of God, and designed to be a counterpart of God; but Satan has labored to obliterate the image of God in man, and to imprint upon him his own image. Man is very dear to God, because he was formed in His own image. This fact should impress us with the importance of teaching by precept and example the sin of defiling, by the indulgence of appetite, or by any other sinful practice, the body which is designed to represent God to the world. . . .

In order to understand the value which God places upon man, we need to comprehend the plan of redemption, the costly sacrifice which our Savior made to save the human race from eternal ruin. Jesus died to regain possession of the one pearl of great price. . . . The life of God's children is a life of self-denial, of self-sacrifice, a life of humility. Those who are not partakers of His sufferings cannot hope to share in His glory. . . . We are to be judged according to the manner in which we use the knowledge of the truth which has been presented to us.

The Lord gave His only begotten Son to ransom us from sin. We are His workmanship, we are His representatives in the world, and He expects that we shall reveal the true value of man by our purity of life, and the earnest efforts put forth to recover the pearl of great price. Our character is to be modeled after the divine similitude, and to be reformed by that faith that works by love and purifies the soul. The grace of God will beautify, ennoble, and sanctify the character. The servant of the Lord who works intelligently will be successful. Our Savior said, "Greater works than these shall he do; because I go unto my Father."

What are these "greater works"? If our lips are touched with the living coal from off the altar, we shall reveal to the world the wonderful love manifested by God in giving Jesus, His only begotten Son, to the world, "that whosoever believeth in him should *not perish*, but have everlasting life."

The mystery of the incarnation of Christ, the account of His sufferings, His crucifixion, His resurrection, and His ascension, open to all humanity the marvelous love of God. This imparts a power to the truth. The attributes of God were made known through the life and works of Christ. He was the representative of the divine character (*Review and Herald*, June 18, 1895).

God's creation is but a reservoir of means made ready for Him to employ instantly to do His pleasure (*The SDA Bible Commentary*, Ellen White Comments, vol. 1, p. 1081).

The Creator Planned for Our Happiness

And the Lord God planted a garden eastward in Eden; and there he put the man whom he had formed. Genesis 2:8.

Notwithstanding all that has been said and written regarding the dignity of manual labor, the feeling prevails that it is degrading. Popular opinion has, in many minds, changed the order of things, and men have come to think that it is not fitting for a man who works with his hands to take his place among gentlemen. Men work hard to obtain money; and having gained wealth, they suppose that their money will make their sons gentlemen. But many such fail to train their sons as they themselves were trained, to hard, useful labor. Their sons spend the money earned by the labor of others, without understanding its value. Thus they misuse a talent that the Lord designed should accomplish much good.

The Lord's purposes are not the purposes of men. He did not design that men should live in idleness. In the beginning He created man a gentleman; but though rich in all that the Owner of the universe could supply, Adam was not to be idle. No sooner was he created than his work was given him. He was to find employment and happiness in tending the things that God had created, and in response to his labor his wants were to be abundantly supplied from the fruits of the Garden of Eden.

While our first parents obeyed God, their labor in the garden was a pleasure, and the earth yielded of its abundance for their wants. But when man departed from obedience, he was doomed to wrestle with the seeds of Satan's sowing and to earn his bread by the sweat of his brow. Henceforth he must battle in toil and hardship against the power to which he had yielded his will.

It was God's purpose to alleviate by toil the evil brought into the world by man's disobedience. By toil the temptations of Satan might be made ineffectual and the tide of evil stayed. And though attended with anxiety, weariness, and pain, labor is still a source of happiness and development, and a safeguard against temptation. Its discipline places a check on self-indulgence and promotes industry, purity, and firmness. Thus it becomes a part of God's great plan for our recovery from the Fall (*Counsels to Parents, Teachers, and Students*, pp. 273, 274).

The Creator of man has arranged the living machinery of our bodies. . . . Every law governing the human machinery is to be considered just as truly divine in origin, in character, and in importance as the Word of God. Every careless, inattentive action, any abuse put upon the Lord's wonderful mechanism by disregarding His specified laws in the human habitation, is a violation of God's law. We may behold and admire the work of God in the natural world, but the human habitation is the most wonderful (*Medical Ministry*, p. 221).

God's Love Expressed in Creation

For by him were all things created, that are in heaven, and that are in earth, visible and invisible, whether they be thrones, or dominions, or principalities, or powers: all things were created by him, and for him. Colossians 1:16.

God is love" (1 John 4:16). His nature, His law, is love. . . . Every manifestation of creative power is an expression of infinite love. The sovereignty of God involves fullness of blessing to all created beings. . . .

The history of the great conflict between good and evil, from the time it first began in heaven to the final overthrow of rebellion and the total eradication of sin, is also a demonstration of God's unchanging love.

The Sovereign of the universe was not alone in His work of beneficence. He had an associate—a coworker who could appreciate His purposes, and could share His joy in giving happiness to created beings. "In the beginning was the Word, and the Word was with God, and the Word was God. The same was in the beginning with God" (John 1:1, 2). Christ, the Word, the only begotten of God, was one with the eternal Father—one in nature, in character, in purpose—the only being that could enter into all the counsels and purposes of God. "His name shall be called Wonderful, Counsellor, The mighty God, The everlasting Father, The Prince of Peace" (Isaiah 9:6). . . .

The Father wrought by His Son in the creation of all heavenly beings. "By him were all things created, . . . whether they be thrones, or dominions, or principalities, or powers: all things were created by him, and for him" (Colossians 1:16). Angels are God's ministers, radiant with the light ever flowing from His presence and speeding on rapid wing to execute His will. But the Son, the anointed of God, the "express image of his person," "the brightness of his glory," "upholding all things by the word of his power," holds supremacy over them all (Hebrews 1:3). . . .

The law of love being the foundation of the government of God, the happiness of all intelligent beings depends upon their perfect accord with its great principles of righteousness. God desires from all His creatures the service of love—service that springs from an appreciation of His character. He takes no pleasure in a forced obedience; and to all He grants freedom of will, that they may render Him voluntary service.

So long as all created beings acknowledged the allegiance of love, there was perfect harmony throughout the universe of God. It was the joy of the heavenly host to fulfill the purpose of their Creator. They delighted in reflecting His glory and showing forth His praise. And while love to God was supreme, love for one another was confiding and unselfish. There was no note of discord to mar the celestial harmonies (*Patriarchs and Prophets*, pp. 33-35).

Worship the Creator

Worship him that made heaven, and earth, and the sea, and the fountains of waters
Revelation 14:7.

The duty to worship God is based upon the fact that He is the Creator and that to Him all other beings owe their existence. And wherever, in the Bible, His claim to reverence and worship, above the gods of the heathen, is presented, there is cited the evidence of His creative power. "All the gods of the nations are idols: but the Lord made the heavens" (Psalm 96:5). "To whom then will ye liken me, or shall I be equal? saith the Holy One. Lift up your eyes on high, and behold who hath created these things." "Thus saith the Lord that created the heavens; God Himself that formed the earth and made it: . . . I am the Lord; and there is none else" (Isaiah 40:25, 26; 45:18).

Says the psalmist: "Know ye that the Lord he is God: it is he that hath made us, and not we ourselves." "O come, let us worship and bow down: let us kneel before the Lord our maker" (Psalm 100:3; 95:6). And the holy beings who worship God in heaven state, as the reason why their homage is due to Him: "Thou art worthy, O Lord, to receive glory and honour and power: for thou hast created all things" (Revelation 4:11).

In Revelation 14, men are called upon to worship the Creator; and the prophecy brings to view a class that, as the result of the threefold message, are keeping the commandments of God. One of these commandments points directly to God as the Creator. The fourth precept declares: "The seventh day is the sabbath of the Lord thy God: . . . for in six days the Lord made heaven and earth, the sea, and all that in them is, and rested the seventh day: wherefore the Lord blessed the sabbath day, and hallowed it" (Exodus 20:10, 11). Concerning the Sabbath, the Lord says, further, that it is "a sign, . . . that ye may know that I am the Lord your God" (Ezekiel 20:20). And the reason given is: "For in six days the Lord made heaven and earth, and on the seventh day he rested, and was refreshed" (Exodus 31:17). . . .

So long as the fact that He is our Creator continues to be a reason why we should worship Him, so long the Sabbath will continue as its sign and memorial. Had the Sabbath been universally kept, man's thoughts and affections would have been led to the Creator as an object of reverence and worship, and there would never have been an idolater, an atheist, or an infidel. The keeping of the Sabbath is a sign of loyalty to the true God, "him that made heaven, and earth, and the sea, and the fountains of waters." It follows that the message which commands men to worship God and keep His commandments will especially call upon them to keep the fourth commandment (*The Great Controversy*, pp. 436-438).

Earth's First Week

For in six days the Lord made heaven and earth, the sea and all that in them is, and rested the seventh day: wherefore the Lord blessed the sabbath day, and hallowed it. Exodus 20:11.

The weekly cycle of seven literal days, six for labor, and the seventh for rest, which has been preserved and brought down through Bible history, originated in the great facts of the first seven days.

When God spake His law with an audible voice from Sinai, He introduced the Sabbath by saying, "Remember the sabbath day, to keep it holy." He then declares definitely what shall be done on the six days, and what shall not be done on the seventh. He then, in giving the reason for thus observing the week, points them back to His example on the first seven days of time. "For in six days the Lord made heaven and earth, the sea, and all that in them is, and rested the seventh day: wherefore the Lord blessed the sabbath day and hallowed it."

This reason appears beautiful and forcible when we understand the record of Creation to mean literal days. The first six days of each week are given to man in which to labor, because God employed the same period of the first week in the work of creation. The seventh day God has reserved as a day of rest, in commemoration of His rest during the same period of time after He had performed the work of creation in six days.

But the infidel supposition, that the events of the first week required seven vast, indefinite periods for their accomplishment, strikes directly at the foundation of the Sabbath of the fourth commandment. It makes indefinite and obscure that which God has made very plain. . . .

Infidel geologists claim that the world is very much older than the Bible record makes it. They reject the Bible record, because of those things which are to them evidences from the earth itself, that the world has existed tens of thousands of years. And many who profess to believe the Bible record are at a loss to account for wonderful things which are found in the earth, with the view that Creation week was only seven literal days, and the world is now only about six thousand years old. . . .

Without Bible history, geology can prove nothing. Relics found in the earth do give evidence of a state of things differing in many respects from the present. But the time of their existence, and how long a period these things have been in the earth, are only to be understood by Bible history. . . . When men leave the Word of God in regard to the history of Creation, and seek to account for God's creative works upon natural principles, they are upon a boundless ocean of uncertainty. Just how God accomplished the work of Creation in six literal days He has never revealed to mortals. His creative works are just as incomprehensible as His existence (*Spiritual Gifts*, vol. 3, pp. 90-93).

The Sabbath Points to the Creator

Verily my sabbaths ye shall keep: for it is a sign between me and you throughout your generations; that ye may know that I am the Lord that doth sanctify you. Exodus 31:13.

The Sabbath was given to all mankind to commemorate the work of creation. The great Jehovah, when He had laid the foundations of the earth, when He had dressed the whole world in its garb of beauty, and created all the wonders of the land and the sea, instituted the Sabbath day and made it holy. When the morning stars sang together, and all the sons of God shouted for joy, the Sabbath was set apart as God's memorial. God sanctified and blessed the day in which He has rested from all His wondrous work. And this Sabbath, sanctified of God, was to be kept for a perpetual covenant. It was a memorial that was to stand from age to age, till the close of earth's history.

God brought the Hebrews out of their Egyptian bondage, and commanded them to observe His Sabbath, and keep the law given in Eden. Every week He worked a miracle to establish in their minds the fact that in the beginning of the world He had instituted the Sabbath. . . .

There are those who hold that the Sabbath was given only for the Jews; but God has never said this. He committed the Sabbath to His people Israel as a sacred trust; but the very fact that the desert of Sinai, and not Palestine, was the place selected by Him in which to proclaim His law, reveals that He intended it for all mankind. The law of ten commandments is as old as creation. Therefore the Sabbath institution has no special relation to the Jews, any more than to all other created beings. God has made the observance of the Sabbath obligatory upon all men. "The sabbath," it is plainly stated, "was made for man." Let every one, therefore, who is in danger of being deceived on this point give heed to the Word of God rather than the assertions of men.

In Eden, God said to Adam concerning the tree of knowledge, "In the day that thou eatest thereof thou shalt surely die." "And the serpent said unto the woman, Ye shall not surely die: for God doth know that in the day ye eat thereof, then your eyes shall be opened, and ye shall be as gods, knowing good and evil." Adam listened to the voice of Satan speaking through his wife; he believed another voice than that which spoke the law in Eden. . . .

As the tree of knowledge was the test of Adam's obedience, so the fourth command is the test that God has given to prove the loyalty of all His people. The experience of Adam is to be a warning to us so long as time shall last. It warns us not to receive any assurance from the mouth of men or of angels that will detract one jot or tittle from the sacred law of Jehovah (*Review and Herald*, Aug. 30, 1898).

The Heavens Declare the Glory of God

The heavens declare the glory of God; and the firmament sheweth his handywork.
Psalm 19:1.

The Creator has given abundant evidence that His power is unlimited, that He can establish kingdoms, and overturn kingdoms. He upholds the world by the word of His power. He made the night, marshaling the shining stars in the firmament. He calls them all by name. The heavens declare the glory of God, and the firmament showeth His handiwork, showing men that this little world is but a jot in God's creation. . . .

The inhabitants of the unfallen worlds look with pity and reproach on man's pride and self-importance. The wealthy and the honored of the world are not the only ones who glorify self. Many who profess to revere God talk of their wisdom and their might. They act as if God is under obligations to them, as if He cannot carry on His work without their aid. Let such gaze into the starry heavens, and with admiration and awe study the marvelous works of God. Let them think of the wisdom He displays in maintaining perfect order in the vast universe, and of the little reason that man has to boast of his attainments.

All that man has—life, the means of existence, happiness, and other blessings unnumbered that come to him day by day—is from the Father above. Man is a debtor for all he proudly claims as his own. God gives His precious gifts, that they may be used in His service. Every particle of the glory of man's success belongs to God. It is His manifold wisdom that is displayed in the works of men, and to Him belongs the praise (*Youth's Instructor*, Apr. 4, 1905).

By and by the gates of heaven will be thrown open to admit God's children, and from the lips of the King of glory the benediction will fall on their ears like richest music, "Come, ye blessed of my Father, inherit the kingdom prepared for you from the foundation of the world" (Matthew 25:34).

Then the redeemed will be welcomed to the home that Jesus is preparing for them. There their companions will not be the vile of earth, liars, idolaters, the impure, and unbelieving; but they will associate with those who have overcome Satan and through divine grace have formed perfect characters. Every sinful tendency, every imperfection, that afflicts them here has been removed by the blood of Christ, and the excellence and brightness of His glory, far exceeding the brightness of the sun, is imparted to them (*Steps to Christ*, pp. 125, 126).

His by Creation and Redemption

Thy hands have made me and fashioned me. Psalm 119:73.

Let us take in the idea of the privilege we have. There are so many who, when they are in trouble, fall into temptation and lose their bearings. They forget the invitations God has abundantly given, and begin to look and plan for human help. They go to human beings for aid, and this is the way in which their experience becomes feeble, and confused. In all our trials we are directed to seek the Lord most earnestly, remembering that we are His property, His children by adoption. No human being can understand our necessities as Christ. We shall receive help if we ask Him in faith. We are His by creation, we are His by redemption. By the cords of divine love we are bound to the Source of all power and strength. If we will only make God our dependence, asking Him for what we want as a little child asks his father for what he wants, we shall obtain a rich experience. We shall learn that God is the source of all strength and power.

If when you ask, you do not immediately feel any special exercise of feeling, do not think that your prayer is not answered. The One who says, "Ask, and it shall be given you; seek, and ye shall find; knock, and it shall be opened unto you: for every one that asketh receiveth; and he that seeketh findeth; and to him that knocketh it shall be opened," *will hear and answer you.* Let then His Word be your trust, ask and seek, and have the privilege of finding. Christ has encouraged you. He says, "Come unto me, *all ye that labour and are heavy laden,* and I *will give you rest.* Take my yoke upon you"—the yoke of restraint and obedience—"and learn of me, for I am meek and lowly in heart: and ye shall find rest unto your souls."

We are to find rest by wearing His yoke and bearing His burdens. In being coworkers with Christ in the great work for which He gave His life, we shall find true rest. When we were sinners He gave His life for us. He wants us to come to Him and learn of Him. Thus we are to find rest. *He* says He will give us rest. Then do not lay your burdens upon any human being. "Learn of Me; for I am meek and lowly in heart." In doing this you will find in your own experience the rest that Christ gives, the rest that comes from wearing His yoke and lifting His burdens.

God has been greatly dishonored by His people leaning upon human beings. He has not told us to do this. He has told us that He will teach us, He will guide us. . . . Think of how many promises He has given us, which we may grasp by the hand of faith. . . . He wants us to become acquainted with Him, to speak to Him, to tell Him of our difficulties, and obtain an experience in asking of One who never misjudges and never makes a mistake (manuscript 144, 1901).

February

11

The Soul
Re-created in the Image of God

The words that I speak unto you, they are spirit, and they are life. John 6:63.

The central theme of the Bible, the theme about which every other in the whole book clusters, is the redemption plan, the restoration in the human soul of the image of God. From the first intimation of hope in the sentence pronounced in Eden to that last glorious promise of the Revelation, "They shall see his face; and his name shall be in their foreheads" (Revelation 22:4), the burden of every book and every passage of the Bible is the unfolding of this wondrous theme—man's uplifting—the power of God, "which giveth us the victory through our Lord Jesus Christ."

He who grasps this thought has before him an infinite field for study. He has the key that will unlock to him the whole treasure house of God's Word. . . .

The creative energy that called the worlds into existence is in the Word of God. This word imparts power; it begets life. Every command is a promise; accepted by the will, received into the soul, it brings with it the life of the Infinite One. It transforms the nature, and re-creates the soul in the image of God.

The life thus imparted is in like manner sustained. "By every word that proceedeth out of the mouth of God" shall man live.

The mind, the soul, is built up by that upon which it feeds; and it rests with us to determine upon what it shall be fed. It is within the power of everyone to choose the topics that shall occupy the thoughts and shape the character. . . .

With the Word of God in his hands, every human being, wherever his lot in life may be cast, may have such companionship as he shall choose. In its pages he may hold converse with the noblest and best of the human race, and may listen to the voice of the Eternal as He speaks with men. As he studies and meditates upon the themes into which "the angels desire to look," he may have their companionship. He may follow the steps of the heavenly Teacher, and listen to His words as when He taught on mountain and plain and sea.

He may dwell in this world in the atmosphere of heaven, imparting to earth's sorrowing and tempted ones thoughts of hope and longings for holiness; himself coming closer and still closer into fellowship with the Unseen; like him of old who walked with God, drawing nearer and nearer the threshold of the eternal world, until the portals shall open, and he shall enter there. He will find himself no stranger. The voices that will greet him are the voices of the holy ones, who, unseen, were on earth his companions—voices that here he learned to distinguish and to love. He who through the Word of God has lived in fellowship with heaven will find himself at home in heaven's companionship (*Education*, pp. 125-127).

Power Over the Tempest

And he arose, and rebuked the wind, and said unto the sea, Peace, be still. And the wind ceased, and there was a great calm. And he said unto them, Why are ye so fearful? how is it that ye have no faith? Mark 4:39, 40.

It had been an eventful day in the life of Jesus. Beside the Sea of Galilee He had spoken His first parables, by familiar illustrations again explaining to the people the nature of His kingdom. . . .

All day He had been teaching and healing; and as evening came on the crowds still pressed upon Him. . . . Now the close of the day found Him so utterly wearied that He determined to seek retirement in some solitary place across the lake. . . .

The Savior was at last relieved from the pressure of the multitude, and, overcome with weariness and hunger, He lay down in the stern of the boat, and soon fell asleep. The evening had been calm and pleasant, and quiet rested upon the lake; but suddenly darkness overspread the sky, the wind swept wildly down the mountain gorges along the eastern shore, and a fierce tempest burst upon the lake. . . .

The waves, lashed into fury by the howling winds, dashed fiercely over the disciples' boat, and threatened to engulf it. Those hardy fishermen had spent their lives upon the lake, and had guided their craft safely through many a storm; but now their strength and skill availed nothing. They were helpless in the grasp of the tempest, and hope failed them as they saw that their boat was filling.

Absorbed in their efforts to save themselves, they had forgotten that Jesus was on board. Now, seeing their labor vain and only death before them, they remembered at whose command they had set out to cross the sea. In Jesus was their only hope. In their helplessness and despair they cried, "Master, Master!" But the dense darkness hid Him from their sight. Their voices were drowned by the roaring of the tempest. . . .

Suddenly a flash of lightning pierces the darkness, and they see Jesus lying asleep, undisturbed by the tumult. In amazement and despair they exclaim, "Master, carest thou not that we perish?" . . . As the lightning's glare reveals Him, they see the peace of heaven in His face; they read in His glance self-forgetful, tender love, and, their hearts turning to Him, cry, "Lord, save us: we perish."

Never did a soul utter that cry unheeded. As the disciples grasp their oars to make a last effort, Jesus rises. He stands in the midst of His disciples, while the tempest rages. . . . He lifts His hand, so often employed in deeds of mercy, and says to the angry sea, "Peace, be still." . . . As Jesus rested by faith in the Father's care, so we are to rest in the care of our Savior (*The Desire of Ages*, pp. 333-336).

Created Anew

Be not conformed to this world: but be ye transformed by the renewing of your mind, that ye may prove what is that good, and acceptable, and perfect, will of God. Romans 12:2.

Christ died on the cross to save the world from perishing in sin. He asks your cooperation in this work. You are to be His helping hand. With earnest, unwearying effort you are to seek to save the lost. Remember that it was your sins that made the cross necessary. When you accepted Christ as your Savior you pledged yourself to unite with Him in bearing the cross. For life and for death you are bound up with Him, a part of the great plan of redemption.

The transforming power of Christ's grace molds the one who gives himself to God's service. Imbued with the Spirit of the Redeemer, he is ready to deny self, ready to take up the cross, ready to make any sacrifice for the Master. No longer can he be indifferent to the souls perishing around him. He is lifted above self-serving. He has been created anew in Christ, and self-serving has no place in his life. He realizes that every part of his being belongs to Christ, who has redeemed him from the slavery of sin; that every moment of his future has been bought with the precious lifeblood of God's only-begotten Son.

Have you so deep an appreciation of the sacrifice made on Calvary that you are willing to make every other interest subordinate to the work of saving souls? The same intensity of desire to save sinners that marked the life of the Savior marks the life of His true follower. The Christian has no desire to live for self. He delights to consecrate all that he has and is to the Master's service. He is moved by an inexpressible desire to win souls to Christ. . . .

How can I best glorify Him whose I am by creation and by redemption? This is to be the question that we are to ask ourselves. With anxious solicitude the one who is truly converted seeks to rescue those who are still in Satan's power. He refuses to do anything that would hinder him in his work. If he has children he realizes that his work must begin in his own family. His children are exceedingly precious to him. Remembering that they are the younger members of the Lord's family, he strives with all his power to place them where they will stand on the Lord's side. He has pledged himself to serve, honor, and obey Christ; and he puts forth patient, untiring effort so to train his children that they will never be hostile to the Savior.

On fathers and mothers, God has placed the responsibility of saving their children from the power of the enemy. This is their work, a work that they should on no account neglect. Those parents who have a living connection with Christ will not rest until they see their children safe in the fold. They will make this the burden of their life (*Testimonies*, vol. 7, pp. 9-11).

Creation Provides Evidence for Faith

The secret things belong unto the Lord our God: but those things which are revealed belong unto us and to our children for ever. Deuteronomy 29:29.

The Word of God is given as a lamp unto our feet, and a light unto our path. Those who cast His Word behind them, and seek by their own blind philosophy to trace out the wonderful mysteries of Jehovah will stumble in darkness. A guide has been given to mortals whereby they may trace Jehovah and His work as far as will be for their good. Inspiration, in giving us the history of the Flood, has explained wonderful mysteries, that geology, independent of inspiration, never could.

It has been the special work of Satan to lead fallen man to rebel against God's government, and he has succeeded too well in his efforts. He has tried to obscure the law of God, which in itself is very plain. He has manifested a special hate against the fourth precept of the Decalogue, because it defines the living God, the Maker of the heavens and the earth. The plainest precepts of Jehovah are turned from, to receive infidel fables.

Man will be left without excuse. God has given sufficient evidence upon which to base faith if he wish to believe. In the last days the earth will be almost destitute of true faith. Upon the merest pretense, the Word of God will be considered unreliable, while human reasoning will be received, though it be in opposition to plain Scripture facts. Men will endeavor to explain from natural causes the work of creation, which God has never revealed. But human science cannot search out the secrets of the God of heaven, and explain the stupendous works of creation, which were a miracle of Almighty power, any sooner than it can show how God came into existence.

"The secret things belong unto the Lord our God: but those things which are revealed belong unto us and to our children for ever." . . . God's ways are not as our ways, neither are His thoughts as our thoughts. Human science can never account for His wondrous works. God so ordered that men, beasts, and trees, many times larger than those now upon the earth, and other things, should be buried in the earth at the time of the Flood, and there be preserved to evidence to man that the inhabitants of the old world perished by a flood. God designed that the discovery of these things in the earth should establish the faith of men in inspired history. But men, with their vain reasoning, make a wrong use of these things which God designed should lead them to exalt Him (*Spiritual Gifts*, vol. 3, pp. 94-96).

All Truth Agrees

The Lord made the heavens. . . . Give unto the Lord the glory due unto his name.
1 Chronicles 16:26-29.

There are men who think they have made wonderful discoveries in science. They quote the opinions of learned men as though they considered them infallible, and teach the deductions of science as truths that cannot be controverted. And the Word of God, which is given as a lamp to the feet of the world-weary traveler, is judged by this standard, and pronounced wanting. The scientific research in which these men have indulged has proved a snare to them. It has clouded their minds, and they have drifted into skepticism. They have a consciousness of power; and instead of looking to the Source of all wisdom, they triumph in the smattering of knowledge they may have gained. They have exalted their human wisdom in opposition to the wisdom of the great and mighty God, and have dared to enter into controversy with Him.

God has permitted a flood of light to be poured upon the world in discoveries in science and art; but when professedly scientific men lecture and write upon these subjects from a merely human standpoint, they will assuredly come to wrong conclusions. The greatest minds, if not guided by the Word of God in their research, become bewildered in their attempts to investigate the relations of science and revelation. The Creator and His works are beyond their comprehension; and because they cannot explain these by natural laws, Bible history is considered unreliable. Those who doubt the reliability of the records of the Old and New Testaments will be led to go a step farther, and doubt the existence of God; and then, having let go their anchor, they are left to beat about upon the rocks of infidelity. Moses wrote under the guidance of the Spirit of God, and a correct theory of geology will never claim discoveries that cannot be reconciled with his statements. The idea that many stumble over, that God did not create matter when He brought the world into existence, limits the power of the Holy One of Israel.

Many, when they find themselves incapable of measuring the Creator and His works by their own imperfect knowledge of science, doubt the existence of God and attribute infinite power to nature. These persons have lost the simplicity of faith, and are removed far from God in mind and spirit. There should be a settled faith in the divinity of God's holy Word. The Bible is not to be tested by men's ideas of science, but science is to be brought to the test of this unerring standard. When the Bible makes statements of facts in nature, science may be compared with the written Word, and a correct understanding of both will always prove them to be in harmony. One does not contradict the other. All truth, whether in nature or revelation, agrees (*Signs of the Times*, Mar. 13, 1884).

Unlimited in Power

He spake, and it was done; he commanded, and it stood fast. Psalm 33:9.

Scientific research will open to the minds of the really wise vast fields of thought and information. They will see God in His works, and will praise Him. He will be to them first and best, and the mind will be centered upon Him. Skeptics, who read the Bible for the sake of caviling, through ignorance claim to find decided contradictions between science and revelation. But man's measurement of God will never be correct. The mind unenlightened by God's Spirit will ever be in darkness in regard to His power.

Spiritual things are spiritually discerned. Those who have no vital union with God are swayed one way and another; they put men's opinions in the front, and God's Word in the background. They grasp human assertions, that judgment against sin is contrary to God's benevolent character, and, while dwelling upon infinite benevolence, try to forget that there is such a thing as infinite justice.

When we have right views of the power, greatness, and majesty of God, and of the weakness of man, we shall despise the assumptions of wisdom made by earth's so-called great men, who have none of Heaven's nobility in their characters. There is nothing for which men should be praised or exalted. There is no reason why the opinions of the learned should be trusted, when they are disposed to measure divine things by their own perverted conceptions. Those who serve God are the only ones whose opinion and example it is safe to follow. A sanctified heart quickens and intensifies the mental powers. A living faith in God imparts energy; it gives calmness and repose of spirit, and strength and nobility of character.

Men of science think that with their enlarged conceptions they can comprehend the wisdom of God, that which He has done or can do. The idea largely prevails that He is bounded and restricted by His own laws. Men either deny and ignore His existence, or think to explain everything, even the operations of His Spirit upon the human heart, by natural laws; and they no longer reverence His name or fear His power. While they think they are gaining everything, they are chasing bubbles, and losing precious opportunities to become acquainted with God. They do not believe in the supernatural, not realizing that the Author of nature's laws can work above those laws. They deny the claims of God, and neglect the interests of their own souls; but His existence, His character, His laws, are facts that the reasoning of men of the highest attainments cannot overthrow. . . .

Nature is a power, but the God of nature is unlimited in power. His works interpret His character (*Signs of the Times*, Mar. 13, 1884).

Power to Multiply

Elisha said, "Give to the men, that they may eat." But his servant said, "How am I to set this before a hundred men?" So he repeated, "Give them to the men, that they may eat." 2 Kings 4:42, 43, RSV.

And there came a man from Baal-shalisha, and brought the man of God bread of the firstfruits, twenty loaves of barley, and full ears of corn in the husk thereof. And he said, Give unto the people, that they may eat.

"And his servitor said, What, should I set this before an hundred men? He said again, Give the people, that they may eat: for thus saith the Lord, They shall eat, and shall leave thereof. So he set it before them, and they did eat, and left thereof, according to the word of the Lord" (2 Kings 4:42-44).

He who worked this miracle in behalf of one hundred men in the Old Testament times wrought a similar wonder for five thousand when as a Man He preached the gospel to men. In the wilderness Christ supplied His people not only with bread but with clear flowing streams. . . .

It is the grace of God on the small portion that makes it all-sufficient. God's hand can multiply it an hundredfold. From His resources He can spread a table in the wilderness for more than a million people. By the touch of His hand God can increase His scanty provision, and make it sufficient for all. It was His power that increased the loaves and corn in the hands of the sons of the prophets.

The Lord has given His life to the trees and vines of His creation. His word can increase or decrease the fruit of the land. If men would open their understanding to discern the relation between nature and nature's God, faithful acknowledgments of the Creator's power would be heard. Without the life of God, nature would die. His creative works are dependent upon Him. He bestows life-giving properties on all that nature produces. We are to regard the trees laden with fruit as the gift of God, just as much as though He placed the fruit in our hands (manuscript 114, 1899).

In feeding the five thousand, Jesus lifts the veil from the world of nature, and reveals the power that is constantly exercised for our good. In the production of earth's harvests God is working a miracle every day. Through natural agencies the same work is accomplished that was wrought in the feeding of the multitude. . . . It is God who is every day feeding millions from earth's harvest fields. Men are called upon to cooperate with God in the care of the grain and the preparation of the loaf, and because of this they lose sight of the divine agency. . . . He desires us to recognize Him in His gifts, that they may be, as He intended, a blessing to us (*The Desire of Ages*, pp. 367, 368).

Joseph Honored the Creator

The king . . . made him master of his household, ruler over all he possessed, to discipline his princes as he pleased and teach his elders wisdom. Psalm 105:20-22, NIV.

From the dungeon Joseph was exalted to be ruler over all the land of Egypt. It was a position of high honor, yet it was beset with difficulty and peril. One cannot stand upon a lofty height without danger. As the tempest leaves unharmed the lowly flower of the valley, while it uproots the stately tree upon the mountaintop, so those who have maintained their integrity in humble life may be dragged down to the pit by the temptations that assail worldly success and honor. But Joseph's character bore the test alike of adversity and prosperity. The same fidelity to God was manifest when he stood in the palace of the Pharaohs as when in a prisoner's cell. He was still a stranger in a heathen land, separated from his kindred, the worshipers of God; but he fully believed that the divine hand had directed his steps, and in constant reliance upon God he faithfully discharged the duties of his position. . . .

In his early years he had consulted duty rather than inclination; and the integrity, the simple trust, the noble nature, of the youth bore fruit in the deeds of the man. A pure and simple life had favored the vigorous development of both physical and intellectual powers. Communion with God through His works and the contemplation of the grand truths entrusted to the inheritors of faith had elevated and ennobled his spiritual nature, broadening and strengthening the mind as no other study could do. Faithful attention to duty in every station, from the lowliest to the most exalted, had been training every power for its highest service. He who lives in accordance with the Creator's will is securing to himself the truest and noblest development of character. . . .

There are few who realize the influence of the little things of life upon the development of character. Nothing with which we have to do is really small. The varied circumstances that we meet day by day are designed to test our faithfulness and to qualify us for greater trusts. By adherence to principle in the transactions of ordinary life, the mind becomes accustomed to hold the claims of duty above those of pleasure and inclination (*Patriarchs and Prophets*, pp. 222, 223).

As a shield from temptation and an inspiration to purity and truth, no other influence can equal the sense of God's presence. "All things are naked and opened unto the eyes of him with whom we have to do." He is "of purer eyes than to behold evil, and canst not look on iniquity." This thought was Joseph's shield amidst the corruptions of Egypt. To the allurements of temptation his answer was steadfast: "How . . . can I do this great wickedness, and sin against God?" Such a shield, faith, if cherished, will bring to every soul (*Education*, p. 255).

Our Vital Force

And all the days that Adam lived were nine hundred and thirty years: and he died. Genesis 5:5.

The book of Genesis gives quite a definite account of social and individual life, and yet we have no record of an infant's being born blind, deaf, crippled, deformed, or imbecile. There is not an instance upon record of a natural death in infancy, childhood, or early manhood. There is no account of men and women dying of disease. Obituary notices in the book of Genesis run thus: "And all the days that Adam lived were nine hundred and thirty years: and he died." "And all the days of Seth were nine hundred and twelve years: and he died." Concerning others, the record states: He lived to a good old age; and he died. It was so rare for a son to die before the father that such an occurrence was considered worthy of record: "And Haran died before his father Terah." Haran was a father of children before his death.

God endowed man with so great vital force that he has withstood the accumulation of disease brought upon the race in consequence of perverted habits, and has continued for six thousand years. This fact of itself is enough to evidence to us the strength and electrical energy that God gave to man at his creation. It took more than two thousand years of crime and indulgence of base passions to bring bodily disease upon the race to any great extent. If Adam, at his creation, had not been endowed with twenty times as much vital force as men now have, the race, with their present habits of living in violation of natural law, would have become extinct. At the time of Christ's first advent the race had degenerated so rapidly that an accumulation of disease pressed upon that generation, bringing in a tide of woe and a weight of misery inexpressible. . . .

God did not create the race in its present feeble condition. This state of things is not the work of Providence, but the work of man; it has been brought about by wrong habits and abuses, by violating the laws that God had made to govern man's existence. Through the temptation to indulge appetite, Adam and Eve first fell from their high, holy, and happy estate. And it is through the same temptation that the race have become enfeebled. They have permitted appetite and passion to take the throne, and to bring into subjection reason and intellect. . . .

The strange absence of principle which characterizes this generation, and which is shown in their disregard of the laws of life and health, is astonishing. Ignorance prevails upon this subject, while light is shining all around them. With the majority, their principal anxiety is, What shall I eat? what shall I drink? and wherewithal shall I be clothed? . . . How great is the contrast between this generation and those who lived during the first two thousand years! (*Testimonies*, vol. 3, pp. 138-141).

Yielding to the Master Potter

But now, O Lord, thou art our father; we are the clay, and thou our potter; and we all are the work of thy hand. Isaiah 64:8.

While the human agent is devising and planning for himself something that God has withheld him from doing, he has a hard time. He complains and frets, and has still increased difficulties. But when he submits to be as clay in the hands of the potter, then God works the man into a vessel of honor. The clay submits to be worked. If God had His way, hundreds would be worked and made into vessels as He sees best.

Let the hand of God work the clay for His own service. He knows just what kind of vessel He wants. To every man He has given his work. God knows what place he is best fitted for. Many are working contrary to the will of God, and they spoil the web. The Lord wants everyone to be submissive under His divine guidance. He will place men where they will submit to be worked into oneness with Christ, bearing His divine similitude. If self will submit to be worked, if you will cooperate with God, if you will pray in unity, work in unity, all taking your place as threads in the web of life, you will grow into a beautiful fabric that will rejoice the universe of God.

The Potter cannot mold and fashion unto honor that which has never been placed in His hands. The Christian life is one of daily surrender, submission, and continual overcoming. Every day fresh victories will be gained. Self must be lost sight of, and the love of God must be constantly cultivated. Thus we grow up into Christ. Thus the life is fashioned according to the divine model.

Every child of God is to do his very best to uplift the standard of truth. He is to work in God's order. If self is exalted, Christ is not magnified. In His Word God compares Himself to a potter, and His people to the clay. His work is to mold and fashion them after His own similitude. The lesson they are to learn is the lesson of submission. Self is not to be made prominent. If due attention is given to the divine instruction, if self is surrendered to the divine will, the hand of the Potter will produce a shapely vessel (*The SDA Bible Commentary*, Ellen G. White Comments, vol. 4, p. 1154).

The potter takes the clay in his hands and molds and fashions it according to his own will. He kneads it and works it. He tears it apart and then presses it together. . . . Thus it becomes a vessel fit for use. So the great Master Worker desires to mold and fashion us. And as the clay is in the hands of the potters, so are we to be in His hands. We are not to try to do the work of the potter. Our part is to yield ourselves to the molding of the Master Worker (*Testimonies*, vol. 8, pp. 186, 187).

God's Words Created His Works

*By the word of the Lord were the heavens made;
and all the host of them by the breath of his mouth. Psalm 33:6.*

The material world is under God's control. The laws that govern all nature are obeyed by nature. Everything speaks and acts the will of the Creator. The clouds, the rain, the dew, the sunshine, the showers, the wind, the storm, all are under the supervision of God, and yield implicit obedience to Him who employs them. The tiny spear of grass bursts its way through the earth, first the blade, then the ear, and then the full corn in the ear. The Lord uses these, His obedient servants, to do His will. The fruit is first seen in the bud, enclosing the future pear, peach, or apple, and the Lord develops these in their proper season, because they do not resist His working. They do not oppose the order of His arrangements. His works, as seen in the natural world, are not one half comprehended or appreciated. These silent preachers will teach human beings their lessons, if they will only be attentive hearers.

Can it be that man, made after the image of God, endowed with the faculties of reason and speech, shall alone be unappreciative of the gifts God has bestowed upon him, and which, if improved, can be enlarged. Shall those who might be elevated and ennobled, fitted to be colaborers with the greatest Teacher the world ever knew, be content to remain imperfect and incomplete in character, producing disorder when they might become vessels unto honor? Shall the bodies and souls of God's purchased inheritance be so hampered with worldbound habits and unholy practices that they will never reflect the beauty of the character of Him who has done all things well in order that imperfect man, through the grace of Christ, might do all things well, and hear at last Christ's benediction, "Well done, thou good and faithful servant: enter thou into the joy of thy lord"?

God spoke, and His words created His works in the natural world. God's creation is but a reservoir of means made ready for Him to employ instantly to do His pleasure. Nothing is useless, but the curse has caused tares to be sown by the enemy. Shall rational beings alone cause confusion in our world? Shall we not live to God? Shall we not honor Him? Our God and Savior is all-wise, all-sufficient. He came to our world that His perfection might be revealed in us. . . .

Our faith must increase. We must be more like Jesus in conduct and disposition. The light that shines on our path, the truth that commends itself to our intelligence, if obeyed, will sanctify and transform the soul. . . . The knowledge of truth, the heavenly wisdom, spiritual endowments, are heaven's goods, committed to us for wise improvement (letter 131, 1897).

February
22

God's Creative Energy Upholds the Universe

He covers the sky with clouds; he supplies the earth with rain and makes grass grow on the hills. He provides food for the cattle and for the young ravens when they call.
Psalm 147:8, 9, NIV.

While the Bible should hold the first place in the education of children and youth, the book of nature is next in importance. God's created works testify to His love and power. He has called the world into being, with all that it contains. God is a lover of the beautiful; and in the world which He has fitted up for us He has not only given us everything necessary for our comfort, but He has filled the heavens and the earth with beauty. We see His love and care in the rich fields of autumn, and His smile in the glad sunshine. His hand has made the castle-like rocks and the towering mountains. The lofty trees grow at His command; He has spread earth's green velvet carpet and dotted it with shrubs and flowers.

Why has He clothed the earth and trees with living green, instead of with dark, somber brown? Is it not that they may be more pleasing to the eye? And shall not our hearts be filled with gratitude as we read the evidences of His wisdom and love in the wonders of His creation?

The same creative energy that brought the world into existence is still exerted in upholding the universe and continuing the operations of nature. The hand of God guides the planets in their orderly march through the heavens. It is not because of inherent power that year by year the earth continues her motion round the sun and produces her bounties. The word of God controls the elements. He covers the heavens with clouds and prepares rain for the earth. He makes the valleys fruitful and "grass to grow upon the mountains" (Psalm 147:8). It is through His power that vegetation flourishes, that the leaves appear and the flowers bloom.

The whole natural world is designed to be an interpreter of the things of God. To Adam and Eve in their Eden home, nature was full of the knowledge of God, teeming with divine instruction. To their attentive ears it was vocal with the voice of wisdom. Wisdom spoke to the eye and was received into the heart, for they communed with God in His created works. As soon as the holy pair transgressed the law of the Most High, the brightness from the face of God departed from the face of nature. Nature is now marred and defiled by sin. But God's object lessons are not obliterated; even now, rightly studied and interpreted, she speaks of her Creator. . . . The children and youth, all classes of students, need the lessons to be derived from this source. In itself the beauty of nature leads the soul away from sin and worldly attractions, and toward purity, peace, and God (*Counsels to Parents, Teachers, and Students*, pp. 185, 186).

God's Power in Nature and Us

For since the creation of the world God's invisible qualities—his eternal power and divine nature—have been clearly seen, being understood from what has been made, so that men are without excuse. Romans 1:20, NIV.

In the cultivation of the soil the thoughtful worker will find that treasures little dreamed of are opening up before him. No one can succeed in agriculture or gardening without attention to the laws involved. The special needs of every variety of plant must be studied. Different varieties require different soil and cultivation, and compliance with the laws governing each is the condition of success.

The attention required in transplanting, that not even a root fiber shall be crowded or misplaced, the care of the young plants, the pruning and watering, the shielding from frost at night and sun by day, keeping out weeds, disease, and insect pests, the training and arranging, not only teach important lessons concerning the development of character, but the work itself is a means of development. In cultivating carefulness, patience, attention to detail, obedience to law, it imparts a most essential training.

The constant contact with the mystery of life and the loveliness of nature, as well as the tenderness called forth in ministering to these beautiful objects of God's creation, tends to quicken the mind and refine and elevate the character; and the lessons taught prepare the worker to deal more successfully with other minds (*Education*, pp. 111, 112).

The same power that upholds nature is working also in man. The same great laws that guide alike the star and the atom control human life. The laws that govern the heart's action, regulating the flow of the current of life to the body, are the laws of the mighty Intelligence that has the jurisdiction of the soul. From Him all life proceeds. Only in harmony with Him can be found its true sphere of action. For all the objects of His creation the condition is the same—a life sustained by receiving the life of God, a life exercised in harmony with the Creator's will. To transgress His law, physical, mental, or moral, is to place one's self out of harmony with the universe, to introduce discord, anarchy, ruin.

To him who learns thus to interpret its teachings, all nature becomes illuminated; the world is a lesson book, life a school. The unity of man with nature and with God, the universal dominion of law, the results of transgression, cannot fail of impressing the mind and molding the character

As the dwellers in Eden learned from nature's pages, as Moses discerned God's handwriting on the Arabian plains and mountains, and the Child Jesus on the hillsides of Nazareth, so the children of today may learn of Him. The unseen is illustrated by the seen. On everything upon the earth . . . from the boundless ocean to the tiniest shell on the shore, they may behold the image and superscription of God (*ibid.*, pp. 99, 100).

The Heavenly Sower

Behold, a sower went forth to sow. Matthew 13:3.

In the East the state of affairs was so unsettled, and there was so great danger from violence that the people dwelt chiefly in walled towns, and the husbandmen went forth daily to their labor outside the walls. So Christ, the heavenly Sower, went forth to sow. He left His home of security and peace, left the glory that He had with the Father before the world was, left His position upon the throne of the universe. He went forth, a suffering, tempted man; went forth in solitude, to sow in tears, to water with His blood, the seed of life for a world lost.

His servants in like manner must go forth to sow. When called to become a sower of the seed of truth, Abraham was bidden, "Get thee out of thy country, and from thy kindred, and from thy father's house, unto a land that I will shew thee" (Genesis 12:1). "And he went out, not knowing whither he went" (Hebrews 11:8). . . . In toil and tears, in solitude, and through sacrifice, must the seed be sown.

"The sower soweth the word." Christ came to sow the world with truth. Ever since the Fall of man, Satan has been sowing the seeds of error. It was by a lie that he first gained control over men, and thus he still works to overthrow God's kingdom in the earth and to bring men under his power. A sower from a higher world, Christ came to sow the seeds of truth. He who had stood in the councils of God, who had dwelt in the innermost sanctuary of the Eternal, could bring to men the pure principles of truth. Ever since the Fall of man, Christ had been the Revealer of truth to the world. By Him the incorruptible seed, "the word of God, which liveth and abideth for ever," is communicated to men (1 Peter 1:23). In that first promise spoken to our fallen race in Eden, Christ was sowing the gospel seed. But it is to His personal ministry among men, and to the work which He thus established, that the parable of the sower especially applies.

The word of God is the seed. Every seed has in itself a germinating principle. In it the life of the plant is enfolded. So there is life in God's word. Christ says, "The words that I speak unto you, they are spirit, and they are life" (John 6:63). . . . In every command and in every promise of the word of God is the power, the very life of God, by which the command may be fulfilled and the promise realized. He who by faith receives the word is receiving the very life and character of God.

Every seed brings forth fruit after its kind. Sow the seed under right conditions, and it will develop its own life in the plant. Receive into the soul by faith the incorruptible seed of the word, and it will bring forth a character and a life after the similitude of the character and the life of God (*Christ's Object Lessons*, pp. 36-38).

Growth Comes From God

They shall revive as the corn, and grow as the vine. Hosea 14:7.

The change of heart by which we become children of God is in the Bible spoken of as birth. Again, it is compared to the germination of the good seed sown by the husbandman. In like manner those who are just converted to Christ are, "as newborn babes," to "grow up" to the stature of men and women in Christ Jesus (1 Peter 2:2; Ephesians 4:15). Or like the good seed sown in the field, they are to grow up and bring forth fruit. Isaiah says that they shall "be called trees of righteousness, the planting of the Lord, that he might be glorified" (Isaiah 61:3). So from natural life, illustrations are drawn, to help us better to understand the mysterious truths of spiritual life.

Not all the wisdom and skill of man can produce life in the smallest object in nature. It is only through the life which God Himself has imparted, that either plant or animal can live. So it is only through the life from God that spiritual life is begotten in the hearts of men. Unless a man is "born from above," he cannot become a partaker of the life which Christ came to give (John 3:3, margin).

As with life, so it is with growth. It is God who brings the bud to bloom and the flower to fruit. It is by His power that the seed develops, "first the blade, then the ear, after that the full corn in the ear" (Mark 4:28). And the prophet Hosea says of Israel, that "he shall grow as the lily" (Hosea 14:5). "They shall revive as the corn, and grow as the vine" (verse 7). And Jesus bids us "consider the lilies how they grow" (Luke 12:27). The plants and flowers grow not by their own care or anxiety or effort, but by receiving that which God has furnished to minister to their life. The child cannot, by any anxiety or power of its own, add to its stature. No more can you, by anxiety or effort of yourself, secure spiritual growth. The plant, the child, grows by receiving from its surroundings that which ministers to its life—air, sunshine, and food. What these gifts of nature are to animal and plant, such is Christ to those who trust in Him. . . .

In the matchless gift of His Son, God has encircled the whole world with an atmosphere of grace as real as the air which circulates around the globe. All who choose to breathe this life-giving atmosphere will live and grow up to the stature of men and women in Christ Jesus.

As the flower turns to the sun, that the bright beams may aid in perfecting its beauty and symmetry, so should we turn to the Sun of Righteousness, that heaven's light may shine upon us, that our character may be developed into the likeness of Christ (*Steps to Christ*, pp. 67, 68).

Totally Dependent Upon the Creator

For in him we live, and move, and have our being. Acts 17:28.

For God so loved the world, that he gave his only begotten Son, that whosoever believeth in him should not perish, but have everlasting life." Here the conditions are plainly stated by Jesus Christ, the Sinbearer. When you deliberately decide to go contrary to the word spoken by Jesus Christ, "Seek ye first the kingdom of God, and his righteousness; and all these things shall be added unto you," how can you expect to be religiously inclined?

To enlarge our views of His condescension and beneficence, He presents the picture of the judgment—the separation of the just and the unjust—and shows us He identifies His interests with suffering humanity. He is teaching in the open field where the eye can take in the beauties of nature and the creatures of God's creation. "Consider the ravens: for they neither sow nor reap . . . : how much more are ye better than the fowls? And which of you with taking thought can add to his stature one cubit? If ye then be not able to do that thing which is least, why take ye thought for the rest?" (Luke 12:24-26).

Here is presented definitely that man is dependent upon God for every breath he draws. The beating heart, the throbbing pulse, every nerve and muscle in the living organism, are kept in order and activity by the power of an infinite God. "Consider the lilies of the field, how they grow; they toil not, neither do they spin: and yet I say unto you, That even Solomon in all his glory was not arrayed like one of these. Wherefore, if God so clothe the grass of the field, which today is, and tomorrow is cast into the oven, shall he not much more clothe you, O ye of little faith? Therefore take no thought, saying, What shall we eat? or, What shall we drink? or, Wherewithal shall we be clothed? (for after all these things do the Gentiles seek:) for your heavenly Father knoweth that ye have need of all these things. But seek ye first the kingdom of God, and his righteousness, and all these things shall be added unto you" (Matthew 6:28-33).

Here Christ leads the mind abroad to contemplate the open fields of nature, and His power touches the eye and the senses, to discern the wonderful works of divine power. He directs attention first to nature, then up through nature to nature's God, who upholds the worlds by His power. He points to the opening bud. . . . He watches over little birds. Not a sparrow falleth to the ground without the notice of your heavenly Father. . . .

Christ represents the divine attention given upon [various elements of] His creation that seem so insignificant, and to the objects of nature which His own hands have created. Every lofty tree, every shrub, every blooming flower, the lily of the field, and the earth clothed with its garment of living green are kept in order and occupy their time and season to bear testimony that God loves man (manuscript 73, 1893).

One Pulse of Life in All Creation

Consider the lilies of the field, how they grow. Matthew 6:28.

The hillsides and the fields were bright with flowers, and, pointing to them in the dewy freshness of the morning, Jesus said, "Consider the lilies of the field, how they grow." The graceful forms and delicate hues of the plants and flowers may be copied by human skill, but what touch can impart life to even one flower or blade of grass? Every wayside blossom owes its being to the same power that set the starry worlds on high. Through all created things thrills one pulse of life from the great heart of God. The flowers of the field are clothed by His hand in richer robes than have ever graced the forms of earthly kings. . . .

It is He who made the flowers and who gave to the sparrow its song who says, "Consider the lilies," "Behold the birds." In the loveliness of the things of nature you may learn more of the wisdom of God than the schoolmen know. On the lily's petals, God has written a message for you, written in language that your heart can read only as it unlearns the lessons of distrust and selfishness and corroding care. Why has He given you the singing birds and the gentle blossoms, but from the overflowing love of a Father's heart, that would brighten and gladden your path of life? . . . He has filled the earth and air and sky with glimpses of beauty to tell you of His loving thought for you. The beauty of all created things is but a gleam from the shining of His glory. If He has lavished such infinite skill upon the things of nature, for your happiness and joy, can you doubt that He will give you every needed blessing?

"Consider the lilies." Every flower that opens its petals to the sunshine obeys the same great laws that guide the stars, and how simple and beautiful and how sweet its life! Through the flowers, God would call our attention to the loveliness of Christlike character. He who has given such beauty to the blossoms desires far more that the soul should be clothed with the beauty of the character of Christ. . . .

Who would dream of the possibilities of beauty in the rough brown bulb of the lily? But when the life of God, hidden therein, unfolds at His call in the rain and the sunshine, men marvel at the vision of grace and loveliness. Even so will the life of God unfold in every human soul that will yield itself to the ministry of His grace, which, free as the rain and the sunshine, comes with its benediction to all. It is the word of God that creates the flowers, and the same word will produce in you the graces of His Spirit (*Thoughts From the Mount of Blessing*, pp. 95-97).

He Supplies Our Needs

Do not be anxious about your life, what you shall eat or what you shall drink, nor about your body, what you shall put on. Is not life more than food, and the body more than clothing? Matthew 6:25, RSV.

He who has given you life knows your need of food to sustain it. He who created the body is not unmindful of your need of raiment. Will not He who has bestowed the greater gift bestow also what is needed to make it complete?

Jesus pointed His hearers to the birds as they warbled their carols of praise, unencumbered with thoughts of care, for "they sow not, neither do they reap"; and yet the great Father provides for their needs. And He asks, "Are not ye of much more value than they?"

"No sparrow falls without His care,
No soul bows low but Jesus knows;
For He is with us everywhere,
And marks each bitter tear that flows.
And He will never, never, never
Forsake the soul that trusts Him ever." . . .

God's law is the law of love. He has surrounded you with beauty to teach you that you are not placed on earth merely to delve for self, to dig and build, to toil and spin, but to make life bright and joyous and beautiful with the love of Christ—like the flowers, to gladden other lives by the ministry of love.

Fathers and mothers, let your children learn from the flowers. Take them with you into garden and field and under the leafy trees, and teach them to read in nature the message of God's love. Let the thoughts of Him be linked with bird and flower and tree. Lead the children to see in every pleasant and beautiful thing an expression of God's love for them. Recommend your religion to them by its pleasantness. Let the law of kindness be in your lips.

Teach the children that because of God's great love their natures may be changed and brought into harmony with His. Teach them that He would have their lives beautiful with the graces of the flowers. Teach them, as they gather the sweet blossoms, that He who made the flowers is more beautiful than they. Thus the tendrils of their hearts will be entwined about Him. He who is "altogether lovely" will become to them as a daily companion and familiar friend, and their lives will be transformed into the image of His purity (*Thoughts From the Mount of Blessing*, pp. 95-98).

[God] would adorn our characters with His own rich graces. He would have our words as fragrant as the flowers of the field (*Review and Herald*, May 19, 1896).

Christ Took Upon Himself Human Nature

And the Word was made flesh, and dwelt among us, (and we beheld his glory, the glory as of the only begotten of the Father,) full of grace and truth. John 1:14.

As one who understands his subject, John ascribes all power to Christ, and speaks of His greatness and majesty. He flashes forth divine rays of precious truth, as light from the sun. He presents Christ as the only Mediator between God and humanity.

The doctrine of the incarnation of Christ in human flesh is a mystery, "even the mystery which hath been hid from ages and from generations." It is the great and profound mystery of godliness. "The Word was made flesh, and dwelt among us." Christ took upon Himself human nature, a nature inferior to His heavenly nature. Nothing so shows the wonderful condescension of God as this. He "so loved the world, that he gave his only begotten Son." John presents this wonderful subject with such simplicity that all may grasp the ideas set forth, and be enlightened.

Christ did not make-believe take human nature; He did verily take it. He did in reality possess human nature. "As the children are partakers of flesh and blood, he also himself likewise took part of the same." He was the son of Mary; He was of the seed of David according to human descent. He is declared to be a man, even the Man Christ Jesus. "This man," writes Paul, "was counted worthy of more glory than Moses, inasmuch as he who hath builded the house hath more honor than the house."

But while God's Word speaks of the humanity of Christ when upon this earth, it also speaks decidedly regarding His preexistence. The Word existed as a divine being, even as the eternal Son of God, in union and oneness with His Father. From everlasting He was the Mediator of the covenant, the One in whom all nations of the earth, both Jews and Gentiles, if they accepted Him, were to be blessed. "The Word was with God, and the Word was God." Before men or angels were created, the Word was with God, and was God. . . .

God and Christ knew from the beginning of the apostasy of Satan and of the fall of Adam through the deceptive power of the apostate. The plan of salvation was designed to redeem the fallen race, to give them another trial. Christ was appointed to the office of Mediator from the creation of God, set up from everlasting to be our substitute and surety. Before the world was made, it was arranged that the divinity of Christ should be enshrouded in humanity. "A body," said Christ, "hast thou prepared me." But He did not come in human form until the fullness of time had expired. Then He came to our world, a babe in Bethlehem (*Review and Herald*, Apr. 5, 1906).

The Birth of Christ an Unfathomable Mystery

The virgin will be with child and will give birth to a son, and will call him Immanuel.
Isaiah 7:14, NIV.

We cannot understand how Christ became a little, helpless babe. He could have come to earth in such beauty that He would have been unlike the sons of men. His face could have been bright with light, and His form could have been tall and beautiful. He could have come in such a way as to charm those who looked upon Him; but this was not the way that God planned He should come among the sons of men.

He was to be like those who belonged to the human family and to the Jewish race. His features were to be like those of other human beings, and He was not to have such beauty of person as to make people point Him out as different from others. He was to come as one of the human family, and to stand as a man before heaven and earth. He had come to take man's place, to pledge Himself in man's behalf, to pay the debt that sinners owed. He was to live a pure life on the earth, and show that Satan had told a falsehood when he claimed that the human family belonged to him forever, and that God could not take men out of his hands.

Men first beheld Christ as a babe, as a child. . . .

The more we think about Christ's becoming a babe here on earth, the more wonderful it appears. How can it be that the helpless babe in Bethlehem's manger is still the divine Son of God? Though we cannot understand it, we can believe that He who made the worlds, for our sakes became a helpless babe. Though higher than any of the angels, though as great as the Father on the throne of heaven, He became one with us. In Him God and man became one, and it is in this fact that we find the hope of our fallen race. Looking upon Christ in the flesh, we look upon God in humanity, and see in Him the brightness of divine glory, the express image of God the Father (*Selected Messages,* book 3, pp. 127, 128).

In contemplating the incarnation of Christ in humanity, we stand baffled before an unfathomable mystery, that the human mind cannot comprehend. The more we reflect upon it, the more amazing does it appear. How wide is the contrast between the divinity of Christ and the helpless infant in Bethlehem's manger! How can we span the distance between the mighty God and a helpless child? And yet the Creator of worlds, He in whom was the fullness of the Godhead bodily, was manifest in the helpless babe in the manger. Far higher than any of the angels, equal with the Father in dignity and glory, and yet wearing the garb of humanity! Divinity and humanity were mysteriously combined, and man and God became one. It is in this union that we find the hope of our fallen race (*Signs of the Times,* July 30, 1896).

Two Natures Blended in One

For verily he took not on him the nature of angels; but he took on him the seed of Abraham. Wherefore in all things it behoved him to be made like unto his brethren.
Hebrews 2:16, 17.

Was the human nature of the Son of Mary changed into the divine nature of the Son of God? No; the two natures were mysteriously blended in one person—the man Christ Jesus. In Him dwelt all the fullness of the Godhead bodily. When Christ was crucified, it was His human nature that died. Deity did not sink and die; that would have been impossible. Christ, the sinless One, will save every son and daughter of Adam who accepts the salvation proffered them, consenting to become the children of God. The Savior has purchased the fallen race with His own blood.

This is a great mystery, a mystery that will not be fully, completely understood in all its greatness until the translation of the redeemed shall take place. Then the power and greatness and efficacy of the gift of God to man will be understood. But the enemy is determined that this gift shall be so mystified that it will become as nothingness (*The SDA Bible Commentary,* Ellen G. White Comments, vol. 5, p. 1113).

We shall have false sentiments to meet. Never, never can we afford to place confidence in human greatness as some have done, looking to men as the angels in heaven looked to the rebellious Lucifer, and thus finally losing the sense of the presence of Christ and God.

Who by searching can find out God to perfection? The Gospels set forth the character of Christ as infinitely perfect. I wish I could speak of this so that the whole world could hear the object of Christ's mission and work. . . .

"Search the scriptures," said Christ; "for in them ye think ye have eternal life, and they are they which testify of me." The sufferings of the Redeemer, the humility of His human-divine character, are not understood, and therefore His virtues are not practiced. The treasures of knowledge to be obtained from God are inexhaustible.

The most gifted men on the earth could all find abundant employment, from now until the judgment, for all their God-given powers in exalting the character of Christ. But they would still fail to present Him as He is. The mysteries of redemption, embracing Christ's divine-human character, His incarnation, His atonement for sin, could employ the pens and the highest mental powers of the wisest men from now until Christ shall be revealed in the clouds of heaven in power and great glory. But though these men should seek with all their power to give a representation of Christ and His work, the representation would fall far short of the reality. . . .

The theme of redemption will employ the minds and tongues of the redeemed through everlasting ages. The reflection of the glory of God will shine forth forever and ever from the Savior's face (letter 280, 1904)

The Spirit in Christ From Youth

And when he was twelve years old, they went up to Jerusalem after the custom of the feast.
Luke 2:42.

At the age of twelve the Holy Spirit was abiding upon Jesus, and He felt something of the burden of the mission for which He had come to our world. His soul was stirred into action. As one who would learn, He asked questions of no ordinary character, by which He flashed light into the minds of His hearers, and brought them to an understanding of the prophecies and the true mission and work of the Messiah they were expecting.

The Jewish people were cherishing erroneous ideas. They were anticipating grand and wonderful things, hoping for their own personal exaltation above the nations of the earth at the Messiah's appearing. They were looking for the glory that will attend the second coming of Christ, and overlooking the humiliation that would attend His first advent.

But Jesus, in His questions about the prophecies of Isaiah that pointed to His first appearing, flashed light into the minds of those who were willing to receive the truth. He Himself had given these prophecies before His incarnation in humanity, and as the Holy Spirit brought these things to His mind, and impressed Him with regard to the great work that He was to accomplish, He imparted light and knowledge to those around Him.

Though He increased in knowledge, and the grace of God was upon Him, yet He did not become lifted up in pride, or feel that He was above doing the most humble toil. He took His share of the burden, together with His father, mother, and brethren. . . . Though His wisdom had astonished the doctors, yet He meekly subjected Himself to His human guardians, bore His part in the family burdens, and worked with His own hands as any toiler would work. It is stated of Jesus that (as He advanced in years) He "increased in wisdom and stature, and in favour with God and man."

The knowledge He was daily obtaining of His wonderful mission did not disqualify Him for performing the most humble duties. He cheerfully took up the work that devolves upon youth who dwell in humble households pressed by poverty. He understood the temptations of children; for He bore their sorrows and trials. Firm and steadfast was His purpose to do the right. Though enticed to evil, He refused to depart in a single instance from the strictest truth and rectitude. He maintained perfect filial obedience; but His spotless life aroused the envy and jealousy of His brethren. His childhood and youth were anything but smooth and joyous. His brethren did not believe on Him, and were annoyed because He did not in all things act as they did, and become one of them in the practice of evil. In His home life He was cheerful, but never boisterous. He ever maintained the attitude of a learner. He took great delight in nature, and God was His teacher (*Signs of the Times*, July 30, 1896).

Jesus Assured of His Sonship

Now when all the people were baptized, it came to pass that Jesus also was baptized; and while he prayed, the heaven was opened. Luke 3:21, NKJV.

When Jesus came to be baptized, John recognized in Him a purity of character that he had never before perceived in any man. The very atmosphere of His presence was holy and awe-inspiring. Among the multitudes that had gathered about him at the Jordan, John had heard dark tales of crime, and had met souls bowed down with the burden of myriad sins; but never had he come in contact with a human being from whom there breathed an influence so divine. All this was in harmony with what had been revealed to John regarding the Messiah. . . .

Jesus did not receive baptism as a confession of guilt on His own account. He identified Himself with sinners, taking the steps that we are to take, and doing the work that we must do. His life of suffering and patient endurance after His baptism was also an example to us.

Upon coming up out of the water, Jesus bowed in prayer on the river bank. A new and important era was opening before Him (*The Desire of Ages*, pp. 110, 111).

Never had angels listened to such a prayer. They were solicitous to bear to the praying Redeemer messages of assurance and love. But no; the Father Himself will minister to His Son. Direct from the throne proceeded the light of the glory of God. The heavens were opened, and beams of light and glory proceeded therefrom and assumed the form of a dove, in appearance like burnished gold. The dovelike form was emblematical of the meekness and gentleness of Christ.

The people stood spellbound with fear and amazement. Their eyes were fastened upon Christ, whose bowed form was bathed in the beautiful light and glory that ever surround the throne of God. His upturned face was glorified as they had never before seen the face of man. The thunders rolled and the lightnings flashed from the opening heavens, and a voice came therefrom in terrible majesty, saying, "This is my beloved Son, in whom I am well pleased." . . . Jehovah's voice assured Christ of His Sonship with the Eternal (*Youth's Instructor*, March 1874).

The glory that rested upon Christ is a pledge of the love of God for us. It tells us of the power of prayer—how the human voice may reach the ear of God, and our petitions find acceptance in the courts of heaven. . . . The light which fell from the open portals upon the head of our Saviour will fall upon us as we pray for help to resist temptation. The voice which spoke to Jesus says to every believing soul, This is My beloved child, in whom I am well pleased (*The Desire of Ages,* p. 113).

Jesus, Our Example

For he hath made him to be sin for us, who knew no sin; that we might be made the righteousness of God in him. 2 Corinthians 5:21.

In the submission of Christ to the ordinance of baptism, He shows the sinner one of the important steps in true conversion. Christ had no sins to wash away, but in consenting to become a substitute for man, the sins of guilty man were imputed to Him. . . . While God accepts Christ as the sinner's substitute, He gives the sinner a chance, with Christ's divine power to help him, to stand the test which Adam failed to endure.

Christ came to John, repenting on the sinner's account, believing in behalf of the sinner, that through the plan He had devised, of taking humanity, and in suffering and dying for man, the sinner would, through repentance, faith, and baptism, be accepted of God. He was buried by John in the liquid grave, and came up out of the water to represent to man, in His holy life, the true pattern for him to copy.

The steps in conversion, plainly marked out, are repentance, faith in Christ as the world's Redeemer, faith in His death, burial, and resurrection, shown by baptism, and His ascension on high to plead in the sinner's behalf. At the very commencement of His public ministry, He presents Himself in the character He sustains to man throughout His mediatorial work. He identifies Himself with sinners as their substitute, taking upon Himself their sins, numbering Himself with the transgressors, and doing the work the sinner is required to do in repentance, faith, and willing obedience. What an example is here given in the life of Christ for sinners to imitate! If they will not follow the example given them, they will be without excuse.

Dear children and youth, your heavenly Father and the dear Savior are your very best friends. You have every evidence that it is possible for you to have of their love for you. "He that spared not his own Son, but delivered him up for us all, how shall he not with him also freely give us all things?"

God will not withhold anything from us that will really be for our good. Jesus would have us happy in this world, and enjoy with Him the glory of the next world. God has given to children and youth invitations to surrender to Him. "My son, give me thine heart." A promise is given—"Those that seek me early shall find me." . . .

All who live have sins to wash away. . . . True repentance of sin, faith in the merits of Jesus Christ, and baptism into His death, to be raised out of the water to live a new life, are the first steps in the new birth which Christ told Nicodemus he must experience in order to be saved. The words of Christ to Nicodemus are not only spoken to him, but to every man, woman, and child, that should live in the world. . . . We are safe in following the example of Christ (*Youth's Instructor*, February 1874).

March

7

He Showed Us How to Overcome

It is written again, Thou shalt not tempt the Lord thy God. Matthew 4:7.

In the wilderness of temptation Christ met the great leading temptations that would assail man. There He encountered, single-handed, the wily, subtle foe, and overcame him. The first great temptation was upon appetite; the second, presumption; the third, love of the world. Satan has overcome his millions by tempting them to the indulgence of appetite. Through the gratification of the taste, the nervous system becomes excited and the brain power enfeebled, making it impossible to think calmly or rationally. The mind is unbalanced. Its higher, nobler faculties are perverted to serve animal lusts, and the sacred, eternal interests are not regarded. When this object is gained, Satan can come with his two other leading temptations and find ready access. His manifold temptations grow out of these three great leading points.

Presumption is a common temptation, and as Satan assails men with this, he obtains the victory nine times out of ten. Those who profess to be followers of Christ, and claim by their faith to be enlisted in the warfare against all evil in their nature, frequently plunge without thought into temptations from which it would require a miracle to bring them forth unsullied. Meditation and prayer would have preserved them and led them to shun the critical, dangerous position in which they placed themselves when they gave Satan the advantage over them. The promises of God are not for us rashly to claim while we rush on recklessly into danger, violating the laws of nature and disregarding prudence and the judgment with which God has endowed us. This is the most flagrant presumption.

The thrones and kingdoms of the world and the glory of them were offered to Christ if He would only bow down to Satan. Never will man be tried with temptations as powerful as those which assailed Christ. Satan came with worldly honor, wealth, and the pleasures of life, and presented them in the most attractive light to allure and deceive. "All these things," said he to Christ, "will I give thee, if thou wilt fall down and worship me." Christ repelled the wily foe and came off victor. . . .

Christ's example is before us. He overcame Satan, showing us how we may also overcome. Christ resisted Satan with Scripture. He might have had recourse to His own divine power, and used His own words; but He said: "It is written." . . . If the Sacred Scriptures were studied and followed, the Christian would be fortified to meet the wily foe. . . .

When the religion of Christ rules in the heart, conscience approves, and peace and happiness reign; perplexity and trouble may surround, yet there is light in the soul. Submission, love, and gratitude to God keep sunshine in the heart, though the day may be ever so cloudy (*Testimonies*, vol. 4, pp. 44-47).

We Have Found the Messias

We have found him, of whom Moses in the law, and the prophets, did write. John 1:45.

Philip called Nathanael. The latter had been among the throng when the Baptist pointed to Jesus as the Lamb of God. As Nathanael looked upon Jesus, he was disappointed. Could this man, who bore the marks of toil and poverty, be the Messiah? Yet Nathanael could not decide to reject Jesus, for the message of John had brought conviction to his heart.

At the time when Philip called him, Nathanael had withdrawn to a quiet grove to meditate upon the announcement of John and the prophecies concerning the Messiah. He prayed that if the one announced by John was the deliverer, it might be made known to him, and the Holy Spirit rested upon him with assurance that God had visited His people and raised up a horn of salvation for them. . . .

The message, "We have found him, of whom Moses in the law, and the prophets, did write," seemed to Nathanael a direct answer to his prayer. But Philip had yet a trembling faith. He added doubtfully, "Jesus of Nazareth, the son of Joseph." Again prejudice arose in Nathanael's heart. He exclaimed, "Can there any good thing come out of Nazareth?"

Philip entered into no controversy. He said, "Come and see." "Jesus saw Nathanael coming to him, and saith of him, Behold an Israelite indeed, in whom is no guile!" In surprise Nathanael exclaimed, "Whence knowest thou me? Jesus answered and said unto him, Before that Philip called thee, when thou wast under the fig tree, I saw thee."

It was enough. The divine Spirit that had borne witness to Nathanael in his solitary prayer under the fig tree now spoke to him in the words of Jesus. Though in doubt, and yielding somewhat to prejudice, Nathanael had come to Christ with an honest desire for truth, and now his desire was met. His faith went beyond that of the one who had brought him to Jesus. He answered and said, "Rabbi, Thou art the Son of God; thou art the King of Israel."

If Nathanael had trusted to the rabbis for guidance, he would never have found Jesus. It was by seeing and judging for himself that he became a disciple. So in the case of many today whom prejudice withholds from good. How different would be the result if they would "come and see"!

While they trust to the guidance of human authority, none will come to a saving knowledge of the truth. Like Nathanael, we need to study God's Word for ourselves, and pray for the enlightenment of the Holy Spirit. He who saw Nathanael under the fig tree will see us in the secret place of prayer. Angels from the world of light are near to those who in humility seek for divine guidance (*The Desire of Ages*, pp. 139-141).

March

9

Brothers to Sinners and Saints

Every one that loveth is born of God, and knoweth God. 1 John 4:7.

In all who suffer for My name, said Jesus, you are to recognize Me. As you would minister to Me, so you are to minister to them. This is the evidence that you are My disciples.

All who have been born into the heavenly family are in a special sense the brethren of our Lord. The love of Christ binds together the members of His family, and wherever that love is made manifest there the divine relationship is revealed. "Every one that loveth is born of God, and knoweth God" (1 John 4:7).

Those whom Christ commends in the judgment may have known little of theology, but they have cherished His principles. Through the influence of the divine Spirit they have been a blessing to those about them. Even among the heathen are those who have cherished the spirit of kindness; before the words of life had fallen upon their ears, they have befriended the missionaries, even ministering to them at the peril of their own lives. Among the heathen are those who worship God ignorantly, those to whom the light is never brought by human instrumentality, yet they will not perish. Though ignorant of the written law of God, they have heard His voice speaking to them in nature, and have done the things that the law required. Their works are evidence that the Holy Spirit has touched their hearts, and they are recognized as the children of God.

How surprised and gladdened will be the lowly among the nations, and among the heathen, to hear from the lips of the Savior, "Inasmuch as ye have done it unto one of the least of these my brethren, ye have done it unto me"! How glad will be the heart of Infinite Love as His followers look up with surprise and joy at His words of approval!

But not to any class is Christ's love restricted. He identifies Himself with every child of humanity. That we might become members of the heavenly family, He became a member of the earthly family. He is the Son of man, and thus a brother to every son and daughter of Adam. His followers are not to feel themselves detached from the perishing world around them. They are a part of the great web of humanity; and Heaven looks upon them as brothers to sinners as well as to saints. The fallen, the erring, and the sinful, Christ's love embraces; and every deed of kindness done to uplift a fallen soul, every act of mercy, is accepted as done to Him (*The Desire of Ages*, p. 638).

An Example of Obedience

Being found in fashion as a man, he humbled himself, and became obedient unto death.
Philippians 2:8.

Since Jesus came to dwell with us, we know that God is acquainted with our trials, and sympathizes with our griefs. Every son and daughter of Adam may understand that our Creator is the friend of sinners. For in every doctrine of grace, every promise of joy, every deed of love, every divine attraction presented in the Savior's life on earth, we see "God with us."

Satan represents God's law of love as a law of selfishness. He declares that it is impossible for us to obey its precepts. The fall of our first parents, with all the woe that has resulted, he charges upon the Creator, leading men to look upon God as the author of sin, and suffering, and death. Jesus was to unveil this deception. As one of us He was to give an example of obedience. For this He took upon Himself our nature, and passed through our experiences. "In all things it behoved him to be made like unto his brethren" (Hebrews 2:17).

If we had to bear anything which Jesus did not endure, then upon this point Satan would represent the power of God as insufficient for us. Therefore Jesus was "in all points tempted like as we are" (Hebrews 4:15). He endured every trial to which we are subject. And He exercised in His own behalf no power that is not freely offered to us. As man, He met temptation, and overcame in the strength given Him from God. He says, "I delight to do thy will, O my God: yea, thy law is within my heart" (Psalm 40:8). As He went about doing good, and healing all who were afflicted by Satan, He made plain to men the character of God's law and the nature of His service. His life testifies that it is possible for us also to obey the law of God.

By His humanity, Christ touched humanity; by His divinity, He lays hold upon the throne of God. As the Son of man, He gave us an example of obedience; as the Son of God, He gives us power to obey. It was Christ who from the bush on Mount Horeb spoke to Moses saying, "I AM THAT I AM. . . . Thus shalt thou say unto the children of Israel, I AM hath sent me unto you" (Exodus 3:14). This was the pledge of Israel's deliverance. So when He came "in the likeness of men," He declared Himself the I AM. The Child of Bethlehem, the meek and lowly Savior, is God "manifest in the flesh" (1 Timothy 3:16) (*The Desire of Ages*, p. 24).

Mercy Toward the Demoniacs

And when he was come to the other side into the country of the Gergesenes, there met him two possessed with devils, coming out of the tombs, exceeding fierce. Matthew 8:28.

In the early morning the Savior and His companions came to shore. . . . But no sooner had they stepped upon the beach than their eyes were greeted by a sight more terrible than the fury of the tempest. From some hiding place among the tombs, two madmen rushed upon them as if to tear them in pieces. . . .

The disciples and their companions fled in terror; but presently they noticed that Jesus was not with them. . . . He was standing where they had left Him. He who had stilled the tempest . . . did not flee before these demons. . . .

With authority He bade the unclean spirits come out of them. His words penetrated the darkened minds of the unfortunate men. . . . A marvelous change had come over the demoniacs. Light had shone into their minds. Their eyes beamed with intelligence. The countenances, so long deformed into the image of Satan, became suddenly mild, the bloodstained hands were quiet, and with glad voices the men praised God for their deliverance. . . .

The people of Gergesa had before them the living evidence of Christ's power and mercy. They saw the men who had been restored to reason; but they were so fearful of endangering their earthly interests that He who had vanquished the prince of darkness before their eyes was treated as an intruder, and the Gift of heaven was turned from their doors. . . .

But far different was the feeling of the restored demoniacs. They desired the company of their deliverer. In His presence they felt secure from the demons that had tormented their lives and wasted their manhood. As Jesus was about to enter the boat, they kept close to His side, knelt at His feet, and begged Him to keep them near Him, where they might ever listen to His words. But Jesus bade them go home and tell what great things the Lord had done for them. . . .

As soon as Jesus pointed out their duty they were ready to obey. Not only did they tell their own households and neighbors about Jesus, but they went throughout Decapolis, everywhere declaring His power to save. . . . In doing this work they could receive a greater blessing than if, merely for benefit to themselves, they had remained in His presence. It is in working to spread the good news of salvation that we are brought near to the Savior. . . . They could not instruct the people as the disciples who had been daily with Christ were able to do. But they bore in their own persons the evidence that Jesus was the Messiah. They could tell what they knew; what they themselves had seen, and heard, and felt of the power of Christ (*The Desire of Ages*, pp. 337-340).

We Must Believe in Him

Daughter, be of good comfort: thy faith hath made thee whole; go in peace. Luke 8:48.

On the way to the ruler's house, Jesus had met, in the crowd, a poor woman who for twelve years had suffered from a disease that made her life a burden. She had spent all her means upon physicians and remedies, only to be pronounced incurable. But her hopes revived when she heard of the cures that Christ performed. She felt assured that if she could only go to Him she would be healed. . . . She had begun to despair, when, in making His way through the multitude, He came near where she was.

The golden opportunity had come. She was in the presence of the Great Physician! But amid the confusion she could not speak to Him, nor catch more than a passing glimpse of His figure. Fearful of losing her one chance of relief, she pressed forward, saying to herself, "If I may but touch his clothes, I shall be whole." As He was passing, she reached forward, and succeeded in barely touching the border of His garment. But in that moment she knew that she was healed. In that one touch was concentrated the faith of her life, and instantly her pain and feebleness gave place to the vigor of perfect health. . . .

Suddenly Jesus stopped, and the people halted with Him. He turned, and looking about asked in a voice distinctly heard above the confusion of the multitude, "Who touched Me?" . . .

The Savior could distinguish the touch of faith from the casual contact of the careless throng. Such trust should not be passed without comment. He would speak to the humble woman words of comfort that would be to her a wellspring of joy—words that would be a blessing to His followers to the close of time. . . .

Jesus insisted on knowing who had touched Him. Finding concealment vain, she came forward tremblingly, and cast herself at His feet. With grateful tears she told the story of her suffering, and how she had found relief. Jesus gently said, "Daughter, be of good comfort: thy faith hath made thee whole; go in peace." . . . It was not through the outward contact with Him, but through the faith which took hold on His divine power, that the cure was wrought. . . .

It is not enough to believe *about* Christ; we must believe *in* Him. The only faith that will benefit us is that which embraces Him as a personal Savior; which appropriates His merits to ourselves. Many hold faith as an opinion. Saving faith is a transaction by which those who receive Christ join themselves in covenant relation with God. Genuine faith is life. A living faith means an increase of vigor, a confiding trust, by which the soul becomes a conquering power (*The Desire of Ages*, pp. 343, 347).

He Is the Sun of Righteousness

Unto you that fear my name shall the Sun of righteousness arise with healing in his wings.
Malachi 4:2.

In the fisherman's home at Capernaum the mother of Peter's wife is lying sick of "a great fever," and "they tell him of her." Jesus "touched her hand, and the fever left her," and she arose and ministered to the Savior and His disciples (Luke 4:38; Mark 1:30; Matthew 8:15).

Rapidly the tidings spread. The miracle had been wrought upon the Sabbath, and for fear of the rabbis the people dared not come for healing until the sun was set. Then from the homes, the shops, the marketplaces, the inhabitants of the city pressed toward the humble dwelling that sheltered Jesus. The sick were brought upon litters, they came leaning upon staffs, or, supported by friends, they tottered feebly into the Savior's presence. . . .

Never before had Capernaum witnessed a day like this. The air was filled with the voice of triumph and shouts of deliverance.

Not until the last sufferer had been relieved did Jesus cease His work. It was far into the night when the multitude departed and silence settled down upon the home of Simon. The long, exciting day was past, and Jesus sought rest. But while the city was wrapped in slumber, the Savior, "rising up a great while before day," "went out, and departed into a solitary place, and there prayed" (Mark 1:35).

Early in the morning Peter and his companions came to Jesus, saying that already the people of Capernaum were seeking Him. With surprise they heard Christ's words, "I must preach the kingdom of God to other cities also; for therefore am I sent" (Luke 4:43).

In the excitement which then pervaded Capernaum there was danger that the object of His mission would be lost sight of. Jesus was not satisfied to attract attention to Himself merely as a wonder-worker or as a healer of physical disease. He was seeking to draw men to Him as their Savior. While the people were eager to believe that He had come as a king to establish an earthly reign, He desired to turn their minds from the earthly to the spiritual. Mere worldly success would interfere with His work. . . .

No self-assertion mingled with His life. . . . None of the means that men employ to win allegiance or command homage did Jesus use. . . .

The Sun of Righteousness did not burst upon the world in splendor, to dazzle the senses with His glory. It is written of Christ, "His going forth is prepared as the morning" (Hosea 6:3). Quietly and gently the daylight breaks upon the earth, dispelling the darkness and waking the world to life. So did the Sun of Righteousness arise, "with healing in his wings" (Malachi 4:2) (*The Ministry of Healing*, pp. 29-32).

He Is Always Near

But that ye may know that the Son of man hath power on earth to forgive sins, (then saith he to the sick of the palsy,) Arise, take up thy bed, and go unto thine house. Matthew 9:6.

With a new hope the sick man looks upon Jesus. The expression of His countenance, the tones of His voice, are like no other. Love and power seem to breathe from His very presence. The cripple's faith takes hold upon Christ's word. Without question he sets his will to obey, and, as he does this, his whole body responds.

Every nerve and muscle thrills with new life, and healthful action comes to his crippled limbs. Springing to his feet, he goes on his way with firm, free step, praising God and rejoicing in his newfound strength. . . . Acting on the word of Christ, he was made whole.

By sin we have been severed from the life of God. Our souls are palsied. Of ourselves we are no more capable of living a holy life than was the impotent man capable of walking. Many realize their helplessness; they are longing for that spiritual life which will bring them into harmony with God, and are striving to obtain it. But in vain. In despair they cry, "O wretched man that I am! who shall deliver me from this body of death?" (Romans 7:24, margin). Let these desponding, struggling ones look up. The Savior is bending over the purchase of His blood, saying with inexpressible tenderness and pity, "Wilt thou be made whole?" He bids you arise in health and peace. Do not wait to feel that you are made whole. Believe the Savior's word. Put your will on the side of Christ. Will to serve Him, and in acting upon His word you will receive strength. Whatever may be the evil practice, the master passion which through long indulgence binds both soul and body, Christ is able and longs to deliver. He will impart life to the soul that is "dead in trespasses" (Ephesians 2:1). . . .

When temptations assail you, when care and perplexity surround you, when, depressed and discouraged, you are ready to yield to despair, look to Jesus, and the darkness that encompasses you will be dispelled by the bright shining of His presence. When sin struggles for the mastery in your soul, and burdens the conscience, look to the Savior. His grace is sufficient to subdue sin. Let your grateful heart, trembling with uncertainty, turn to Him. Lay hold on the hope set before you. Christ waits to adopt you into His family. His strength will help your weakness; He will lead you step by step. Place your hand in His, and let Him guide you.

Never feel that Christ is far away. He is always near. His loving presence surrounds you. Seek Him as one who desires to be found of you. He desires you not only to touch His garments, but to walk with Him in constant communion (*The Ministry of Healing,* pp. 84, 85).

He Understands Our Motives

And he called his disciples to him, and said to them, "Truly, I say to you, this poor widow has put in more than all those who are contributing to the treasury. Mark 12:43, RSV.

Jesus was in the court where were the treasure chests, and He watched those who came to deposit their gifts. Many of the rich brought large sums, which they presented with great ostentation. Jesus looked upon them sadly, but made no comment on their liberal offerings. Presently His countenance lighted as He saw a poor widow approach hesitatingly, as though fearful of being observed. As the rich and haughty swept by, to deposit their offerings, she shrank back as if hardly daring to venture farther. And yet she longed to do something, little though it might be, for the cause she loved.

She looked at the gift in her hand. It was very small in comparison with the gifts of those around her, yet it was her all. Watching her opportunity, she hurriedly threw in her two mites, and turned to hasten away. But in doing this she caught the eye of Jesus, which was fastened earnestly upon her.

The Savior called His disciples to Him, and bade them mark the widow's poverty. Then His words of commendation fell upon her ear: "Of a truth I say unto you, that this poor widow hath cast in more than they all." Tears of joy filled her eyes as she felt that her act was understood and appreciated. Many would have advised her to keep her pittance for her own use; given into the hands of the well-fed priests, it would be lost sight of among the many costly gifts brought to the treasury. But Jesus understood her motive. She believed the service of the Temple to be of God's appointment, and she was anxious to do her utmost to sustain it. She did what she could, and her act was to be a monument to her memory through all time, and her joy in eternity. Her heart went with her gift; its value was estimated, not by the worth of the coin, but by the love to God and the interest in His work that had prompted the deed. . . .

It is the motive that gives character to our acts, stamping them with ignominy or with high moral worth. Not the great things which every eye sees and every tongue praises does God account most precious. The little duties cheerfully done, the little gifts which make no show, and which to human eyes may appear worthless, often stand highest in His sight. A heart of faith and love is dearer to God than the most costly gift. . . . It was this unselfish spirit and childlike faith that won the Savior's commendation.

Among the poor there are many who long to show their gratitude to God for His grace and truth. . . . Let them lay up their mites in the bank of heaven. If given from a heart filled with love for God, these seeming trifles become consecrated gifts, priceless offerings, which God smiles upon and blesses (*The Desire of Ages,* pp. 614, 615).

His Compassion

He took them up in his arms, put his hands upon them, and blessed them. Mark 10:16.

As Jesus ministers in the streets of the cities, mothers with their sick and dying little ones in their arms press through the throng, seeking to come within reach of His notice.

Behold these mothers, pale, weary, almost despairing, yet determined and persevering. Bearing their burden of suffering, they seek the Savior. As they are crowded back by the surging throng, Christ makes His way to them step by step, until He is close by their side. Hope springs up in their hearts. Their tears of gladness fall as they catch His attention, and look into the eyes expressing such pity and love.

Singling out one of the group, the Savior invites her confidence, saying, "What shall I do for thee?" She sobs out her great want, "Master, that thou wouldest heal my child." Christ takes the little one from her arms, and disease flees at His touch. The pallor of death is gone; the life-giving current flows through the veins; the muscles receive strength. Words of comfort and peace are spoken to the mother; and then another case, just as urgent, is presented. Again Christ exercises His life-giving power, and all give praise and honor to Him who doeth wonderful things.

We dwell much on the greatness of Christ's life. We speak of the wonderful things that He accomplished, of the miracles that He wrought. But His attention to things accounted small is even higher proof of His greatness.

Among the Jews it was customary for children to be brought to some rabbi, that he might lay his hands upon them in blessing; but the disciples thought the Savior's work too important to be interrupted in this way. When the mothers came desiring Him to bless their little ones, the disciples looked on them with disfavor. They thought these children too young to be benefited by a visit to Jesus, and concluded that He would be displeased at their presence. But the Savior understood the care and burden of the mothers who were seeking to train their children according to the Word of God. He had heard their prayers. He Himself had drawn them into His presence. . . .

Christ is today the same compassionate Savior as when He walked among men. He is as verily the helper of mothers now as when He gathered the little ones to His arms in Judea. The children of our hearths are as much a purchase of His blood as were the children of long ago. . . .

Let mothers come to Jesus with their perplexities. They will find grace sufficient to aid them in the care of their children. The gates are open for every mother who would lay her burdens at the Savior's feet. He who said, "Suffer the little children to come unto me, and forbid them not" (Mark 10:14), still invites mothers to bring their little ones to be blessed by Him (*The Ministry of Healing,* pp. 38-42).

Sympathy to All

The spirit of the Lord God is upon me; because the Lord hath anointed me to . . . give unto them beauty for ashes, the oil of joy for mourning, the garment of praise for the spirit of heaviness. Isaiah 61:1-3.

Christ was a close observer, noticing many things that others passed by. He was ever helpful, ever ready to speak words of hope and sympathy to the discouraged and the bereaved. He allowed the crowd to press round Him, and complained not, though sometimes almost lifted off His feet. When He met a funeral, He did not pass by indifferently. Sadness came over His face as He looked upon death, and He wept with the mourners.

As the children gathered the wildflowers growing so abundantly around them, and crowded up to present to Him their little offerings, He received them gladly, smiled upon them, and expressed His joy at seeing so many varieties of flowers.

These children were His heritage. He knew that He had come to ransom them from the enemy by dying on the cross of Calvary. He spoke words to them that ever after they carried in their hearts. They were delighted to think that He appreciated their gifts and spoke so lovingly to them.

Christ watched children at their play, and often expressed His approval when they gained an innocent victory over something they were determined to do. He sang to children in sweet and blessed words. They knew that He loved them. He never frowned on them. He shared childish joys and sorrows. Often he would gather flowers, and after pointing out their beauties to the children, would leave them with them as a gift. He had made the flowers, and He delighted to point out their beauties.

It has been said that Jesus never smiled. This is not correct. A child in its innocence and purity called forth from His lips joyous song.

To those who followed Him He explained the Word of God so clearly that they loved to be in His company. He led their minds from the inferior things of earth to the holy principles of truth and righteousness. He prepared them to understand what is comprehended in transformation of character after the divine similitude. His words encouraged faith. He carried the minds of His hearers from this world, with its busy cares, to the higher, nobler world, which so many had lost sight of. He showed that every moment of life is fraught with eternal significance. He declared that the things of this world are of minor importance in comparison with the things of the world to come (manuscript 20, 1902).

A Fountain of Pleasure and Joy

Thou wilt shew me the path of life: in thy presence is fulness of joy; at thy right hand there are pleasures for evermore. Psalm 16:11.

The beauty of the mind, the purity of the soul, revealed in the countenance, will have more power to attract and exert an influence upon hearts than any outward adorning. . . .

A cultivated mind, adorned with the grace of meekness and humility, a pure and upright heart, will be reflected in the countenance, and command love and respect. . . .

[Children and youth] can, through cultivation of the intellect, depending upon God for success, develop firm and beautiful characters. The fear of God, the contemplation of the glories of nature in His created works, will never dwarf the intellect, but will have a tendency to strengthen every faculty of the soul.

It is the precious privilege of children and youth to yield their minds to the control of the Spirit of God and become intellectual Christians. Their mental and moral powers may grow in harmonious proportions. Their understanding may be strong, their consciences, pure, and their characters, lovely. . . .

If you would find happiness and peace in all you do, you must do everything in reference to the glory of God. If you would have peace in your hearts, you must seek earnestly to imitate the life of Christ. Then there will be no need of affecting cheerfulness, or of your seeking for pleasure in the indulgence of pride and the frivolities of the world. You will have a serenity and happiness in rightdoing that you can never realize in a course of wrong.

Jesus took human nature, passing through infancy, childhood, and youth, that He might know how to sympathize with all, and leave an example for all children and youth. He is acquainted with the temptations and weaknesses of children. He has, in His love, opened the fountain of pleasure and joy for the soul that trusts in Him. By seeking to honor Christ and to follow His example, children and youth can be truly happy. They may feel their accountability to labor with Jesus Christ in the great plan of saving souls.

If youth will feel their responsibility before God, they will be elevated above everything that is mean, selfish, and impure. Life to such will be full of importance. They will realize that they have something great and glorious to live for. This will have an influence upon youth to make them earnest, cheerful, and strong under all the burdens, discouragements, and difficulties of life, as was their divine Pattern. . . . The consciousness that you are doing those things which God can approve will make you strong in His strength; and by copying the Pattern, you may, like Him, increase in wisdom, and in favor with God and man (*Youth's Instructor,* September 1873).

Always Presenting the Word of God

What is written in the law? How do you read it? Luke 10:26.

The Savior made each work of healing an occasion of implanting divine principles in the mind and soul. This was the purpose of His work. He imparted earthly blessings, that He might incline the hearts of men to receive the gospel of His grace.

Christ might have occupied the highest place among the teachers of the Jewish nation, but He preferred rather to take the gospel to the poor. He went from place to place, that those in the highways and byways might hear the words of truth. By the sea, on the mountainside, in the streets of the city, in the synagogue, His voice was heard explaining the Scriptures. Often He taught in the outer court of the Temple, that the Gentiles might hear His words.

So unlike the explanations of Scripture given by the scribes and Pharisees was Christ's teaching, that the attention of the people was arrested. The rabbis dwelt upon tradition, upon human theory and speculation. Often that which men had taught and written about the Scripture was put in place of the Scripture itself. The subject of Christ's teaching was the Word of God. He met questioners with a plain, "It is written," "What saith the Scripture?" "How readest thou?" At every opportunity, when an interest was awakened by either friend or foe, He presented the Word. With clearness and power He proclaimed the gospel message. His words shed a flood of light on the teachings of patriarchs and prophets, and the Scriptures came to men as a new revelation. Never before had His hearers perceived in the Word of God such depth of meaning.

Never was there such an evangelist as Christ. He was the Majesty of heaven, but He humbled Himself to take our nature, that He might meet men where they were. To all people, rich and poor, free and bond, Christ, the Messenger of the covenant, brought the tidings of salvation. His fame as the great Healer spread throughout Palestine. The sick came to the places through which He would pass, that they might call on Him for help. Hither, too, came many anxious to hear His words and to receive a touch of His hand. Thus He went from city to city, from town to town, preaching the gospel and healing the sick—the King of glory in the lowly garb of humanity.

He attended the great yearly festivals of the nation, and to the multitude absorbed in outward ceremony He spoke of heavenly things, bringing eternity within their view. To all He brought treasures from the storehouse of wisdom. He spoke to them in language so simple that they could not fail of understanding. . . . With tender, courteous grace, He ministered to the sin-sick soul, bringing healing and strength (*Gospel Workers,* pp. 43-45).

Seek Help From Jesus, Not Sinful Humans

Lo, I am with you alway, even unto the end of the world. Matthew 28:20.

Christ took humanity upon Himself. He laid aside His royal robe and kingly crown, and stepped down from His high command in the heavenly courts. Clothing His divinity with humanity, Christ encircled the race with His long human arm. He stands at the head of humanity, not as a sinner but as a Savior. It is because there is no spot or stain of sin upon His divine soul that He can stand there as the sinner's surety. Because He is sinless He can take away our sins and place us on vantage ground with God, if we will believe in Him and trust Him as the One that will be our sanctification and righteousness. . . .

He has promised that if you ask wisdom from Him, He will give it to you. But it is not always essential for us to know all the whys and wherefores. We dishonor God by striving to get someone who we think understands our case to help us. Has He not given us His only begotten Son? Is not Christ close beside us, and will He not give us the help we need? "Lo, I am with you alway," He says, "even unto the end of the world." His Word repeats the promise over and over again. . . .

It is no marvel to me that at the present time there is so much weakness where there should be strength. The reason of this is that instead of drinking of the pure water of Lebanon, we are seeking to quench our thirst from cisterns in the lowlands, which contain not the water of life. We trust in human beings and are disappointed and often misled. . . .

We have done great dishonor to our Master in turning away from Christ to seek wisdom from finite human beings. Shall we continue to cherish the sin of unbelief, which doth so easily beset us, or shall we cast away this weight of unbelief, and go to the Source of strength believing that we shall receive pity and compassion from the One who knows our frame, who loves us so well that He gave His own life for us, who bore in His own body the strokes which fell because of our transgression of the law of God. All this He did that we might become prisoners of hope.

We are not polite to Christ. We do not recognize His presence. We do not realize that He is to be our honored guest, that we are encircled by His long human arm, while with His divine arm He grasps the throne of the Infinite. We forget that the threshold of heaven is flooded with the glory proceeding from the throne of God, that the light may fall directly on those who are seeking the help that Christ alone can give. He said to the woman of Samaria, "If thou knewest the gift of God, and who it is that saith to thee, Give me to drink; thou wouldest have asked of him, and he would have given thee living water" (John 4:10) (manuscript 144, 1901).

March
21

Jesus the Prince of Peace

Whatsoever ye would that men should do to you, do ye even so to them. Matthew 7:12.

Wherever the power of intellect, of authority, or of force is employed, and love is not manifestly present, the affections and will of those whom we seek to reach assume a defensive, repelling position, and their strength of resistance is increased. Jesus was the Prince of Peace. He came into the world to bring resistance and authority into subjection to Himself. Wisdom and strength He could command, but the means He employed with which to overcome evil were the wisdom and strength of love. . . .

"Whatsoever ye would that men should do to you, do ye even so to them." Blessed results would appear as the fruit of such a course. "With what measure ye mete, it shall be measured to you again." Here are strong motives which should constrain us to love one another with a pure heart, fervently. Christ is our example. He went about doing good. He lived to bless others. Love beautified and ennobled all His actions. We are not commanded to do to *ourselves* what we wish others to do unto us; we are to *do unto others* what we wish them to do to us under like circumstances. The measure we mete is always measured to us again. Pure love is simple in its operations, and is distinct from any other principle of action. . . . Love should be cherished and cultivated, for its influence is divine (*Testimonies*, vol. 2, pp. 135, 136).

In Jesus you may love with fervor, with earnestness. This love may increase in depth and expand without limit. . . . Love to God will ensure love to your neighbor, and you will engage in the duties of life with a deep, unselfish interest. Pure principles should underlie your actions. Inward peace will bring even your thoughts into a healthful channel. . . .

Peace of mind, which comes from pure and holy motives and actions, will give free and vigorous spring to all the organs of the body. Inward peace and a conscience void of offense toward God will quicken and invigorate the intellect like dew distilled upon the tender plants. . . . The meditations are pleasing because they are sanctified. The serenity of mind which you may possess will bless all with whom you associate. This peace and calmness will, in time, become natural, and will reflect its precious rays upon all around you, to be again reflected upon you.

The more you taste this heavenly peace and quietude of mind, the more it will increase. It is an animated, living pleasure which does not throw all the moral energies into a stupor, but awakens them to increased activity. Perfect peace is an attitude of heaven which angels possess (*ibid.*, pp. 326, 327).

Christ's Matchless Tenderness

The Lord God hath given me the tongue of the learned, that I should know how to speak a word in season to him that is weary. Isaiah 50:4.

As the dew and the still showers fall upon the withering plants, so let words fall gently when seeking to win men from error. God's plan is first to reach the heart. We are to speak the truth in love, trusting in Him to give it power for the reforming of the life. The Holy Spirit will apply to the soul the word that is spoken in love.

Naturally we are self-centered and opinionated. But when we learn the lessons that Christ desires to teach us, we become partakers of His nature; henceforth we live His life. The wonderful example of Christ, the matchless tenderness with which He entered into the feelings of others, weeping with those who wept, rejoicing with those who rejoiced, must have a deep influence upon the character of all who follow Him in sincerity. By kindly words and acts they will try to make the path easy for weary feet. . . .

All around us are afflicted souls. Here and there, everywhere, we may find them. Let us search out these suffering ones and speak a word in season to comfort their hearts. Let us ever be channels through which shall flow the refreshing waters of compassion.

In all our associations it should be remembered that in the experience of others there are chapters sealed from mortal sight. On the pages of memory are sad histories that are sacredly guarded from curious eyes. There stand registered long, hard battles with trying circumstances, perhaps troubles in the home life, that day by day weaken courage, confidence, and faith. Those who are fighting the battle of life at great odds may be strengthened and encouraged by little attentions that cost only a loving effort. To such the strong, helpful grasp of the hand by a true friend is worth more than gold or silver. Words of kindness are as welcome as the smile of angels.

There are multitudes struggling with poverty, compelled to labor hard for small wages, and able to secure but the barest necessities of life. Toil and deprivation, with no hope of better things, make their burden very heavy. When pain and sickness are added, the burden is almost insupportable. Careworn and oppressed, they know not where to turn for relief. Sympathize with them in their trials, their heartaches, and disappointments. This will open the way for you to help them. Speak to them of God's promises, pray with and for them, inspire them with hope.

Words of cheer and encouragement spoken when the soul is sick and the pulse of courage is low—these are regarded by the Savior as if spoken to Himself. As hearts are cheered, the heavenly angels look on in pleased recognition (*The Ministry of Healing*, pp. 157-159).

Reaching Forward to Perfection

Be ye therefore perfect, even as your Father which is in heaven is perfect. Matthew 5:48.

God intends that improvement shall be the lifework of all His followers and that it shall be guided and controlled by correct experience. The true man is one who is willing to sacrifice his own interest for the good of others and who exercises himself in binding up the brokenhearted. The true object of life has scarcely begun to be understood by many. . . .

Intellect alone does not make the man, according to the divine standard. There is a power in intellect if sanctified and controlled by the Spirit of God. It is superior to riches and to physical power, yet it must be cultivated in order to make the man. . . .

That which will bless humanity is spiritual life. If the man is in harmony with God, he will depend continually upon Him for strength. "Be ye therefore perfect, even as your Father which is in heaven is perfect." It is our lifework to be reaching forward to the perfection of Christian character, striving continually for conformity to the will of God. The efforts begun upon earth will continue through eternity. God's standard of man is elevated to the highest meaning of the term, and if he acts up to his God-given manhood he will promote happiness in this life, which will lead to glory and an eternal reward in the life to come.

The members of the human family are entitled to the name of men and women only when they employ their talents, in every possible way, for the good of others. The life of Christ is before us as a pattern, and it is when ministering, like angels of mercy, to the wants of others that man is closely allied to God. It is the nature of Christianity to make happy families and happy society. Discord, selfishness, and strife will be put away from every man and woman who possesses the true spirit of Christ.

Those who are partakers of Christ's love have no right to think that there is a limit to their influence and work in trying to benefit humanity. Did Christ become weary in His efforts to save fallen man? Our work is to be continuous and persevering. We shall find work to do until the Master shall bid us lay our armor at His feet. God is a moral governor, and we must wait, submissive to His will, ready and willing to spring to our duty whenever work needs to be done (*Testimonies*, vol. 4, pp. 519, 520).

Our Savior took up the true relationship of a human being as the Son of God. We are sons and daughters of God. . . . We must follow where Christ leads the way. For thirty years He lived the life of a perfect man, meeting the highest standard of perfection (*The SDA Bible Commentary*, Ellen G. White Comments, vol. 5, pp. 1085, 1086).

Our Elder Brother Brings Us Rest

Take my yoke upon you, and learn of me; for I am meek and lowly in heart: and ye shall find rest unto your souls. Matthew 11:29.

Jesus looked upon the distressed and heart-burdened, those whose hopes were blighted, and who with earthly joys were seeking to quiet the longing of the soul, and He invited all to find rest in Him.

Tenderly He bade the toiling people, "Take my yoke upon you, and learn of me; for I am meek and lowly in heart: and ye shall find rest unto your souls" (Matthew 11:29).

In these words, Christ was speaking to every human being. Whether they know it or not, all are weary and heavy-laden. All are weighed down with burdens that only Christ can remove. The heaviest burden that we bear is the burden of sin. If we were left to bear this burden, it would crush us. But the Sinless One has taken our place. "The Lord hath laid on him the iniquity of us all" (Isaiah 53:6).

He has born the burden of our guilt. He will take the load from our weary shoulders. He will give us rest. The burden of care and sorrow also He will bear. He invites us to cast all our care upon Him; for He carries us upon His heart.

The Elder Brother of our race is by the eternal throne. He looks upon every soul who is turning his face toward Him as the Savior. He knows by experience what are the weaknesses of humanity, what are our wants, and where lies the strength of our temptations; for He was "in all points tempted like as we are, yet without sin" (Hebrews 4:15). He is watching over you, trembling child of God. Are you tempted? He will deliver. Are you weak? He will strengthen. Are you ignorant? He will enlighten. Are you wounded? He will heal. The Lord "telleth the number of the stars"; and yet "He healeth the broken in heart, and bindeth up their wounds" (Psalm 147:4, 3).

Whatever your anxieties and trials, spread out your case before the Lord. Your spirit will be braced for endurance. The way will be open for you to disentangle yourself from embarrassment and difficulty. The weaker and more helpless you know yourself to be, the stronger will you become in His strength. The heavier your burdens, the more blessed the rest in casting them upon your Burden Bearer.

Circumstances may separate friends; the restless waters of the wide sea may roll between us and them. But no circumstances, no distance, can separate us from the Savior. Wherever we may be, He is at our right hand, to support, maintain, uphold, and cheer. Greater than the love of a mother for her child is Christ's love for His redeemed. It is our privilege to rest in His love, to say, "I will trust Him; for He gave His life for me." Human love may change, but Christ's love knows no change. When we cry to Him for help, His hand is stretched out to save (*The Ministry of Healing*, pp. 71, 72).

March
25

Choose Him as Our Trusted Friend

Henceforth I call you not servants; . . . but I have called you friends; for all things that I have heard of my Father I have made known unto you. John 15:15.

Wickedness prevails at the present day. The perils of the last days thicken around us, and because iniquity abounds the love of many waxes cold. This need not be if all would come to Jesus, and in confiding faith trust in Him. His meekness and lowliness, cherished in the heart, will bring peace and rest, and give moral power to every soul.

The shortness of time is frequently urged as an incentive for seeking righteousness and making Christ our friend. This should not be the great motive with us; for it savors of selfishness. Is it necessary that the terrors of the day of God should be held before us, that we may be compelled to right action through fear? It ought not to be so. Jesus is attractive. He is full of love, mercy, and compassion. He proposes to be our friend, to walk with us through all the rough pathways of life. He says to us, I am the Lord thy God; walk with Me, and I will fill thy path with light. Jesus, the Majesty of heaven, proposes to elevate to companionship with Himself those who come to Him with their burdens, their weaknesses, and their cares. He will count them as His children, and finally give them an inheritance of more value than the empires of kings, a crown of glory richer than has ever decked the brow of the most exalted earthly monarch.

It is our duty to love Jesus as our Redeemer. He has a right to command our love, but He invites us to give Him our heart. He calls us to walk with Him in the path of humble, truthful obedience. His invitation to us is a call to a pure, holy, and happy life—a life of peace and rest, of liberty and love—and to a rich inheritance in the future, immortal life. Which will we choose—liberty in Christ, or bondage and tyranny in the service of Satan? . . . If we choose to live with Christ through the ceaseless ages of eternity, why not choose Him now as our most loved and trusted friend, our best and wisest counselor.

It is our privilege to have daily a calm, close, happy walk with Jesus. We need not be alarmed if the path lies through conflicts and sufferings. We may have the peace which passeth understanding; but it will cost us battles with the powers of darkness, struggles severe against selfishness and inbred sin. The victories gained daily through persevering, untiring effort in well-doing will be precious through Christ who has loved us, who gave Himself for us, that He might redeem us from all iniquity, and purify unto Himself a "peculiar people, zealous of good works." . . .

The Son of the Highest suffered shame on the cross, that sinners might not suffer everlasting shame and contempt, but be ransomed, and crowned with eternal glory (*Signs of the Times*, Mar. 17, 1887).

Order and Perfection Seen in All He Did

Then cometh Simon Peter . . . and went into the sepulchre, and seeth the linen clothes lie, and the napkin, that was about his head, not lying with the linen clothes, but wrapped together in a place by itself. John 20:6, 7.

A young man clothed in shining garments was sitting by the tomb. It was the angel who had rolled away the stone. He had taken the guise of humanity that he might not alarm these friends of Jesus. Yet about him the light of the heavenly glory was still shining, and the women were afraid. They turned to flee, but the angel's words stayed their steps. "Fear not ye," he said; "for I know that ye seek Jesus, which was crucified. He is not here: for he is risen, as he said. Come, see the place where the Lord lay. And go quickly, and tell his disciples that he is risen from the dead."

Again they look into the tomb, and again they hear the wonderful news. Another angel in human form is there, and he says, "Why seek ye the living among the dead? He is not here, but is risen: remember how he spake unto you when he was yet in Galilee, saying, The Son of man must be delivered into the hands of sinful men, and be crucified, and the third day rise again."

He is risen, He is risen! the women repeat the words again and again. No need now for the anointing spices. The Savior is living, and not dead. They remember now that when speaking of His death He said that He would rise again. What a day is this to the world! Quickly the women departed from the sepulcher "with fear and great joy; and did run to bring his disciples word."

Mary had not heard the good news. She went to Peter and John with the sorrowful message, "They have taken away the Lord out of the sepulchre, and we know not where they have laid him." The disciples hurried to the tomb, and found it as Mary had said. They saw the shroud and the napkin, but they did not find their Lord. Yet even here was testimony that He had risen. The graveclothes were not thrown heedlessly aside, but carefully folded, each in a place by itself. John "saw, and believed." He did not yet understand the scripture that Christ must rise from the dead; but he now remembered the Savior's words foretelling His resurrection.

It was Christ Himself who had placed those graveclothes with such care. When the mighty angel came down to the tomb, he was joined by another, who with his company had been keeping guard over the Lord's body. As the angel from heaven rolled away the stone, the other entered the tomb, and unbound the wrappings from the body of Jesus. But it was the Savior's hand that folded each, and laid it in its place. In His sight who guides alike the star and the atom, there is nothing unimportant. Order and perfection are seen in all His work (*The Desire of Ages,* pp. 788, 789).

Lift Him Up the Risen Savior

Now is Christ risen from the dead, and become the firstfruits of them that slept.
1 Corinthians 15:20.

The time had come for Christ to ascend to His Father's throne. As a divine conqueror He was about to return with the trophies of victory to the heavenly courts. Before His death He had declared to His Father, "I have finished the work which thou gavest me to do" (John 17:4). After His resurrection He tarried on earth for a season, that His disciples might become familiar with Him in His risen and glorified body. Now He was ready for the leave-taking. He had authenticated the fact that He was a living Savior. His disciples need no longer associate Him with the tomb. They could think of Him as glorified before the heavenly universe.

As the place of His ascension, Jesus chose the spot so often hallowed by His presence while He dwelt among men. . . . Christ stood upon Olivet, with yearning heart overlooking Jerusalem. The groves and glens of the mountain had been consecrated by His prayers and tears. Its steeps had echoed the triumphant shouts of the multitude that proclaimed Him king. On its sloping descent He had found a home with Lazarus at Bethany. In the Garden of Gethsemane at its foot He had prayed and agonized alone. From this mountain He was to ascend to heaven. Upon its summit His feet will rest when He shall come again. Not as a man of sorrows, but as a glorious and triumphant king He will stand upon Olivet, while Hebrew hallelujahs mingle with Gentile hosannas, and the voices of the redeemed as a mighty host shall swell the acclamation, Crown Him Lord of all! . . .

Upon reaching the Mount of Olives, Jesus led the way across the summit, to the vicinity of Bethany. Here He paused, and the disciples gathered about Him. Beams of light seemed to radiate from His countenance as He looked lovingly upon them. He upbraided them not for their faults and failures; words of the deepest tenderness were the last that fell upon their ears from the lips of their Lord.

With hands outstretched in blessing, and as if in assurance of His protecting care, He slowly ascended from among them, drawn heavenward by a power stronger than any earthly attraction. As He passed upward, the awestricken disciples looked with straining eyes for the last glimpse of their ascending Lord. A cloud of glory hid Him from their sight; and the words came back to them as the cloudy chariot of angels received Him, "Lo, I am with you alway, even unto the end of the world." At the same time there floated down to them the sweetest and most joyous music from the angel choir (*The Desire of Ages,* pp. 829-831).

Ascended to Heaven in Human Form

Ye men of Galilee, why stand ye gazing up into heaven? this same Jesus, which is taken up from you into heaven, shall so come in like manner as ye have seen him go into heaven. Acts 1:11.

While the disciples were still gazing upward, voices addressed them which sounded like richest music. They turned, and saw two angels in the form of men, who spoke to them, saying, "Ye men of Galilee, why stand ye gazing up into heaven? this same Jesus . . . shall so come in like manner as ye have seen him go into heaven."

These angels were of the company that had been waiting in a shining cloud to escort Jesus to His heavenly home. The most exalted of the angel throng, they were the two who had come to the tomb at Christ's resurrection, and they had been with Him throughout His life on earth. With eager desire all heaven had waited for the end of His tarrying in a world marred by the curse of sin. The time had now come for the heavenly universe to receive their King. . . .

Christ had ascended to heaven in the form of humanity. The disciples had beheld the cloud receive Him. The same Jesus who had walked and talked and prayed with them; who had broken bread with them; who had been with them in their boats on the lake; and who had that very day toiled with them up the ascent of Olivet—the same Jesus had now gone to share His Father's throne. And the angels had assured them that the very One whom they had seen go up into heaven would come again even as He had ascended. He will come "with clouds; and every eye shall see him." . . . Well might the disciples rejoice in the hope of their Lord's return.

When the disciples went back to Jerusalem, the people looked upon them with amazement. After the trial and crucifixion of Christ, it had been thought that they would appear downcast and ashamed. Their enemies expected to see upon their faces an expression of sorrow and defeat. Instead of this there was only gladness and triumph. Their faces were aglow with a happiness not born of earth. They did not mourn over disappointed hopes, but were full of praise and thanksgiving to God. With rejoicing they told the wonderful story of Christ's resurrection and His ascension to heaven, and their testimony was received by many.

The disciples no longer had any distrust of the future. They knew that Jesus was in heaven, and that His sympathies were with them still. They knew that they had a friend at the throne of God, and they were eager to present their requests to the Father in the name of Jesus. . . . They extended the hand of faith higher and higher, with the mighty argument, "It is Christ that died, yea rather, that is risen again . . . who also maketh intercession for us" (Romans 8:34). And Pentecost brought them fullness of joy in the presence of the Comforter, even as Christ had promised (*The Desire of Ages*, pp. 831-833).

Glorified Before the Universe

I have glorified thee on the earth: I have finished the work which thou gavest me to do. John 17:4.

By raising Christ from the dead, the Father glorified His Son before the Roman guard, before the satanic host, and before the heavenly universe. A mighty angel, clothed with the panoply of heaven, descended, scattering the darkness from his track, and, breaking the Roman seal, rolled back the stone from the sepulcher as if it had been a pebble, undoing in a moment the work that the enemy had done. The voice of God was heard, calling Christ from His prison house. The Roman guard saw heavenly angels falling in reverence before Him whom they had crucified, and He proclaimed above the rent sepulcher of Joseph, "I am the resurrection, and the life." Can we be surprised that the soldiers fell as dead men to the earth?

Christ's ascension to heaven, amid the cloud of heavenly angels, glorified Him. His concealed glory shone forth with all the brightness that mortal man could endure and live. He came to our world as a man; He ascended to His heavenly home as God. His human life was full of sorrow and grief, because of His cruel rejection by those He came to save; but men were permitted to see Him strengthened, to behold Him ascending in glory and triumph, surrounded by a convoy of angels. The same holy beings that announced His advent to the world were permitted to attend Him at His ascension, and to demand a triumphal entrance for the royal and glorified Being. "Lift your heads, O ye gates," they cry as they near the heavenly portals. . . . "Who is this King of glory?" And from thousands and ten thousands of voices the answer comes: "The Lord strong and mighty, the Lord mighty in battle." . . .

Thus the prayer of Christ was answered. He was glorified with the glory which He had with His Father before the world was. But amid this glory, Christ does not lose sight of His toiling, struggling ones upon earth. He has a request to make of His Father. He waves back the heavenly host until He is in the direct presence of Jehovah, and then He presents His petition in behalf of His chosen ones.

"Father," He says, "I will that they also, whom thou hast given me, be with me where I am." And then the Father declares, "Let all the angels of God worship him." The heavenly host prostrate themselves before Him, and raise their song of triumph and joy. Glory encircles the King of heaven, and was beheld by all the heavenly intelligences. No words can describe the scene which took place as the Son of God was publicly reinstated in the place of honor and glory which He voluntarily left when He became a man (*Signs of the Times,* May 10, 1899).

In the Father's Arms

I ascend unto my Father, and your Father; and to my God, and your God. John 20:17.

Before the foundations of the earth were laid, the Father and the Son had united in a covenant to redeem man if he should be overcome by Satan. They had clasped Their hands in a solemn pledge that Christ should become the surety for the human race. This pledge Christ has fulfilled. When upon the cross He cried out, "It is finished," He addressed the Father. The compact had been fully carried out. Now He declares: Father, it is finished. I have done Thy will, O My God. I have completed the work of redemption. If Thy justice is satisfied, "I will that they also, whom thou hast given me, be with me where I am" (John 19:30; 17:24).

The voice of God is heard proclaiming that justice is satisfied. Satan is vanquished. Christ's toiling, struggling ones on earth are "accepted in the beloved" (Ephesians 1:6). Before the heavenly angels and the representatives of unfallen worlds, they are declared justified. Where He is, there His church shall be. "Mercy and truth are met together; righteousness and peace have kissed each other" (Psalm 85:10). The Father's arms encircle His Son, and the word is given, "Let all the angels of God worship him" (Hebrews 1:6).

With joy unutterable, rulers and principalities and powers acknowledge the supremacy of the Prince of life. The angel host prostrate themselves before Him, while the glad shout fills all the courts of heaven, "Worthy is the Lamb that was slain to receive power, and riches, and wisdom, and strength, and honour, and glory, and blessing" (Revelation 5:12).

Songs of triumph mingle with the music from angel harps, till heaven seems to overflow with joy and praise. Love has conquered. The lost is found. Heaven rings with voices in lofty strains proclaiming, "Blessing, and honor, and glory, and power, be unto him that sitteth upon the throne, and unto the Lamb for ever and ever" (verse 13).

From that scene of heavenly joy, there comes back to us on earth the echo of Christ's own wonderful words, "I ascend unto my Father, and your Father; and to my God, and your God" (John 20:17). The family of heaven and the family of earth are one. For us our Lord ascended, and for us He lives. "Wherefore he is able also to save them to the uttermost that come unto God by him, seeing he ever liveth to make intercession for them" (Hebrews 7:25) (*The Desire of Ages,* pp. 834, 835).

At the Right Hand of God

I see the heavens opened, and the Son of man standing on the right hand of God.
Acts 7:56.

Stephen, the foremost of the seven deacons, was a man of deep piety and broad faith. . . .

As the priests and rulers saw the power that attended the preaching of Stephen, they were filled with bitter hatred. Instead of yielding to the evidence that he presented, they determined to silence his voice by putting him to death. . . .

The priests and rulers could not prevail against the clear, calm wisdom of Stephen. They determined to make an example of him, and while they thus satisfied their revengeful hatred, prevent others, through fear, from adopting his belief. Witnesses were hired to bear false testimony that they had heard him speak blasphemous words against the Temple and the law. . . .

When Stephen was questioned as to the truth of the charges against him, he began his defense in a clear, thrilling voice, which rang through the council hall. . . . He saw the resistance that met his words, and knew that he was giving his last testimony. When he connected Christ with the prophecies, and spoke as he did of the Temple, the priest, pretending to be horror-stricken, rent his robe. To Stephen, this act was a signal that his voice would soon be silenced forever. Although in the midst of his sermon, he abruptly concluded it. . . . The prisoner read his fate in the cruel faces about him, but he did not waver. The fear of death was gone. The enraged priests and the excited mob had no terror for him. The scene before him faded from his vision. To him the gates of heaven were ajar, and looking in, he saw the glory of the courts of God, and Christ, as if just risen from His throne, standing ready to sustain His servant, who was about to suffer martyrdom for His sake. In words of triumph Stephen exclaimed, "I see the heavens opened, and the Son of man standing on the right hand of God."

As he described the glorious scene opened before him, it was more than his persecutors could endure. Stopping their ears, that they might not hear his words, and uttering loud cries, they ran furiously upon him with one accord. "And they stoned Stephen, calling upon God, and saying, Lord Jesus, receive my spirit. And he kneeled down, and cried with a loud voice, Lord, lay not this sin to their charge. And when he had said this, he fell asleep." . . .

The signet of God upon Stephen's face, and his words, which reached the very souls of those who heard them, remained in the minds of the beholders, and testified to the truth of that which he had proclaimed (*Review and Herald,* Feb. 23, 1911).

The Bread of Life

And Jesus said unto them, I am the bread of life.
John 6:35.

I am the bread of life," the Author, Nourisher, and Supporter of eternal, spiritual life. . . . Christ represents Himself under the similitude of heavenly bread. To eat His flesh and to drink His blood means to receive Him as a heaven-sent teacher. Belief in Him is essential to spiritual life. Those who feast on the Word never hunger, never thirst, never desire any higher or more exalted good.

Christ exclaimed the meaning of His words so clearly that none need stumble over them. His statement regarding eating the flesh and drinking the blood of the Son of God is to be taken in a spiritual sense. We eat Christ's flesh and drink His blood when by faith we lay hold upon Him as our Savior.

Christ used the figure of eating and drinking to represent that nearness to Him which all must have who are at last partakers with Him in His glory. The temporal food we eat is assimilated, giving strength and solidity to the body. In a similar manner, as we believe and receive the words of the Lord Jesus, they become a part of our spiritual life, bringing light and peace, hope and joy, and strengthening the soul as physical food strengthens the body.

It is not enough for us to know and respect the words of the Scriptures. We must enter into the understanding of them, studying them earnestly. . . . Christians will reveal the degree to which they do this by the healthiness of their spiritual character. We must know the practical application of the Word to our own individual character-building. We are to be holy temples, in which God can live and walk and work. Never must we strive to lift ourselves above the servants whom God has chosen to do His work and to honor His holy name. "All ye are brethren." Let us apply this Word to our individual selves, comparing scripture with scripture.

In our daily lives, before our brethren and before the world, we are to be living interpreters of the Scriptures, doing honor to Christ by revealing His meekness and His lowliness of heart. As we eat and digest the bread of life, we shall reveal a symmetrical character. By our unity, by esteeming others better than ourselves, we are to bear to the world a living testimony of the power of the truth. . . .

When men submit entirely to God, eating the bread of life and drinking the water of salvation, they will grow up into Christ. Their characters are composed of that which the mind eats and drinks. Through the Word of life, which they receive and obey, they become partakers of the divine nature. Then . . . Christ, not man, is exalted (*The SDA Bible Commentary*, Ellen G. White Comments, vol. 5, p. 1135).

April
2

The Word Our Spiritual Food

He that cometh to me shall never hunger; and he that believeth on me shall never thirst. John 6:35.

There are many in this age of the world who act as if they were at liberty to question the words of the Infinite, to review His decisions and statutes, endorsing, revising, reshaping, and annulling at their pleasure. We are never safe while we are guided by human opinions, but we are safe when we are guided by a "Thus saith the Lord." We cannot trust the salvation of our souls to any lower standard than the decisions of an infallible Judge.

Those who make God their guide and His Word their counselor behold the lamp of life. God's living oracles guide their feet in straight paths. Those who are thus led do not dare to judge the Word of God, but ever hold that His Word judges them. They get their faith and religion from the Word of the living God. It is the guide and counselor that direct their path. The Word is indeed a light to their feet and a lamp to their path. They walk under the direction of the Father of light, with whom is no variableness, neither shadow or turning. He whose tender mercies are over all His works makes the path of the just as a shining light, which shineth more and more unto the perfect day.

The Word of God is to be our spiritual food. "I am the bread of life," Christ said; "he that cometh to me shall never hunger; and he that believeth on me shall never thirst." The world is perishing for pure, unadulterated truth. Christ is the truth. His words are truth, and they have a greater value and a deeper significance than appears on the surface. . . . Minds that are quickened by the Holy Spirit will discern the value of these sayings. . . .

By his conscience every honest Jew was convinced that Jesus Christ was the Son of God, but the heart, in its pride and ambition, would not surrender. When the truth is held as the truth only by the conscience, when the heart is not stimulated and made receptive, the mind only is affected. But when the truth is received as truth by the heart, it has passed through the conscience, and captivated the soul by its pure principles. It is placed in the heart by the Holy Spirit, who reveals its beauty to the mind, that its transforming power may be seen in the character. . . .

True religion is embodied in the Word of God, and consists in being under the guidance of the Holy One in thought, word, and deed. He who is the Way, the Truth, and the Life takes the humble, earnest, wholehearted seeker, and says, Follow Me. He leads him the narrow way to holiness and heaven. . . . And all who decide to follow the Lord fully will be led in the royal path (*Review and Herald*, Mar. 29, 1906).

The Bread of Life and the Robe of Righteousness

For the bread of God is he who comes down from heaven and gives life to the world.
John 6:33, NIV.

If ye . . . know how to give good gifts unto your children: how much more shall your heavenly Father give the Holy Spirit to them that ask Him?" (Luke 11:13). The Holy Spirit, the representative of Himself, is the greatest of all gifts. All "good things" are comprised in this. The Creator Himself can give us nothing greater, nothing better. When we beseech the Lord to pity us in our distress, and to guide us by His Holy Spirit, He will never turn away our prayer.

It is possible even for a parent to turn away from his hungry child, but God can never reject the cry of the needy and longing heart. With what wonderful tenderness He has described His love! To those who in days of darkness feel that God is unmindful of them, this is the message from the Father's heart: "Zion said, The Lord hath forsaken me, and my Lord hath forgotten me. Can a woman forget her sucking child, that she should not have compassion on the son of her womb? yea, they may forget, yet will I not forget thee. Behold, I have graven thee upon the palms of my hands" (Isaiah 49:14-16).

Every promise in the Word of God furnishes us with subject matter for prayer, presenting the pledged word of Jehovah as our assurance. Whatever spiritual blessing we need, it is our privilege to claim through Jesus. We may tell the Lord, with the simplicity of a child, exactly what we need. We may state to Him our temporal matters, asking Him for bread and raiment as well as for the bread of life and the robe of Christ's righteousness. Your heavenly Father knows that you have need of all these things, and you are invited to ask Him concerning them. It is through the name of Jesus that every favor is received. God will honor that name, and will supply your necessities from the riches of His liberality.

But do not forget that in coming to God as a father you acknowledge your relation to Him as a child. You not only trust His goodness, but in all things yield to His will, knowing that His love is changeless. You give yourself to do His work. It was to those whom He had bidden to seek first the kingdom of God and His righteousness that Jesus gave the promise, "Ask, and ye shall receive" (John 16:24).

The gifts of Him who has all power in heaven and earth are in store for the children of God. Gifts so precious that they come to us through the costly sacrifice of the Redeemer's blood; gifts that will satisfy the deepest craving of the heart, gifts lasting as eternity, will be received and enjoyed by all who will come to God as little children. Take God's promises as your own, plead them before Him as His own words, and you will receive fullness of joy (*Thoughts From the Mount of Blessing*, pp. 132-134).

Jesus Sowed the Seed of the Living Word

It is written, Man shall not live by bread alone,
but by every word that proceedeth out of the mouth of God.
Matthew 4:4.

The subject of Christ's teaching and preaching was the Word of God. He met questioners with a plain, "It is written." "What saith the Scriptures?" "How readest thou?" At every opportunity, when an interest was awakened by either friend or foe, He sowed the seed of the Word. He who is the Way, the Truth, and the Life, Himself the living Word, points to the Scriptures, saying, "They are they which testify of Me." . . .

Christ's servants are to do the same work. In our day, as of old, the vital truths of God's Word are set aside for human theories and speculations. Many professed ministers of the gospel do not accept the whole Bible as the inspired word. One wise man rejects one portion; another questions another part. They set up their judgment as superior to the Word; and the Scripture which they do teach rests upon their own authority. Its divine authenticity is destroyed. Thus the seeds of infidelity are sown broadcast; for the people become confused and know not what to believe.

There are many beliefs that the mind has no right to entertain. In the days of Christ the rabbis put a forced, mystical construction upon many portions of Scripture. Because the plain teaching of God's Word condemned their practices, they tried to destroy its force. The same thing is done today. The Word of God is made to appear mysterious and obscure in order to excuse transgression of His law. Christ rebuked these practices in His day. He taught that the Word of God was to be understood by all. He pointed to the Scriptures as of unquestionable authority, and we should do the same. The Bible is to be presented as the word of the infinite God, as the end of all controversy and the foundation of all faith.

The Bible has been robbed of its power, and the results are seen in a lowering of the tone of spiritual life. . . . [Yet] there are many who are crying out for the living God, longing for the divine presence. . . .

Christ's favorite theme was the paternal tenderness and abundant grace of God; He dwelt much upon the holiness of His character and His law; He presented Himself to the people as the Way, the Truth, and the Life. Let these be the themes of Christ's ministers. Present the truth as it is in Jesus. Make plain the requirements of the law and the gospel. Tell the people of Christ's life of self-denial and sacrifice; of His humiliation and death; of His resurrection and ascension; of His intercession for them in the courts of God; of His promise, "I will come again, and receive you unto myself" (John 14:3) (*Christ's Object Lessons*, pp. 39, 40).

Feed on the Bread of Life

My Father giveth you the true bread from heaven.
John 6:32.

We are baptized in the name of the Father, and of the Son, and of the Holy Ghost, and these three great, infinite powers are unitedly pledged to work in our behalf if we will cooperate with them. We are buried with Christ in baptism as an emblem of His death.

We are raised from the water as an emblem of His resurrection. We are to live as newborn souls, that we may be raised at the last great day. . . . You are pledged to live in newness of life; for you are dead, and your life is hid with Christ in God. "If ye then be risen with Christ, *seek those things which are above*, where Christ sitteth on the right hand of God." This is where you are to place your treasure. Finite man cannot do your believing. Come to the great source of power for your strength.

Christ's prayer on the banks of the Jordan includes everyone who will believe in Him. The promise that you are accepted in the Beloved comes to you. Hold it with the grip of unyielding faith. God said, "This is my beloved Son, *in whom I am well pleased*." This means that through the dark shadow which Satan has thrown athwart your pathway Christ has cleaved the way for you to the throne of the infinite God. He has laid hold of almighty power, and you are accepted in the Beloved.

In every respect you are to honor God by being partakers of His divine nature that you may have the assurance of sins pardoned which would testify of the love of God. But there is not in our experience that pleasantness and joyousness that there should be. Christ says that if *He* is in us, *our joy will be full*. Let us then be partakers of the *divine* nature, having escaped the corruption that is in the world through lust. Let us not, by living inconsistent, earthly, sensual lives, heap reproach upon Christ. Let us rise above the malarious atmosphere that pervades the world, and breathe the breath of God. Let us feed upon the bread of life.

Christ declares that if we eat *His* flesh and drink *His* blood, we shall have eternal life. His word will be to us as the leaves of the tree of life if we will believe in Christ as our personal Savior. If we eat the bread that came down from heaven, we shall have a live connection with God. We shall bring eternity into our reckoning. We shall live as in the presence of the whole heavenly host. The angels are watching and guarding us.

God loves us, but we fail to cherish that love. We are losing in spirituality. God wants us to recognize His ownership in every human being. He has His claims. They are mine, He says. I have bought them with a *price*. "Ye are not your own. . . . Therefore glorify God in your body, and in your spirit, which are God's." Will you do this? Will you pray in faith? Will you honor Christ by taking Him at His word? (manuscript 144, 1901).

The Bread of Life Revives the Spiritual Nature

This is the bread which cometh down from heaven, that a man may eat thereof, and not die. John 6:50.

There is a great need of taking self in hand when we find ourselves watching to make capital out of the missteps of a brother, a sister, or a friend. Although we do not acknowledge that the object of defaming another is to exalt self, self-exaltation is behind the practice of noting the shortcomings of others. Let every soul remember it is best to be on guard, and to make straight paths for his own feet, lest the lame . . . be turned out of the way. None of us are in danger of being too devotional, or of possessing too much Christlikeness of character. The remedy for unlikeness to Christ, for giving occasion for your good to be evil spoken of, is to live humbly, to keep looking unto Jesus in prayerful watchfulness, until changed into the likeness of His beautiful character.

The soul cannot be satisfied with forms, maxims, and traditions. The cry of the soul must be, give me the *bread of life*; lift up a full cup to my parched, spiritual nature, that I may be revived and refreshed; but do not intrude and interpose yourself between me and my Redeemer. Let me see Him as my helper, as the man of sorrows, acquainted with grief. Thou, O Lord, must be my helper. Thou wast wounded for my transgressions, bruised for my iniquities, . . . and with Thy stripes I am healed.

Christ was crucified for our sins, and was raised from the rent sepulcher for our justification; and He proclaims in triumph, "I am the resurrection, and the life." Jesus lives as our intercessor to plead before the Father. He has carried the sins of the whole world, and has not made one mortal man a sin-bearer for others. No man can bear the weight of his own sins. The crucified One bore them all, and every soul who believes in Him shall not perish, but have everlasting life.

The disciples of Christ will be fitted by His grace for every trial and test as he strives for perfection of character. By looking away from Jesus to some other one, or to something else, he may sometimes make mistakes; but as soon as he is warned of his danger, he again fastens his eyes upon Jesus, in whom his hope of eternal life is centered, and he plants his feet in the footprints of his Lord, and travels on securely. He rejoices, saying, "He is my living intercessor before God. He prays in my behalf. He is my advocate, and clothes me with the perfection of His own righteousness. This is all I require to enable me to bear shame and reproach for His dear name's sake. If He permits me to endure persecution, He will give me grace and the comfort of His presence, so that His name shall be thereby glorified" (*Review and Herald*, May 12, 1896).

Bible Study Strengthens the Intellect

Whatsoever things were written aforetime were written for our learning, that we through patience and comfort of the scriptures might have hope.
Romans 15:4.

There is nothing more calculated to strengthen the intellect than a study of the Bible. No other book is so potent to elevate the thoughts, to give vigor to the faculties, as the broad, ennobling truths of the Bible. If God's Word were studied as it should be, men would have a breadth of mind, a nobility of character, that is rarely seen in these times.

No knowledge is so firm, so consistent, so far-reaching, as that obtained from a study of the Word of God. If there were not another book in the wide world, the Word of God, lived out through the grace of Christ, would make man perfect in this world, with a character fitted for the future, immortal life. Those who study the Word, taking it in faith as the truth, and receiving it into the character, will be complete in Him who is all and in all. Thank God for the possibilities set before humanity. . . .

The time devoted to a study of God's Word and to prayer will bring a hundredfold in return.

The Word of God is the living seed, and as this seed is sown in the mind, the human agent must give diligent care to the successive stages of its growth. How is this to be done? After the Word has been prayerfully received, it is to be cherished, and practiced in the daily life. It is to spring up and bear fruit, putting forth first the blade, then the ear, then the full corn in the ear.

It is not enough to study the Bible as other books are studied. In order for it to be understood savingly, the Holy Spirit must move on the heart of the searcher. The same Spirit that inspired the Word must inspire the reader of the Word. Then will be heard the voice of heaven. "Thy Word, O God, is truth" will be the language of the soul.

The mere reading of the Word will not accomplish the result designed of Heaven; it must be studied, and cherished in the heart. The knowledge of God is not gained without mental effort. We should diligently study the Bible, asking God for the aid of the Holy Spirit, that we may understand His Word. We should take one verse, and concentrate the mind on the task of ascertaining the thought which God has put in that verse for us. We should dwell on the thought till it becomes our own, and we know "what saith the Lord." . . .

The Word of God is the bread of life. Those who eat and digest this Word, making it a part of every action and of every attribute of character, grow strong in the strength of God. It gives immortal vigor to the soul, perfecting the experience and bringing joys that will abide forever (*Signs of the Times*, June 25, 1902).

Treasures of Truth Revealed

Blessed are they which do hunger and thirst after righteousness: for they shall be filled.
Matthew 5:6.

All who receive the gospel message into the heart will long to proclaim it. The heaven-born love of Christ must find expression. Those who have put on Christ will relate their experience, tracing step by step the leadings of the Holy Spirit—their hungering and thirsting for the knowledge of God and of Jesus Christ whom He has sent, the results of their searching of the Scriptures, their prayers, their soul agony, and the words of Christ to them, "Thy sins be forgiven thee." It is unnatural for any to keep these things secret, and those who are filled with the love of Christ will not do so.

In proportion as the Lord has made them the depositaries of sacred truth will be their desire that others shall receive the same blessing. And as they make known the rich treasures of God's grace, more and still more of the grace of Christ will be imparted to them. They will have the heart of a little child in its simplicity and unreserved obedience. Their souls will pant after holiness, and more and more of the treasures of truth and grace will be revealed to them to be given to the world.

The great storehouse of truth is the Word of God—the written Word, the book of nature, and the book of experience in God's dealing with human life. Here are the treasures from which Christ's workers are to draw. In the search after truth they are to depend upon God, not upon human intelligences, the great men whose wisdom is foolishness with God. Through His own appointed channels the Lord will impart a knowledge of Himself to every seeker.

If the follower of Christ will believe His Word and practice it, there is no science in the natural world that he will not be able to grasp and appreciate. There is nothing but that will furnish him means for imparting the truth to others. Natural science is a treasure house of knowledge from which every student in the school of Christ may draw. As we contemplate the beauty of nature, as we study its lessons in the cultivation of the soil, in the growth of the trees, in all the wonders of earth and sea and sky, there will come to us a new perception of truth. And the mysteries connected with God's dealings with men, the depths of His wisdom and judgment as seen in human life—these are found to be a storehouse rich in treasure.

But it is in the written Word that a knowledge of God is most clearly revealed to fallen man. This is the treasure house of the unsearchable riches of Christ. . . . The truths of redemption are capable of constant development and expansion. Though old, they are ever new, constantly revealing to the seeker for truth a greater glory and a mightier power (*Christ's Object Lessons*, pp. 125-127).

The Truth in Christ Is Measureless

As the living Father hath sent me, and I live by the Father: so he that eateth me, even he shall live by me. John 6:57.

Truth in Christ and through Christ is measureless. The student of Scripture looks, as it were, into a fountain that deepens and broadens as he gazes into its depths.

Not in this life shall we comprehend the mystery of God's love in giving His Son to be the propitiation for our sins. The work of our Redeemer on this earth is and ever will be a subject that will put to the stretch our highest imagination. Man may tax every mental power in the endeavor to fathom this mystery, but his mind will become faint and weary. The most diligent searcher will see before him a boundless, shoreless sea.

The truth as it is in Jesus can be experienced, but never explained. Its height and breadth and depth pass our knowledge. We may task our imagination to the utmost, and then we shall see only dimly the outlines of a love that is unexplainable, that is as high as heaven, but that stooped to the earth to stamp the image of God on all mankind.

Yet it is possible for us to see all that we can bear of the divine compassion. This is unfolded to the humble, contrite soul. We shall understand God's compassion just in proportion as we appreciate His sacrifice for us. As we search the Word of God in humility of heart, the grand theme of redemption will open to our research. It will increase in brightness as we behold it, and as we aspire to grasp it, its height and depth will ever increase.

Our life is to be bound up with the life of Christ; we are to draw constantly from Him, partaking of Him, the living Bread that came down from heaven, drawing from a fountain ever fresh, ever giving forth its abundant treasures. If we keep the Lord ever before us, allowing our hearts to go out in thanksgiving and praise to Him, we shall have a continual freshness in our religious life.

Our prayers will take the form of a conversation with God as we would talk with a friend. He will speak His mysteries to us personally. Often there will come to us a sweet joyful sense of the presence of Jesus. Often our hearts will burn within us as He draws nigh to commune with us as He did with Enoch. When this is in truth the experience of the Christian, there is seen in his life a simplicity, a humility, meekness, and lowliness of heart, that show to all with whom he associates that he has been with Jesus and learned of Him.

In those who possess it, the religion of Christ will reveal itself as a vitalizing, pervading principle, a living, working, spiritual energy. There will be manifest the freshness and power and joyousness of perpetual youth (*Christ's Object Lessons*, pp. 128-130).

Compare Scripture With Scripture

For precept must be upon precept, precept upon precept; line upon line, line upon line; here a little, and there a little. Isaiah 28:10.

We are thankful that we have a sure word of prophecy, so that none of us need be deceived. We know that there are heresies and fables in our world at the present time, and we want to know what is truth. It becomes us to search carefully for ourselves that we may gain this knowledge. We cannot do this with a mere reading of the Scriptures, but we must compare scripture with scripture. We must search the Scriptures for ourselves, so that we shall not be led astray; and while many may be led astray because there are all kinds of doctrines in our world, there is one truth. Many may come to you and tell you that they have the truth, but it is your privilege to search the Scriptures for yourself. "To the law and to the testimony: if they speak not according to this word, it is because there is no light in them." We must be acquainted with the Scriptures ourselves, that we may understand the true reason of the hope that is within us.

The apostle tells us that we are to give to every man that asks us a reason of the hope that is within us, with meekness and fear. "The entrance of thy words giveth light; it giveth understanding unto the simple." It is not enough to merely read, but the Word of God must enter into our hearts and our understanding, in order that we may be established in the blessed truth. If we should neglect to search the Scriptures for ourselves, that we may know what is truth, then if we are led astray, we are accountable for it. We must search the Scriptures carefully, so that we will know every condition that the Lord has given us; and if we have minds of limited capacity, by diligently searching the word of God we may become mighty in the Scriptures, and may explain them to others. . . .

If you are established in the Scriptures, you will feel the responsibility and will search the Scriptures for yourselves, so that you may be a help to others. Now, the small churches, although they are but few, may be a power for the truth. Every one should feel that a solemn responsibility rests upon him to build up his little church in the most holy faith. The very fact that there are only a few, should cause every individual member to seek most earnestly for a living connection with God; because the giving of the truth to those around you depends upon the influences that you exert.

Christ has said, "Ye are the light of the world"; therefore you must put forth every effort to let that light shine. The only way for you to know that you have the true light from heaven, is to compare the light you have received with the Scriptures. . . . The word was given to Joshua, "Be strong and of a good courage"; for there is a great work before you (*Review and Herald*, Apr. 3, 1888).

The Bible Is Its Own Expositor

Study to shew thyself approved unto God, a workman that needeth not to be ashamed, rightly dividing the word of truth. 2 Timothy 2:15.

The Bible is its own expositor. Scripture is to be compared with scripture. The student should learn to view the Word as a whole and to see the relation of its parts. He should gain a knowledge of its grand central theme—of God's original purpose for the world, of the rise of the great controversy, and of the work of redemption. He should understand the nature of the two principles that are contending for the supremacy, and should learn to trace their working through the records of history and prophecy, to the great consummation. He should see how this controversy enters into every phase of human experience; how in every act of life he himself reveals the one or the other of the two antagonistic motives; and how, whether he will or not, he is even now deciding upon which side of the controversy he will be found.

Every part of the Bible is given by inspiration of God, and is profitable. The Old Testament, no less than the New, should receive attention. As we study the Old Testament, we shall find living springs bubbling up where the careless reader discerns only a desert.

The Old Testament sheds light upon the New, and the New upon the Old. Each is a revelation of the glory of God in Christ. Christ as manifested to the patriarchs, as symbolized in the sacrificial service, as portrayed in the law, and as revealed by the prophets is the riches of the Old Testament. Christ in His life, His death, and His resurrection; Christ as He is manifested by the Holy Spirit, is the treasure of the New. Both Old and New present truths that will continually reveal new depths of meaning to the earnest seeker (*Counsels to Parents, Teachers, and Students,* pp. 462, 463).

Christ reproached His disciples with their slowness of comprehension. . . . After His resurrection, as He was walking to Emmaus with two of the disciples, He opened their understanding, that they might comprehend the Scriptures, so explaining the Old Testament to them that they saw in its teachings a meaning that the writers themselves had not seen.

Christ's words are the bread of life. As the disciples ate the words of Christ, their understanding was quickened. They understood better the value of the Savior's teachings. In their comprehension of these teachings they stepped from the obscurity of dawn to the radiance of noonday. So will it be with us as we study God's Word (*Signs of the Times*, Apr. 4, 1906).

The work of explaining the Bible by the Bible itself is the work that should be done by all our ministers who are fully awake to the times in which we live (letter 376, 1906).

April
12

Sound Doctrine

The time will come when they will not endure sound doctrine; but after their own lusts shall they heap to themselves teachers, having itching ears; and they shall turn away their ears from the truth, and shall be turned unto fables. But watch thou in all things, endure afflictions, do the work of an evangelist, make full proof of thy ministry.
2 Timothy 4:3-5.

"Sound doctrine" is Bible truth—truth that will promote piety and devotion, confirming God's people in the faith. Sound doctrine means much to the receiver; and it means much, too, to the teacher, the minister of righteousness; for wherever the gospel is preached, every laborer, whatever his line of service, is either true or untrue to his responsibility as the Lord's messenger.

Paul wrote again, "It is a faithful saying: For if we be dead with him, we shall also live with him: if we suffer, we shall also reign with him: if we deny him, he also will deny us: if we believe not, yet he abideth faithful: he cannot deny himself. Of these things put them in remembrance, charging them before the Lord that they strive not about words to no profit, but to the subverting of the hearers" (2 Timothy 2:11-14).

Some who in Paul's day listened to the truth raised questions of no vital importance, presenting the ideas and opinions of men, and seeking to divert the mind of the teacher from the great truths of the gospel, to the discussions of nonessential theories and the settlement of unimportant disputes. Paul knew that the laborer for God must be wise enough to see the design of the enemy, and refuse to be misled or diverted. The conversion of souls must be the burden of his work; he must preach the Word of God, but avoid controversy. . . .

The ministers of Christ today are in the same danger. Satan is constantly at work to divert the mind into wrong channels, so that the truth may lose its force upon the heart. . . .

Men of ability have devoted a lifetime of study and prayer to the searching of the Scriptures, and yet there are many portions of the Bible that have not been fully explored. Some passages of Scripture will never be perfectly comprehended until in the future life Christ shall explain them. There are mysteries to be unraveled, statements that human minds cannot harmonize. And the enemy will seek to arouse argument upon these points, which might better remain undiscussed.

A devoted, spiritual worker will avoid bringing up minor theoretical differences, and will devote his energies to the proclamation of the great testing truths to be given to the world. He will point the people to the work of redemption, the commandments of God, the near coming of Christ; and it will be found that in these subjects there is food enough for thought (*Gospel Workers*, pp. 311-313).

The Bible—A Perfect Whole

Holy men of God spake as they were moved by the Holy Ghost. 2 Peter 1:21.

Before the entrance of sin, Adam enjoyed open communion with his Maker; but since man separated himself from God by transgression, the human race has been cut off from this high privilege. By the plan of redemption, however, a way has been opened whereby the inhabitants of the earth may still have connection with heaven. God has communicated with men by His Spirit, and divine light has been imparted to the world by revelations to His chosen servants. "Holy men of God spake as they were moved by the Holy Ghost" (2 Peter 1:21).

During the first twenty-five hundred years of human history, there was no written revelation. Those who have been taught of God communicated their knowledge to others, and it was handed down from father to son, through successive generations. The preparation of the written word began in the time of Moses. Inspired revelations were then embodied in an inspired book. This work continued during the long period of sixteen hundred years—from Moses, the historian of Creation and the law, to John, the recorder of the most sublime truths of the gospel.

The Bible points to God as its author; yet it was written by human hands; and in the varied style of its different books it presents the characteristics of the several writers. The truths revealed are all "given by inspiration of God" (2 Timothy 3:16); yet they are expressed in the words of men. The Infinite One by His Holy Spirit has shed light into the minds and hearts of His servants. He has given dreams and visions, symbols and figures; and those to whom the truth was thus revealed have themselves embodied the thought in human language.

The Ten Commandments were spoken by God Himself, and were written by His own hand. They are of divine, and not of human composition. But the Bible, with its God-given truths expressed in the language of men, presents a union of the divine and the human. Such a union existed in the nature of Christ, who was the Son of God and the Son of man. Thus it is true of the Bible, as it was of Christ, that "the Word was made flesh, and dwelt among us" (John 1:14).

Written in different ages by men who differed widely in rank and occupation, and in mental and spiritual endowments, the books of the Bible present a wide contrast in style, as well as a diversity in the nature of the subjects unfolded. Different forms of expression are employed by different writers; often the same truth is more strikingly presented by one than by another. . . . And the truths thus revealed unite to form a perfect whole, adapted to meet the wants of men in all the circumstances and experiences of life (*The Great Controversy*, pp. v, vi).

The Glory of a Divine Power

Every scripture inspired of God is also profitable for teaching, for reproof, for correction, for instruction which is in righteousness; that the man of God may be complete, furnished completely unto every good work. 2 Timothy 3:16, 17, RV.

God has been pleased to communicate His truth to the world by human agencies, and He Himself, by His Holy Spirit, qualified men and enabled them to do this work. He guided the mind in the selection of what to speak and what to write. The treasure was entrusted to earthen vessels, yet it is, nonetheless, from Heaven. The testimony is conveyed through the imperfect expression of human language, yet it is the testimony of God; and the obedient, believing child of God beholds in it the glory of a divine power, full of grace and truth.

In His Word, God has committed to men the knowledge necessary for salvation. The Holy Scriptures are to be accepted as an authoritative, infallible revelation of His will. They are the standard of character, the revealer of doctrines, and the test of experience. . . .

Yet the fact that God has revealed His will to men through His Word has not rendered needless the continued presence and guiding of the Holy Spirit. On the contrary, the Spirit was promised by our Savior, to open the Word to His servants, to illuminate and apply its teachings. And since it was the Spirit of God that inspired the Bible, it is impossible that the teaching of the Spirit should ever be contrary to that of the Word.

The Spirit was not given—nor can it ever be bestowed—to supersede the Bible; for the Scriptures explicitly state that the Word of God is the standard by which all teaching and experience must be tested. Says the apostle John, "Believe not every spirit, but try the spirits whether they are of God: because many false prophets are gone out into the world" (1 John 4:1). And Isaiah declares, "To the law and to the testimony: if they speak not according to this word, it is because there is no light in them" (Isaiah 8:20). . . .

In harmony with the Word of God, His Spirit was to continue its work throughout the period of the gospel dispensation. During the ages while the Scriptures of both the Old and the New Testament were being given, the Holy Spirit did not cease to communicate light to individual minds, apart from the revelations to be embodied in the Sacred Canon. The Bible itself relates how, through the Holy Spirit, men received warning, reproof, counsel, and instruction, in matters in no way relating to the giving of the Scriptures. And mention is made of prophets in different ages, of whose utterances nothing is recorded. In like manner, after the close of the canon of the Scriptures, the Holy Spirit was still to continue its work, to enlighten, warn, and comfort the children of God (*The Great Controversy*, pp. vi-viii).

The Knowledge of the Lord

The earth shall be full of the knowledge of the Lord, as the waters cover the sea. Isaiah 11:9.

A failure to study and obey God's Word has brought confusion into the world. Men have left the guardianship of Christ for the guardianship of the great rebel, the prince of darkness. Strange fire has been mingled with the sacred. The accumulation of things that minister to lust and ambition has brought upon the world the judgment of heaven.

When in difficulty, philosophers and men of science try to satisfy their minds without appealing to God. They ventilate their philosophy in regard to the heavens and the earth, accounting for plagues, pestilences, epidemics, earthquakes, and famines, by their supposed science. Questions relating to creation and providence they attempt to solve by saying, This is a law of nature.

Disobedience has closed the door to a vast amount of knowledge that might have been gained from the Word of God. Had men been obedient, they would have understood the plan of God's government. The heavenly world would have opened its chambers of grace and glory for exploration. In form, in speech, in song, human beings would have been altogether superior to what they are now. The mystery of redemption, the incarnation of Christ, His atoning sacrifice, would not be vague in our minds. They would be not only better understood, but altogether more highly appreciated.

A failure to study God's Word is the great cause of mental weakness and inefficiency. In turning from this Word to feed on the writings of uninspired men, the mind becomes dwarfed and cheapened. It is not brought in contact with deep, broad principles of eternal truth. The understanding adapts itself to the comprehension of the things with which it is familiar, and in this devotion to finite things it is weakened, its power is contracted, and after a time it becomes unable to expand.

All this is false education. The work of every teacher should be to fasten the minds of the youth upon the grand truths of the Word of Inspiration. This is the education essential for this life and the life to come.

And let it not be thought that this will prevent the study of the sciences or cause a lower standard in education. The knowledge of God is as high as heaven and as broad as the universe. There is nothing so ennobling and invigorating as a study of the great themes which concern our eternal life. Let the youth seek to grasp these God-given truths, and their minds will expand and grow strong in the effort. It will bring every student who is a doer of the Word into a broader field of thought, and secure for him a wealth of knowledge that is imperishable (*Counsels to Parents, Teachers, and Students*, pp. 440–442).

Spiritual Food for Growth and Strength

And we also thank God continually because, when you received the word of God, which you heard from us, you accepted it not as the word of men, but as it actually is, the word of God, which is at work in you who believe.
1 Thessalonians 2:13, NIV.

The Bible contains all that is needful for the saving of the soul, and at the same time it is adapted to strengthen and discipline the mind. . . . It will be found far more effective than any other book in guiding wisely in the affairs of this life, as well as in aiding the soul to climb the ladder that reaches to heaven. The Bible gives the true seeker an advanced mental drill; he comes from the contemplation of divine things with his faculties enriched. Self is humbled, while God and His truth are exalted. It is because men are unacquainted with the truths of the Bible that there is so much lifting up of man, and so little honor given to God.

In searching the pages of God's Word, we move through scenes majestic and eternal. We behold Jesus, the Son of God, coming to our world, and engaging in the mysterious conflict that discomfited the power of darkness. How wonderful, how almost incredible, it is that the infinite God would consent to the humiliation of His only-begotten Son! . . .

God's Word is the spiritual food by which the Christian must grow strong in spirit and in intellect, that he may do battle for truth and righteousness. The Bible teaches that every besetting sin must be put away, that the warfare against evil must be waged until every wrong is overcome. The human agent must place himself as a willing student in the school of Christ. As he accepts the grace freely offered him, the presence of the Savior in the thoughts and in the heart will give him decision of purpose to lay aside every weight, that the heart may be filled with all the fullness of God.

The simplicity of true godliness must be brought into the education of our young people, if they are to know how to escape the corruption that is in the world. They must be taught that the true followers of Christ will serve God not only when it is in accordance with their inclinations, but also when it involves self-denial and cross-bearing. Besetting sins must be battled with and overcome. Objectionable traits of character, whether hereditary or cultivated, must be compared with the great rule of righteousness, and then conquered in the strength of Christ. Day by day, hour by hour, a vigorous work of self-denial and of sanctification must go on within; then the works will bear witness that Jesus is abiding in the heart by faith. Sanctification does not close the avenues of the soul to knowledge, but expands the mind, and inspires it to search for truth as for hidden treasure (*Counsels to Parents, Teachers, and Students*, pp. 448, 449).

Constantly Increasing in Discernment

The Comforter, which is the Holy Ghost, whom the Father will send in my name, he shall teach you all things. John 14:26.

The young man who makes the Bible his guide need not mistake the path of duty and of safety. That Book will teach him to preserve his integrity of character, to be truthful, to practice no deception. It will teach him that he must never transgress God's law in order to accomplish a desired object, even though to obey involves a sacrifice. It will teach him that the blessing of heaven will not rest upon him if he departs from the path of rightdoing; that although men may appear to prosper in disobedience, they will surely reap the fruit of their sowing.

Those only who read the Scriptures as the voice of God speaking to them are true learners. They tremble at the voice of God, for to them it is a living reality. They open their understanding to divine instruction, and pray for grace, that they may obtain a preparation for service. As the heavenly torch is placed in his hand, the seeker for truth sees his own frailty, his infirmity, the hopelessness of looking to himself for righteousness. He sees that there is in him nothing that can recommend him to God. He prays for the Holy Spirit, the representative of Christ, to be his constant guide, to lead him into all truth. He repeats the promise, "The Comforter, which is the Holy Ghost, whom the Father will send in my name, he shall teach you all things" (John 14:26). . . .

Those who receive into their hearts the holy principles of truth will work with increasing energy. No circumstances can alter their determination to attain to the highest possible standard. And that which they have received they will impart to others. As they themselves drink from the fountain of living water, from them will flow living streams to bless and refresh others.

The diligent Bible student will constantly increase in knowledge and discernment. His intellect will grasp elevated subjects and lay hold of the truth of eternal realities. His motives of action will be right. He will use his talent of influence to help others to understand more perfectly their God-given responsibilities. His heart will be a wellspring of joy as he sees success attend his efforts to impart to others the blessings he has received.

The talent of knowledge, sanctified and put to use in the Master's service, is never lost. A self-sacrificing effort to do good will be crowned with success. "We are labourers together with God" (1 Corinthians 3:9). The Lord will cooperate with the human worker. To Him is to be given the praise and the glory for what we are able to accomplish (*Counsels to Parents, Teachers, and Students*, pp. 449-451).

For This Life and the Life to Come

The entrance of thy words giveth light; it giveth understanding unto the simple.
Psalm 119:130.

For the mind and the soul, as well as for the body, it is God's law that strength is acquired by effort. It is exercise that develops. In harmony with this law, God has provided in His Word the means for mental and spiritual development.

The Bible contains all the principles that men need to understand in order to be fitted either for this life or for the life to come. And these principles may be understood by all. . . .

And even greater is the power of the Bible in the development of the spiritual nature. Man, created for fellowship with God, can only in such fellowship find his real life and development. Created to find in God his highest joy, he can find in nothing else that which can quiet the cravings of the heart, can satisfy the hunger and thirst of the soul. He who with sincere and teachable spirit studies God's Word, seeking to comprehend its truths, will be brought in touch with its Author; and, except by his own choice, there is no limit to the possibilities of his development.

In its wide range of style and subjects the Bible has something to interest every mind and appeal to every heart. In its pages are found history the most ancient; biography the truest to life; principles of government for the control of the state, for the regulation of the household—principles that human wisdom has never equaled. It contains philosophy the most profound, poetry the sweetest and the most sublime, the most impassioned and the most pathetic. Immeasurably superior in value to the productions of any human author are the Bible writings, even when thus considered; but of infinitely wider scope, of infinitely greater value, are they when viewed in their relation to the grand central thought. Viewed in the light of this thought, every topic has a new significance. In the most simply stated truths are involved principles that are as high as heaven and that compass eternity.

The central theme of the Bible, the theme about which every other in the whole book clusters, is the redemption plan, the restoration in the human soul of the image of God. From the first intimation of hope in the sentence pronounced in Eden to that last glorious promise of the Revelation, "They shall see his face; and his name shall be in their foreheads" (Revelation 22:4), the burden of every book and every passage of the Bible is the unfolding of this wondrous theme—man's uplifting—the power of God, "which giveth us the victory through our Lord Jesus Christ" (1 Corinthians 15:57).

He who grasps this thought has before him an infinite field for study. He has the key that will unlock to him the whole treasure house of God's Word (*Education*, pp. 123-126).

Sanctified by Truth

Sanctify them through thy truth; thy word is truth.
John 17:17.

It is through the truth, by the power of the Holy Spirit, that we are to be sanctified—transformed into the likeness of Christ. And in order for this change to be wrought in us, there must be an unconditional, wholehearted acceptance of the truth, an unreserved surrender of the soul to its transforming power. . . .

Many persons cling tenaciously to their peculiarities. Even after they profess to accept the truth, to yield themselves to Christ, the same old habits are indulged, the same self-esteem is manifested, the same false notions entertained. Although such ones claim to be converted, it is evident that they have not yielded themselves to the transforming power of the truth. . . .

The new birth consists in having new motives, new tastes, new tendencies. Those who are begotten unto a new life by the Holy Spirit have become partakers of the divine nature, and in all their habits and practices, they will give evidence of their relationship to Christ. . . .

The command, "Be ye therefore perfect, even as your Father which is in heaven is perfect," would never have been given if every provision had not been made whereby we may become as perfect in our sphere as God is in His. We are to be ever advancing from light to a greater light, holding fast what we have already received, and praying for more. Thus we shall never be left in darkness (*Review and Herald*, Apr. 12, 1892).

The last message of mercy is to be given to the world by the proclamation of gospel truth. *Truth, Bible truth*—this is what the people need. On our knees we are to claim the promises of God's Word, asking that we may receive pure, unadulterated truth, and that we may realize the necessity of giving this truth to others. Then men and women will be converted. The hand of God will be recognized in the raising up of new churches. The Lord will baptize with the apostolic spirit many who will go forth to do missionary work in places where the people know not the truth.

True missionary work will furnish the churches with a sure foundation, a foundation having this seal, "The Lord knoweth them that are his." Then God will be glorified in His people. Christian missions will be built upon Jesus Christ. Under the supervision of God the work will go forward, and innumerable evidences will be given of the genuineness of the work. The workers will not seek to glorify self, but will praise God as the designer and organizer of every holy, ennobling work. They not only *profess* to be believers; they *are* believers. They are sanctified by the truth; for truth *acted* as well as *preached* has a purifying influence upon the character (*Signs of the Times*, Aug. 21, 1901).

The Holy Spirit in the Life

I will pray the Father, and he shall give you another Comforter, that he may abide with you for ever. John 14:16.

There are souls famishing for the bread of life, thirsting for the waters of salvation; and woe unto that man who by pen or voice shall turn them aside into false paths! The Spirit of God is appealing to men, presenting to them their moral obligation to love and serve Him with heart, might, mind, and strength, and to love their neighbors as themselves. The Holy Spirit moves upon the inner self until it becomes conscious of the divine power of God, and every spiritual faculty is quickened to decided action. . . .

A deep, thorough work is to be wrought in the soul, which the world cannot see. Those who know not what it is to have an experience in the things of God, who . . . have not the witness of the Spirit that they are accepted of Jesus Christ, are in need of being born again. . . . What can the world know of Christian experience? Verily, nothing. "Except ye eat the flesh of the Son of man, and drink his blood, ye have no life in you." The Great Teacher explained this instruction, saying, "It is the spirit that quickeneth; the flesh profiteth nothing: the words that I speak unto you, they are spirit, and they are life."

In this age, the Word of God is not considered reliable. The word of Christ, that cuts directly across human desires and indulgences, and condemns popular habits and practices—the Word which was made flesh and dwelt among us—is ignored and despised. The teachings and example of Christ are not made the criterion for the life of the professed follower of Christ. Many who name the name of Christ are walking in the light of the sparks of their own kindling, rather than following in the footsteps of their professed Master. They do not represent the same character that Christ represented in His pure, sincere love to God, and in His love for fallen man. They do not take God at His word, and identify their interests with Jesus Christ. They do not form the habit of communing with Jesus, of taking Him as a guide and counselor, and thus learn the trade of living a well-defined Christian life.

Those who not only hear but do the words of Christ make manifest in character the operation of the Holy Spirit. The result of the internal operation of the Holy Spirit is demonstrated in the outward conduct. The life of the Christian is hid with Christ in God, and God acknowledges those who are His, declaring, "Ye are My witnesses." They testify that divine power is influencing their hearts and shaping their conduct. Their works give evidence that the Spirit is moving upon the inward man; those who are associated with them are convinced that they are making Jesus Christ their pattern (*Review and Herald*, May 12, 1896).

The Word of God Our Safeguard

To the law and to the testimony: if they speak not according to this word, it is because there is no light in them. Isaiah 8:20.

Our watchword is to be "To the law and to the testimony: if they speak not according to this word, it is because there is no light in them." We have a Bible full of the most precious truth. It contains the alpha and the omega of knowledge. The Scriptures, given by inspiration of God, are "profitable for doctrine, for reproof, for correction, for instruction in righteousness: that the man of God may be perfect, throughly furnished unto all good works" (2 Timothy 3:16, 17). Take the Bible as your study book. All can understand its instruction.

Christ calls upon His people to believe and practice His Word. Those who receive and assimilate this Word, making it a part of every action, of every attribute of character, will grow strong in the strength of God. It will be seen that their faith is of heavenly origin. They will not wander into strange paths. Their minds will not turn to a religion of sentimentalism and excitement. Before angels and before men, they will stand as those who have strong, consistent Christian characters.

In the golden censer of truth, as presented in Christ's teachings, we have that which will convict and convert souls. Proclaim, in the simplicity of Christ, the truths that He came to this world to proclaim, and the power of your message will make itself felt. Do not advocate theories or tests that Christ has never mentioned, and that have no foundation in the Bible. We have grand, solemn truths for the people. "It is written" is the test that must be brought home to every soul.

Let us go to the Word of God for guidance. Let us seek for a "Thus saith the Lord." We have had enough of human methods. A mind trained only in worldly science will fail to understand the things of God; but the same mind, converted and sanctified, will see the divine power in the Word. Only the mind and heart cleansed by the sanctification of the Spirit can discern heavenly things. . . .

In the name of the Lord I call upon you to awake to your duty. Let your hearts be yielded to the power of the Holy Spirit, and they will be made susceptible to the teachings of the Word. Then you will be able to discern the deep things of God.

May God bring His people under the deep movings of His Spirit! May He arouse them to see their peril, and to prepare for what is coming upon the earth! (*Gospel Workers*, pp. 309, 310).

When questions arise upon which we are uncertain, let us ask, What saith the Scripture? . . . Let those who wish for something new seek for that newness of life resulting from the new birth. Let them purify their souls by obeying the truth, and act in harmony with the instruction that Christ has given (*ibid.*, pp. 314, 315).

The Bread of Life for the Hungry

He that eateth my flesh, and drinketh my blood, dwelleth in me, and I in him.
John 6:56.

The Lord has made every provision that the uplifted Savior may be revealed to sinners. Although they are dead in trespasses and sins, their attention must be aroused by the preaching of Christ and Him crucified. . . .

The infinite value of the sacrifice required for our redemption reveals the fact that sin is a tremendous evil. God might have wiped out this foul blot from His creation by sweeping the sinner from the face of the earth. But He "so loved the world, that he gave his only begotten Son, that whosoever believeth in him should not perish, but have everlasting life" (John 3:16). Why are not all who claim to love God seeking to enlighten their neighbors and their associates, that they may not longer neglect this great salvation? . . .

Christ is able, Christ is willing, Christ is longing, to save all who will come unto Him! Talk to souls in peril and get them to behold Jesus upon the cross, dying to make it possible for Him to pardon. Talk to the sinner with your own heart overflowing with the tender, pitying love of Christ. Let there be deep earnestness; but not a harsh, loud note should be heard from the one who is trying to win the soul to look and live. First have your own soul consecrated to God. As you look upon our Intercessor in heaven, let your heart be broken. Then, softened and subdued, you can address repenting sinners as one who realizes the power of redeeming love. Pray with these souls, by faith bringing them to the foot of the cross; carry their minds up with your mind, and fix the eye of faith where you look, upon Jesus the Sin Bearer. Get them to look away from their poor, sinful selves to the Savior, and the victory is won. They behold for themselves the Lamb of God that taketh away the sin of the world. They see the Way, the Truth, the Life. The Sun of Righteousness shed its bright beams into the heart. The strong tide of redeeming love pours into the parched and thirsty soul, and the sinner is saved to Jesus Christ.

Christ crucified—talk it, pray it, sing it, and it will break and win hearts. This is the power and wisdom of God to gather souls for Christ. . . . The melting love of God in the hearts of the workers will be recognized by those for whom they labor. Souls are thirsting for the waters of life. Do not be empty cisterns. If you reveal the love of Christ to them, you may lead the hungering, thirsting ones to Jesus, and He will give them the bread of life and the water of salvation (*Testimonies*, vol. 6, pp. 66, 67).

All Heaven Is Watching

Search the scriptures; for in them ye think ye have eternal life: and they are they which testify of me.
John 5:39.

This is an age of unrest, and the youth drink deeply of its spirit. Would that they could be made to realize the importance and the peril of the position they occupy! Would that parents and Sabbath school teachers could be led to see their duty to guide them wisely! Never before have there been so many important interests at stake. Never were such momentous issues before any generation as await the one now coming upon the stage of action. Never were the youth of any age or country so earnestly observed by the angels of God as are the youth today. All heaven is watching with intense interest for every indication of the characters they are forming—whether, when brought to the test, they will stand firmly for God and the right, or be swayed by worldly influences.

God has a great work to be done in a short time. He has committed to the youth talents of intellect, time, and means, and He holds them responsible for the use they make of these good gifts. He calls upon them to come to the front, to resist the corrupting, bewitching influences of this fast age, and to become qualified to labor in His cause. They cannot become fitted for usefulness without putting heart and energy into the work of preparation. Christian principles must be developed by being cherished and brought into active exercise. Self-control must be gained by earnest effort aided by the grace of God. . . .

When the young choose the service of Christ, and prove that through divine aid they have the moral principle to govern self, they are a power for good, and an influence goes out from them that leads others to glorify God. . . .

It is a divine law that blessings come at some cost to the receiver. Those who would become wise in the sciences must study; and those who would become wise in regard to Bible truth, that they may impart that knowledge to others, must be diligent students of God's Holy Word. There is no other way; they must search the Scriptures diligently, interestedly, prayerfully. Precious words of promise and encouragement, of warning, reproof, and instruction, are there found. They will learn of Christ's love, the value of His blood, and the wonderful privileges afforded by His grace. . . .

The Bible should ever be the Christian's textbook; of all books it should be made the most attractive to the young. If they drink deep of its spirit, they will be prepared to withstand the wiles of Satan, and to resist the temptations of this infidel age. By its simple beauty of language, its elevated sentiment, its unerring truthfulness, its tenderness and pathos, the Word of God is well calculated to impress the mind and impart rich lessons (*Youth's Instructor*, May 7, 1884).

Seek for the Living Bread

If ye then be risen with Christ, seek those things which are above, where Christ sitteth on the right hand of God. Set your affections on things above, not on things on the earth. Colossians 3:1, 2.

When temporal matters absorb the mind and engage the attention, the whole strength of the being is engaged in the service of man, and men look upon the worship due to God as a trifling matter. Religious interests are made subservient to the world. But Jesus, who has paid the ransom for the souls of the human family, requires that men shall subordinate temporal interests to the heavenly interests. He would have them cease to indulge in hoarding up earthly treasures, in spending money upon luxuries, and in surrounding themselves with all those things which they do not need. He would not have them destroy spiritual power, but directs their attention to heavenly things.

He urges that men should seek more earnestly and continually for the bread of life than for the bread which perishes. He says, "Labour not for the meat which perisheth, but for that meat which endureth unto everlasting life, which the Son of man shall give unto you: for him hath God the Father sealed." . . . It is the Word of God that is essential for our spiritual growth. "It is the spirit that quickeneth; the flesh profiteth nothing: the words that I speak unto you, they are spirit, and they are life." Those who are doers of the words of Christ will bring heaven into their life.

Christ is our Redeemer, our owner, and He is intensely interested that we shall have peace in this world. He seeks to present before us the attractions of heaven; for where the treasure is, there will the heart be also. To lay up treasure in heaven is to use our God-given capabilities in acquiring means and influence that may be used for the glory of God. Every dollar we earn is the Lord's property, and should be used in reference to the time when we shall be called to give an account of our stewardship. No one of us will be able to evade the future reckoning. By choosing to lay up treasure in heaven, our characters will be molded after the likeness of Christ. The world will see that our hopes and plans are made in reference to the advancement of the truth and the salvation of perishing souls. They will see that Christ is all in all to those who love Him. . . .

In securing treasure in heaven, we place ourselves in living connection with God, who owns all the treasures of the earth, and supplies all temporal mercies that are essential for life. Every soul may secure the eternal inheritance. The Lord opens the fact before His people that there is full room for the exercise of their faculties, for the fulfillment of their loftiest aims, for the acquirements of the choicest and most enduring treasure. They may lay up treasures where neither fire nor flood nor any manner of adversity can touch (*Review and Herald*, Apr. 7, 1896).

Success for Your Efforts

For the Lord is a sun and shield: the Lord will give grace and glory: no good thing will he withhold from them that walk uprightly.
Psalm 84:11.

Jesus has said: "Ask, and it shall be given you; seek, and ye shall find; knock, and it shall be opened unto you: for every one that asketh receiveth; and he that seeketh findeth; and to him that knocketh it shall be opened." . . . Be earnest; be resolute. Present the promise of God, and then believe without a doubt. Do not wait to feel special emotions before you think the Lord answers. Do not mark out some particular way that the Lord must work for you before you believe you receive the things you ask of Him; but trust His word, and leave the whole matter in the hands of the Lord, with full faith that your prayer will be honored, and the answer will come at the very time and in the very way your heavenly Father sees is for your good; and then live out your prayers. Walk humbly and keep moving forward.

"For the Lord is a sun and shield: the Lord will give grace and glory: no good thing will he withhold from them that walk uprightly." "O fear the Lord, ye his saints: for there is no want to them that fear him" . . . "The Lord is nigh unto them that are of a broken heart; and saveth such as be of a contrite spirit." Here are promises, rich and abundant, upon condition that you cease to do evil and learn to do well. Then set your aim in life high, as did Joseph and Daniel and Moses; and take into consideration the cost of character-building, and then build for time and eternity.

Satan will oppose your efforts to advance. Your path will not always be smooth, but there are encouragements in God's rich promises. The Lord has pledged His word that in every effort toward righteousness He will help us. We are weak and without wisdom, but God has said: "If any of you lack wisdom, let him ask of God, that giveth to all men liberally, and upbraideth not; and it shall be given him." Only learn to be thorough, never to let go your hold upon God, to persevere in His service, and you will be an overcomer through the blood of the Lamb. In doing this work for yourself you are having an influence on many others whom you associate with.

Words spoken in season, how good are they! How much strength a word of hope, courage, and determination in a right course will give one who is inclined to slide into habits that are demoralizing! The firm purpose you may possess in carrying out good principles will have an influence to balance souls in the right direction. There is no limit to the good you may do. If you make the Word of God the rule of your life, and govern your actions by its precepts, making all your purposes and exertions in the fulfilling of your duty a blessing . . . success will crown your efforts (*Youth's Instructor*, Sept. 1, 1886).

April
26

Our Only Safeguard in Trial and Temptation

Thy word is a lamp unto my feet, and a light unto my path. Psalm 119:105.

God has given us His Word as a lamp to our feet and a light to our path. Its teachings have a vital bearing on our prosperity in all the relations of life. Even in our temporal affairs it will be a wiser guide than any other counselor. Its divine instruction is the only way to success. There is no social position, no phase of human experience, for which the study of the Bible is not an essential preparation.

The Bible is the great standard of right and wrong, clearly defining sin and holiness. Its living principles, running through our lives like threads of gold, are our only safeguard in trial and temptation.

The Bible is a chart, showing us the waymarks of truth. Those who are acquainted with this chart will be enabled to tread with certainty in the path of duty, wherever they may be called to go.

The Bible contains a simple and complete system of theology and philosophy. It is the book that makes us wise unto salvation. It tells us how to reach the abodes of eternal happiness. It tells us of the love of God as shown in the plan of redemption, imparting the knowledge essential for all—the knowledge of Christ. He is the Sent of God; He is the Author of our salvation. But apart from the Word of God, we could have no knowledge that such a person as the Lord Jesus ever visited our world, nor any knowledge of His divinity, as indicated by His previous existence with the Father.

The Bible was not written for the scholar alone; on the contrary, it was designed for the common people. The great truths necessary for our salvation are made as clear as noonday, and none will mistake and lose their way except those who follow their own judgment instead of the plainly revealed will of God.

The Word of God strikes at every wrong trait of character, molding the whole man, internally and externally, abasing his pride and self-exaltation, leading him to bring the Spirit of Christ into the smaller as well as the larger duties of life. It teaches him to be unswerving in his allegiance to justice and purity, and at the same time always to be kind and compassionate.

The appreciation of the Bible grows with its study. Whichever way the student may turn, he will find displayed the infinite wisdom and love of God. To him who is truly converted, the Word of God is the joy and consolation of the life. The Spirit of God speaks to him, and his heart becomes like a watered garden (*Signs of the Times,* June 25, 1902).

The heart that is stored with the precious truths of God's Word is fortified against the temptations of Satan, against impure thoughts and unholy actions (*Youth's Instructor,* July 28, 1892).

Daily Bread Assured

Give us this day our daily bread. Matthew 6:11.

Like a child, you shall receive day by day what is required for the day's need. Every day you are to pray, "Give us this day our daily bread." Be not disturbed if you have not sufficient for tomorrow. You have the assurance of His promise, "Thou shalt dwell in the land, and verily thou shalt be fed." David says, "I have been young, and now am old; yet have I not seen the righteous forsaken, nor his seed begging bread."

That God who sent the ravens to feed Elijah by the brook Cherith will not pass by one of His faithful, self-sacrificing children. Of him that walketh righteously it is written, "Bread shall be given him; his waters shall be sure." "They shall not be ashamed in the evil time: and in the days of famine they shall be satisfied." "He that spared not his own Son, but delivered him up for us all, how shall he not with him also freely give us all things?"

He who lightened the cares and anxieties of His widowed mother, and helped to provide for the household of Nazareth, sympathizes with every mother in her struggle to provide her children food. He who had compassion on the multitude because they "fainted, and were scattered abroad" still has compassion on the suffering poor. His hand is stretched out toward them in blessing and in the very prayer which He gave His disciples, He teaches us to remember the poor (*Signs of the Times*, Nov. 4, 1903).

The prayer for daily bread includes not only food to sustain the body, but that spiritual bread which will nourish the soul unto life everlasting. Jesus bids us, "Labour not for the meat which perisheth, but for that meat which endureth unto everlasting life" (John 6:27). He says, "I am the living bread which came down from heaven: if any man eat of this bread, he shall live for ever" (verse 51). Our Savior is the bread of life, and it is by beholding His love, by receiving it into the soul, that we feed upon the bread which came down from heaven.

We receive Christ through His Word, and the Holy Spirit is given to open the Word of God to our understanding, and bring home its truths to our hearts. We are to pray day by day that as we read His Word, God will send His Spirit to reveal to us the truth that will strengthen our souls for the day's need.

In teaching us to ask every day for what we need—both temporal and spiritual blessings—God has a purpose to accomplish for our good. He would have us realize our dependence upon His constant care, for He is seeking to draw us into communion with Himself. In this communion with Christ, through prayer and the study of the great and precious truths of His Word, we shall as hungry souls be fed; as those that thirst, we shall be refreshed at the fountain of life (*Thoughts From the Mount of Blessing*, pp. 112, 113).

Lessons From Timothy

And that from a child thou hast known the holy scriptures, which are able to make thee wise unto salvation through faith which is in Christ Jesus. 2 Timothy 3:15.

Silas, Paul's companion in labor, was a tried worker, gifted with the spirit of prophecy; but the work to be done was so great that there was need of training more laborers for active service. In Timothy, Paul saw one who appreciated the sacredness of the work of a minister; who was not appalled at the prospect of suffering and persecution; and who was willing to be taught. Yet the apostle did not venture to take the responsibility of giving Timothy, an untried youth, a training in the gospel ministry, without first fully satisfying himself in regard to his character and his past life.

Timothy's father was a Greek and his mother a Jewess. From a child he had known the Scriptures. The piety that he saw in his home life was sound and sensible. The faith of his mother and his grandmother in the sacred oracles was to him a constant reminder of the blessing in doing God's will. The Word of God was the rule by which these two godly women had guided Timothy. The spiritual power of the lessons that he had received from them kept him pure in speech and unsullied by the evil influences with which he was surrounded. Thus his home instructors had cooperated with God in preparing him to bear burdens.

Paul saw that Timothy was faithful, steadfast, and true, and he chose him as a companion in labor and travel. Those who had taught Timothy in his childhood were rewarded by seeing the son of their care linked in close fellowship with the great apostle. Timothy was a mere youth when he was chosen by God to be a teacher, but his principles had been so established by his early education that he was fitted to take his place as Paul's helper. And though young, he bore his responsibilities with Christian meekness. . . .

Paul loved Timothy, his "own son in the faith" (1 Timothy 1:2). The great apostle often drew the younger disciple out, questioning him in regard to Scripture history, and as they traveled from place to place, he carefully taught him how to do successful work. Both Paul and Silas . . . sought to deepen the impression . . . of the sacred, serious nature of the work of the gospel minister.

In his work, Timothy constantly sought Paul's advice and instruction. He did not move from impulse, but exercised consideration and calm thought, inquiring at every step, Is this the way of the Lord? The Holy Spirit found in him one who could be molded and fashioned as a temple for the indwelling of the divine Presence.

As the lessons of the Bible are wrought into the daily life, they have a deep and lasting influence upon the character. These lessons Timothy learned and practiced (*The Acts of the Apostles*, pp. 203-205).

Sitting at the Feet of Jesus

One thing is needful: and Mary hath chosen that good part, which shall not be taken away from her. Luke 10:42.

Our Savior appreciated a quiet home and interested listeners. He longed for human tenderness, courtesy, and affection. Those who received the heavenly instruction He was always ready to impart were greatly blessed. As the multitudes followed Christ through the open fields, He unfolded to them the beauties of the natural world. He sought to open the eyes of their understanding, that they might see how the hand of God upholds the world. . . . But the multitudes were slow of hearing, and in the home at Bethany Christ found rest from the weary conflict of public life. Here He opened to an appreciative audience the volume of Providence. In these private interviews He unfolded to His hearers that which He did not attempt to tell to the mixed multitude. He needed not to speak to His friends in parables.

As Christ gave His wonderful lessons, Mary sat at His feet, a reverent and devoted listener. On one occasion, Martha, perplexed with the care of preparing the meal, went to Christ, saying, "Lord, dost thou not care that my sister hath left me to serve alone? bid her therefore that she help me." This was the time of Christ's first visit to Bethany. The Savior and His disciples had just made the toilsome journey on foot from Jericho. Martha was anxious to provide for their comfort, and in her anxiety she forgot the courtesy due to her Guest. Jesus answered her with mild and patient words, "Martha, Martha, thou art careful and troubled about many things: but one thing is needful: and Mary hath chosen that good part, which shall not be taken away from her." Mary was storing her mind with the precious words falling from the Savior's lips, words that were more precious to her than earth's most costly jewels.

The "one thing" that Martha needed was a calm, devotional spirit, a deeper anxiety for knowledge concerning the future, immortal life, and the graces necessary for spiritual advancement. She needed less anxiety for the things which pass away, and more for those things which endure forever. Jesus would teach His children to seize every opportunity of gaining that knowledge which will make them wise unto salvation. The cause of Christ needs careful, energetic workers. There is a wide field for the Marthas, with their zeal in active religious work. But let them first sit with Mary at the feet of Jesus. Let diligence, promptness, and energy be sanctified by the grace of Christ; then the life will be an unconquerable power for good (*The Desire of Ages*, pp. 524, 525).

Results From Eating the Bread of Life

So faith, hope, love abide, these three; but the greatest of these is love.
1 Corinthians 13:13, RSV.

We have an abundance of sermonizing. What is most needed . . . is love for perishing souls, that love which comes in rich currents from the throne of God. True Christianity diffuses love through the whole being. It touches every vital part, the brain, the heart, the helping hands, the feet, enabling men to stand firmly where God requires them to stand, so that they will not make crooked paths for their feet, lest the lame be turned out of the way. The burning, consuming love of Christ for perishing souls is the life of the whole system of Christianity.

What is the Bible interpretation of God? "God is love." By giving Christ to our world, God manifested His love for mankind. "God so loved the world, that he gave his only begotten Son, that whosoever believeth in him should not perish, but have everlasting life." Yes, "everlasting life." This is the love which is the fulfilling of the law. Only he whose heart is filled with compassion for fallen man, who loves to a purpose, showing his love by the performance of Christlike deeds, will be able to endure the seeing of Him who is invisible. He only who loves his fellowmen to a purpose can know God. He who loves not those for whom the Father has done so much know not God. This is the reason there is so little genuine vitality in our churches. Theology is valueless unless it is saturated with the love of Christ.

God is supreme. His love in the human heart will lead to the doing of work that will bear fruit after the similitude of the character of God. . . .

"Charity [love] suffereth long, and is kind; charity envieth not; charity vaunteth not itself, is not puffed up, doth not behave itself unseemly, *seeketh not her own,* is not easily provoked, *thinketh no evil;* rejoiceth not in iniquity, but rejoiceth in the truth." O blessed leaves of the tree of life! "And now abideth faith, hope, charity, these three; but the greatest of these is charity."

"Bless the Lord, O my soul: and all that is within me, bless his holy name," because our Guidebook is so very plain and definite. Others may not follow the plain "It is written," which Christ used on every occasion to meet the fallen foe, but let us follow the Savior's example. The less we give expression to our own human opinions, the purer and more marked with grace will be our conversation. The Lord calls for sanctified speech, because it is a savor of life unto life (letter 156, 1900).

The Claims of the Law of God

Open thou mine eyes, that I may behold wondrous things out of thy law. Psalm 119:18.

Christ came to a people who were deceived and deluded by the demon of ambition. At that time they were under the Roman yoke, but they expected One to come who would establish a kingdom from which would be excluded every other people on the earth. He was to break the heathen yoke, to lift up His people, and set them with princes. All nations were to be summoned to appear before the One sent by God, and there called upon to surrender themselves or be consumed.

Prophets were continually arising and claiming to have special messages to this effect. Judah was to be honored as the place of power and glory. The kingdoms of the world and the riches of the Gentiles were to be placed at their feet, and they were to be exalted as priests and kings unto God. Those who did not believe in these great things for the Jewish nation were pronounced infidels. If their prayers did not abound in these glowing expectations, they were treated as worse than useless. . . . The people were so infatuated by the falsehoods of Satan that their minds were wholly unprepared for the real Christ.

Christ's work was to set before men the character of His kingdom, showing that names and positions and titles are nothing, but that pure virtue and a holy character is accounted as everything in the sight of heaven. In His sermon on the mount, the very first sentences that came from His lips were calculated to lay those ambitions low in the dust. "Blessed are the poor in spirit," He said, "for theirs is the kingdom of heaven. Blessed are they that mourn: for they shall be comforted. Blessed are the meek: for they shall inherit the earth. Blessed are they which do hunger and thirst after righteousness: for they shall be filled. Blessed are the merciful: for they shall obtain mercy. Blessed are the pure in heart: for they shall see God. Blessed are the peacemakers: for they shall be called the children of God. Blessed are they which are persecuted for righteousness' sake; for theirs is the kingdom of heaven."

This whole sermon was an exposition of the law. Christ presented the far-reaching claims of the law of God. He tried to correct their high imaginings by exalting true sentiments, and proclaiming a blessing upon those traits of character that were entirely opposite to the attributes they were cherishing. He presented before them a kingdom where human ambitions and earthly passions cannot find an entrance. . . .

Christ's work was . . . that He might lift souls who were perishing in ignorance of true godliness into a pure and holy atmosphere (*Signs of the Times*, Jan. 10, 1900).

God's Law Stands Forever

All his commandments are sure. They stand fast for ever and ever. Psalm 111:7, 8.

The temple of God was opened in heaven, and there was seen in His temple the ark of his testament" (Revelation 11:19). The ark of God's testament is in the Holy of Holies, the second apartment of the sanctuary. In the ministration of the earthly tabernacle, which served "unto the example and shadow of heavenly things," this apartment was opened only upon the great Day of Atonement for the cleansing of the sanctuary. Therefore the announcement that the temple of God was opened in heaven and the ark of His testament was seen points to the opening of the Most Holy Place of the heavenly sanctuary in 1844 as Christ entered there to perform the closing work of the atonement.

Those who by faith followed their great High Priest as He entered upon His ministry in the Most Holy Place beheld the ark of His testament. As they had studied the subject of the sanctuary they had come to understand the Savior's change of ministration, and they saw that He was now officiating before the ark of God, pleading His blood in behalf of sinners.

The ark in the tabernacle on earth contained the two tables of stone, upon which were inscribed the precepts of the law of God. The ark was merely a receptacle for the tables of the law, and the presence of these divine precepts gave to it its value and sacredness. When the temple of God was opened in heaven, the ark of His testament was seen. Within the Holy of Holies, in the sanctuary in heaven, the divine law is sacredly enshrined—the law that was spoken by God Himself amid the thunders of Sinai and written with His own finger on the tables of stone.

The law of God in the sanctuary in heaven is the great original, of which the precepts inscribed upon the tables of stone and recorded by Moses in the Pentateuch were an unerring transcript. Those who arrived at an understanding of this important point were thus led to see the sacred, unchanging character of the divine law. They saw, as never before, the force of the Savior's words: "Till heaven and earth pass, one jot or one tittle shall in no wise pass from the law" (Matthew 5:18).

The law of God, being a revelation of His will, a transcript of His character, must forever endure, "as a faithful witness in heaven." Not one command has been annulled; not a jot or tittle has been changed. Says the psalmist: "Forever, O Lord, thy word is settled in heaven." "All his commandments are sure. They stand fast for ever and ever" (Psalm 111:7, 8) (*The Great Controversy*, pp. 433, 434).

Keeping the Sabbath

I am the Lord your God; follow my decrees and be careful to keep my laws. Keep my Sabbaths holy, that they may be a sign between us. Then you will know that I am the Lord your God. Ezekiel 20:19, 20, NIV.

At the time of the Exodus from Egypt, the Sabbath institution was brought prominently before the people of God. While they were still in bondage, their taskmasters had attempted to force them to labor on the Sabbath by increasing the amount of work required each week. . . . But the Israelites were delivered from bondage and brought to a place where they might observe unmolested all the precepts of Jehovah.

At Sinai the law was spoken; and a copy of it, on two tables of stone, "written with the finger of God," was delivered to Moses (Exodus 31:18). And through nearly forty years of wandering the Israelites were constantly reminded of God's appointed rest day, by the withholding of the manna every seventh day and the miraculous preservation of the double portion that fell on the preparation day.

Before entering the Promised Land, the Israelites were admonished by Moses to "keep the sabbath day to sanctify it" (Deuteronomy 5:12). The Lord designed that by a faithful observance of the Sabbath command, Israel should continually be reminded of their accountability to Him as their Creator and their Redeemer. While they should keep the Sabbath in the proper spirit, idolatry could not exist; but should the claims of this precept of the Decalogue be set aside as no longer binding, the Creator would be forgotten and men would worship other gods.

"I gave them my sabbaths," God declared, "to be a sign between me and them, that they might know that I am the Lord that sanctify them." Yet "they despised my judgments, and walked not in my statutes, but polluted my sabbaths: for their heart went after their idols." And in His appeal to them to return to Him, He called their attention anew to the importance of keeping the Sabbath holy. "I am the Lord your God," He said; "walk in my statutes, and keep my judgments, and do them; and hallow my sabbaths; and they shall be a sign between me and you, that ye may know that I am the Lord your God" (Ezekiel 20:12, 16, 19, 20). . . .

Christ, during His earthly ministry, emphasized the binding claims of the Sabbath; in all His teaching He showed reverence for the institution He Himself had given. In His days the Sabbath had become so perverted that its observance reflected the character of selfish and arbitrary men rather than the character of God. Christ set aside the false teaching by which those who claimed to know God had misrepresented Him. Although followed with merciless hostility by the rabbis, He did not even appear to conform to their requirements, but went straight forward keeping the Sabbath according to the law of God (*Prophets and Kings*, pp. 180-183).

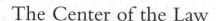

The Center of the Law

Remember the sabbath day, to keep it holy. Exodus 20:8.

In the very bosom of the Decalogue is the fourth commandment, as it was first proclaimed: "Remember the sabbath day, to keep it holy. Six days shalt thou labour, and do all thy work: but the seventh day is the sabbath of the Lord thy God: in it thou shalt not do any work, thou, nor thy son, nor thy daughter, thy manservant, nor thy maidservant, nor thy cattle, nor thy stranger that is within thy gates: for in six days the Lord made heaven and earth, the sea, and all that in them is, and rested the seventh day: wherefore the Lord blessed the sabbath day, and hallowed it" (Exodus 20:8-11). . . .

Christ had opened the door, or ministration, of the Most Holy Place, light was shining from that open door of the sanctuary in heaven, and the fourth commandment was shown to be included in the law which is there enshrined; what God has established, no man could overthrow (*The Great Controversy*, pp. 434, 435).

God has given us His commandments, not only to be believed in, but to be obeyed. The great Jehovah, when He had laid the foundations of the earth, had dressed the whole world in the garb of beauty, and had filled it with things useful to man—when He had created all the wonders of the land and the sea—instituted the Sabbath day and made it holy. God blessed and sanctified the seventh day, because He rested upon it from all His wondrous work of creation. The Sabbath was made for man, and God would have him put by his labor on that day, as He Himself rested after His six days' work of creation.

Those who reverence the commandments of Jehovah will, after light has been given them in reference to the fourth precept of the Decalogue, obey it without questioning the feasibility or convenience of such obedience. God made man in His own image and then gave him an example of observing the seventh day, which He sanctified and made holy. He designed that upon that day man should worship Him and engage in no secular pursuits. No one who disregards the fourth commandment, after becoming enlightened concerning the claims of the Sabbath, can be held guiltless in the sight of God. . . .

At the very beginning of the fourth precept, God said, "*Remember,*" knowing that man, in the multitude of his cares and perplexities, would be tempted to excuse himself from meeting the full requirements of the law, or in the press of worldly business, would forget its sacred importance. . . . But He claims one day, which He has set apart and sanctified. He gives it to man as a day in which he may rest from labor and devote himself to worship and the improvement of his spiritual condition (*Testimonies*, vol. 4, pp. 247-249).

A Special, Distinguishing Sign

The children of Israel shall keep the sabbath, to observe the sabbath throughout their generations, for a perpetual covenant. It is a sign between me and the children of Israel for ever; for in six days the Lord made heaven and earth, and on the seventh day he rested, and was refreshed. Exodus 31:16, 17.

In this scripture the observance of the Sabbath is specified as a special, distinguishing sign between God's people and the people of the world. This gives to parents a most solemn work—the work of teaching their children to obey the Sabbath commandment, in order that they may be numbered among the people of God.

In Exodus 19 we read: "Ye have seen what I did unto the Egyptians, and how I bear you on eagles' wings, and brought you unto myself. Now therefore, if ye will obey my voice indeed, and keep my covenant, then ye shall be a peculiar treasure unto me above all people: for all the earth is mine: and ye shall be unto me a kingdom of priests, and an holy nation. These are the words which thou shalt speak unto the children of Israel."

Wonderful condescension is this! God offers to make the Israelites His peculiar treasure, if they obey His law and glorify His name. Observe the response they made to these words:

"Moses came and called for the elders of the people, and laid before their faces all these words which the Lord commanded him." All this instruction was placed by the elders before the vast multitude assembled. "And all the people answered together, and said, All that the Lord hath spoken we will do. And Moses returned the words of the people unto the Lord" (manuscript 152, 1901).

We cannot overestimate the value of simple faith and unquestioning obedience. It is by following in the path of obedience in simple faith that the character obtains perfection. Adam was required to render strict obedience to God's commandments, and no lower standard is presented to those who desire salvation [today]. . . . [Christ] says, "Whatsoever ye shall ask in my name, that will I do, that the Father may be glorified in the Son. If ye shall ask anything in my name, I will do it. If ye love me, keep my commandments. And I will pray the Father, and he shall give you another Comforter, that he may abide with you for ever; even the Spirit of truth; whom the world cannot receive" (John 14:13-17). . . . The world is leagued against the truth, because it does not desire to obey the truth. Shall I who perceive the truth close my eyes and heart to its saving power because the world chooses darkness rather than light? (letter 119, 1895).

The sacred statutes which Satan has hated and sought to destroy, will be honored throughout a sinless universe (*Patriarchs and Prophets*, p. 342).

May

6

The Law for Man's Happiness

The statutes of the Lord are right, rejoicing the heart: the commandment of the Lord is pure, enlightening the eyes. Psalm 19:8.

In the beginning, God gave His law to mankind as a means of attaining happiness and eternal life. Satan's only hope of thwarting the purpose of God is to lead men and women to disobey this law, and his constant effort has been to misrepresent its teachings and belittle its importance. His master stroke has been an attempt to change the law itself, so as to lead men to violate its precepts while professing to obey it.

One writer has likened the attempt to change the law of God to an ancient mischievous practice of turning in a wrong direction a signpost erected at an important junction where two roads met. The perplexity and hardship which this practice often caused was great.

A signpost was erected by God for those journeying through this world. One arm of this signpost pointed out willing obedience to the Creator as the road to felicity and life, while the other arm indicated disobedience as the path to misery and death. The way to happiness was as clearly defined as was the way to the city of refuge under the Jewish dispensation. But in an evil hour for our race, the great enemy of all good turned the signpost around, and multitudes have mistaken the way.

Through Moses the Lord instructed the Israelites: "Verily my sabbaths ye shall keep: for it is a sign between me and you throughout your generations; that ye may know that I am the Lord that doth sanctify you. Ye shall keep the sabbath therefore; for it is holy unto you: every one that defileth it shall surely be put to death: for whosoever doeth any work . . . in the sabbath day, he shall surely be put to death. Wherefore the children of Israel shall keep the sabbath, to observe the sabbath throughout their generations, for a perpetual covenant. It is a sign between me and the children of Israel for ever: for in six days the Lord made heaven and earth, and on the seventh day he rested, and was refreshed" (Exodus 31:13-17).

In these words the Lord clearly defined obedience as the way to the City of God; but the man of sin has changed the signpost, making it point in a wrong direction. He has set up a false sabbath and has caused men and women to think that by resting on it they were obeying the command of the Creator.

God has declared that the seventh day is the Sabbath of the Lord. When "the heavens and the earth were finished," He exalted this day as a memorial of His creative work. Resting on the seventh day "from all his work which he had made, . . . God blessed the seventh day, and sanctified it" (Genesis 2:1-3) (*Prophets and Kings*, pp. 178-180).

God's Law Never Changes

And he gave unto Moses, when he had made an end of communing with him upon mount Sinai, two tables of testimony, tables of stone, written with the finger of God. Exodus 31:18.

During the Christian dispensation, the great enemy of man's happiness has made the Sabbath of the fourth commandment an object of special attack. Satan says, "I will work at cross purposes with God. I will empower my followers to set aside God's memorial, the seventh-day Sabbath. Thus I will show the world that the day sanctified and blessed by God has been changed. That day shall not live in the minds of the people. I will obliterate the memory of it. I will place in its stead a day that does not bear the credentials of God, a day that cannot be a sign between God and His people. I will lead those who accept this day to place upon it the sanctity that God placed upon the seventh day." . . .

Through the setting up of a false sabbath, the enemy thought to change times and laws. But has he really succeeded in changing God's law? The words of the thirty-first chapter of Exodus are the answer. He who is the same yesterday, today, and forever has declared of the seventh-day Sabbath: "It is a sign between me and you throughout your generations." "It is a sign . . . for ever" (Exodus 31:13, 17). The changed signpost is pointing the wrong way, but God has not changed. He is still the mighty God of Israel. "Behold, the nations are as a drop of a bucket, and are counted as the small dust of the balance: behold, he taketh up the isles as a very little thing" (Isaiah 40:15). . . . And He is just as jealous for His law now as He was in the days of Ahab and Elijah.

But how is that law disregarded! Behold the world today in open rebellion against God. This is in truth a froward generation, filled with ingratitude, formalism, insincerity, pride, and apostasy. Men neglect the Bible and hate truth. Jesus sees His law rejected, His love despised, His ambassadors treated with indifference. He has spoken by His mercies, but these have been unacknowledged; He has spoken by warnings, but these have been unheeded. The temple courts of the human soul have been turned into places of unholy traffic. Selfishness, envy, pride, malice—all are cherished. . . .

Those who believe that word just as it reads are held up to ridicule. There is a growing contempt for law and order, directly traceable to a violation of the plain commands of Jehovah (*Prophets and Kings,* pp. 183-185).

Jehovah engraved His ten commandments on tables of stone, that all the inhabitants of the earth might understand His eternal, unchangeable character (*Counsels to Parents, Teachers, and Students,* p. 248).

The First Great Commandment

Thou shalt love the Lord thy God with all thy heart, and with all thy soul, and with all thy mind, and with all thy strength: this is the first commandment. Mark 12:30.

I saw that whatever divides the affections, or takes away from the heart supreme love for God, or prevents unlimited confidence and entire trust in Him, assumes the character and takes the form of an idol. I was pointed to the first great commandment: "Thou shalt love the Lord thy God with all thy heart, and with all thy soul, and with all thy mind." There is allowed no separation of our affections from God. Nothing is to divide our supreme love for Him or our delight in Him. Your will, wishes, plans, desires, and pleasures must all be in subjection.

You have something to learn, to exalt the Lord God in your heart, in your conversation, in all your acts; and then Jesus can teach you, and help you, as you cast your net on the right side of the ship, to bring it to shore full of fishes. But without the help of Christ in casting your net, you may toil, weeks, months, and years without seeing much fruit of your labor. . . .

Study yourself. Try every motive. . . . Seek to exhibit Christ (*Testimonies,* vol. 1, pp. 436, 437).

When one is fully emptied of self, when every false god is cast out of the soul, the vacuum is filled by the inflowing of the Spirit of Christ. Such a one has the faith that purifies the soul from defilement. He is conformed to the Spirit, and he minds the things of the Spirit. He has no confidence in self. Christ is all and in all. He receives with meekness the truth that is constantly being unfolded, and gives the Lord all the glory, saying, "God hath revealed them unto us by his Spirit." "Now we have received, not the spirit of the world, but the spirit which is of God; that we might know the things that are freely given to us of God" (*Gospel Workers,* p. 287).

The voice that spoke to Israel from Sinai is speaking in these last days to men and women, saying, "Thou shalt have no other gods before me" (Exodus 20:3). The law of God was written with His own finger on tables of stone, thus showing that it could never be changed or abrogated. It is to be preserved through the eternal ages, immutable as the principles of His government. Men have set their will against the will of God, but this cannot silence His words of wisdom and command, though they may set their speculative theories in opposition to the teachings of revelation, and exalt human wisdom above a plain "Thus saith the Lord" (*Counsels to Parents, Teachers, and Students*, p. 248).

The spirit of worldliness may contaminate the many and control the few, the cause of God may hold its ground only by great exertion and continual sacrifice, yet in the end the truth will triumph gloriously (*Prophets and Kings,* p. 186).

No Other Gods

Thou shalt have no other gods before me. Exodus 20:3.

Christ gave His life that all who would might be freed from sin and reinstated in the favor of the Creator.

It was the anticipation of a redeemed, holy universe that prompted Christ to make this great sacrifice. . . . Are we followers of God as dear children, or are we servants of the prince of darkness? Are we worshipers of Jehovah, or of Baal? of the living God, or of idols?

No outward shrines may be visible, there may be no image for the eye to rest upon, yet we may be practicing idolatry. It is as easy to make an idol of cherished ideas or objects as to fashion gods of wood or stone. Thousands have a false conception of God and His attributes. They are as verily serving a false god as were the servants of Baal. Are we worshiping the true God as He is revealed in His Word, in Christ, in nature, or are we adoring some philosophical idol enshrined in His place? God is a God of truth. Justice and mercy are the attributes of His throne. He is a God of love, of pity and tender compassion. Thus He is represented in His Son, our Savior. He is a God of patience and long-suffering. If such is the being whom we adore and to whose character we are seeking to assimilate, we are worshiping the true God.

If we are following Christ, His merits, imputed to us, come up before the Father as sweet odor. And the graces of our Savior's character, implanted in our hearts, will shed around us a precious fragrance. The spirit of love, meekness, and forbearing pervading our life will have power to soften and subdue hard hearts and win to Christ bitter opposers of the faith.

"Let nothing be done through strife or vainglory; but in lowliness of mind let each esteem other better than themselves. Look not every man on his own things, but every man also on the things of others." . . .

Vainglory, selfish ambition, is the rock upon which many souls have been wrecked and many churches rendered powerless. Those who know least of devotion, who are least connected with God, are the ones who will most eagerly seek the highest place. They have no sense of their weakness and their deficiencies of character. . . . The soul that is constantly looking unto Jesus will see His self-denying love and deep humility, and will copy His example. Pride, ambition, deceit, hatred, selfishness, must be cleansed from the heart. With many these evil traits are partially subdued, but not thoroughly uprooted from the heart. Under favorable circumstances they spring up anew and ripen into rebellion against God. Here lies a terrible danger. To spare any sin is to cherish a foe that only awaits an unguarded moment to cause our ruin. . . . Divine grace is our only hope (*Testimonies,* vol. 5, pp. 173-175).

Honor for Those Who Honor God

Know ye not, that to whom ye yield yourselves servants to obey, his servants ye are to whom ye obey; whether of sin unto death, or of obedience unto righteousness? Romans 6:16.

When the mind has been long permitted to dwell only on earthly things, it is a difficult matter to change the habits of thought. That which the eye sees and the ear hears too often attracts the attention and absorbs the interest. But if we would enter the city of God, and look upon Jesus in His glory, we must become accustomed to beholding Him with the eye of faith here. The words and the character of Christ should be often the subject of our thoughts and of our conversation; and each day some time should be especially devoted to prayerful meditation upon these sacred themes.

Sanctification is a daily work. Let none deceive themselves with the belief that God will pardon and bless them while they are trampling upon one of His requirements. The willful commission of a known sin silences the witnessing voice of the Spirit, and separates the soul from God. Whatever may be the ecstasies of religious feeling, Jesus cannot abide in the heart that disregards the divine law. God will honor those only who honor Him.

"To whom ye yield yourselves servants to obey, his servants ye are to whom ye obey." If we indulge anger, lust, covetousness, hatred, selfishness, or any other sin, we become servants of sin. "No man can serve two masters." If we serve sin, we cannot serve Christ. The Christian will feel the promptings of sin, for the flesh lusteth against the Spirit; but the Spirit striveth against the flesh, keeping up a constant warfare. Here is where Christ's help is needed. Human weakness becomes united to divine strength, and faith exclaims, "Thanks be to God, which giveth us the victory through our Lord Jesus Christ!"

If we would develop a character which God can accept, we must form correct habits in our religious life. Daily prayer is as essential to growth in grace and even to spiritual life itself, as is temporal food to physical well-being. We should accustom ourselves to often lift the thoughts to God in prayer. If the mind wanders, we must bring it back; by persevering effort, habit will finally make it easy. We cannot for one moment separate ourselves from Christ with safety. We may have His presence to attend us at every step, but only by observing the conditions which He has Himself laid down.

Religion must be made the great business of life. Everything else should be held subordinate to this. All our powers of soul, body, and spirit must be engaged in the Christian warfare. We must look to Christ for strength and grace, and we shall gain the victory as surely as Jesus did for us (*Review and Herald,* Nov. 15, 1887).

Obeying God's Law

For what nation is there so great, who hath God so nigh unto them, as the Lord our God is in all things that we call upon him for? And what nation is there so great, that hath statutes and judgments so righteous as all this law, which I set before you this day?
Deuteronomy 4:7, 8.

Concerning His commandments God declared, through Moses, to His people: "Keep therefore and do them; for this is your wisdom and your understanding in the sight of the nations." . . .

The precious instruction that the Lord gave to His people from Mount Sinai was carried to them all through their wilderness wandering, and was repeated by them wheresoever they encamped. God designed that they should give to the surrounding nations a representation of Him and of His law, by the words they would speak, and in a variety of other ways. On many occasions, as they met the people who knew not God, they exalted their Leader as a great and holy Being whom all should always honor and respect and reverence. . . .

The surrounding nations were to become acquainted with the exalted principles of the God-given laws that the leaders were educating the people to observe. Then, instead of demeriting the people thus instructed, they would regard the observance of these laws as a proof that this was a people peculiarly blessed indeed among the nations.

Another remarkable exhibition to the nations round about was the perfect order observed in the camp of the Israelites. They could see the cloud hovering over the place where the tabernacle was to be pitched; they observed the priests and other appointed agencies going about their special work, each one doing the part assigned him in the work of preparing the camp for the night. No one did anything that someone else should do. Whoever would have tried to do another man's work would have suffered the death penalty. Each one attended to his special duty. In the erecting of the tabernacle, part fitted to part, and the house of the Lord was set up with beautiful precision. Not a word was spoken, not an order given, excepting by the one in charge. No one was confused; everything was put together in accordance with the similitude shown to Moses in the mount.

Everything connected with the pitching of the camp was an object lesson to the children, schooling them in habits of precision and carefulness and order. The children that were old enough were required to learn how to pitch the tents in which they lived, and to observe perfect order in all that they did. . . . Constantly they were obtaining an education in regard to heavenly things. Constantly the parents were explaining to their children why the Israelites were traveling in the wilderness; why the law was given at Sinai; and what they expected to do and to be when they reached the Land of Promise (manuscript 152, 1901).

Exalting God's Law

So you shall remember and do all my commandments, and be holy to your God.
Numbers 15:40, RSV.

All the instruction given to the Israelites of old in regard to teaching the commandments to their children is for us. If we become careless, and neglect to urge the necessity of observing these commandments, as I know that many have done, let us all humble our hearts before God, and make earnest, thorough work of repentance. Let us learn to deal mercifully with our children. In their tender years they are to be kindly, patiently, intelligently, lovingly taught in all religious service, the parents making these lessons simple and attractive, in order that they may make known to their little ones the way of the Lord. In the past, the failure of parents to do this work has been felt in future generations. . . .

It requires constant, persevering effort to keep exalted the standard of righteousness; but none who are lax in principles are approved of God. Our religious experience is spoiled by allowing our principles to become perverted. Now, more than in any other period of the world's history, should we heed the admonition, "Be ye also ready: for in such an hour as ye think not the Son of man cometh."

In ancient times cautions were continually given against idolatry. In this age of the world the same danger exists. We should guard our children against having fellowship with the world, and against imitating the works of those who are in darkness. So far as possible, let us keep them from the society of unbelievers. We know that those who do not serve the Lord Jesus serve another leader, and that this leader will make decided efforts to control the minds of those who know the truth.

Satan's deceptive workings are constantly being carried on in every place. Those who truly love God will reveal their love for Him in every and under every circumstance. They will not condescend to engage in the foolish amusements and the entertainments of worldlings. They will not be persuaded to forget the Lord at any time. Christians may and should feel a holy indignation against the lightness and the folly of those who love not God. "Consider thyself," and fall not into temptation by speaking idle, cheap, meaningless words. Speak words that reveal that you are a child of God, and that your heart is filled with His love.

We must be as decidedly a peculiar people, holy unto the Lord, as the Israelites were required to be, else we cannot properly represent our wise, compassionate, glorified Redeemer (manuscript 152, 1901).

The Law and Gospel in Harmony

We all, with open face beholding as in a glass the glory of the Lord, are changed into the same image from glory to glory, even as by the Spirit of the Lord. 2 Corinthians 3:18.

After Christ died on the cross as a sin offering, the ceremonial law could have no force. Yet it was connected with the moral law, and was glorious. The whole bore the stamp of divinity, and expressed the holiness, justice, and righteousness of God. And if the ministration of the dispensation to be done away was glorious, how much more must the reality be glorious, when Christ was revealed, giving His life-giving sanctifying Spirit to all who believe?

The proclamation of the law of Ten Commandments was a wonderful exhibition of the glory and majesty of God. . . .

"Moses said unto the people, Fear not: for God is come to prove you, and that his fear may be before your faces, that ye sin not. And the people stood afar off, and Moses drew near unto the thick darkness where God was" (Exodus 20:20, 21).

The pardon of sin, justification by faith in Jesus Christ, access to God only through a mediator because of their lost condition, their guilt and sin—of these truths the people had little conception. In a great measure they had lost a knowledge of God and of the only way to approach Him. They had lost nearly all sense of what constitutes sin and of what constitutes righteousness. The pardon of sin through Christ, the promised Messiah, whom their offerings typified, was but dimly understood. . . .

The moral law was never a type or a shadow. It existed before man's creation, and will endure as long as God's throne remains. God could not change nor alter one precept of His law in order to save men; for the law is the foundation of His government. It is unchangeable, unalterable, infinite, and eternal. In order for man to be saved, and for the honor of the law to be maintained, it was necessary for the Son of God to offer Himself as a sacrifice for sin. He who knew no sin became sin for us. He died for us on Calvary. His death shows the wonderful love of God for man, and the immutability of His law. . . .

Christ is the sinner's advocate. Those who accept His gospel behold Him with open face. They see the relation of His mission to the law, and they acknowledge God's wisdom and glory as revealed by the Savior. The glory of Christ is revealed in the law, which is a transcript of His character, and His transforming efficacy is felt upon the soul until men become changed into His likeness. They are made partakers of the divine nature, and grow more and more like their Savior, advancing step by step in conformity to the will of God, till they reach perfection. The law and the gospel are in perfect harmony (*Selected Messages*, book 1, pp. 238-240).

Christ's New Commandment

A new commandment I give unto you, That ye love one another; as I have loved you, that ye also love one another. John 13:34.

Do you in your words, in your spirit, in your actions, resemble Christ? If in word and spirit you represent the character of Christ, then you are Christians; for to be a Christian is to be Christlike. The tongue will testify of the principles that characterize the life; it is the sure test of what power controls the heart. We may judge our own spirit and principles by the words that proceed from our lips. The tongue is always to be under the control of the Holy Spirit.

When poor, wounded, bruised souls come to you for words of hope, you are to speak to them the words of Christ. Do you refuse to give them pleasant, courteous, kind words? Those who speak as Christ spoke will never plant bitter words like barbed arrows in the wounded soul. "The Lord hearkened, and heard." Will you bear in mind that the Lord hears the words we speak, and is acquainted with the spirit that prompts our action? Christ is the defense of all that are hidden in Him.

Bear in mind that every unkind word, every ruthless thrust, is recorded in the books of heaven as given to Christ in the person of His suffering ones. Is it not Christlike to speak kind words, comforting words, even though you feel inclined to do otherwise? Is it not Christlike to help lift the burdens when they press heavily upon souls whom God has valued so highly as to give His only begotten Son, that whosoever believeth in Him should not perish, but have everlasting life? . . .

"Dost thou believe on the Son of God?" You are just as dependent upon Christ for all that you receive as is the weakest, poorest, and humblest soul. "Dost thou believe on the Son of God?" A mere speculative belief amounts to nothing. Do you believe on the Son of God as your personal Savior? Then if you believe with all your heart, God dwells in the soul, and the soul in God. You represent Jesus. Those who are in positions of trust are on test and trial, to see if they will be wise men in positions of trust, to reveal whether Christ is working in and through them, so that He can represent His character and express Himself in their words and actions toward His heritage, for whom He has given His own precious life. . . .

Just in proportion as the human agent is a partaker of the divine nature, he will be in sympathy with Christ. Jesus says, "A new commandment I give unto you [That ye tolerate one another? No], That ye love one another; as I have loved you, that ye also love one another. By this shall all men know that ye are my disciples, if ye have love one to another." "This is my commandment, That ye love one another, as I have loved you" (*Review and Herald*, May 26, 1896).

All May Wear the Crown

Know ye not that they which run in a race run all, but one receiveth the prize? So run, that ye may obtain. 1 Corinthians 9:24.

The competitors in the ancient games, after they had submitted to self-denial and rigid discipline, were not even then sure of the victory. "Know ye not," Paul asked, "that they which run in a race run all, but one receiveth the prize?" However eagerly and earnestly the runners might strive, the prize could be awarded to but one. One hand only could grasp the coveted garland. Some might put forth the utmost effort to obtain the prize, but as they reached forth the hand to secure it, another, an instant before them, might grasp the coveted treasure.

Such is not the case in the Christian warfare. Not one who complies with the conditions will be disappointed at the end of the race. Not one who is earnest and persevering will fail of success. The race is not to the swift, nor the battle to the strong. The weakest saint, as well as the strongest, may wear the crown of immortal glory. All may win who, through the power of divine grace, bring their lives into conformity to the will of Christ. The practice, in the details of life, of the principles laid down in God's Word, is too often looked upon as unimportant—a matter too trivial to demand attention. But in view of the issue at stake, nothing is small that will help or hinder. Every act casts its weight into the scale that determines life's victory or defeat. And the reward given to those who win will be in proportion to the energy and earnestness with which they have striven. . . .

Paul knew that his warfare against evil would not end so long as life should last. Ever he realized the need of putting a strict guard upon himself, that earthly desires might not overcome spiritual zeal. With all his power he continued to strive against natural inclinations. Ever he kept before him the ideal to be attained, and this ideal he strove to reach by willing obedience to the law of God. His words, his practices, his passions—all were brought under the control of the Spirit of God.

It was this singlehearted purpose to win the race for eternal life that Paul longed to see revealed in the lives of the Corinthian believers. He knew that in order to reach Christ's ideal for them, they had before them a life struggle from which there would be no release. He entreated them to strive lawfully, day by day seeking for piety and moral excellence. He pleaded with them to lay aside every weight and to press forward to the goal of perfection in Christ (*The Acts of the Apostles*, pp. 313-315).

One goal he kept ever before him, and strove earnestly to reach—"the righteousness which is of God by faith" (Philippians 3:9) (*ibid.*, p. 314).

The Royal Law Measures Character

If you really fulfil the royal law, according to scripture, . . . you do well. James 2:8, RSV.

The standard by which to measure character is the royal law. The law is the sin detector. By the law is the knowledge of sin. But the sinner is constantly being drawn to Jesus by the wonderful manifestation of His love in that He humiliated Himself to die a shameful death upon the cross. What a study is this! Angels have striven, earnestly longed, to look into this wonderful mystery. It is a study that can tax the highest human intelligence, that man, fallen, deceived by Satan, taking Satan's side of the question, can be conformed to the image of the Son of the infinite God—that man shall be like Him, that, because of the righteousness of Christ given to man, God will love man, fallen but redeemed, even as He loved His Son. Read it right out of the living oracles.

This is the mystery of godliness. This picture is of the highest value. It is to be meditated upon, placed in every discourse, hung in memory's hall, uttered by human lips, and traced by human beings who have tasted and known that the Lord is good. It is to be the groundwork of every discourse. . . .

A Christian is the highest type of a man because he is Christlike. . . . He feels his weakness, he lays hold with earnest purpose and living faith upon the strength of God, and is an overcomer. Great becomes his peace, his joy, for it comes from the Lord, and there is nothing more acceptable in the sight of God than the continual humiliation of the soul before Him. These evidences are unmistakable proofs that the Lord has touched hearts by His Holy Spirit. More wonderful than miracles of physical healing is the miracle wrought in the child of God in wrestling with natural defects and overcoming them. The universe of God looks upon him with joy far greater than on any splendid outward display. The inward character is molded after the divine Pattern. . . .

Holding up Christ as our only source of strength, presenting His matchless love in having the guilt of the sins of men charged to His account and His own righteousness imputed to man, in no case does away with the law or detracts from its dignity. Rather, it places it where the correct light shines upon and glorifies it. This is done only through the light reflected from the cross of Calvary. The law is complete and full in the great plan of salvation, only as it is presented in the light shining from the crucified and risen Savior. This can be only spiritually discerned. It kindles in the heart of the beholder ardent faith, hope, and joy that Christ is his righteousness. This joy is only for those who love and keep the words of Jesus, which are the words of God (manuscript 24, 1888).

The Principle of Love in the Law

We love him, because he first loved us. 1 John 4:19.

There is no evidence of genuine repentance unless it works reformation. If he restore the pledge, give again that he had robbed, confess his sins, and love God and his fellowmen, the sinner may be sure that he has passed from death unto life.

When, as erring, sinful beings, we come to Christ and become partakers of His pardoning grace, love springs up in the heart. Every burden is light, for the yoke that Christ imposes is easy. Duty becomes a delight, and sacrifice a pleasure. The path that before seemed shrouded in darkness, becomes bright with beams from the Sun of Righteousness.

The loveliness of the character of Christ will be seen in His followers. It was His delight to do the will of God. Love to God, zeal for His glory, was the controlling power in our Savior's life. Love beautified and ennobled all His actions. Love is of God. The unconsecrated heart cannot originate or produce it. It is found only in the heart where Jesus reigns. "We love, because he first loved us" (1 John 4:19, RV). In the heart renewed by divine grace, love is the principle of action. It modifies the character, governs the impulses, controls the passions, subdues enmity, and ennobles the affections. This love, cherished in the soul, sweetens the life and sheds a refining influence on all around.

There are two errors against which the children of God—particularly those who have just come to trust in His grace—especially need to guard. The first . . . is that of looking to their own works, trusting to anything they can do, to bring themselves into harmony with God. He who is trying to become holy by his own works in keeping the law, is attempting an impossibility. All that man can do without Christ is polluted with selfishness and sin. It is the grace of Christ alone, through faith, that can make us holy.

The opposite and no less dangerous error is that belief in Christ releases men from keeping the law of God; that since by faith alone we become partakers of the grace of Christ, our works have nothing to do with our redemption.

But notice here that obedience is not a mere outward compliance, but the service of love. The law of God is an expression of His very nature; it is an embodiment of the great principle of love, and hence is the foundation of His government in heaven and earth. If our hearts are renewed in the likeness of God, if the divine love is implanted in the soul, will not the law of God be carried out in the life? When the principle of love is implanted in the heart, when man is renewed after the image of Him that created him, the new covenant promise is fulfilled. . . . Obedience—the service and allegiance of love—is the true sign of discipleship (*Steps to Christ*, pp. 59, 60).

The Plan of Redemption

According as his divine power hath given unto us all things that pertain unto life and godliness, through the knowledge of Him that hath called us to glory and virtue. 2 Peter 1:3.

The plan of salvation is but dimly comprehended by the Christian world. Man, as now taught by men who claim to have a knowledge of the Scriptures, can never know the extent of his fallen, degraded condition; but the mission of Christ will reveal the truth as it is in Jesus. Man can know the depths to which he has sunk only by beholding the wondrous chain of redemption employed to draw him up. The extent of our ruin can be discerned only in the light of the law of God exhibited in the cross of Calvary. The wonderful plan of redemption must be discerned in the death of Christ.

The world by its own wisdom cannot acquire a correct knowledge of the true and living God. When Christ came to this world, clothing His divinity with humanity, the treatment He received from the highest authorities of a nation that professed to know God, made fully manifest the strength of human wisdom and reason. Their reason could not form a correct idea of God through His way and works.

Only through faith in Christ is it possible for man to live the law. Man is not able to save himself, but the Son of God fights his battles for him, and places him on vantage ground by giving him His divine attributes. And as man accepts the righteousness of Christ, he is a partaker of the divine nature. He may keep the commandments of God, and live. Says Peter: . . . "Whereby are given unto us exceeding great and precious promises: that by these ye might be partakers of the divine nature, having escaped the corruption that is in the world through lust."

The truth as it is in Jesus is obedience to every precept of Jehovah. It is heart work. Bible sanctification is not the spurious sanctification which will not search the Scriptures, but will trust to good feeling and impulses rather than to the seeking for truth as for hidden treasure. Bible sanctification will lead its possessors to know the requirements of God and to obey them. There is a pure and holy heaven in store for those who keep God's commandments. It is worth lifelong, persevering, untiring effort. Satan is on your right hand and on your left; he is before you and behind. He supplies his falsehoods to every soul who is not cherishing the truth as it is in Jesus. He, the destroyer, is upon you to palsy your every effort. But there is a crown of life to be won, a life that measures with the life of God. And those who do not close their hearts and minds to conviction will learn what the love of a holy and righteous God is; for it is an amazing principle, which works in a mysterious and wonderful manner to secure the salvation of the race (*Review and Herald*, Feb. 8, 1898).

The Truth as It Is in Jesus

If so be that ye have heard him, and have been taught by him, as the truth is in Jesus. Ephesians 4:21.

When prophets stood in defense of the truth, it was the word of God that was given to them. They understood the work of salvation to be accomplished by the Messiah to come. But after Christ came, after He died as man's sacrifice, after the typical sacrifices were fulfilled by the Antitype, the old truth in the typical service was revealed more clearly. In Christ, the representative of the Father, a wonderful truth was revealed to the world. The light from the cross of Calvary, reflected back upon the Jewish age, gives character and significance to the whole Jewish economy; and on this side of the cross, in a special manner, we have the truth as it is in Jesus. Truth communicated through our Redeemer becomes indeed present truth.

What a truth is presented as we gaze upon Jesus in connection with the cross of Calvary, as we see this Wonderful, this Counselor, this mysterious Victim, stooping beneath the amazing burden of our race! That the transgressor might have another trial, that men might be brought into favor with God the Father, the eternal Son of God interposed Himself to bear the punishment of transgression. One clothed with humanity, who was yet one with the Deity, was our ransom. The very earth shook and reeled at the spectacle of God's dear Son suffering the wrath of God for man's transgression. The heavens were clothed in sackcloth to hide the sight of the Divine Sufferer.

It was the transgression of the law of God that made this suffering necessary. And yet men harbor the thought, and give expression to the suggestions of Satan through those who trample upon the law of God, that all this suffering was to make that law of none effect. Deceived and blinded by the great transgressor, they tell the people that there is no law, or that, if they keep the commandments of God in this dispensation, they have fallen from grace. What a delusion is this that Satan has fastened upon human minds!

When the theory that the law of Jehovah is not binding upon the human family is adopted and taught, man is blinded to his terrible ruin. He cannot discern it. Then God has no moral standard by which to measure character, and to govern the heavenly universe, the worlds unfallen, and this fallen world. Could God have abolished the law in order to meet man in his fallen condition, and yet have maintained His honor as Governor of the universe, Christ need not have died. But the death of Christ is the convincing, everlasting argument that the law of God is as unchanging as His throne (*Review and Herald*, Feb. 8, 1898).

May
20

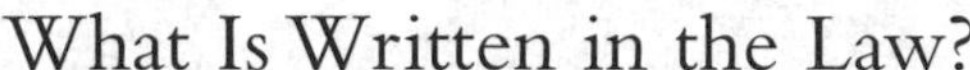

What Is Written in the Law?

Thou shalt love the Lord thy God with all thy heart, and with all thy soul, and with all thy strength, and with all thy mind; and thy neighbor as thyself. Luke 10:27.

Among the Jews the question "Who is my neighbor?" caused endless dispute. They had no doubt as to the heathen and the Samaritans. These were strangers and enemies. But where should the distinction be made among the people of their own nation, and among the different classes of society? Whom should the priest, the rabbi, the elder, regard as neighbor? . . .

This question Christ answered in the parable of the good Samaritan. He showed that our neighbor does not mean merely one of the church or faith to which we belong. It has no reference to race, color, or class distinction. Our neighbor is every person who needs our help. Our neighbor is every soul who is wounded and bruised by the adversary. Our neighbor is everyone who is the property of God.

The parable of the good Samaritan was called forth by a question put to Christ by a doctor of the law. As the Savior was teaching, "a certain lawyer stood up, and tempted him, saying, Master, what shall I do to inherit eternal life?" The Pharisees had suggested this question to the lawyer, in the hope that they might entrap Christ in His words, and they listened eagerly for His answer. But the Savior entered into no controversy. He required the answer from the questioner himself. "What is written in the law?" He asked. "How readest thou?" The Jews still accused Jesus of lightly regarding the law given from Sinai, but He turned the question of salvation upon the keeping of God's commandments. . . .

The lawyer was not satisfied with the position and works of the Pharisees. He had been studying the Scriptures with a desire to learn their real meaning. He had a vital interest in the matter, and he asked in sincerity, "What shall I do?" In his answer as to the requirements of the law, he passed by all the mass of ceremonial and ritualistic precepts. For these he claimed no value, but presented the two great principles on which hang all the law and the prophets. The Savior's commendation of this answer placed Him on vantage ground with the rabbis. They could not condemn Him for sanctioning that which had been advanced by an expositor of the law.

"This do, and thou shalt live," Christ said. In His teaching He ever presented the law as a divine unity, showing that it is impossible to keep one precept and break another; for the same principle runs through all. Man's destiny will be determined by his obedience to the whole law (*Christ's Object Lessons*, pp. 376-378).

In Harmony With God's Law

A certain Samaritan, as he journeyed, came where he was: and when he saw him, he had compassion on him, and went to him, . . . and took care of him. Luke 10:33, 34.

Christ knew that no one could obey the law in his own strength. He desired to lead the lawyer to clearer and more critical research, that he might find the truth. Only by accepting the virtue and grace of Christ can we keep the law. Belief in the propitiation for sin enables fallen man to love God with his whole heart and his neighbor as himself.

The lawyer knew that he had kept neither the first four nor the last six commandments. He was convicted under Christ's searching words, but instead of confessing his sin, he tried to excuse it. Rather than acknowledge the truth, he endeavored to show how difficult of fulfillment the commandment is. Thus he hoped both to parry conviction and to vindicate himself in the eyes of the people. The Saviour's words had shown that his question was needless, since he was able to answer it himself. Yet he put another question, saying, "Who is my neighbour?"

Again Christ refused to be drawn into controversy. He answered the question by relating an incident, the memory of which was fresh in the minds of His hearers. "A certain man," He said, "went down from Jerusalem to Jericho, and fell among thieves, which stripped him of his raiment, and wounded him, and departed, leaving him half dead." . . .

As he lay thus, a priest came that way; he saw the man lying wounded and bruised, weltering in his own blood; but he left him without rendering any assistance. He "passed by on the other side." Then a Levite appeared. Curious to know what had happened, he stopped and looked at the sufferer. He was convicted of what he ought to do, but it was not an agreeable duty. He wished that he had not come that way so that he would not have seen the wounded man. He persuaded himself that the case was no concern of his, and he too "passed by on the other side."

But a Samaritan, traveling the same road, saw the sufferer, and he did the work that others had refused to do. With gentleness and kindness he ministered to the wounded man. "When he saw him, he had compassion on him, and went to him, and bound up his wounds, pouring in oil and wine, and set him on his own beast, and brought him to an inn, and took care of him. And on the morrow when he departed, he took out two pence, and gave them to the host, and said unto him, Take care of him; and whatsoever thou spendest more, when I come again, I will repay thee." The priest and the Levite both professed piety, but the Samaritan showed that he was truly converted. It was no more agreeable for him to do the work than for the priest and the Levite, but in spirit and works he proved himself to be in harmony with God (*Christ's Object Lessons*, pp. 378-380).

The Complete Savior

For by grace are ye saved through faith; and that not of yourselves: it is the gift of God. Ephesians 2:8.

The thought that the righteousness of Christ is imputed to us, not because of any merit on our part, but as a free gift from God, is a precious thought. The enemy of God and man is not willing that this truth should be clearly presented; for he knows that if the people receive it fully, his power will be broken. If he can control minds so that doubt and unbelief and darkness shall compose the experience of those who claim to be the children of God, he can overcome them with temptation.

That simple faith which takes God at His word should be encouraged. God's people must have that faith which will lay hold of divine power; "for by grace are ye saved through faith; and that not of yourselves: it is the gift of God" (Ephesians 2:8). Those who believe that God for Christ's sake has forgiven their sins, should not, through temptation, fail to press on to fight the good fight of faith. Their faith should grow stronger until their Christian life, as well as their words, shall declare, "The blood of Jesus Christ . . . cleanseth us from all sin" (1 John 1:7).

If we would have the spirit and power of the third angel's message, we must present the law and the gospel together, for they go hand in hand. As a power from beneath is stirring up the children of disobedience to make void the law of God, and to trample upon the truth that Christ is our righteousness, a power from above is moving upon the hearts of those who are loyal to exalt the law, and to lift up Jesus as a complete Savior. Unless divine power is brought into the experience of the people of God, false theories and ideas will take minds captive, Christ and His righteousness will be dropped out of the experience of many, and their faith will be without power or life. . . .

The people must be instructed that Christ is unto them salvation and righteousness. It is Satan's studied purpose to keep souls from believing in Christ as their only hope; for the blood of Christ that cleanseth from all sin is efficacious in behalf of those only who believe in its merit, and who present it before the Father as did Abel in his offering. . . .

The burden of our message is not only the commandments of God, but the faith of Jesus. A bright light shines upon our pathway today, and it leads to increased faith in Jesus. We must receive every ray of light, and walk in it. . . . As increased light is given, men must be reformed, elevated, and refined by it (*Gospel Workers*, pp. 161, 162).

Then you will have right to the tree of life, and eat of the leaves and immortal fruit . . . and live for ever in perfect happiness (*Youth's Instructor*, August 1852).

The Law Is Complete in Itself

I the Lord speak righteousness, I declare things that are right. Isaiah 45:19.

With the setting aside of the Bible has come a turning away from God's law. The doctrine that men are released from obedience to the divine precepts has weakened the force of moral obligation and opened the floodgates of iniquity upon the world. Lawlessness, dissipation, and corruption are sweeping in like an overwhelming flood. Everywhere are seen envy, evil surmising, hypocrisy, estrangement, emulation, strife, betrayal of sacred trusts, indulgence of lust. The whole system of religious principles and doctrines, which should form the foundation and framework of social life, seems to be a tottering mass, ready to fall in ruins. . . .

There is no such thing as weakening or strengthening the law of Jehovah. As it has been, so it is. It always has been, and always will be, holy, just, and good, complete in itself. It cannot be repealed or changed. To "honor" or "dishonor" it is but the speech of men.

Between the laws of men and the precepts of Jehovah will come the last great conflict of the controversy between truth and error. Upon this battle we are now entering—a battle not between rival churches contending for the supremacy, but between the religion of the Bible and the religions of fable and tradition. The agencies which have united against truth are now actively at work. God's Holy Word, which has been handed down to us at so great a cost of suffering and bloodshed, is little valued. There are few who really accept it as the rule of life.

Infidelity prevails to an alarming extent, not in the world only, but in the church. Many have come to deny doctrines which are the very pillars of the Christian faith. The great facts of Creation as presented by the inspired writers, the fall of man, the atonement, the perpetuity of the law—these all are practically rejected by a large share of the professedly Christian world. Thousands who pride themselves in their knowledge regard it as an evidence of weakness to place implicit confidence in the Bible, and a proof of learning to cavil at the Scriptures and to spiritualize and explain away their most important truths.

Christians should be preparing for what is soon to break upon the world as an overwhelming surprise, and this preparation they should make by diligently studying the Word of God and striving to conform their lives to its precepts. The tremendous issues of eternity demand of us something besides an imaginary religion, a religion of words and forms, where truth is kept in the outer court. God calls for a revival and a reformation. The words of the Bible, and the Bible alone, should be heard from the pulpit (*Prophets and Kings*, pp. 624-626).

Christ Magnifies the Law

The Lord is well pleased for his righteousness' sake; he will magnify the law, and make it honourable. Isaiah 42:21.

Were the law understood apart from Christ, it would have a crushing power upon sinful men, blotting the sinner out of existence. But by understanding the law in connection with Christ, receiving Him by faith as his substitute and surety, man sees himself as a prisoner of hope. The truth as it is in Jesus is an acquaintance with the holy, just, and good law of God, as this law is elevated, and its immutability demonstrated, in Christ. He magnified the law, expanded its every precept, and in His obedience left man an example, that he also may meet its demands. . . .

The agonies of the garden of Gethsemane, the insult, the mockery, the abuse, heaped upon God's dear Son, the horrors and ignominy of the Crucifixion, furnish sufficient and thrilling demonstrations that God's justice, when it punishes, does the work thoroughly. The fact that His own Son, the surety for man, was not spared is an argument that will stand to all eternity before saint and sinner, before the universe of God, to testify that He will not excuse the transgressor of His law.

God is love. He has shown that love in the gift of His only begotten Son. Yet the love of God does not excuse sin. God does not excuse sin in Satan, in Adam, or in Cain, nor will He excuse sin in any of the children of men. The perverted nature of man may distort the love of God into an attribute of weakness; but light is shining from the cross of Calvary, that man may have correct views and hold theories that are not perverted.

God has given His law for the regulation of the conduct of nations, of families, and of individuals. There is not one worker of wickedness, though his sin is the least and the most secret, that escapes the denunciation of that law. The whole work of the father of lies is recorded in the statute books of heaven; and those who lend themselves to the service of Satan, to present to men his lies by precept and practice, will receive according to their deeds. Every offense against God, however minute, is set down in the reckoning. And when the sword of justice is taken in hand, it will do the work that was done to the Divine Sufferer. Justice will strike; for God's hatred of sin is intense and overwhelming.

The truth as it is in Jesus will teach most important lessons. It will show that the love of God is broad and deep; that it is infinite; and that in awarding the penalty to the disobedient, those who have made void God's law, it will be uncompromising. This is the love and justice of God combined. It reaches to the very depth of human woe and degradation, to lift up the fallen and oppressed who lay hold of the truth by repentance and faith in Jesus (*Review and Herald*, Feb. 8, 1898).

Obedience to Physical and Moral Laws

I beseech you therefore, brethren, by the mercies of God, that ye present your bodies a living sacrifice, holy, acceptable unto God, which is your reasonable service.
Romans 12:1.

We should preserve our strength to labor in the cause of God when our labor is needed. We should be careful not to take upon ourselves burdens that others can and should bear. We should encourage a cheerful, hopeful, peaceful frame of mind; for our health depends upon our so doing. The work that God requires us to do will not prevent our caring for our health, that we may recover from the effect of overtaxing labor. The more perfect our health, the more perfect will be our labor. When we overtax our strength, and become exhausted, we are liable to take cold, and at such times there is danger of disease assuming a dangerous form. We must not leave the care of ourselves with God, when He has placed that responsibility with us (*Testimonies,* vol. 3, p. 13).

God created man a little lower than the angels and bestowed upon him attributes that will, if properly used, make him a blessing to the world and cause him to reflect the glory to the Giver. But although made in the image of God, man has, through intemperance, violated principle and God's law in his physical nature. Intemperance of any kind benumbs the perceptive organs and so weakens the brain-nerve power that eternal things are not appreciated, but placed upon a level with the common. The higher powers of the mind, designed for elevated purposes, are brought into slavery to the baser passions. If our physical habits are not right, our mental and moral powers cannot be strong; for great sympathy exists between the physical and the moral. The apostle Peter understood this and raised his voice of warning to his brethren: "Dearly beloved, I beseech you as strangers and pilgrims, abstain from fleshly lusts, which war against the soul."

There is but little moral power in the professed Christian world. Wrong habits have been indulged, and physical and moral laws have been disregarded, until the general standard of virtue and piety is exceedingly low. Habits which lower the standard of physical health enfeeble mental and moral strength. . . .

Those who have had the light upon the subjects of eating and dressing with simplicity in obedience to physical and moral laws, and who turn from the light which points out their duty, will shun duty in other things. If they blunt their consciences to avoid the cross which they will have to take up to be in harmony with natural law, they will, in order to shun reproach, violate the Ten Commandments. . . . There are many among professed Sabbathkeepers . . . who are more firmly wedded to worldly fashions and lusts than they are to healthy bodies, sound minds, or sanctified hearts (*ibid.,* pp. 50, 51).

Results of Obedience to Physical Laws

These are the commandments, the statutes, and the judgments, which the Lord your God commanded to teach you, that ye might do them in the land whither ye go to possess it: that thou mightest fear the Lord thy God, to keep all his statutes and his commandments, which I command thee . . . all the days of thy life; and that thy days may be prolonged. Deuteronomy 6:1, 2.

In this scripture we are taught that obedience to God's requirements brings the obedient under the laws that control the physical being. Those who would preserve themselves in health must bring into subjection all appetites and passions. They must not indulge lustful passion and intemperate appetite, for they are to remain under control to God, and their physical, mental, and moral powers are to be so wisely employed that the bodily mechanism will remain in good working order.

Health, life, and happiness are the result of obedience to physical laws governing our bodies. If our will and way are in accordance with God's will and way; if we do the pleasure of our Creator, He will keep the human organism in good condition, and restore the moral, mental, and physical powers, in order that He may work through us to His glory. Constantly His restoring power is manifested in our bodies. If we cooperate with Him in this work, health and happiness, peace and usefulness, are the sure results (*The SDA Bible Commentary,* Ellen G. White Comments, vol. 1, p. 1118).

"And the Lord commanded us to do all these statutes, to fear the Lord our God, for our good always, that he might preserve us alive, as it is at this day. And it shall be our righteousness, if we observe to do all these commandments before the Lord our God, as he hath commanded us." The fear here spoken of is not a servile fear, but a godly fear.

God gave these laws to Israel to preserve them in a happy, healthful state. If there had existed no Satan to tempt them, these special instructions would not have been needed; but unless the people had something to guide them, they would surely be led astray by the specious devisings of the enemy of all righteousness. Their only safety was to be found in hearkening with all diligence to the word of the Lord.

Parents who desire to train their children aright should heed the instruction given in these scriptures, and allow their little ones to do nothing in disregard of God's commandments so plainly given. Let fathers and mothers faithfully teach their children these precepts, and impress upon their tender minds that fact that in obedience there is life, health, happiness. . . .

The great object we should always keep in view, when obtaining a knowledge of God's laws, is that we are to become acquainted with His will in order that we may obey Him (manuscript 151, 1901).

Christ Is the Center of the Law

Do we then make void the law through faith? God forbid: yea, we establish the law.
Romans 3:31.

Of all professing Christians, Seventh-day Adventists should be foremost in uplifting Christ before the world. The proclamation of the third angel's message calls for the presentation of the Sabbath truth. This truth, with others included in the message, is to be proclaimed; but the great center of attraction, Christ Jesus, must not be left out. It is at the cross of Christ that mercy and truth meet together, and righteousness and peace kiss each other. The sinner must be led to look to Calvary; with the simple faith of a little child he must trust in the merits of the Savior, accepting His righteousness, believing in His mercy.

Through the love of God the treasures of the grace of Christ have been laid open before the church and the world. "God so loved the world, that he gave his only begotten Son, that whosoever believeth in him should not perish, but have everlasting life" (John 3:16). What marvelous, unfathomable love, which led Christ to die for us while we were yet sinners! And what a loss the soul suffers who, understanding the strong claims of the law, fails to acknowledge that where sin abounds, the grace of Christ does much more abound!

When the law is presented as it should be, it reveals the love of God. But it is no wonder that hearts are not melted even by truth when it is presented in a cold, lifeless manner; no wonder that faith staggers at the promises of God, when ministers and workers fail to present Jesus in His relation to the law. . . .

Let the teacher of truth make known to the sinner what God really is—a Father waiting with yearning love to receive the returning prodigal, not hurling at him accusations of wrath, but preparing a feast to welcome his return. O that we might all learn the way of the Lord in winning souls!

God would draw minds from the conviction of logic to a conviction deeper, higher, purer, and more glorious. Often human logic has nearly quenched the light that God would have shine forth in clear rays to convince men that the Lord of nature is worthy of all praise and glory, because He is the Creator of all things (*Gospel Workers,* pp. 156-158).

Lift up Jesus, you that teach the people, lift Him up in sermon, in song, in prayer. Let all your powers be directed to pointing souls, confused, bewildered, lost to "the Lamb of God." Lift Him up, the risen Savior, and say to all who hear, Come to Him who "hath loved us, and hath given himself for us" (Ephesians 5:2). Let the science of salvation be the burden of every sermon, the theme of every song. Let it be poured forth in every supplication. . . . Show forth the grace and completeness of the Savior (*ibid.,* p. 160).

May
28

In the School of Christ

O that thou hadst hearkened to my commandments! then had thy peace been as a river, and thy righteousness as the waves of the sea. Isaiah 48:18.

We are to enter the school of Christ, to learn from Him meekness and lowliness. Redemption is that process by which the soul is trained for heaven. This training means a knowledge of Christ. It means emancipation from ideas, habits, and practices that have been gained in the school of the prince of darkness. The soul must be delivered from all that is opposed to loyalty to God.

In the heart of Christ, where reigned perfect harmony with God, there was perfect peace. He was never elated by applause, nor dejected by censure or disappointment. Amid the greatest opposition and the most cruel treatment, He was still of good courage. But many who profess to be His followers have an anxious, troubled heart, because they are afraid to trust themselves with God. They do not make a complete surrender to Him; for they shrink from the consequences that such a surrender may involve. Unless they do make this surrender, they cannot find peace.

It is the love of self that brings unrest. When we are born from above, the same mind will be in us that was in Jesus, the mind that led Him to humble Himself that we might be saved. Then we shall not be seeking the highest place. We shall desire to sit at the feet of Jesus, and learn of Him. We shall understand that the value of our work does not consist in making a show and noise in the world, and in being active and zealous in our own strength. The value of our work is in proportion to the impartation of the Holy Spirit. Trust in God brings holier qualities of mind, so that in patience we may possess our souls.

The yoke is placed upon the oxen to aid them in drawing the load, to lighten the burden. So with the yoke of Christ. When our will is swallowed up in the will of God, and we use His gifts to bless others, we shall find life's burden light. He who walks in the way of God's commandments is walking in company with Christ, and in His love the heart is at rest. When Moses prayed, "Shew me now thy way, that I may know thee," the Lord answered him, "My presence shall go with thee, and I will give thee rest." And through the prophets the message was given, "Thus saith the Lord, Stand ye in the ways, and see, and ask for the old paths, where is the good way, and walk therein, and ye shall find rest to your souls" (Exodus 33:13, 14; Jeremiah 6:16). And He says, "O that thou hadst hearkened to my commandments! then had thy peace been as a river, and thy righteousness as the waves of the sea" (Isaiah 48:18) (*The Desire of Ages,* pp. 330, 331).

The Robe of Christ's Own Righteousness

I counsel thee to buy of me . . . white raiment, that you mayest be clothed, and that the shame of thy nakedness do not appear. Revelation 3:18.

The white robe of innocence was worn by our first parents when they were placed by God in holy Eden. They lived in perfect conformity to the will of God. All the strength of their affections was given to their heavenly Father. A beautiful soft light, the light of God, enshrouded the holy pair. This robe of light was a symbol of their spiritual garments of heavenly innocence. Had they remained true to God, it would ever have continued to enshroud them. But when sin entered, they severed their connection with God, and the light that had encircled them departed. Naked and ashamed, they tried to supply the place of the heavenly garments by sewing together fig leaves for a covering.

This is what the transgressors of God's law have done ever since the day of Adam and Eve's disobedience. They have sewed together fig leaves to cover the nakedness caused by transgression. They have worn the garments of their own devising, by works of their own they have tried to cover their sins, and make themselves acceptable with God.

But this they can never do. Nothing can man devise to supply the place of his lost robe of innocence. No fig-leaf garments, no worldly citizen dress, can be worn by those who sit down with Christ and angels at the marriage supper of the Lamb.

Only the covering which Christ Himself has provided can make us meet to appear in God's presence. This covering, the robe of His own righteousness, Christ will put upon every repenting, believing soul. . . .

This robe, woven in the loom of heaven, has in it not one thread of human devising. Christ in His humanity wrought out a perfect character, and this character He offers to impart to us. "All our righteousnesses are as filthy rags." Everything that we of ourselves can do is defiled by sin. But the Son of God "was manifested to take away our sins; and in him is no sin." . . .

By His perfect obedience He has made it possible for every human being to obey God's commandments. When we submit ourselves to Christ, the heart is united with His heart, the will is merged in His will, the mind becomes one with His mind, the thoughts are brought into captivity to Him; we live His life. This is what it means to be clothed with the garment of His righteousness. Then as the Lord looks upon us, He sees, not the fig-leaf garment, not the nakedness and deformity of sin, but His own robe of righteousness, which is perfect obedience to the law of Jehovah (*Christ's Object Lessons,* pp. 310-312).

Transforming Power of Obedience to God's Law

Yet I have left me seven thousand in Israel, all the knees which have not bowed unto Baal. 1 Kings 19:18.

Today, as in the days of Elijah, the line of demarcation between God's commandment-keeping people and the worshipers of false gods is clearly drawn. "How long halt ye between two opinions?" Elijah cried; "if the Lord be God, follow him: but if Baal, then follow him" (1 Kings 18:21). And the message for today is: "Babylon the great is fallen, is fallen. . . . Come out of her, my people, that ye be not partakers of her sins, and that ye receive not of her plagues. For her sins have reached unto heaven, and God hath remembered her iniquities" (Revelation 18:2-5).

The time is not far distant when the test will come to every soul. The observance of the false sabbath will be urged upon us. The contest will be between the commandments of God and the commandments of men. Those who have yielded step by step to worldly demands and conformed to worldly customs will then yield to the powers that be, rather than subject themselves to derision, insult, threatened imprisonment, and death. At that time the gold will be separated from the dross. True godliness will be clearly distinguished from the appearance and tinsel of it. Many a star that we have admired for its brilliance will then go out in darkness. Those who have assumed the ornaments of the sanctuary, but are not clothed with Christ's righteousness, will then appear in the shame of their own nakedness.

Among earth's inhabitants, scattered in every land, there are those who have not bowed the knee to Baal. Like the stars of heaven, which appear only at night, these faithful ones will shine forth when darkness covers the earth and gross darkness the people. In heathen Africa, in the Catholic lands of Europe and of South America, in China, in India, in the islands of the sea, and in all the dark corners of the earth, God has in reserve a firmament of chosen ones that will yet shine forth amidst the darkness, revealing clearly to an apostate world the transforming power of obedience to His law. Even now they are appearing in every nation, among every tongue and people; and in the hour of deepest apostasy, when Satan's supreme effort is made to cause "all, both small and great, rich and poor, free and bond," to receive, under penalty of death, the sign of allegiance to a false rest day, these faithful ones, "blameless and harmless, the sons of God, without rebuke," will "shine as lights in the world" (Revelation 13:16; Philippians 2:15). The darker the night, the more brilliantly will they shine (*Prophets and Kings,* pp. 187-189).

Teachers to Uphold God's Law

The law of the Lord is perfect, converting the soul. Psalm 19:7.

Wherever Ezra labored, there sprang up a revival in the study of the Holy Scriptures. Teachers were appointed to instruct the people; the law of the Lord was exalted and made honorable. The books of the prophets were searched and the passages foretelling the coming of the Messiah brought hope and comfort to many a sad and weary heart.

More than two thousand years have passed since Ezra "prepared his heart to seek the law of the Lord, and to do it" (Ezra 7:10), yet the lapse of time has not lessened the influence of his pious example. Through the centuries the record of his life of consecration has inspired many with the determination "to seek the law of the Lord, and to do it."

Ezra's motives were high and holy; in all that he did he was actuated by a deep love for souls. The compassion and tenderness that he revealed toward those who had sinned, either willfully or through ignorance, should be an object lesson to all who seek to bring about reforms. The servants of God are to be as firm as a rock where right principles are involved; and yet, withal, they are to manifest sympathy and forbearance. Like Ezra, they are to teach transgressors the way of life by inculcating principles that are the foundation of all rightdoing.

In this age of the world, when Satan is seeking, through manifold agencies, to blind the eyes of men and women to the binding claims of the law of God, there is need of men who can cause many to "tremble at the commandment of our God" (Ezra 10:3). There is need of true reformers, who will point transgressors to the great Lawgiver and teach them that "the law of the Lord is perfect, converting the soul" (Psalm 19:7). There is need of men mighty in the Scriptures, men whose every word and act exalts the statutes of Jehovah, men who seek to strengthen faith. Teachers are needed, oh, so much, who will inspire hearts with reverence and love for the Scriptures.

The widespread iniquity prevalent today may in a great degree be attributed to a failure to study and obey the Scriptures, for when the Word of God is set aside, its power to restrain the evil passions of the natural heart is rejected....

In the last days of this earth's history the voice that spoke from Sinai is still declaring, "Thou shalt have no other gods before me" (Exodus 20:3). Man has set his will against the will of God, but he cannot silence the word of command. The human mind cannot evade its obligation to a higher power. Theories and speculations may abound; men may try to set science in opposition to revelation, and thus do away with God's law; but stronger and still stronger comes the command, "Thou shalt worship the Lord thy God, and Him only shalt thou serve" (Matthew 4:10) (*Prophets and Kings,* pp. 623-625).

June
1

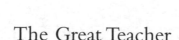

The Great Teacher

For this cause came I into the world, that I should bear witness unto the truth. John 18:37.

Christ was the greatest teacher the world has ever known. He came to this earth to shed abroad the bright beams of truth, that men might gain a fitness for heaven. "For this cause came I into the world that I should bear witness unto the truth." He came to reveal the character of the Father, that men might be led to worship Him in spirit and in truth.

Man's need for a divine teacher was known in heaven. The pity and sympathy of God were aroused in behalf of human beings, fallen and bound to Satan's chariot car; and when the fullness of time was come, He sent forth His Son. The One appointed in the councils of heaven came to this earth as man's instructor. The rich benevolence of God gave Him to our world, and to meet the necessities of human nature He took humanity upon Himself. To the astonishment of the heavenly host, the eternal Word came to this world as a helpless babe. Fully prepared, He left the royal courts and mysteriously allied Himself with fallen human beings. "The Word was made flesh, and dwelt among us" (John 1:14).

When Christ left His high command, He might have taken upon Him any condition in life that He chose. But greatness and rank were nothing to Him, and He chose the most humble walk of life. No luxury, ease, or self-gratification came into His experience. The truth of heavenly origin was to be His theme; He was to sow the world with truth, and He lived in such a way as to be accessible to all.

That during His childhood Christ should grow in wisdom and in favor with God and man was not a matter of astonishment; for it was according to the laws of His divine appointment that His talents should develop and His faculties strengthen. He did not seek an education in the schools of the rabbis, for God was His instructor. As He grew older He continued to increase in wisdom. He applied Himself diligently to a study of the Scriptures, for He knew them to be full of invaluable instruction. He was faithful in the discharge of His home duties; and the early morning hours, instead of being spent in bed, often found Him in a retired place, searching the Scriptures and praying to His heavenly Father.

All the prophecies concerning His work and mediation were familiar to Him, especially those having reference to His humiliation, atonement, and intercession. The object of His life on earth was ever before Him, and He rejoiced to think that the gracious purpose of the Lord should prosper in His hands. . . .

His words comforted, strengthened, and blessed those who were longing for the peace that He alone could give (*Counsels to Parents, Teachers, and Students,* pp. 259, 260).

June
2

The Teacher Sent by God

We know that thou art a teacher come from God: for no man can do these miracles that thou doest, except God be with him. John 3:2.

Christ maintained an all-sided, firm self-possession in His remarkable sympathy for others. He did good with a tranquillity and patient continuance never equaled by any human being. The Pharisees and Sadducees were always on His track; and many of them, as they listened to His words, and noted His calmness, even when assailed by passionate, uncourteous men, believed on Him. . . .

All the contempt and bitterness that Christ met day by day could not rob Him of His self-possession. When He was reviled, He reviled not again. . . . He never overstepped the bounds of decorum. Who was He? The Majesty of heaven, the King of glory. The storm raised by His opponents beat about Him, but He heeded it not. He could afford to be calm; for He was the living embodiment of truth.

And those today who bear the message of truth to the world should study the life of Christ, and practice His lessons. Never forget that you are children of the heavenly King, sons and daughters of the Lord of hosts. Maintain a calm repose in God, even when meeting with those who are moved by a power from beneath to uphold falsehood. Be sure that the best weapons they possess are not able to destroy the truth, however they may strive to blacken it by misrepresentation. "If God be for us, who can be against us?" . . .

He was the teacher sent by God to instruct mankind. As one in whom all restorative power is found, Christ spoke of drawing all men unto Him, and of giving the life everlasting. In Him there is power to heal every physical and every spiritual disease.

Christ came to our world with a consciousness of more than human greatness, to accomplish a work that was to be infinite in its results. Where do you find Him when doing this work? In the house of Peter the fisherman. Resting by Jacob's well, telling the Samaritan woman of the living water. He generally taught in the open air, but sometimes in the Temple, for He attended the gatherings of the Jewish people. But oftenest He taught when sitting on a mountainside, or in a fisherman's boat. He entered into the lives of these humble fishermen. His sympathy was enlisted in behalf of the needy, the suffering, the despised; and many were attracted to Him. . . . And to those who are longing for rest and peace today just as truly as those who listened to His words in Judea, He is saying, "Come unto me, all ye that labour and are heavy laden, and I will give you rest" (*Signs of the Times,* June 24, 1897).

Disciples of the Heavenly Teacher

We have found the Messias, which is, being interpreted, the Christ. John 1:41.

While two disciples were standing near, John again saw Jesus among the people. Again the face of the prophet was lighted up with glory from the Unseen, as he cried, "Behold the Lamb of God!" The words thrilled the hearts of the disciples. They did not fully understand them. What meant the name that John had given Him—"the Lamb of God"? John himself had not explained it.

Leaving John, they went to seek Jesus. One of the two was Andrew, the brother of Simon; the other was John the evangelist. These were Christ's first disciples. Moved by an irresistible impulse, they followed Jesus—anxious to speak with Him, yet awed and silent, lost in the overwhelming significance of the thought, "Is this the Messiah?"

Jesus knew that the disciples were following Him. They were the first fruits of His ministry, and there was joy in the heart of the divine Teacher as these souls responded to His grace. Yet turning, He asked only, "What seek ye?" He would leave them free to turn back or to speak of their desire.

Of one purpose only were they conscious. One presence filled their thought. They exclaimed, "Rabbi, . . . where dwellest *thou*?" In a brief interview by the wayside they could not receive that for which they longed. They desired to be alone with Jesus, to sit at His feet, and hear His words. "He saith unto them, Come and see. They came and saw where he dwelt, and abode with him that day."

If John and Andrew had possessed the unbelieving spirit of the priests and rulers they would not have been found as learners at the feet of Jesus. They would have come to Him as critics, to judge His words. Many thus close the door to the most precious opportunities. But not so did these first disciples. They had responded to the Holy Spirit's call in the preaching of John the Baptist. Now they recognized the voice of the heavenly Teacher. To them the words of Jesus were full of freshness and truth and beauty. A divine illumination was shed upon the teaching of the Old Testament Scriptures. The many-sided themes of truth stood out in new light.

It is contrition and faith and love that enable the soul to receive wisdom from heaven. Faith working by love is the key of knowledge, and everyone that loveth "knoweth God" (1 John 4:7). . . .

"The day following Jesus would go forth into Galilee, and findeth Philip, and saith unto him, Follow me." Philip obeyed the command, and straightway he also became a worker for Christ (*The Desire of Ages*, pp. 138, 139).

Christ Invites Our Confidence

[Jesus] said . . . , follow me. Luke 9:58, 59.

The fall of our first parents broke the golden chain of implicit obedience of the human will to the divine. Obedience has no longer been deemed an absolute necessity. The human agents follow their own imaginations which the Lord said of the inhabitants of the old world was evil and that continually. The Lord Jesus declares, I have kept my Father's commandments. How? As a man! "Lo, I come to do thy will, O God." To the accusations of the Jews He stood forth in His pure, virtuous, holy character and challenged them, "Which of you convinceth me of sin?" The world's Redeemer came not only to be a sacrifice for sin, but to be an example to man in all things. He was a teacher, such an educator as the world never saw or heard before. He spoke as one having authority, and yet He invites the confidence of all. . . .

The only begotten Son of the infinite God has, by His Word, His practical example, left us a plain pattern which we are to copy. By His words He has educated us to obey God, and by His own practice He has showed us how we can obey God. This is the very work He wants every man to do, to obey God intelligently and by precept and example teach others what they must do in order to be obedient children of God.

Jesus has helped the whole world to an intelligent knowledge of His divine mission and work. He came to represent the character of the Father to our world, and as we study the life, the words, and works of Jesus Christ, we are helped in every way in the education of obedience to God; and as we copy the example He has given us, we are living epistles known and read of all men. We are the living human agencies to represent in character Jesus Christ to the world. Not only did Christ give explicit rules showing how we may become obedient children, but He showed us in His own life and character just how to do those things which are right and acceptable with God, so there is no excuse why we should not do those things which are pleasing in His sight.

We are ever to be thankful that Jesus has proved to us by actual facts that man can keep the commandments of God, giving contradiction to Satan's falsehood that man cannot keep them. The Great Teacher came to our world to stand at the head of humanity, to thus elevate and sanctify humanity by His holy obedience to all of God's requirements showing it is possible to obey all the commandments of God. He has demonstrated that a lifelong obedience is possible. Thus He gives men to the world, as the Father gave the Son, to exemplify in their life the life of Jesus Christ. . . .

Jesus says, "Follow me" (manuscript 1, 1892).

Christ Teaches Heavenly Things

Teach me thy way, O Lord; I will walk in thy truth: unite my heart to fear thy name.
Psalm 86:11.

That which in the counsels of heaven the Father and the Son deemed essential for man's salvation is clearly presented in the Holy Scriptures. The infinite truths of salvation are stated so plainly that finite beings who desire to know the truth cannot fail to understand. Divine revelations have been made for their instruction in righteousness, that they may glorify God and help their fellowmen.

These truths are found in the Word of God—the standard by which we are to judge between right and wrong. Obedience to this Word is the best shield for the youth against the temptations to which they are exposed while acquiring an education. From this Word they learn how to honor God, and how to be faithful to humanity, cheerfully performing the duties and meeting the trials that each day brings, and courageously bearing its burdens.

Christ, the Great Teacher, sought to win the minds of men from the contemplation of earthly things, that He might teach them of heavenly things. Had the teachers of His day been willing to be instructed by Him, had they united with Him in sowing the world with the seeds of truth, the world would be far different from what it now is. Had the scribes and Pharisees joined their forces with the Savior, the knowledge of Christ would have restored the moral image of God in their souls.

But the leaders of Israel turned from the fountain of true knowledge. They studied the Scriptures only to sustain their traditions and enforce their man-made observances. By their interpretation they made them express sentiments that God had never given. Their mystical construction made indistinct that which He had made plain. They disputed over technicalities, and practically denied the most essential truths. God's Word was robbed of its power, and evil spirits worked their will.

Christ's words contain nothing that is nonessential. The Sermon on the Mount is a wonderful production, yet so simple that a child can study it without misunderstanding. The mount of beatitudes is a symbol of the spiritual elevation on which Christ ever stood. Every word He uttered came from God, and He spoke with the authority of heaven. "The words that I speak unto you, they are spirit, and they are life" (John 6:63). His teaching is full of ennobling, saving truth, to which men's highest ambitions and most profound investigations can bear no comparison. He was alive to the terrible ruin hanging over the race, and He came to save souls by His own righteousness, bringing to the world definite assurance of hope and complete relief (*Counsels to Parents, Teachers, and Students,* pp. 438, 439).

Daily Speak the Words of Christ

If ye continue in my word, then are ye my disciples indeed. John 8:31.

It is the will of God that each professing Christian shall perfect a character after the divine similitude. By studying the character of Christ revealed in the Bible, by practicing His virtues, the believer will be changed into the same likeness of goodness and mercy. Christ's work of self-denial and sacrifice brought into the daily life will develop the faith that works by love and purifies the soul. There are many who wish to evade the cross-bearing part, but the Lord speaks to all when He says, "If any man will come after me, let him deny himself, and take up his cross, and follow me" (Matthew 16:24).

A great work is to be accomplished by the setting forth of the saving truths of the Bible. This is the means ordained of God to stem the tide of moral corruption in the earth. Christ gave His life to make it possible for man to be restored to the image of God. It is the power of His grace that draws men together in obedience to the truth. Those who would experience more of the sanctification of the truth in their own souls should present this truth to those who are ignorant of it. Never will they find a more elevating, ennobling work. . . .

No man is qualified for this work unless he is daily learning to speak the words of the Teacher sent from God. Now is the time to sow the gospel seed. The seed we sow must be that which will produce the choicest fruit. We have no time to lose. The work of our schools is to become more and more in character like the work of Christ. Only the power of the grace of God working on human hearts and minds will make and keep the atmosphere of our schools and churches clean. . . .

In the messages that have been sent us from time to time, we have truths that will accomplish a wonderful work of reform in our characters if we will give them place. They will prepare us for entrance into the city of God. It is our privilege to make continual advancement to a higher grade of Christian living. . . .

We need to be converted from our faulty lives to the faith of the gospel. Christ's followers have no need to try to shine. If they will behold constantly the life of Christ they will be changed in mind and heart into the same image. Then they will shine without any superficial attempt. The Lord asks for no display of goodness. In the gift of His Son He has made provision that our inward lives may be imbued with the principles of heaven. It is the appropriation of this provision that will lead to a manifestation of Christ to the world. When the people of God experience the new birth, their honesty, their uprightness, their fidelity, their steadfast principles, will unfailingly reveal it (*Counsels to Parents, Teachers, and Students,* pp. 249-251).

Jesus' Teaching—Simple, but With Authority

He taught them as one having authority, and not as the scribes. Matthew 7:29.

At Capernaum Jesus dwelt in the intervals of His journeys to and fro, and it came to be known as "his own city." . . .

It was a great thoroughfare of travel. People from many lands passed through the city, and tarried for rest in their journeyings to and fro. Here Jesus could meet all nations and all ranks, the rich and great as well as the poor and lowly, and His lessons would be carried to other countries and into many households. Investigation of the prophecies would thus be excited, attention would be directed to the Savior, and His mission would be brought before the world.

Notwithstanding the action of the Sanhedrin against Jesus, the people eagerly awaited the development of His mission. All heaven was astir with interest. Angels were preparing the way for His ministry, moving upon men's hearts, and drawing them to the Savior.

In Capernaum the nobleman's son whom Christ had healed was a witness to His power. And the court official and his household joyfully testified of their faith. When it was known that the Teacher Himself was among them, the whole city was aroused. Multitudes flocked to His presence. On the Sabbath the people crowded the synagogue until great numbers had to turn away, unable to find entrance.

All who heard the Savior "were astonished at his doctrine: for his word was with power" (Luke 4:32). . . .

Jesus had nothing to do with the various subjects of dissension among the Jews. It was His work to present the truth. His words shed a flood of light upon the teachings of the patriarchs and prophets, and the Scriptures came to men as a new revelation. Never before had His hearers perceived such a depth of meaning in the Word of God.

Jesus met the people on their own ground, as one who was acquainted with their perplexities. He made truth beautiful by presenting it in the most direct and simple way. His language was pure, refined, and clear as a running stream. His voice was as music to those who had listened to the monotonous tones of the rabbis. But while His teaching was simple, He spoke as one having authority. This characteristic set His teaching in contrast with that of all others. The rabbis spoke with doubt and hesitancy, as if the Scriptures might be interpreted to mean one thing or exactly the opposite. The hearers were daily involved in greater uncertainty. But Jesus taught the Scriptures as of unquestionable authority. Whatever His subject, it was presented with power, as if His words could not be controverted. . . . In every theme God was revealed (*The Desire of Ages,* pp. 252-254).

Important Spiritual Lessons Taught

Whatsoever ye do, do it heartily, as to the Lord, and not unto men. Colossians 3:23.

The life of Christ from His earliest years was a life of earnest activity. He lived not to please Himself. He was the Son of the infinite God, yet He worked at the carpenter's trade with His father Joseph. His trade was significant. He had come into the world as the character builder, and as such all His work was perfect. Into all His secular labor He brought the same perfection as into the characters He was transforming by His divine power. He is our pattern.

Parents should teach their children the value and right use of time. Teach them that to do something which will honor God and bless humanity is worth striving for. Even in their early years they can be missionaries for God. . . .

Whatever the line of work in which we engage, the Word of God teaches us to be "not slothful in business; fervent in spirit; serving the Lord" (Romans 12:11). "Whatsoever thy hand findeth to do, do it with thy might" (Ecclesiastes 9:10), "knowing that of the Lord ye shall receive the reward of the inheritance; for ye serve the Lord" (Colossians 3:24) (*Christ's Object Lessons,* pp. 345, 346).

The lessons given to the children regarding the common duties of the home may be presented in such a way that through them the Lord can make lasting impressions on their hearts. Make these common things of life texts on which to hang the lessons of the Word of God. Show your children that all their work in mechanical lines they must learn to work perfectly. By bringing exactness and skill into their everyday duties they will learn spiritual lessons that will remain with them through all their days. God requires that good judgment and skill shall be exercised in our planning and labors. In giving instruction for the building of the earthly sanctuary, the great Teacher laid down principles that were to be for the spiritual help of Israel through all their future experience. The wisdom and perfection brought into that work was typical of the work to be done in their lives in preparing their hearts for the indwelling of the Spirit of God.

Parents, do you ask what your work is? It is to take up your home responsibilities, doing the best you can, and seeking daily, hourly, to set before your children an example worthy of imitation. . . . Let your lessons be such as will bring joy and happiness into their lives, and will lead them to desire the service of Christ. Teach them to use their God-given powers in His service. Thus they will be following the example of the child Jesus (*Signs of the Times,* Nov. 14, 1911).

Jesus Taught Industry by His Own Example

Whatsoever thy hand findeth to do, do it with thy might. Ecclesiastes 9:10.

In the simple garb of a common laborer [Jesus] walked the streets of the little town, going to and returning from His humble work. He did not employ His divine power to lessen His burdens or to lighten His toil.

As Jesus worked in childhood and youth, mind and body were developed. He did not use His physical powers recklessly, but in such a way as to keep them in health, that He might do the best work in every line. He was not willing to be defective, even in the handling of tools. He was perfect as a workman, as He was perfect in character. By His own example He taught that it is our duty to be industrious, that our work should be performed with exactness and thoroughness, and that such labor is honorable. The exercise that teaches the hands to be useful and trains the young to bear their share of life's burdens gives physical strength, and develops every faculty. All should find something to do that will be beneficial to themselves and helpful to others. God appointed work as a blessing, and only the diligent worker finds the true glory and joy of life. The approval of God rests with loving assurance upon children and youth who cheerfully take their part in the duties of the household, sharing the burdens of father and mother. Such children will go out from the home to be useful members of society.

Throughout His life on earth, Jesus was an earnest and constant worker. He expected much; therefore He attempted much. . . . Jesus did not shirk care and responsibility. . . . The positiveness and energy, the solidity and strength of character, manifested in Christ are to be developed in us, through the same discipline that He endured. And the grace that He received is for us. . . .

Jesus carried into His labor cheerfulness and tact. It requires much patience and spirituality to bring Bible religion into the home life and into the workshop, to bear the strain of worldly business, and yet keep the eye single to the glory of God. This is where Christ was a helper. He was never so full of worldly care as to have no time or thought for heavenly things. Often He expressed the gladness of His heart by singing psalms and heavenly songs. Often the dwellers in Nazareth heard His voice raised in praise and thanksgiving to God. He held communion with heaven in song; and as His companions complained of weariness from labor, they were cheered by the sweet melody from His lips. His praise seemed to banish the evil angels, and, like incense, fill the place with fragrance. The minds of His hearers were carried away from their earthly exile, to the heavenly home (*The Desire of Ages,* pp. 72, 73).

Christ Delegates Power to Us

And the Lord said, Simon, Simon, behold, Satan hath desired to have you, that he may sift you as wheat: but I have prayed for thee, that thy faith fail not. Luke 22:31, 32.

As the Prince of life, He had power with God and prevailed for His people. This Savior, who prayed for those that felt no need of prayer, and wept for those that felt no need of tears, is now before the throne, to receive and present to His Father the petitions of those for whom He prayed on earth. The example of Christ is for us to follow. Prayer is a necessity in our labor for the salvation of souls. God alone can give the increase of the seed we sow.

We fail many times because we do not realize that Christ is with us by His Spirit as truly as when, in the days of His humiliation, He moved visibly upon the earth. The lapse of time has wrought no change in His parting promise to His apostles as He was taken up from them into heaven: "Lo, I am with you alway, even unto the end of the world" (Matthew 28:20). He has ordained that there should be a succession of men who derive authority from the first teachers of the faith for the continual preaching of Christ and Him crucified. The Great Teacher has delegated power to His servants, who "have this treasure in earthen vessels." Christ will superintend the work of His ambassadors if they wait for His instruction and guidance. . . .

With an earnestness and faith that will not be denied, they will plead with God that they may be strengthened and fortified for duty and for trial, and that their lips may be sanctified by a touch of the living coal from off the altar, to speak the words of God to the people. "The Lord hath given me the tongue of the learned, that I should know how to speak a word in season to him that is weary: he wakeneth morning by morning, he wakeneth mine ear to hear as the learned" (Isaiah 50:4).

Christ said to Peter: "Simon, Simon, behold, Satan hath desired to have you, that he may sift you as wheat: but I have prayed for thee, that thy faith fail not" (Luke 22:31, 32). Who can estimate the result of the prayers of the world's Redeemer? When Christ shall see the travail of His soul and be satisfied, then will be seen and realized the value of His earnest prayers while His divinity was veiled with humanity.

Jesus pleaded, not for one only, but for all His disciples: "Father, I will that they also whom thou hast given me, be with me where I am" (John 17:24). His eye pierced the dark veil of the future and read the life history of every son and daughter of Adam. He felt the burdens and sorrows of every tempest-tossed soul, and that earnest prayer included with His living disciples all His followers to the close of time. . . . That prayer . . . embraces even us. . . . When all human support fails, then Jesus comes to our aid, and His presence scatters the darkness and lifts the cloud of gloom (*Testimonies,* vol. 4, pp. 528-530).

Learning From the Divine Teacher

And He shall sit as a refiner and purifier of silver: and He shall purify the sons of Levi, and purge them as gold and silver, that they may offer unto the Lord an offering in righteousness. Malachi 3:3.

Here is the process, the refining, purifying process, to be carried on by the Lord of hosts. The work is most trying to the soul, but it is only through this process that the rubbish and defiling impurities can be removed. Our trials are all necessary to bring us close to our heavenly Father, in obedience to His will, that we may offer to the Lord an offering in righteousness. God has given each of us capabilities, talents to improve. We need a new and living experience in the divine life, in order to do the will of God. No amount of past experience will suffice for the present, or will strengthen us to overcome the difficulties in our path. We must have new grace and fresh strength daily in order to be victorious.

We are seldom, in all respects, placed in the same condition twice. . . . Each has his own experience, peculiar in its character and circumstances, to accomplish a certain work. God has a work, a purpose, in the life of each and all of us. Every act, however small, has its place in our life experience. We must have the continual light and experience that come from God. We all need them, and God is more than willing we should have them, if we will take them. He has not closed the windows of heaven to our prayers, but there are those who have felt satisfied to pass on without the divine help they so much need. . . .

We need to learn of the divine Teacher as much now as at any period of our lives, and even more. And the more experience we gain, the nearer we draw toward the pure light of heaven, the more shall we discern in ourselves that needs reforming. We may all do a good work in blessing others, if we will seek counsel of God, and follow on in obedience and faith. The path of the just is a progressive one, from strength to strength, from grace to grace, and from glory to glory. The divine illumination will increase more and more, corresponding with our onward movements, qualifying us to meet the responsibilities and emergencies before us.

Real godliness is diffusive and communicative. The psalmist says, "I have not hid thy righteousness within my heart; I have declared thy faithfulness and thy salvation. I have not concealed thy lovingkindness and thy truth from the great congregation" (Psalm 40:10). Wherever the love of God is, there is always a desire to express it. It is hard for us to submit to the crucifixion of self. . . .

We may be thoroughly converted and transformed, and be indeed children of God, enjoying not only the knowledge of His will, but leading others, by our example, in the same path of humble obedience and consecration (*Review and Herald,* June 22, 1886).

Christ's Teaching Embraced the World

When Jesus finished saying these things, the crowds were amazed at his teaching.
Matthew 7:28, NIV.

C[hrist] did not deal in abstract theories, but in that which is essential to the development of character; that which will enlarge man's capacity for knowing God, and increase his power to do good. He spoke of those truths that relate to the conduct of life and that unite man with eternity.

Instead of directing the people to study men's theories about God, His Word, or His works, He taught them to behold Him, as manifested in His works, in His Word, and by His providences. He brought their minds in contact with the mind of the Infinite.

The people "were astonished at his teaching" (Matthew 7:28, ASV); "for his word was with power" (Luke 4:32). Never before spoke one who had such power to awaken thought, to kindle aspiration, to arouse every capability of body, mind, and soul.

Christ's teaching, like His sympathies, embraced the world. Never can there be a circumstance of life, a crisis in human experience, which has not been anticipated in His teaching, and for which its principles have not a lesson. The Prince of teachers, His words will be found a guide to His co-workers till the end of time. . . . Before His mind's eye was outspread every scene of human effort and achievement, of temptation and conflict, of perplexity and peril. All hearts, all homes, all pleasures and joys and aspirations, were known to Him.

He spoke not only for, but to, all mankind. To the little child, in the gladness of life's morning; to the eager, restless heart of youth; to men in the strength of their years, bearing the burden of responsibility and care; to the aged in their weakness and weariness—to all, His message was spoken—to every child of humanity, in every land and in every age.

In His teaching were embraced the things of time and the things of eternity—things seen, in their relation to things unseen, the passing incidents of common life and the solemn issues of the life to come.

The things of this life He placed in their true relation, as subordinate to those of eternal interest; but He did not ignore their importance. He taught that heaven and earth are linked together, and that a knowledge of divine truth prepares man better to perform the duties of daily life.

To Him nothing was without purpose. The sports of the child, the toils of the man, life's pleasures and cares and pains, all were means to the one end—the revelation of God for the uplifting of humanity (*Education*, pp. 81, 82).

June
13

To Know God Is to Obey Him

If ye shall ask any thing in my name I will do it. If ye love me keep my commandments. John 14:14, 15.

In my name," Christ bade His disciples pray. In Christ's name His followers are to stand before God. Through the value of the sacrifice made for them, they are of value in the Lord's sight. Because of the imputed righteousness of Christ they are accounted precious. For Christ's sake the Lord pardons those that fear Him. He does not see in them the vileness of the sinner. He recognizes in them the likeness of His Son, in whom they believe.

The Lord is disappointed when His people place a low estimate upon themselves. He desires His chosen heritage to value themselves according to the price He has placed upon them. God wanted them, else He would not have sent His Son on such an expensive errand to redeem them. He has a use for them, and He is well pleased when they make the very highest demands upon Him, that they may glorify His name. They may expect larger things if they have faith in His promises.

But to pray in Christ's name means much. It means that we are to accept His character, manifest His spirit, and work His works. The Savior's promise is given on condition. "If ye love me," He says, "keep my commandments." He saves men, not in sin, but from sin; and those who love Him will show their love by obedience.

All true obedience comes from the heart. It was heart work with Christ. And if we consent, He will so identify Himself with our thoughts and aims, so blend our hearts and minds into conformity to His will, that when obeying Him we shall be but carrying out our own impulses. The will, refined and sanctified, will find its highest delight in doing His service. When we know God as it is our privilege to know Him, our life will be a life of continual obedience. Through an appreciation of the character of Christ, through communion with God, sin will become hateful to us.

As Christ lived the law in humanity, so we may do if we will take hold of the Strong for strength. But we are not to place the responsibility of our duty upon others, and wait for them to tell us what to do. We cannot depend for counsel upon humanity. The Lord will teach us our duty just as willingly as He will teach somebody else. If we come to Him in faith, He will speak His mysteries to us personally. Our hearts will often burn within us as One draws nigh to commune with us as He did with Enoch. Those who decide to do nothing in any line that will displease God will know, after presenting their case before Him, just what course to pursue. And they will receive not only wisdom, but strength. Power for obedience, for service, will be imparted to them, as Christ has promised (*The Desire of Ages,* pp. 667, 668).

The Holy Spirit Given to Teach Us

When he, the Spirit of truth, is come, he will guide you into all truth. John 16:13.

Before offering Himself as the sacrificial victim, Christ sought for the most essential and complete gift to bestow upon His followers, a gift that would bring within their reach the boundless resources of grace. "I will pray the Father," He said, "and he shall give you another Comforter, that he may abide with you for ever; even the Spirit of truth; whom the world cannot receive, because it seeth him not, neither knoweth him: but ye know him; for he dwelleth with you, and shall be in you. I will not leave you orphans: I will come to you" (John 14:16-18, margin).

Before this the Spirit had been in the world; from the very beginning of the work of redemption He had been moving upon men's hearts. But while Christ was on earth, the disciples had desired no other helper. Not until they were deprived of His presence would they feel their need of the Spirit, and then He would come.

The Holy Spirit is Christ's representative, but divested of the personality of humanity, and independent thereof. Cumbered with humanity, Christ could not be in every place personally. Therefore it was for their interest that He should go to the Father, and send the Spirit to be His successor on earth. No one could then have any advantage because of his location or his personal contact with Christ. By the Spirit the Savior would be accessible to all. In this sense He would be nearer to them if He had not ascended on high. . . .

At all times and in all places, in all sorrows and in all afflictions, when the outlook seems dark and the future perplexing, and we feel helpless and alone, the Comforter will be sent in answer to the prayer of faith. Circumstances may separate us from every earthly friend; but no circumstance, no distance, can separate us from the heavenly Comforter. Wherever we are, wherever we may go, He is always at our right hand to support, sustain, uphold, and cheer. . . .

The Comforter is called "the Spirit of truth." His work is to define and maintain the truth. He first dwells in the heart as the Spirit of truth, and thus He becomes the Comforter. There is comfort and peace in the truth, but no real peace or comfort can be found in falsehood. It is through false theories and traditions that Satan gains his power over the mind. By directing men to false standards, he misshapes the character. Through the Scriptures the Holy Spirit speaks to the mind, and impresses truth upon the heart. Thus He exposes error, and expels it from the soul. It is by the Spirit of truth, working through the Word of God, that Christ subdues His chosen people to Himself (*The Desire of Ages,* pp. 668-671).

June
15

Christ's Method of Teaching

How beautiful upon the mountains are the feet of him that bringeth good tidings, that publisheth peace; . . . that saith unto Zion, Thy God reigneth. Isaiah 52:7.

In all the sermons and in all the Bible studies, let the people see that on every point a plain "Thus saith the Lord" is given for the faith and doctrines which we advocate.

This was the method of Christ's teaching. As He spoke to the people, they would question as to His meaning. To those who were humbly seeking for light, He was always ready to explain His words. But Christ did not encourage criticism or caviling, nor should we. When men try to provoke a discussion of controverted points of doctrine, tell them that the meeting was not appointed for that purpose. When you do answer a question, be sure to have the hearers see and acknowledge that it is answered. Do not let a question drop, telling them to ask it again. Feel your way step by step, and know how much you have gained (*Testimonies,* vol. 6, p. 69).

We must talk the truth in private and in public, presenting every argument, urging every motive of infinite weight, to draw men to the Savior uplifted on the cruel cross. God desires every man to attain unto eternal life. Mark how all through the Word of God there is manifest the spirit of urgency, of imploring men and women to come to Christ, to deny appetites and passions that corrupt the soul. With all our powers we must urge them to look unto Jesus and to accept His life of self-denial and sacrifice. We must show that we expect them to give joy to the heart of Christ by using every one of His gifts in honoring His name. . . .

Let much time be spent in prayer and close searching of the Word. Let all obtain the real facts of faith in their own souls through belief that the Holy Spirit will be imparted to them because they have a real hungering and thirsting after righteousness. Teach them how to surrender themselves to God, how to believe, how to claim the promises. Let the deep love of God be expressed in words of encouragement, in words of intercession.

Let there be far more wrestling with God for the salvation of souls. Work disinterestedly, determinedly, with a spirit never to let go. Compel souls to come in to the marriage supper of the Lamb. Let there be more praying, believing, and receiving, and more working together with God. . . .

Men must be convicted of the evil of sin. The eyes of the transgressor must be enlightened. Let all who have been drawn to Christ tell the story of His love. Let everyone who has felt the converting power of Christ upon his own soul do what he can in the name of the Lord (*ibid.,* pp. 65, 66).

The Humble Searcher May Learn

Shew me thy way, O Lord; teach me thy paths. Psalm 25:4.

Revelation is not the creation or invention of something new, but the manifestation of that which, until revealed, was unknown to human beings. The great and eternal truths contained in the gospel are revealed through diligent searching and humbling of ourselves before God. We have a divine Teacher who leads the mind of the humble searcher for truth; and by the Holy Spirit's guidance, the truths of the Word are revealed to him. And there can be no more certain and efficient knowledge of the truth than to be thus guided into all truth. Through the impartation of the Holy Spirit, we are to understand God's Word. We are admonished to seek the truth as if searching for hidden treasure.

The Lord opens the understanding of the true seeker. The Holy Spirit enables the human mind to grasp the facts of revelation, and divine light communicates with the soul. This is the opening of the eyes to behold the genuine treasure, and the mind lays hold upon the glories of a better world. The soul pants after the excellence of Christ Jesus (manuscript 59, 1906).

Jesus was the greatest teacher the world ever knew. He presented truth in clear, forcible statements, and the illustrations He used were of the purest and highest order. He never mingled cheap symbols and figures with His divine instruction, or sought to pander to curiosity or to gratify the class that will listen simply to be amused. He did not bring sacred truth down to the level of the common. . . . His words were of the purest and most elevated. . . . He did not humble the truth to meet man in his fallen condition, and lower the standard of righteousness to suit his degradation; but He humbled Himself, and became obedient unto death, even the death of the cross, in order that He might save the race that had been degraded by transgression. It was not His purpose to abolish by His death the law of God, but rather to show the immutability of its sacred claims. It was His purpose to "magnify the law, and make it honourable," so that every one who should look upon the cross of Calvary with its uplifted Victim should see the unanswerable argument of the perfect truth of the law. . . .

He rescued truth, eternal truth, from the base companionship of error, and commanded it to shine forth in all its brightness and heavenly luster. He set the truth on high, in order that like a light it might illuminate the moral darkness of the world. . . . Jesus restored truth that had been cast out, to its royal order, and invested it with its true importance and dignity. Christ Himself was the truth and the life (*Review and Herald,* Aug. 6, 1895).

June
17

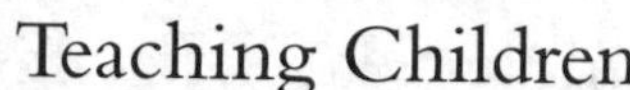

Teaching Children

Suffer the little children to come unto me, and forbid them not: for of such is the kingdom of heaven. Mark 10:14.

Jesus knows the burdens of every mother's heart. He who had a mother that struggled with poverty and privation sympathizes with every mother in her labors. He who made a long journey in order to relieve the anxious heart of a Canaanite woman will do as much for the mothers of today. He who gave back to the widow of Nain her only son, and in His agony upon the cross remembered His own mother, is touched today by the mother's sorrow. In every grief and every need, He will comfort and help. . . .

In the children who were brought in contact with Him, Jesus saw the men and women who should be heirs of His grace and subjects of His kingdom, and some of whom would become martyrs for His sake. He knew that these children would listen to Him and accept Him as their Redeemer far more readily than would grown-up people, many of whom were the worldly-wise and hard-hearted. In teaching, He came down to their level. He, the Majesty of heaven, answered their questions and simplified His important lessons to meet their childish understanding. He planted in their minds the seeds of truth, which in after years would spring up and bear fruit unto eternal life.

When Jesus told the disciples not to forbid the children to come to Him, He was speaking to His followers in all ages—to officers of the church, ministers, helpers, and all Christians. Jesus is drawing the children, and He bids us, "Suffer them to come"; as if He would say, They will come, if you do not hinder them. . . .

As the Holy Spirit moves upon the hearts of the children, cooperate with His work. Teach them that the Savior is calling them, that nothing can afford Him greater joy than for them to give themselves to Him in the bloom and freshness of their years.

The Savior regards with infinite tenderness the souls whom He has purchased with His blood. They are the claim of His love. He looks upon them with unutterable longing. His heart is drawn out, not only to the best-trained and most attractive children, but to those who by inheritance and through neglect have objectionable traits of character. Many parents do not understand how much they are responsible for these traits in their children. . . . Jesus looks upon these children with pity. He traces from cause to effect.

The Christian worker may be Christ's agent in drawing these faulty and erring ones to the Savior. By wisdom and tact he may bind them to his heart, he may give courage and hope, and through the grace of Christ may see them transformed in character, so that of them it may be said, "Of such is the kingdom of God" (*The Ministry of Healing,* pp. 42-44).

By the Ties of Human Sympathy

There cometh a woman of Samaria to draw water: Jesus saith unto her, Give me to drink. John 4:7.

He [Christ] passed by no human being as worthless, but sought to apply the healing remedy to every soul. In whatever company He found Himself He presented a lesson appropriate to the time and the circumstances. Every neglect or insult shown by men to their fellowmen only made Him more conscious of their need of His divine-human sympathy. He sought to inspire with hope the roughest and most unpromising, setting before them the assurance that they might become blameless and harmless, attaining such a character as would make them manifest as the children of God. . . .

Though He was a Jew, Jesus mingled freely with the Samaritans, setting at nought the Pharisaic customs of His nation. In face of their prejudices He accepted the hospitality of this despised people. He slept with them under their roofs, ate with them at their tables—partaking of the food prepared and served by their hands—taught in their streets, and treated them with the utmost kindness and courtesy. And while He drew their hearts to Him by the tie of human sympathy, His divine grace brought to them the salvation which the Jews rejected.

Christ neglected no opportunity of proclaiming the gospel of salvation. Listen to His wonderful words to that one woman of Samaria. He was sitting by Jacob's well, as the woman came to draw water. To her surprise He asked a favor of her. "Give me to drink," He said. He wanted a cool draft, and He wished also to open the way whereby He might give to her the water of life. "How is it," said the woman, "that thou, being a Jew, askest drink of me, which am a woman of Samaria? for the Jews have no dealings with the Samaritans." Jesus answered, "If thou knewest the gift of God, and who it is that saith to thee, Give me to drink; thou wouldest have asked of him, and he would have given thee living water" (John 4:7-10). . . .

How much interest Christ manifested in this one woman! How earnest and eloquent were His words! When the woman heard them, she left her waterpot, and went into the city, saying to her friends, "Come, see a man, which told me all things that ever I did: is not this the Christ?" We read that "many of the Samaritans of that city believed on him" (verses 29, 39). And who can estimate the influence which these words have exerted for the saving of souls in the years that have passed since then?

Wherever hearts are open to receive the truth, Christ is ready to instruct them. He reveals to them the Father, and the service acceptable to Him who reads the heart. For such He uses no parables. To them, as to the woman at the well, He says, "I that speak unto thee am he" (*The Ministry of Healing*, pp. 25-28).

June
19

A Satisfying Fountain

If thou knewest the gift of God, and who it is that saith to thee, Give me to drink; thou wouldest have asked of him, and he would have given thee living water. John 4:10.

What said Christ to the Samaritan woman at Jacob's well? . . . "The water that I shall give . . . shall be . . . a well of water springing up into everlasting life." The water that Christ referred to was the revelation of His grace in His Word; His Spirit, His teaching, is as a satisfying fountain to every soul. Every other source to which they shall resort will prove unsatisfying. But the word of truth is as cool streams, represented as the waters of Lebanon, which are always satisfying. In Christ is fullness of joy forevermore. The desires and pleasures and amusements of the world are never satisfying nor healing to the soul. But Jesus says, "Whoso eateth my flesh, and drinketh my blood, hath eternal life."

Christ's gracious presence in His Word is ever speaking to the soul, representing Him as the well of living water to refresh the thirsting soul. It is our privilege to have a living, abiding Savior. He is the source of spiritual power implanted within us, and His influence will flow forth in words and actions, refreshing all within the sphere of our influence, begetting in them desires and aspirations for strength and purity, for holiness and peace, and for that joy which brings no sorrow with it. This is the result of an indwelling Savior.

Jesus said, "Lo, I am with you alway, even unto the end of the world." He walked once a man on earth, His divinity clothed with humanity, a suffering, tempted man, beset with Satan's devices. He was tempted in all points like as we are, and He knows how to succor those that are tempted. Now He is at the right hand of God. He is in heaven as our advocate, to make intercession for us. We must always take comfort and hope as we think of this. He is thinking of those who are subject to temptations in this world. He thinks of us individually, and knows our every necessity. When tempted, just say, He cares for me, He makes intercession for me, He loves me, He has died for me. I will give myself unreservedly to Him.

We grieve the heart of Christ when we go mourning over ourselves as though we were our own savior. No; we must commit the keeping of our souls to God as unto a faithful Creator. He ever lives to make intercession for the tried, tempted ones. Open your heart to the bright beams of the Sun of Righteousness, and let not one breath of doubt, one word of unbelief, escape your lips, lest you sow the seeds of doubt. There are rich blessings for us; let us grasp them by faith. I entreat you to have courage in the Lord. Divine strength is ours; and let us talk courage and strength and faith. . . . Bear a living testimony for God under all circumstances (*Testimonies to Ministers*, pp. 390, 391).

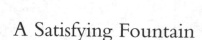

True Higher Education

Teach me to do thy will; for thou art my God; thy spirit is good; lead me into the land of uprightness. Psalm 143:10.

Rejoice in the Lord alway: and again I say, Rejoice." Those who do this have a joyous life. No unpleasantness comes from their lips or from the atmosphere surrounding the soul, for they do not feel that they are better than others. Hide in Jesus Christ; then all the time the truth of God will be fitting you up for the future, immortal life. When you have confidence in the Mighty One, your experience is not borrowed; it is your own. Whatever your disposition may be, God is able to so mold that disposition that it will be sweet and Christlike. By living faith you separate from everything not in accordance with the mind of God, and thus bring a heaven into your life here below. Will you do this? If you do, you will have sunshine at every step. . . .

True higher education is that which is received by sitting at the feet of Jesus. Humble yourselves under the mighty hand of God, and He will lift you up. You need not struggle to lift yourself. Commit your work to Him; do it in faithfulness, in sincerity, in truth, in righteousness; and you will find that every day it brings its reward, and that the light of heaven is shining upon you. His light, His grace, His salvation, are thus revealed. . . .

We know so little of Jesus Christ that we can but dimly comprehend what He will do for us. God desires us to learn of Him. . . . Let your character-building be in accordance with the beautiful pattern revealed to men in the life of Christ.

In all your work you should do as the husbandman does in producing the fruits of the earth. Apparently he throws away the seed; but, buried in the soil, the seed, in dying, germinates. The power of the living God gives it life and vitality, and there is seen, "first the blade, then the ear, after that the full corn in the ear." Study this wonderful process. Oh, there is so much to learn, so much to understand, that it seems as though we cannot learn everything during this life—and we cannot. But if we now improve our minds to the utmost of our ability, we shall through the eternal ages carry forward the study of God's ways and works, continually reaching higher and still higher.

We need now minds that can understand the simplicity of godliness. More than we desire anything else, we should desire to have Jesus Christ abiding in the soul-temple, because He cannot abide there without being revealed and shown forth in fruits and good works. . . . God wants every one of you to be His helping hand; and if you yield yourself to Him, He will teach and work through you, that you may be able to impart to others. Then you will be able to say, "O God, 'thy gentleness hath made me great'!" (manuscript 91, 1901).

June
21

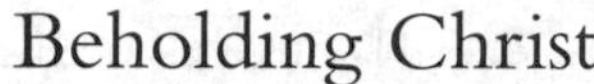

Beholding Christ

God hath said, I will dwell in them, and walk in them; and I will be their God, and they shall be my people. 2 Corinthians 6:16.

As the mind dwells upon Christ, the character is molded after the divine similitude. The thoughts are pervaded with a sense of His goodness, His love. We contemplate His character, and thus He is in all our thoughts. His love encloses us.

If we gaze even a moment upon the sun in its meridian glory, when we turn away our eyes, the image of the sun will appear in everything upon which we look. Thus it is when we behold Jesus; everything we look upon reflects His image, the Sun of righteousness. We cannot see anything else, or talk of anything else. His image is imprinted upon the eye of the soul and affects every portion of our daily life, softening and subduing our whole nature. By beholding, we are conformed to the divine similitude, even the likeness of Christ. To all with whom we associate we reflect the bright and cheerful beams of His righteousness. We have become transformed in character; for heart, soul, mind, are irradiated by the reflection of Him who loved us and gave Himself for us. Here again there is the realization of a personal, living influence dwelling in our hearts by faith.

When His words of instruction have been received, and have taken possession of us, Jesus is to us an abiding presence, controlling our thoughts and ideas and actions. We are imbued with the instruction of the greatest Teacher the world ever knew. A sense of human accountability and of human influence gives character to our views of life and of daily duties. Jesus Christ is everything to us—the first, the last, the best in everything. Jesus Christ, His Spirit, His character, colors everything; it is the warp and the woof, the very texture of our entire being. The words of Christ are spirit and life. We cannot, then, center our thoughts upon self; it is no more we that live, but Christ that liveth in us, and He is the hope of glory. Self is dead, but Christ is a living Savior.

Continuing to look unto Jesus, we reflect His image to all around us. We cannot stop to consider our disappointments, or even to talk of them; for a more pleasant picture attracts our sight—the precious love of Jesus. He dwells in us by the word of truth (*Testimonies to Ministers*, pp. 388-390).

We have a high calling in Christ Jesus; we are carrying forward a vast and holy work, and God calls upon each one to uplift His standard in the sight of this world and of the universe of heaven, by the power of the Lord Jehovah, in whom is "everlasting strength" (*ibid.*, p. 386).

We Are Blessed as We Teach Others

He that watereth shall be watered also himself. Proverbs 11:25.

The teaching of Christ was the expression of an inwrought conviction and experience, and those who learn of Him become teachers after the divine order. The Word of God, spoken by one who is himself sanctified through it, has a life-giving power that makes it attractive to the hearers, and convicts them that it is a living reality. When one has received the truth in the love of it, he will make this manifest in the persuasion of his manner and the tones of his voice. He makes known that which he himself has heard, seen, and handled of the Word of life, that others may have fellowship with him through the knowledge of Christ. His testimony, from lips touched with a live coal from off the altar, is truth to the receptive heart, and works sanctification upon the character.

And he who seeks to give light to others will himself be blessed. "There shall be showers of blessing." "He that watereth shall be watered also himself." God could have reached His object in saving sinners without our aid; but in order for us to develop a character like Christ's, we must share in His work. In order to enter into His joy—the joy of seeing souls redeemed by His sacrifice—we must participate in His labors for their redemption.

Nathanael's first expression of his faith, so full and earnest and sincere, fell like music on the ears of Jesus. And He "answered and said unto him, Because I said unto thee, I saw thee under the fig tree, believest thou? thou shalt see greater things than these." The Savior looked forward with joy to His work in preaching good tidings to the meek, binding up the broken-hearted, and proclaiming liberty to the captives of Satan. At thought of the precious blessings He had brought to men, Jesus added, "Verily, verily, I say unto you, Hereafter ye shall see heaven open, and the angels of God ascending and descending upon the Son of man."

Here Christ virtually says, On the bank of the Jordan the heavens were opened, and the Spirit descended like a dove upon Me. That scene was but a token that I am the Son of God. If you believe on Me as such, your faith shall be quickened. You shall see that the heavens are opened, and are never to be closed. I have opened them to you. The angels of God are ascending, bearing the prayers of the needy and distressed to the Father above, and descending, bringing blessing and hope, courage, help, and life, to the children of men

The angels of God are ever passing from earth to heaven, and from heaven to earth. . . . And thus Christ is the medium of communication of men with God, and of God with men (*The Desire of Ages*, pp. 142, 143).

June
23

Students in the School of Christ

His delight is in the law of the Lord; and in his law doth he meditate day and night. Psalm 1:2.

The mind that dwells much on the revealed will of God to man will become strong in the truth. Those who read and study with an earnest desire for divine light, whether they are ministers or not, will soon discover in the Scriptures a beauty and harmony which will captivate their attention, elevate their thoughts, and give them an inspiration and an energy of argument that will be powerful to convict and convert souls. . . .

The psalmist declares of the good man: "His delight is in the law of the Lord; and in his law doth he meditate day and night." He refers to his own experience, and exclaims: "O how love I thy law! it is my meditation all the day." "Mine eyes prevent the night watches, that I might meditate in thy word." . . .

Said Jesus to His disciples: "Learn of me; for I am meek and lowly in heart." I would plead with those who have accepted the position of teachers, to first become humble learners, and ever to remain as pupils in the school of Christ to receive from the Master lessons of meekness and lowliness of heart. Humility of spirit, combined with earnest activity, will result in the salvation of souls so dearly purchased by the blood of Christ. . . . "Faith without works is dead." He needs that faith that works by love and purifies the soul. A living faith in Christ will bring every action of the life and every emotion of the soul into harmony with God's truth and righteousness.

Fretfulness, self-exaltation, pride, passion, and every other trait of character unlike our holy Pattern must be overcome; and then humility, meekness, and sincere gratitude to Jesus for His great salvation will continually flow out from the pure fountain of the heart. The voice of Jesus should be heard in the message coming from the lips of His ambassador. . . .

If those who sound the solemn notes of warning for this time could realize their accountability to God they would see the necessity for fervent prayer. When the cities were hushed in midnight slumber, when every man had gone to his own house, Christ, our Example, would repair to the Mount of Olives, and there, amid the overshadowing trees, would spend the entire night in prayer. He who was Himself without the taint of sin—a treasure house of blessing; whose voice was heard in the fourth watch of the night by the terrified disciples upon the stormy sea, in heavenly benediction; and whose word could summon the dead from their graves—He it was who made supplication with strong crying and tears. He prayed not for Himself, but for those whom He came to save (*Testimonies*, vol. 4, pp. 526-528).

Bear a Living Testimony

As thou hast sent me into the world, even so have I also sent them into the world. John 17:18.

Because of the increasing power of Satan's temptations, the times in which we live are full of peril for the children of God, and we need to learn constantly of the Great Teacher, that we may take every step in surety and righteousness. Wonderful scenes are opening before us; and at this time a living testimony is to be borne in the lives of God's professed people, so that the world may see that in this age, when evil reigns on every side, there is yet a people who are laying aside their will and are seeking to do God's will—a people in whose hearts and lives God's law is written.

God expects those who bear the name of Christ to represent Him. Their thoughts are to be pure, their words noble and uplifting. The religion of Christ is to be interwoven with all that they do and say. They are to be a sanctified, purified, holy people, communicating light to all with whom they come in contact. It is His purpose that by exemplifying the truth in their lives they shall be a praise in the earth. The grace of Christ is sufficient to bring this about. But let God's people remember that only as they believe and work out the principles of the gospel can they fulfill His purpose. Only as they yield their God-given capabilities to His service will they enjoy the fullness and the power of the promise whereon the church has been called to stand. . . .

The followers of Christ are to be separate from the world in principles and interests; but they are not to isolate themselves from the world. The Savior mingled constantly with men, not to encourage them in anything that was not in accordance with God's will, but to uplift and ennoble them. . . . So the Christian is to abide among men, that the savor of divine love may be as salt to preserve the world from corruption.

Daily beset by temptation, constantly opposed by the leaders of the people, Christ knew that He must strengthen His humanity by prayer. In order to be a blessing to men, He must commune with God, pleading for energy, perseverance, and steadfastness. . . . Without this daily communion with God, no human being can gain power for service. Christ alone can direct the thoughts aright. He alone can give noble aspirations and fashion the character after the divine similitude. If we draw near to Him in earnest prayer, He will fill our hearts with high and holy purposes, and with deep longings for purity and righteousness. . . .

God desires His people to show by their lives the advantage of Christianity over worldliness; to show that they are working on a high, holy plane. . . . He longs to make them channels through which He can pour His boundless love and mercy (*Counsels to Parents, Teachers, and Students,* pp. 322-324).

He Was All He Claimed

He that believeth on me, the works that I do shall he do also; and greater works than these shall he do; because I go unto my Father. John 14:12.

After the Lord's ascension, the disciples realized the fulfillment of His promise. The scenes of the crucifixion, resurrection, and ascension of Christ were a living reality to them. They saw that the prophecies had been literally fulfilled. They searched the Scriptures, and accepted their teaching with a faith and assurance unknown before. They knew that the divine Teacher was all that He had claimed to be. As they told their experience, and exalted the love of God, men's hearts were melted and subdued, and multitudes believed on Jesus.

The Savior's promise to His disciples is a promise to His church to the end of time. God did not design that His wonderful plan to redeem men should achieve only insignificant results. All who will go to work, trusting not in what they themselves can do, but in what God can do for and through them, will certainly realize the fulfillment of His promise. "Greater works than these shall he do," He declares; "because I go unto my Father."

As yet the disciples were unacquainted with the Savior's unlimited resources and power. He said to them, "Hitherto have ye asked nothing in my name" (John 16:24). He explained that the secret of their success would be in asking for strength and grace in His name. He would be present before the Father to make request for them. The prayer of the humble suppliant He presents as His own desire in that soul's behalf. Every sincere prayer is heard in heaven. It may not be fluently expressed; but if the heart is in it, it will ascend to the sanctuary where Jesus ministers, and He will present it to the Father without one awkward, stammering word, beautiful and fragrant with the incense of His own perfection.

The pathway of sincerity and integrity is not a path free from obstruction, but in every difficulty we are to see a call to prayer. There is no one living who has any power that he has not received from God, and the source whence it comes is open to the weakest human being. "Whatsoever ye shall ask in my name," said Jesus, "that will I do, that the Father may be glorified in the Son. If ye shall ask any thing in my name, I will do it" (John 14:13, 14) (*The Desire of Ages,* p. 667).

The Savior was deeply anxious for His disciples to understand for what purpose His divinity was united to humanity. He came to the world to display the glory of God, that man might be uplifted by its restoring power. God was manifested in Him that He might be manifested in them. Jesus revealed no qualities, and exercised no powers, that men may not have through faith in Him. His perfect humanity is that which all His followers may possess, if they will be in subjection to God as He was (*ibid.,* p. 664).

Christ's Favorite Subject

It is expedient for you that I go away: for if I go not away, the Comforter will not come unto you; but if I depart, I will send him unto you. And when he is come, he will reprove the world of sin, and of righteousness, and of judgment. John 16:7, 8.

Christ, the Great Teacher, had an infinite variety of subjects from which to choose, but the one upon which He dwelt most largely was the endowment of the Holy Spirit (*Selected Messages,* book 1, p. 156).

In describing to His disciples the office work of the Holy Spirit, Jesus sought to inspire them with the joy and hope that inspired His own heart. He rejoiced because of the abundant help He had provided for His church. The Holy Spirit was the highest of all gifts that He could solicit from His Father for the exaltation of His people. The Spirit was to be given as a regenerating agent, and without this the sacrifice of Christ would have been of no avail. The power of evil had been strengthening for centuries, and the submission of men to this satanic captivity was amazing. Sin could be resisted and overcome only through the mighty agency of the Third Person of the Godhead, who would come with no modified energy, but in the fullness of divine power. It is the Spirit that makes effectual what has been wrought out by the world's Redeemer. It is by the Spirit that the heart is made pure. Through the Spirit the believer becomes a partaker of the divine nature. Christ has given His Spirit as a divine power to overcome all hereditary and cultivated tendencies to evil, and to impress His own character upon His church.

Of the Spirit Jesus said, "He shall glorify me." The Savior came to glorify the Father by the demonstration of His love; so the Spirit was to glorify Christ by revealing His grace to the world. The very image of God is to be reproduced in humanity. The honor of God, the honor of Christ, is involved in the perfection of the character of His people.

"When he [the Spirit of truth] is come, He will reprove the world of sin, and of righteousness, and of judgment." The preaching of the Word will be of no avail without the continual presence and aid of the Holy Spirit. This is the only effectual teacher of divine truth. Only when the truth is accompanied to the heart by the Spirit will it quicken the conscience or transform the life. One might be able to present the letter of the Word of God, he might be familiar with all its commands and promises; but unless the Holy Spirit sets home the truth, no souls will fall on the Rock and be broken. No amount of education, no advantages, however great, can make one a channel of light without the cooperation of the Spirit of God. . . . This promised blessing, claimed by faith, brings all other blessings in its train. It is given according to the riches of the grace of Christ, and He is ready to supply every soul according to the capacity to receive (*The Desire of Ages,* pp. 671, 672).

The Highest of All Education

And let us not be weary in well doing: for in due season we shall reap, if we faint not.
Galatians 6:9.

Christ calls upon us to labor patiently and perseveringly for the thousands perishing in their sins, scattered in all lands, like wrecks on a desert shore. Those who share in Christ's glory must share also in His ministry, helping the weak, the wretched, and the despondent.

Let those who take up this work make the life of Christ their constant study. Let them be intensely in earnest, using every capability in the Lord's service. Precious results will follow sincere, unselfish effort. From the Great Teacher the workers will receive the highest of all education. But those who do not impart the light they have received will one day realize that they have sustained a fearful loss.

Human beings have no right to think that there is a limit to the efforts that they are to make in the work of soul saving. Did Christ ever become weary in His work? Did He ever draw back from sacrifice and hardship? Church members are to put forth the continuous, persevering efforts that He put forth. They are to be ever ready to spring into action in obedience to the Master's commands. Wherever we see work waiting to be done we are to take it up and do it, constantly looking unto Jesus. If our church members would heed this instruction, hundreds of souls would be won to Jesus. If every church member were a living missionary, the gospel would speedily be proclaimed in all countries, to all peoples, nations, and tongues.

Let sanctified ability be brought into the work of proclaiming the truth for this time. If the forces of the enemy gain the victory now, it will be because the churches neglect their God-given work. For years the work has been kept before us, but many have been asleep. If Seventh-day Adventists will now arouse and do the work assigned them, the truth will be presented to our neglected cities in clear, distinct lines and in the power of the Spirit.

When wholehearted work is done, the efficacy of the grace of Christ will be seen. The watchmen on the walls of Zion are to be wide awake, and they are to arouse others. God's people are to be so earnest and faithful in their work for Him that all selfishness will be separated from their lives. His workers will then see eye-to-eye, and the arm of the Lord, the power of which was seen in the life of Christ, will be revealed. Confidence will be restored, and there will be unity in the churches throughout our ranks. . . . To every worker Christ promises the divine efficiency that will make his labors a success (*Testimonies,* vol. 9, pp. 31-34).

God Himself Was Daniel's Teacher

Them that honour me I will honour. 1 Samuel 2:30.

In acquiring the wisdom of the Babylonians, Daniel and his companions were far more successful than their fellow students; but their learning did not come by chance. They obtained their knowledge by the faithful use of their powers, under the guidance of the Holy Spirit. They placed themselves in connection with the Source of all wisdom, making the knowledge of God the foundation of their education. In faith they prayed for wisdom, and they lived their prayers. They placed themselves where God could bless them. They avoided that which would weaken their powers, and improved every opportunity to become intelligent in all lines of learning. They followed the rules of life that could not fail to give them strength of intellect. They sought to acquire knowledge for one purpose—that they might honor God. They realized that in order to stand as representatives of true religion amid the false religions of heathenism they must have clearness of intellect and must perfect a Christian character. And God Himself was their teacher. Constantly praying, conscientiously studying, keeping in touch with the Unseen, they walked with God as did Enoch.

True success in any line of work is not the result of chance or accident or destiny. It is the outworking of God's providences, the reward of faith and discretion, of virtue and perseverance. Fine mental qualities and a high moral tone are not the result of accident. God gives opportunities; success depends upon the use made of them.

While God was working in Daniel and his companions "to will and to do of His good pleasure" (Philippians 2:13), they were working out their own salvation. Herein is revealed the outworking of the divine principle of cooperation, without which no true success can be attained. Human effort avails nothing without divine power; and without human endeavor, divine effort is with many of no avail. To make God's grace our own, we must act our part. His grace is given to work in us to will and to do, but never as a substitute for our effort.

As the Lord cooperated with Daniel and his fellows, so He will cooperate with all who strive to do His will. And by the impartation of His Spirit He will strengthen every true purpose, every noble resolution. Those who walk in the path of obedience will encounter many hindrances. Strong, subtle influences may bind them to the world; but the Lord is able to render futile every agency that works for the defeat of His chosen ones; in His strength they may overcome every temptation, conquer every difficulty (*Prophets and Kings,* pp. 486, 487).

Taught by the World's Greatest Educator

Cast the net on the right side of the ship, and ye shall find. They cast therefore, and now they were not able to draw it for the multitude of fishes. John 21:6.

Seven of the disciples were in company. They were clad in the humble garb of fishermen; they were poor in worldly goods, but rich in the knowledge and practice of the truth, which in the sight of Heaven gave them the highest rank as teachers. They had not been students in the schools of the prophets, but for three years they had been taught by the greatest Educator the world has ever known. Under His instruction they had become elevated, intelligent, and refined, agents through whom men might be led to a knowledge of the truth. . . .

The evening was pleasant, and Peter, who still had much of his old love for boats and fishing, proposed that they should go out upon the sea and cast their nets. In this plan all were ready to join; they were in need of food and clothing, which the proceeds of a successful night's fishing would supply. So they went out in their boat, but they caught nothing. All night they toiled, without success. Through the weary hours they talked of their absent Lord, and recalled the wonderful events they had witnessed in His ministry beside the sea. They questioned as to their own future, and grew sad at the prospect before them.

All the while a lone watcher upon the shore followed them with His eye, while He Himself was unseen. At length the morning dawned. The boat was but a little way from the shore, and the disciples saw a stranger standing upon the beach, who accosted them with the question, "Children, have ye any meat?" When they answered, "No," He said unto them, "Cast the net on the right side of the ship, and ye shall find. They cast therefore, and now they were not able to draw it for the multitude of fishes."

John recognized the stranger, and exclaimed to Peter, "It is the Lord." . . . Jesus had called them to leave their fishing boats, and had promised to make them fishers of men. It was to bring this scene to their minds, and to deepen its impression, that He had again performed the miracle. His act was a renewal of the commission to the disciples. It showed them that the death of their Master had not lessened their obligation to do the work He had assigned them. Though they were to be deprived of His personal companionship, and of the means of support by their former employment, the risen Savior would still have a care for them. While they were doing His work, He would provide for their needs. And Jesus had a purpose in bidding them cast their net on the right side of the ship. On that side He stood upon the shore. That was the side of faith. If they labored in connection with Him—His divine power combining with their human effort—they could not fail of success (*The Desire of Ages,* pp. 809-811).

Putting the Word of God Into Practice

Therefore whosoever heareth these sayings of Mine, and doeth them, I will liken him unto a wise man, which built his house upon a rock . . . and it fell not: for it was founded upon a rock.
Matthew 7:24, 25.

Jesus ended His teaching on the mount with an illustration that presented with startling vividness the importance of putting in practice the words He had spoken. Among the crowds that thronged about the Savior were many who had spent their lives about the Sea of Galilee. As they sat upon the hillside, listening to the words of Christ, they could see valleys and ravines through which the mountain streams found their way to the sea. In summer these streams often wholly disappeared, leaving only a dry and dusty channel. But when the wintry storms burst upon the hills, the rivers became fierce, raging torrents, at times overspreading the valleys and bearing everything away on their resistless flood. . . . But high upon the hills were houses built upon the rock. In some parts of the land were dwellings built wholly of rock, and many of them had withstood the tempests of a thousand years. . . . And wind and flood and tempest beat upon them in vain.

Like the builders of these houses on the rock, said Jesus, is he who shall receive the words that I have spoken to you, and make them the foundation of his character and life. Centuries before, the prophet Isaiah had written, "The word of our God shall stand for ever" (Isaiah 40:8); and Peter, long after the Sermon on the Mount was given, quoting these words of Isaiah, added, "This is the word which by the gospel is preached unto you (1 Peter 1:25). The Word of God is the only steadfast thing our world knows. It is the sure foundation. "Heaven and earth shall pass away," said Jesus, "but my words shall not pass away" (Matthew 24:35).

The great principles of the law, of the very nature of God, are embodied in the words of Christ on the mount. Whoever builds upon them is building upon Christ, the Rock of Ages. In receiving the word, we receive Christ. And only those who thus receive His words are building upon Him. "Other foundation can no man lay than that is laid, which is Jesus Christ" (1 Corinthians 3:11). "There is none other name under heaven, given among men, whereby we must be saved" (Acts 4:12). Christ, the Word, the revelation of God—the manifestation of His character, His law, His love, His life—is the only foundation upon which we can build a character that will endure. . . .

As you give heed to the light you have, greater light will come. You are building on God's Word, and your character will be builded after the similitude of the character of Christ. Christ, the true foundation, is a living stone; His life is imparted to all that are built upon Him. "Ye also, as living stones, are built up a spiritual house" (1 Peter 2:5, ASV). . . . That building no tempest can overthrow (*Thoughts From the Mount of Blessing*, pp. 147-150).

Christ Is the Chief Shepherd

When the chief Shepherd shall appear, ye shall receive a crown of glory that fadeth not away. 1 Peter 5:4.

A shepherd's life was one of diligence. He was obliged to watch his flocks day and night. Wild beasts were common, and often bold, and would do great injury to flocks of sheep and cattle that were not guarded by a faithful shepherd. Although Jacob had a number of servants to aid him in tending the flocks owned by himself and Laban, yet the responsibility of the whole matter rested upon him. And in some seasons of the year he was obliged to be with the flocks himself, day and night, to protect them in the driest season of the year, that they should not perish with thirst; and in the coldest part of the season, to save them from becoming chilled with the heavy night frosts. Their flocks were also in danger of being stolen by unprincipled shepherds, who wished to enrich themselves by stealing their neighbor's cattle.

A shepherd's life was one of constant care. He was not qualified for a shepherd unless he was merciful, and possessed courage and perseverance. Jacob was chief shepherd, and had shepherds under him who were termed servants. The chief shepherd called these servants, to whom he intrusted the care of the flock, to a strict account if they were not found in a flourishing condition. If there were any of the cattle missing, the chief shepherd suffered the loss.

The relation of Christ to His people is compared to a shepherd. He saw, after the Fall, His sheep in a pitiable condition exposed to sure destruction. He left the honors and glory of His Father's house to become a shepherd, to save the . . . wandering sheep who were ready to perish. His winning voice was heard calling them to His fold, a safe and sure retreat from the hand of robbers; also a shelter from the scorching heat, and a protection from the chilling blasts. His care was continually exercised for the good of His sheep. He strengthened the weak, nourished the suffering, and gathered the lambs of the flock in His arms, and carried them in His bosom. His sheep love Him. He goeth before His sheep, and they hear His voice and follow Him. "And a stranger will they not follow, but will flee from him: for they know not the voice of strangers." Christ says, "I am the good shepherd: the good shepherd giveth His life for the sheep." . . .

Christ is the chief shepherd. He has intrusted the care of His flock to undershepherds. He requires these shepherds to have the same interest for His sheep which He has ever manifested, and to ever feel the responsibility of the charge He has intrusted to them. . . . If they imitate His self-denying example, the flock will prosper under their care. . . . They will be constantly laboring for the welfare of the flock (*Spiritual Gifts*, vol. 3, pp. 122-124).

Christ Is the Door

Then said Jesus unto them . . . , Verily, verily, I say unto you, I am the door of the sheep. John 10:7.

Satan took the field in person against Jesus Christ. Evil angels conspired with evil men to resist good, to trample upon righteousness, and all the energies of evil were confederated together to destroy the champion of God and truth. While success seems to attend the masterly activity of Satan, Jesus takes the field to contest his power. Jesus came "unto his own, and his own received him not." He was charged with an embassage of mercy, sent of the Father at a crisis when rebellion had overspread the world, in order that man should not perish, but have everlasting life through faith in the Son of God. Through Christ they were to bruise the serpent's head, and gain eternal life. . . .

In the parable of the shepherd Jesus puts His own interpretation on His work and mission, and represents Himself as the good shepherd, feeding and taking charge of the sheep. He said, "He that entereth not by the door [by himself] into the sheepfold, but climbeth up some other way, the same is a thief and a robber." Christ said that all who came before Him claiming to be the Messiah were deceivers. All the time of Christ's coming there was much agitation concerning the appearance of the world's Messiah. The Jewish nation expected that a great deliverer would come, and there were men who took advantage of this expectation, turning it to the service of themselves, that they might be thereby profited and glorified. Prophecy had foretold that these deceivers would arise. The deceivers did not come in the way in which it was prophesied that the world's Redeemer should come; but Christ came, answering every specification. Types and symbols had represented Him, and in Him type met antitype. In the life, mission, and death of Jesus every specification was fulfilled.

Jesus was the good shepherd to whom the porter openeth, who knows the sheep, calleth His own by name, and leadeth them out. He it is who is stronger than the thief and the robber, those who enter not in at the door, but climb up some other way. The Pharisees were not able to discern that this parable was spoken against them, the professed leaders of the people, pastors of the flock. Jesus presented Himself in contrast to them, and when they reasoned in their hearts as to what He could mean by the parable, He said, "I am the door [of the sheep]: by me if any man enter in, he shall be saved, and shall go in and out, and find pasture." . . . Christ presented Himself as the only one in whom were qualifications for making a good shepherd.

He is represented as the "Chief Shepherd" (*Signs of the Times*, Dec. 4, 1893).

The Deliverer a Humble Shepherd

God called unto him out of the midst of the bush, and said, Moses, Moses. And he said, Here am I. And he said, Draw not nigh hither: put off thy shoes from off thy feet, for the place whereon thou standest is holy ground. Exodus 3:4, 5.

The time for Israel's deliverance had come. But God's purpose was to be accomplished in a manner to pour contempt on human pride. The deliverer was to go forth as a humble shepherd, with only a rod in his hand; but God would make that rod the symbol of His power. Leading his flocks one day near Horeb, "the mountain of God," Moses saw a bush in flames. . . . A voice from out of the flame called him by name. With trembling lips he answered, "Here am I." He was warned not to approach irreverently. . . .

Humility and reverence should characterize the deportment of all who come into the presence of God. In the name of Jesus we may come before Him with confidence, but we must not approach Him with the boldness of presumption, as though He were on a level with ourselves. There are those who address the great and all-powerful and holy God, who dwelleth in light unapproachable, as they would address an equal, or even an inferior. There are those who conduct themselves in His house as they would not presume to do in the audience chamber of an earthly ruler. These should remember that they are in His sight whom seraphim adore, before whom angels veil their faces. God is greatly to be reverenced; all who truly realize His presence will bow in humility before Him. . . .

As Moses waited in reverent awe before God the words continued: ". . . Come now therefore, and I will send thee unto Pharaoh, that thou mayest bring forth my people the children of Israel out of Egypt."

Amazed and terrified at the command, Moses drew back. . . . Moses saw before him difficulties that seemed insurmountable. What proof could he give his people that God had indeed sent him? . . . Evidence that appealed to his own senses was now given. He was told to cast his rod upon the ground. As he did so, "it became a serpent; and Moses fled from before it." He was commanded to seize it, and in his hand it became a rod. . . . The Lord assured Moses that His own people, as well as Pharaoh, should be convinced that One mightier than the king of Egypt was manifest among them. . . .

God blessed his ready obedience, and he became eloquent, hopeful, self-possessed, and well fitted for the greatest work ever given to man. This is an example of what God does to strengthen the character of those who trust Him fully and give themselves unreservedly to His commands (*Patriarchs and Prophets*, pp. 251-255).

A Shepherd's Crook for a Sceptre

Then Samuel took the horn of oil, and anointed him in the midst of his brethren: and the spirit of the Lord came upon David from that day forward. 1 Samuel 16:13.

As the sons of Jesse passed before Samuel, he would have selected Eliab, who was of high stature, and dignified appearance, but the angel of God stood by him to guide him in the important decision, and instructed him that he should not judge from appearance. Eliab did not fear the Lord. His heart was not right with God. He would make a proud, exacting ruler. None were found among the sons of Jesse but David, the youngest, whose humble occupation was that of tending sheep. He had filled the humble office of shepherd with such faithfulness and courage that God selected him to be captain of his people. In course of time, he was to change his shepherd's crook for the sceptre (*Spiritual Gifts,* vol. 4, pp. 77, 78).

God selected David, a humble shepherd, to rule His people. He was strict in all the ceremonies connected with the Jewish religion, and he distinguished himself by his boldness and unwavering trust in God. He was remarkable for his fidelity and reverence. His firmness, humility, love of justice, and decision of character, qualified him to carry out the high purposes of God, to instruct Israel in their devotions, and to rule them as a generous and wise monarch.

His religious life was sincere and fervent. It was while David was thus true to God, and possessing these exalted traits of character, that God calls him a man after His own heart (*ibid*., pp. 85, 86).

The great honor conferred upon David did not serve to elate him. Notwithstanding the high position which he was to occupy, he quietly continued his employment, content to await the development of the Lord's plan in His own time and way. As humble and modest as before his anointing, the shepherd boy returned to the hills and watched and guarded his flocks as tenderly as ever. . . .

David, in the beauty and vigor of his young manhood, was preparing to take a high position with the noblest of the earth. His talents, as precious gifts from God, were employed to extol the glory of the divine Giver. His opportunities of contemplation and meditation served to enrich him with that wisdom and piety that made him beloved of God and angels. . . . The love that moved him, the sorrows that beset him, the triumphs that attended him, were all themes for his active thought; and as he beheld the love of God in all the providences of his life, his heart throbbed with more fervent adoration and gratitude, his voice rang out in richer melody, his harp was swept with more exultant joy; and the shepherd boy proceeded from strength to strength, from knowledge to knowledge; for the Spirit of the Lord was upon him (*Patriarchs and Prophets*, pp. 641, 642).

July

5

A Connection With the Chief Shepherd

For we are laborers together with God. 1 Corinthians 3:9.

A vital connection with the Chief Shepherd will make the undershepherd a living representative of Christ, a light indeed to the world. An understanding of all points of our faith is essential, but it is of still greater importance that the minister be sanctified through the truth he presents.

The worker who knows the meaning of union with Christ, has a constantly increasing desire and capacity to grasp the meaning of service for God. His knowledge enlarges; for to grow in grace means to have an increased ability to understand the Scriptures. Such a one is indeed a laborer together with God. He realizes that he is but an instrument, and that he must be passive in the Master's hands. Trials come to him; for unless thus tested, he would never know his lack of wisdom and experience. But if he seeks the Lord with humility and trust, every trial will work for his good. He may sometimes seem to fail, but his apparent failure may be God's way of bringing him true advancement, and may mean a better knowledge of himself and a firmer trust in Heaven. He may still make mistakes, but he learns not to repeat these mistakes. He becomes stronger to resist evil, and others reap benefit from his example. . . .

Those who have the deepest experience in the things of God are the farthest removed from pride and self-exaltation. Because they have an exalted conception of the glory of God, they feel that the lowest place in His service is too honorable for them.

When Moses came down from the mount after forty days spent in communion with God, he did not know that his face shone with a brightness that was terrifying to those who beheld.

Paul had a very humble opinion of his advancement in the Christian life. He speaks of himself as the chief of sinners. And again he says, "Not as though I had already attained, either were already perfect" (Philippians 3:12). Yet Paul had been highly honored by the Lord.

Our Savior declared John the Baptist to be the greatest of prophets; yet when asked if he were the Christ, John declared himself unworthy even to unloose his Master's sandals. When His disciples came with the complaint that all men were turning to the new teacher, John reminded them that he was but the forerunner of the Coming One.

Workers with this spirit are needed today. . . . Our Lord calls for laborers who, feeling their own need of the atoning blood of Christ, enter upon their work . . . with full assurance of faith, realizing that they will always need the help of Christ in order to know how to deal with minds (*Gospel Workers,* pp. 142, 143).

The Good Shepherd

I am the good shepherd: the good shepherd giveth his life for the sheep. John 10:11.

Christ . . . likens Himself to a shepherd. "I am the good shepherd," He declares; "the good shepherd giveth his life for the sheep." "I am the good shepherd, and know my sheep, and am known of mine. As the Father knoweth me, even so know I the Father: and I lay down my life for the sheep" (John 10:11, 14, 15).

As an earthly shepherd knows his sheep, so does the divine Shepherd know His flock that are scattered throughout the world. "Ye my flock, the flock of my pasture, are men, and I am your God, saith the Lord God" (Ezekiel 34:31).

In the parable of the lost sheep, the shepherd goes out to search for one sheep—the very least that can be numbered. Discovering that one of his sheep is missing, he does not look carelessly upon the flock that is safely housed, and say, I have ninety and nine, and it will cost me too much trouble to go in search of the straying one. Let him come back, and I will open the door of the sheepfold and let him in. No; no sooner does the sheep go astray than the shepherd is filled with grief and anxiety. Leaving the ninety and nine in the fold, he goes in search of the straying one. However dark and tempestuous the night, however perilous and uncertain the way, however long and tedious the search, he does not falter until the lost is found.

With what relief does he hear in the distance its first faint cry! Following the sound, he climbs the steepest heights; he goes to the very edge of the precipice, at the risk of his own life. Thus he searches while the cry, growing fainter, tells him that his sheep is ready to die.

And when the straying one is found, does he command it to follow him? . . . No; he lays the exhausted sheep on his shoulder, and with cheerful gratitude that his search has not been in vain, he returns to the fold. His gratitude finds expression in songs of rejoicing. And "when he cometh home, he calleth together his friends and neighbours, saying unto them, Rejoice with me; for I have found my sheep which was lost" (Luke 15:6).

So when the lost sinner is found by the Good Shepherd, heaven and earth unite in rejoicing and thanksgiving. For "joy shall be in heaven over one sinner that repenteth, more than over ninety and nine just persons, which need no repentance" (verse 7) (*Gospel Workers,* pp. 181, 182).

In our work, individual effort will accomplish much more than can be estimated. It is for the want of this that souls are perishing. One soul is of infinite value; Calvary speaks its worth. One soul won to Christ will be instrumental in winning others, and there will be an ever-increasing result of blessing and salvation (*ibid.*, p. 184).

The Divine Shepherd

I will set up one shepherd over them, and he shall feed them . . . and he shall be their shepherd. Ezekiel 34:23.

Jesus found access to the minds of His hearers by the pathway of their familiar associations. He had likened the Spirit's influence to the cool, refreshing water. He had represented Himself as the light, the source of life and gladness to nature and to man. Now in a beautiful pastoral picture He represents His relation to those that believe on Him. No picture was more familiar to His hearers than this, and Christ's words linked it forever with Himself. Never could the disciples look on the shepherds tending their flocks without recalling the Savior's lesson. They would see Christ in each faithful shepherd. They would see themselves in each helpless and dependent flock.

This figure the prophet Isaiah had applied to the Messiah's mission, in the comforting words, . . . "He shall feed his flock like a shepherd: he shall gather the lambs with his arm, and carry them in his bosom" (Isaiah 40:11). David had sung, "The Lord is my shepherd; I shall not want" (Psalm 23:1). And the Holy Spirit through Ezekiel had declared: "I will set up one shepherd over them, and he shall feed them." "I will seek that which was lost, and bring again that which was driven away, and will bind up that which was broken, and will strengthen that which was sick." "And I will make with them a covenant of peace." "And they shall no more be a prey to the heathen; . . . but they shall dwell safely, and none shall make them afraid" (Ezekiel 32:23, 16, 25, 28). . . .

Christ is the door to the fold of God. Through this door all His children, from the earliest times, have found entrance. In Jesus, as shown in types, as shadowed in symbols, as manifested in the revelation of the prophets, as unveiled in the lessons given to His disciples, and in the miracles wrought for the sons of men, they have beheld "the Lamb of God, which taketh away the sin of the world" (John 1:29), and through Him they are brought within the fold of His grace. Many have come presenting other objects for the faith of the world; ceremonies and systems have been devised by which men hope to receive justification and peace with God, and thus find entrance to His fold. But the only door is Christ, and all who have interposed something to take the place of Christ, all who have tried to enter the fold in some other way, are thieves and robbers. . . .

"He that entereth in by the door is the shepherd of the sheep." Christ is both the door and the shepherd. He enters in by Himself. It is through His own sacrifice that He becomes the shepherd of the sheep (*The Desire of Ages*, pp. 476-478).

The Shepherd Knows Every Sheep

Fear not; for I have . . . called thee by thy name; thou art mine. Isaiah 43:1.

Of all creatures the sheep is one of the most timid and helpless, and in the East the shepherd's care for his flock is untiring and incessant. Anciently as now there was little security outside of the walled towns. Marauders from the roving border tribes, or beasts of prey from their hiding places in the rocks, lay in wait to plunder the flocks. The shepherd watched his charge, knowing that it was at the peril of his own life. Jacob, who kept the flocks of Laban in the pasture grounds of Haran, describing his own unwearied labor, said, "In the day the drought consumed me, and the frost by night; and my sleep departed from my eyes" (Genesis 31:40). And it was while guarding his father's sheep that the boy David, single-handed, encountered the lion and the bear, and rescued from their teeth the stolen lamb.

As the shepherd leads his flock over the rocky hills, through forest and wild ravines, to grassy nooks by the riverside; as he watches them on the mountains through the lonely night, shielding from robbers, caring tenderly for the sickly and feeble, his life comes to be one with theirs. A strong and tender attachment unites him to the objects of his care. However large the flock, the shepherd knows every sheep. Every one has its name, and responds to the name at the shepherd's call.

As an earthly shepherd knows his sheep, so does the divine shepherd know His flock that are scattered throughout the world. "Ye my flock, the flock of my pasture, are men, and I am your God, saith the Lord God." Jesus says, "I have called thee by thy name; thou art mine." "I have graven thee upon the palms of my hands" (Ezekiel 34:31; Isaiah 43:1; 49:16).

Jesus knows us individually, and is touched with the feeling of our infirmities. He knows us all by name. He knows the very house in which we live, the name of each occupant. He has at times given directions to His servants to go to a certain street in a certain city, to such a house, to find one of His sheep.

Every soul is as fully known to Jesus as if he were the only one for whom the Savior died. The distress of every one touches His heart. The cry for aid reaches His ear. He came to draw all men unto Himself. He bids them, "Follow me," and His Spirit moves upon their hearts to draw them to come to Him. Many refuse to be drawn. Jesus knows who they are. He also knows who gladly hear His call, and are ready to come under His pastoral care. He says, "My sheep hear my voice, and I know them, and they follow me." He cares for each one as if there were not another on the face of the earth (*The Desire of Ages,* pp. 478-480).

The Shepherd Leads the Way

When he putteth forth his own sheep, he goeth before them, and the sheep follow him: for they know his voice. John 10:4.

The Eastern shepherd does not drive his sheep. He depends not upon force or fear; but going before, he calls them. They know his voice, and obey the call. So does the Savior-Shepherd with His sheep. The Scripture says, "Thou leddest thy people like a flock by the hand of Moses and Aaron." Through the prophet, Jesus declares, "I have loved thee with an everlasting love: therefore with lovingkindness have I drawn thee." He compels none to follow Him. "I drew them," He says, "with cords of a man, with bands of love" (Psalm 77:20; Jeremiah 31:3; Hosea 11:4).

It is not the fear of punishment, or the hope of everlasting reward, that leads the disciples of Christ to follow Him. They behold the Savior's matchless love, revealed throughout His pilgrimage on earth, from the manger of Bethlehem to Calvary's cross, and the sight of Him attracts, it softens and subdues the soul. Love awakens in the heart of the beholders. They hear His voice, and they follow Him.

As the shepherd goes before his sheep, himself first encountering the perils of the way, so does Jesus with His people. "When he putteth forth his own sheep, he goeth before them." The way to heaven is consecrated by the Savior's footprints. The path may be steep and rugged, but Jesus has traveled that way; His feet have pressed down the cruel thorns, to make the pathway easier for us. Every burden that we are called to bear He Himself has borne.

Though now He has ascended to the presence of God, and shares the throne of the universe, Jesus has lost none of His compassionate nature. Today the same tender, sympathizing heart is open to all the woes of humanity. Today the hand that was pierced is reached for to bless more abundantly His people that are in the world. "And they shall never perish, neither shall any man pluck them out of my hand."

The soul that has given himself to Christ is more precious in His sight than the whole world. The Savior would have passed through the agony of Calvary that one might be saved in His kingdom. He will never abandon one for whom He has died. Unless His followers choose to leave Him, He will hold them fast.

Through all of our trials we have a never-failing Helper. He does not leave us alone to struggle with temptation, to battle with evil, and be finally crushed with burdens and sorrow. Though now He is hidden from mortal sight, the ear of faith can hear His voice saying, "Fear not; I am with you." "I am he that liveth, and was dead; and, behold, I am alive for evermore" (Revelation 1:18) (*The Desire of Ages*, pp. 480-483).

The Shepherd Gave His Life for the Sheep

I know my sheep and my sheep know me—just as the Father knows me and I know the Father—and I lay down my life for the sheep. John 10:14, 15, NIV.

I have endured your sorrows, experienced your struggles, encountered your temptations. I know your tears; I also have wept. The griefs that lie too deep to be breathed into any human ear, I know. Think not that you are desolate and forsaken. Though your pain touch no responsive chord in any heart on earth, look unto Me, and live. "The mountains shall depart, and the hills be removed; but my kindness shall not depart from thee, neither shall the covenant of my peace be removed, saith the Lord that hath mercy on thee" (Isaiah 54:10).

However much a shepherd may love his sheep, he loves his sons and daughters more. Jesus is not only our shepherd; He is our "everlasting Father." And He says, "I know mine own, and mine own know me, even as the Father knoweth me, and I know the Father" (John 10:14, 15, RV). What a statement is this! The only-begotten Son, He who is in the bosom of the Father, He whom God has declared to be "the man that is my fellow" (Zechariah 13:7)—the communion between Him and the eternal God is taken to represent the communion between Christ and His children on the earth!

Because we are the gift of His Father, and the reward of His work, Jesus loves us. He loves us as His children. Reader, He loves you. Heaven itself can bestow nothing greater, nothing better. Therefore trust.

Jesus thought upon the souls all over the earth who were misled by false shepherds. Those whom He longed to gather as the sheep of His pasture were scattered among wolves, and He said, "Other sheep I have, which are not of this fold: them also I must bring, and they shall hear my voice; and they shall become one flock, one shepherd" (John 10:16, RV).

"Therefore doth my Father love me, because I lay down my life, that I might take it again." That is, My Father has so loved you, that He even loves Me more for giving My life to redeem you. In becoming your substitute and surety, by surrendering My life, by taking your liabilities, your transgressions, I am endeared to My Father. . . .

While as a member of the human family He was mortal, as God He was the fountain of life for the world. He could have withstood the advances of death, and refused to come under its dominion; but voluntarily He laid down His life, that He might bring life and immortality to light. He bore the sin of the world, endured its curse, yielded up His life as a sacrifice, that men might not eternally die. "Surely he hath borne our griefs, and carried our sorrows" (Isaiah 53:4) (*The Desire of Ages*, pp. 483, 484).

The Lost Sheep

Rejoice with me; for I have found my sheep which was lost. Luke 15:6.

I was referred to the parable of the lost sheep. The ninety and nine sheep are left in the wilderness, and search is instituted for the one that has strayed. When the lost sheep is found, the shepherd elevates it to his shoulder and returns with rejoicing. He does not return murmuring and censuring the poor lost sheep for having made him so much trouble, but his return with the burden of the sheep is with rejoicing.

And a still greater demonstration of joy is demanded. Friends and neighbors are called to rejoice with the finder, "for I have found my sheep which was lost." The finding was the theme of rejoicing; the straying was not dwelt upon; for the joy of finding overbalanced the sorrow of the loss and the care, the perplexity and the peril, incurred in searching for the lost sheep and restoring it to safety. "I say unto you, that likewise joy shall be in heaven over one sinner that repenteth, more than over ninety and nine just persons, which need no repentance" (Luke 15:7) (*Testimonies,* vol. 3, p. 99).

Jesus has given the parable of the lost sheep for our study. The true Shepherd leaves the ninety and nine, and goes into the desert at any expense and suffering to Himself. . . . How many of the wandering and lost sheep have you sought for, and brought back to the fold with a heart full of pitying tenderness, forgiveness, and love? How many words of encouragement have you spoken to the wandering sheep, that have cost you pain, anxiety, and much inconvenience? . . . Have you spoken soothing words of hope, courage, and pardon, bearing the wanderer home on your shoulders, rejoicing at every step, and saying, "Rejoice with me; for I have found my sheep which was lost"? . . .

Study the life and character of Christ, and seek to imitate His example. The unconsecrated course of some of those who claim to be believers in the third angel's message has resulted in driving some of the poor sheep into the desert; and who is it that has manifested a shepherd's care for the lost and wandering? Is it not time to be Christians in practice as well as profession? What benevolence, what compassion, what tender sympathy, Jesus has manifested toward suffering humanity! The heart that beats in unison with His great heart of infinite love will give sympathy to every needy soul, and will make it manifest that he has the mind of Christ. . . . Every suffering soul has a claim upon the sympathy of others, and those who are imbued with the love of Christ, filled with His pity, tenderness, and compassion, will respond to every appeal to their sympathy. . . . Every soul who attempts to retrace his wanderings and return to God needs the help of those who have a tender, pitying heart of Christlike love (*Review and Herald*, Oct. 16, 1894).

Estimate of a Lost Sheep

Herein is love, not that we loved God, but that he loved us. 1 John 4:10.

The Pharisees said that if Jesus were a true prophet, He would harmonize with them, and voice their precepts and maxims, and treat the wretched publicans and sinners as they treated them. In giving His Son to die for the sins of the world, the Lord God made manifest what was the estimate He placed upon men; for in giving Jesus to the world, He gave heaven's best gift. For this costly sacrifice the most profound gratitude is demanded from every soul. Whatever may be the nation, kindred, or tongue, whether a man is white or black, he still bears the image of God, and "the proper study of mankind is man," viewed from the fact that he is the purchase of the blood of Christ. To show contempt for, to manifest hatred toward any nation, is to reveal the characteristic of Satan.

God has placed His estimate upon man in giving Jesus to a life of humiliation, poverty, and self-sacrifice, to contempt, rejection, and death, in order that man, His lost sheep, might be saved. Is it then a remarkable thing that all heaven is interested in the ransom of man? Is it a wonderful fact that ten thousand times ten thousand, and thousands of thousands of angels are employed in ascending and descending on the mystic ladder to minister to those who shall be heirs of salvation? Angels do not come to the earth to denounce and to destroy, to rule and to exact homage, but are messengers of mercy to cooperate with the Captain of the Lord's host, to cooperate with the human agents who shall go forth to seek and save the lost sheep. Angels are commanded to encamp round about those who fear and love God.

The sympathy of all heaven is enlisted on behalf of the sheep that is wandering far from the fold. If the Pharisees had been working in harmony with God, in place of uniting with the adversary of God and man, they would not have been found despising the purchase of the blood of Christ. As the delusions of Satan are broken from human minds, as the sinner looks to Calvary, and sees the costly offering that has been given to save an apostate and ruined race, he contemplates and is deeply moved by the love of God, and becomes repentant. "Herein is love, not that we loved God, but that he loved us."

Oh, that we might comprehend the love of God, and even to a faint degree take in the compassion that has been manifested toward fallen man! How would we look and live! By beholding Christ man becomes changed and transformed in character from glory to glory. The conflict between light and darkness is entered upon. Look, poor sinner, represented by the lost sheep after whom the shepherd is seeking, look to the cross! . . . In the poor blind man restored to sight by the compassionate Shepherd was one whom the self-righteous Pharisees thought only worthy of . . . hatred (*Signs of the Times*, Nov. 20, 1893).

Christ Came to Seek the Lost Sheep

I came not to call the righteous, but sinners to repentance. Luke 5:32.

While on earth, Christ accomplished the work for which He left the throne of God in heaven. He worked for humanity, that through His work, humanity might be elevated in the scale of moral value with God. He assumed human nature, that He might elevate the human family, make them partakers of the divine nature, and place them on vantage ground with God. His every action had been in behalf of the fallen world—to seek the sheep that had strayed from the fold, and bring it back to God. . . .

The Lord saw us in a sad condition, and sent to our world the only Messenger that He could trust with His great treasure of pardon and grace. Christ, the only begotten Son of God, was the delegated messenger. He was ordained to do a work that even the angels of heaven could not accomplish. He alone could be trusted to do the work required for the redemption of a world all seared and marred with the curse. And in this gift the Father gave all heaven to the world.

What a change was this for the Son of God, Him who was the adored of angels, the Light of heaven! He might have gone to the pleasant homes of the unfallen worlds, to the pure atmosphere where disloyalty and rebellion had never intruded; and there He would have been received with acclamations of praise and love. But it was a fallen world that needed the Redeemer. "I came not to call the righteous," said He, "but sinners to repentance." He came to represent the Father in bringing the message of hope and salvation to our world. He lived not for Himself; He did not consult His own ease and pleasure; He did not yield to temptation; and He condescended to die in order that sinful men might be redeemed, and live eternally in the mansions He was to prepare for them. His mission was to teach souls who were dying in their sins.

This work Christ has laid upon every one whom He has purchased. The Lord will give ample light to all who will be true and loyal to Him. . . . His mercy and the gracious influences of His Spirit remain the same for all who will receive them. His offer of salvation does not change. It is man who changes His relationship to God. Many place themselves where they cannot recognize His grace and His salvation. . . .

God has left nothing undone that He could do for us. He gave a perfect example of His character in the character of His Son; and it is the work of Christ's followers, as they behold the incomparable excellency of His life and character, to grow in His likeness. As they look unto Jesus and respond to His love, they will reflect the image of Christ (*Review and Herald*, Feb. 15, 1898).

The Lost Sheep a Special Burden

What man of you, having a hundred sheep, if he lose one of them, doth not leave the ninety and nine in the wilderness, and go after that which is lost, until he find it?
Luke 15:4.

It is important work to deal with human minds. Man is God's property, and angels are looking with intense interest to see how man will deal with his fellowman. When heavenly intelligences see those who claim to be the sons and daughters of God putting forth Christlike efforts to help the erring, manifesting a tender, sympathetic spirit for the repentant and the fallen, angels press close to them, and bring to their remembrance the very words that will soothe and uplift the soul. Holy angels are on the track of every one of us. We are not to despise the least of God's little ones, not to exact homage for anyone toward ourselves. The angels are all ministering spirits sent forth to minister to those who shall be heirs of salvation. Shall we be privileged to cooperate with heavenly intelligences? Will God accept us as light bearers to the world?

Jesus Christ has taken the position of one who came to seek and to save that which is lost, and He has exalted the world inasmuch as He died to redeem it, to bring back the one lost sheep to the fold. Jesus has given His precious life, His personal attention, to the least of God's little ones; and angels that excel in strength encamp round about them that fear God. Then let us be upon our guard, and never permit one contemptuous thought to occupy the mind in regard to one of the little ones of God. We should look after the erring with solicitude, and speak encouraging words to the fallen, and fear lest by some unwise action we shall turn them away from the pitying Savior.

Those who love Jesus will love those for whom Christ died. If many of the sinners that are around us had received the light which has blessed us, they would have rejoiced in the truth, and have been in advance of many that have had a long experience and great advantages. Take these lost sheep as your special burden, and watch for souls as they that must give an account. Draw not a glance to yourself, but cry with earnest, heartfelt interest, "Behold the Lamb of God, which taketh away the sin of the world." This is the Christian's message to the world. This is the effective argument. Encourage your heart to put forth earnest endeavors to induce perishing souls to fix their eyes upon Him who was uplifted upon the cross; and remember that as you do this, unseen angels are . . . impressing it upon the heart, and leading the soul to believe in Jesus. The sinner is enabled to see Jesus as He is—full of compassion, pity, and love—and he exclaims, "Thy gentleness hath made me great" (Psalm 18:35) (*Review and Herald*, June 30, 1896).

Finding the Lost Sheep

And if so be that he find [the lost sheep], verily I say unto you, he rejoiceth more of that sheep, than of the ninety and nine which went not astray. Matthew 18:13.

Jesus would impress upon the hearts and minds of His disciples the value of the human soul. He demands cooperation on the part of His followers in rescuing lost sinners. There is one lost sheep, the very least that could be numbered; and yet He represents the shepherd as leaving the ninety and nine, and going into the mountains to seek that one lost wanderer. Then why is it that the sons and daughters of God are so cold of heart, so indifferent to the souls that are perishing around them? Why is it that the members of the church are so willing to let the whole burden rest upon the shoulders of the minister? How great a mistake is this, since every subject of grace is to have a part to act in saving those that are lost.

To every man Christ has given his work, and personal efforts must be put forth to save the perishing. The worker must be much in secret prayer; for this work requires great wisdom in the science of saving souls. Christ said, "I am the light of the world: he that followeth me shall not walk in darkness, but shall have the light of life." He said also to His disciples, "Ye are the light of the world." He made the church the depositary of sacred truth. He left His church a stewardship of sacred truth, and it is the work of the church to carry forward His mission of saving the world. He is the Sun of Righteousness, who is to impart bright rays to His followers; and they, in turn, are to shed His light upon others. They are to be His representatives to the world. Believing in Christ as their personal Savior, they take up the work where He left it. "Without me ye can do nothing," said Christ; but with Him we can do all things. There is a large, a very large number of straying and lost sheep that have perished in the wild deserts of sin, simply because no one went after them, to search for them and to bring them back to the fold. Jesus uses the illustration of a lost sheep to show the need of seeking after those who have wandered from Him; for a sheep once lost will never find its way back to the fold without help. It must be sought for, it must be carried back to the fold.

All heaven is interested in the work of saving the lost. Angels watch with intense interest to see who will leave the ninety and nine, and go out in tempest and storm and rain into the wild desert to seek the lost sheep. The lost are all around us, perishing and sadly neglected. But they are of value to God, the purchase of the blood of Christ. . . . We are to seek to save those that are lost. We are to search for the one lost sheep, and bring him back to the fold; and this represents personal effort (*Review and Herald*, June 30, 1896).

True Sheep Hear the True Shepherd

And other sheep I have, which are not of this fold: them also I must bring, and they shall hear my voice; and there shall be one fold, and one shepherd.
John 10:16.

The truth should be presented with divine tact, gentleness, and tenderness. It should come from a heart that has been softened and made sympathetic. . . . Let our words be gentle as we seek to win souls. God will be wisdom to him who seeks for wisdom from a divine source. We are to seek opportunities on every hand, we are to watch unto prayer, and be ready always to give a reason for the hope that is in us, with meekness and fear. Lest we shall impress unfavorably one soul for whom Christ died we should keep our hearts uplifted to God, so that when the opportunity presents itself, we may have the right words to speak at the right time. If you thus undertake work for God, the Spirit of God will be your helper. The Holy Spirit will apply the word spoken in love for the soul. The truth will have quickening power when spoken under the influence of the grace of Christ.

God's plan is first to get at the heart. Speak the truth, and let Him carry forward the reformatory power and principle. Make no reference to what opponents say, but let the truth alone be advanced. The truth can cut to the quick. Plainly unfold the Word in all its impressiveness.

As trials thicken around us, both separation and unity will be seen in our ranks. Some who are now ready to take up weapons of warfare will in time of real peril make it manifest that they have not built upon the solid rock; they will yield to temptation. Those who have had great light and precious privileges, but have not improved them, will, under one pretext or another, go out from us. Not having received the love of the truth, they will be taken in the delusions of the enemy; they will give heed to seducing spirits and doctrines of devils, and will depart from the faith.

But, on the other hand, when the storm of persecution really breaks upon us, the true sheep will hear the true Shepherd's voice. Self-denying efforts will be put forth to save the lost, and many who have strayed from the fold will come back to follow the great Shepherd. The people of God will draw together and present to the enemy a united front. In view of the common peril, strife for supremacy will cease; there will be no disputing as to who shall be accounted greatest. No one of the true believers will say: "I am of Paul; and I of Apollos; and I of Cephas." The testimony of one and all will be: "I cleave unto Christ; I rejoice in Him as my personal Savior." . . .

The love of Christ, the love of our brethren, will testify to the world that we have been with Jesus and learned of Him. Then will the message of the third angel swell to a loud cry, and the whole earth will be lightened with the glory of the Lord (*Testimonies*, vol. 6, pp. 400, 401).

Joy Over One Sinner That Repenteth

I say unto you, that likewise joy shall be in heaven over one sinner that repenteth, more than over ninety and nine just persons, which need no repentance. Luke 15:7.

Jesus, the Son of the Highest, is combating the powers of Satan, who is laying every possible device whereby he may counteract the work of God. The prize for which the powers of light and darkness are contending is the soul of man. The Good Shepherd is seeking His sheep, and what self-denial, what hardships, what privations He endures! The undershepherds know something of the stern conflict, but little in comparison to what is endured by the Shepherd of the sheep. With what compassion, what sorrow, what persistence, He seeks the lost! How few realize what desperate efforts are put forth by Satan to defeat the Shepherd's purpose. When the Shepherd at last finds His lost sheep, He gathers it in His arms with rejoicing, and bears it back to the fold on His shoulders. And the harps of heaven are touched, and an anthem of rejoicing is sung over the ransom of the wandering and lost sheep. "Joy shall be in heaven over one sinner that repenteth, more than over ninety and nine just persons which need no repentance."...

The Son of man came to seek and to save that which was lost. A lost sheep never finds its way back to the fold of itself. If it is not sought for and saved by the watchful shepherd, it wanders until it perishes. What a representation of the Savior is this! Unless Jesus, the Good Shepherd, had come to seek and to save the wandering, we should have perished. The Pharisees had taught that none but the Jewish nation would be saved, and they treated all other nationalities with contempt. But Jesus attracted the attention of those that the Pharisees despised, and He treated them with consideration and courtesy....

"God so loved the world, that he gave his only begotten Son, that whosoever believeth in him should not perish, but have everlasting life." This love on behalf of man, expressed in the gift of His only-begotten Son, called forth from Satan the most intense hatred, both toward the Giver and toward the priceless Gift. Satan had represented the Father to the world in a false light, and by this great Gift his representations were proved untrue, for here was love without a parallel, proving that man was to be redeemed by an inconceivable cost. Satan had tried to obliterate the image of God in man in order that as God looked upon him in his wretchedness, in his perverseness, in his degradation, He might be induced to give him up as hopelessly lost. But the Lord gave His only begotten Son in order that the most sinful, the most degraded, need not perish, but, by believing on Jesus Christ, may be reclaimed, regenerated, and restored to the image of God, and thus have eternal life (*Signs of the Times*, Nov. 20, 1893).

We Are Undershepherds

Beware of false prophets, which come to you in sheep's clothing, but inwardly they are ravening wolves. Matthew 7:15.

The less you meditate upon Christ and His matchless love and the less you are assimilated to His image, the better will you appear in your own eyes, and the more self-confidence and self-complacency will you possess. A correct knowledge of Christ, a constant looking unto the Author and Finisher of our faith, will give you such a view of the character of a true Christian that you cannot fail to make a right estimate of your own life and character in contrast with those of the great Exemplar. . . .

The fitting up for your work is a life business, a daily, laborious, hand-to-hand struggle with established habits, inclinations, and hereditary tendencies. It requires a constant, earnest, and vigilant effort to watch and control self, to keep Jesus prominent and self out of sight.

It is necessary for you to watch for the weak points in your character, to restrain wrong tendencies, and to strengthen and develop noble faculties that have not been properly exercised. The world will never know the work secretly going on between the soul and God, nor the inward bitterness of spirit, the self-loathing, and the constant efforts to control self; but many of the world will be able to appreciate the result of these efforts. They will see Christ revealed in your daily life. You will be a living epistle, known and read of all men, and will possess a symmetrical character, nobly developed.

"Learn of me," said Christ; "for I am meek and lowly in heart: and ye shall find rest unto your souls." He will instruct those who come to Him for knowledge. There are multitudes of false teachers in the world. The apostle declares that in the last days men will "heap to themselves teachers, having itching ears," because they desire to hear smooth things. Against these Christ has warned us: "Beware of false prophets, which come to you in sheep's clothing, but inwardly they are ravening wolves. Ye shall know them by their fruits." The class of religious teachers here described profess to be Christians. They have the form of godliness and appear to be laboring for the good of souls. . . . They are in conflict with Christ and His teachings, and are destitute of His meek and lowly spirit. . . .

The Good Shepherd came to seek and to save that which was lost. He has manifested in His works His love for His sheep. All the shepherds who work under the Chief Shepherd will possess His characteristics; they will be meek and lowly of heart. Childlike faith brings rest to the soul and also works by love and is ever interested for others. If the Spirit of Christ dwells in them, they will be Christlike and do the works of Christ (*Testimonies,* vol. 4, pp. 375-377).

Brought Back by the Shepherd

As a shepherd seeketh out his flock in the day that he is among his sheep that are scattered; so will I seek out my sheep, and will deliver them out of all places where they have been scattered in the cloudy and dark day. Ezekiel 34:12.

The sheep that has strayed from the fold is the most helpless of all creatures. It must be sought for by the shepherd, for it cannot find its way back. So with the soul that has wandered away from God; he is as helpless as the lost sheep, and unless divine love had come to his rescue he could never find his way to God.

The shepherd who discovers that one of his sheep is missing does not look carelessly upon the flock that is safely housed, and say, "I have ninety and nine, and it will cost me too much trouble to go in search of the straying one. Let him come back, and I will open the door of the sheepfold, and let him in." No; no sooner does the sheep go astray than the shepherd is filled with grief and anxiety. He counts and recounts the flock. When he is sure that one sheep is lost, he slumbers not. He leaves the ninety and nine within the fold, and goes in search of the straying sheep. The darker and more tempestuous the night and the more perilous the way, the greater is the shepherd's anxiety and the more earnest his search. He makes every effort to find that one lost sheep.

With what relief he hears in the distance its first faint cry. Following the sound, he climbs the steepest heights, he goes to the very edge of the precipice, at the risk of his own life. Thus he searches, while the cry, growing fainter, tells him that his sheep is ready to die. At last his effort is rewarded; the lost is found. Then he does not scold it because it has caused him so much trouble. He does not drive it with a whip. He does not even try to lead it home. In his joy he takes the trembling creature upon his shoulders; if it is bruised and wounded, he gathers it in his arms, pressing it close to his bosom, that the warmth of his own heart may give it life. With gratitude that his search has not been in vain, he bears it back to the fold.

Thank God, He has presented to our imagination no picture of a sorrowful shepherd returning without the sheep. The parable does not speak of failure but of success and joy in the recovery. Here is the divine guarantee that not even one of the straying sheep of God's fold is overlooked, not one is left unsuccored. Every one that will submit to be ransomed, Christ will rescue from the pit of corruption and from the briers of sin (*Christ's Object Lessons,* pp. 187, 188).

The Sheep of His Pasture

The Lord is my shepherd; I shall not want. He maketh me to lie down in green pastures; he leadeth me beside the still waters. Psalm 23:1, 2.

As Jesus, the great Teacher, presents His lessons to be learned from the open book of nature, He opens the eye of their understanding to reveal the attention that is given to objects in proportion to the rank they occupy in the scale of creation. If the grass of the field, which today is so beautiful, delighting the senses, [and] is tomorrow cut down and burned, receives so great attention from God, how much more will He not bestow upon man formed in His image. We cannot form exaggerated ideas of the value of the human soul, and the attention given by Heaven to man. He then gives the comforting assurance, "Fear not, little flock; for it is your Father's good pleasure to give you the kingdom."

Jesus is the good Shepherd. His followers are the sheep of His pasture. A shepherd is always with his flock to defend them, to keep them from the wolves, to hunt up the lost sheep and carry them back to the fold, to lead them beside green pastures and beside living waters.

I cannot neglect the great salvation that has been brought to me at such an infinite cost to my heavenly Father, who "so loved the world that he gave his only begotten Son, that whosoever believeth in him should not perish, but have everlasting life." I will not dishonor my Redeemer to lightly esteem His sufferings, His trials, His condescension, His sacrifice, His death, because He so loves us, He would Himself become our sin-bearer. Oh, what love, what inexpressible love! He became a man of sorrows, acquainted with grief. He died on the cross [as if He were] a transgressor, that man might be justified through His merits. . . .

The soul is through the Lifegiver capable of living through eternal ages, and man is to take special care of the soul which Christ has purchased with His own blood. With Christ is Omnipotence. He also is able to keep that which I have committed to His trust against that day. If the preciousness of the soul has not been appreciated, if its temple courts have been defiled with buyers and sellers, and with committing it to the rule and indwelling of Satan in thought or in feeling, I would in deep earnestness beseech you to make no delay, but come before God in sincere prayer without one moment's speculation or hesitation, and say, "O Lord, I have opened the door of my heart to Thy worst enemy, and the worst enemy of my soul. I have acted as though I could save my own soul, as if I could sin and then reform when I choose to do so; but I find a power holding me in his keeping. Thou alone can save me that my soul shall not be eternally ruined. . . . No longer will I withhold it from Thee. I dare not trust it with any power but Thine. . . . I lay it at Thy feet. Thou Lamb of God, wash my soul in the blood of the Lamb; clothe it with Thine own garments of purity and righteousness (manuscript 73, 1893).

"What More Could I Have Done?"

Last of all he sent unto them his son. Matthew 21:37.

Is there no power that can take hold of our sensibilities and show us that we are near the verge of the eternal world? Can we not get our minds on the other side? What can be done to arouse our people? Why, these light afflictions, how we talk about them. Hear what Paul says about them: "For our light affliction, which is but for a moment, worketh for us a far more exceeding and eternal weight of glory" (2 Corinthians 4:17). Would you consider that to be beaten with rods, to be a night and a day in the deep, suffer with hunger, cold, nakedness, and all these things—and worst of all from false brethren—were light afflictions? But he says, These light afflictions. . . .

There is too much self. We want self to die and be hid in Christ Jesus, then we will not talk of discouragement and difficulties and all these small things, but we will talk of the great plan of redemption and the matchless power of Jesus Christ to come to our world and take upon Him human nature that we through Him might be elevated and have a seat at His right hand. What could be more pleasant than that?

If this is not enough, what more could heaven do for the fallen race than has been done? "What more," says Christ, "could I do for My sheep than that I have done?" What more? Will He have to let us go? He will unless you change your attitude toward God, for He has done all He could to save us. According to the light that we have received, so is our accountability before God. Walk in the light as He is in the light. . . .

Evil surmising and evil speaking will be put away. You will talk and we will not be thinking of ourselves and what others are doing, but what God and Jesus are doing. . . . What are they doing? They are cleansing the sanctuary. . . . We should be with Him in this work and be cleansing the sanctuary of our souls of all unrighteousness, that our names may be written in the Lamb's book of life, that our sins may be blotted out when the times of refreshing shall come from the presence of the Lord. It is the most solemn work that was ever given to mortals.

You have no time to be exalting self, but [only to] lift Jesus up. Oh, lift Him up! How can we do this? How can we [be] seeking all the time to be saving ourselves, and exalting ourselves? . . . Says the shepherd of the flock, "Who does He mean—ministers? No. Everyone who has named the name of Christ, who has tasted and knows that the Lord is good. . . .

God will put His power on you, and combine His divine with our human efforts, and we can work out our salvation with fear and trembling. That is a power that Satan cannot resist or overthrow (manuscript 26, 1888).

Feeding the Flock

And they went . . . unto the east side of the valley, to seek pasture for their flocks. And they found fat pasture and good, and the land was wide, and quiet, and peaceable.
1 Chronicles 4:39, 40.

God's word is true philosophy, true science. Human opinions and sensational preaching amount to very little. Those who are imbued with the word of God will teach it in the same simple way that Christ taught it. The world's greatest Teacher used the simplest language and the plainest symbols.

The Lord calls upon His shepherds to feed the flock with pure provender. He would have them present the truth in its simplicity. When this work is faithfully done, many will be convicted and converted by the power of the Holy Spirit. There is need of Bible teachers who will come close to the unconverted, who will search for the lost sheep, who will do personal labor, and will give clear, definite instruction.

Never utter sentiments of doubt. Christ's teaching was always positive in its nature. With a tone of assurance bear an affirmative message. Lift up the Man of Calvary higher and still higher; there is power in the exaltation of the cross of Christ.

It is the student's privilege to have clear and accurate ideas of the truth of the Word, that he may be prepared to present these truths to other minds. He should be rooted and grounded in the faith. Students should be led to think for themselves, to see the force of truth for themselves, and to speak every word from a heart full of love and tenderness. Urge upon their minds the vital truths of the Bible. Let them repeat these truths in their own language, that you may be sure that they clearly comprehend them. Be sure that every point is fastened upon the mind. This may be a slow process, but it is of 10 times more value than rushing over important subjects without giving them due consideration. It is not enough that the student believe the truth for himself. He must be drawn out to state this truth clearly in his own words, that it may be evident that he sees the force of the lesson and makes its application. . . .

Never forget that the greatest lesson to be taught and to be learned is the lesson of copartnership with Christ in the work of salvation. The education to be secured by searching the Scriptures is an experimental knowledge of the plan of salvation. Such an education will restore the image of God in the soul. It will strengthen and fortify the mind against temptation, and fit the learner to become a worker with Christ in His mission of mercy to the world. It will make him a member of the heavenly family, prepare him to share the inheritance of the saints in light. . . . The Bible becomes a lesson book such as God designed it to be, giving clear conceptions to those who strive to grasp its grand and glorious truths. . . . There is shed into the mind a flood of light (*Counsels to Parents, Teachers, and Students,* pp. 433-437).

Special Care of the Flock

Know ye that the Lord he is God; it is he that hath made us, and not we ourselves; we are his people, and the sheep of his pasture. Psalm 100:3.

Jesus] knows the wants of each of His creatures and reads the hidden, unspoken grief of every heart. If one of the little ones for whom He died is injured, He sees it and calls the offender to account. Jesus is the Good Shepherd. He cares for His feeble, sickly, wandering sheep. He knows them all by name. The distress of every sheep and every lamb of His flock touches His heart of sympathizing love, and the cry for aid reaches His ear. One of the greatest sins of the shepherds of Israel is thus pointed out by the prophet: "The diseased have ye not strengthened, neither have ye healed that which was sick, neither have ye bound up that which was broken, neither have ye brought again that which was driven away, neither have ye sought that which was lost; but with force and with cruelty have ye ruled them. And they were scattered, because there is no shepherd. . . . None did search or seek after them." . . .

As Deity He exerts mighty power in our behalf, while as our Elder Brother He feels for all our woes. The Majesty of heaven held not Himself aloof from degraded, sinful humanity. We have not a high priest who is so high, so lifted up, that He cannot notice us or sympathize with us, but one who was in all points tempted like as we are, yet without sin. . . .

You will have many perplexities to meet in your Christian life in connection with the church, but do not try too hard to mold your brethren. If you see that they do not meet the requirements of God's Word, do not condemn; if they provoke, do not retaliate. When things are said that would exasperate, quietly keep your soul from fretting. . . . You must labor for the erring with a heart subdued, softened by the Spirit of God, and let the Lord work through you, the agent. Roll your burden on Jesus. You feel that the Lord must take up the case where Satan is striving for the mastery over some soul; but you are to do what you can in humility and meekness, and put the tangled work, the complicated matters, into the hands of God. Follow the directions in His word, and leave the outcome of the matter to His wisdom. Having done all you can to save your brother, cease worrying, and go calmly about other pressing duties. It is no longer your matter, but God's.

Do not, through impatience, cut the knot of difficulty, making matters hopeless. Let God untangle the snarled-up threads for you. He is wise enough to manage the complications of our lives. He has skill and tact. We cannot always see His plans; we must wait patiently their unfolding and not mar and destroy them. He will reveal them to us in His own good time. Seek for unity; cultivate love and conformity to Christ in all things. He is the source of unity and strength. . . . If you do as God would have you, His blessing will come into the church (*Testimonies,* vol. 5, pp. 346-348).

July
24

The Gentle and Caring Shepherd

He shall feed his flock like a shepherd: he shall gather the lambs with his arm, and carry them in his bosom. Isaiah 40:11.

True workers walk and work by faith. Sometimes they grow weary with watching the slow advance of the work when the battle wages strong between the powers of good and evil. But if they refuse to fail or be discouraged they will see the clouds breaking away and the promise of deliverance fulfilling. Through the mist with which Satan has surrounded them, they will see the shining of the bright beams of the Sun of Righteousness.

Work in faith, and leave results with God. Pray in faith, and the mystery of His providence will bring its answer. At times it may seem that you cannot succeed. But work and believe, putting into your efforts faith, hope, and courage. After doing what you can, wait for the Lord, declaring His faithfulness, and He will bring His word to pass. Wait, not in fretful anxiety, but in undaunted faith and unshaken trust.

"If God be for us, who can be against us? He that spared not his own Son, but delivered him up for us all, how shall he not with him also freely give us all things?" (Romans 8:31, 32) (*Testimonies,* vol. 7, p. 245).

Our heavenly Father has a thousand ways to provide for us of which we know nothing. Those who accept the one principle of making the service of God supreme will find perplexities vanish and a plain path before their feet.

The faithful discharge of today's duties is the best preparation for tomorrow's trials. Do not gather together all tomorrow's liabilities and cares and add them to the burden of today. . . .

Let us be hopeful and courageous. Despondency in God's service is sinful and unreasonable. He knows our every necessity. To the omnipotence of the King of kings our covenant-keeping God unites the gentleness and care of the tender shepherd. His power is absolute, and it is the pledge of the sure fulfillment of His promises to all who trust in Him. He has means for the removal of every difficulty, that those who serve Him and respect the means He employs may be sustained. His love is as far above all other love as the heavens are above the earth. He watches over His children with a love that is measureless and everlasting.

In the darkest days, when appearances seem most forbidding, have faith in God. He is working out His will, doing all things well in behalf of His people. The strength of those who love and serve Him will be renewed day by day.

He is able and willing to bestow upon His servants all the help they need. He will give them the wisdom which their varied necessities demand (*The Ministry of Healing,* pp. 481, 482).

July 25

The Tenderness of the Shepherd

And when he has found [the sheep], he lays it on his shoulders, rejoicing.
Luke 15:5, RSV.

In the commission to His disciples, Christ not only outlined their work, but gave them their message. Teach the people, He said, "to observe all things whatsoever I have commanded you." The disciples were to teach what Christ had taught. That which He had spoken, not only in person, but through all the prophets and teachers of the Old Testament, is here included. Human teaching is shut out. There is no place for tradition, for man's theories and conclusions, or for church legislation. No laws ordained by ecclesiastical authority are included in the commission. None of these are Christ's servants to teach. "The law and the prophets," with the record of His own words and deeds, are the treasure committed to the disciples to be given to the world. Christ's name is their watchword, their badge of distinction, their bond of union, the authority for their course of action, and the source of their success. Nothing that does not bear His superscription is to be recognized in His kingdom.

The gospel is to be presented, not as a lifeless theory, but as a living force to change the life. God desires that the receivers of His grace shall be witnesses to its power. Those whose course has been most offensive to Him He freely accepts; when they repent, He imparts to them His divine Spirit, places them in the highest positions of trust, and sends them forth into the camp of the disloyal to proclaim His boundless mercy. He would have His servants bear testimony to the fact that through His grace men may possess Christlikeness of character, and may rejoice in the assurance of His great love. He would have us bear testimony to the fact that He cannot be satisfied until the human race are reclaimed and reinstated in their holy privileges as His sons and daughters.

In Christ is the tenderness of the shepherd, the affection of the parent, and the matchless grace of the compassionate Savior. His blessings He presents in the most alluring terms. He is not content merely to announce these blessings; He presents them in the most attractive way, to excite a desire to possess them. So His servants are to present the riches of the glory of the unspeakable Gift. The wonderful love of Christ will melt and subdue hearts, when the mere reiteration of doctrines would accomplish nothing. . . . Christ is sitting for His portrait in every disciple. Every one God has predestinated to be "conformed to the image of his Son" (Romans 8:29). In every one Christ's long-suffering love, His holiness, meekness, mercy, and truth are to be manifested to the world (*The Desire of Ages,* pp. 826, 827).

Christ Is Everything to Those Who Receive Him

My sheep hear my voice, and I know them, and they follow me. John 10:27.

The transformation of the human character makes the yoke of Christ easy, and His burden light. Through faith everyone can, if he will become one with Christ in his obedience and his service.

It is God's prerogative to command; it is the duty of man to obey. Nothing is forced upon any soul. The honor of duty is a thing conferred upon him as a Son of God, an heir of heaven. He is to labor for God in interested, truehearted, glad, honorable service. In obeying all His commandments, a spirit of love for God is revealed. In this very atmosphere of love Christ lived and worked.

Each word, each action, is a work for God. Here is faith in God, and faith in men. Christ would never have given His life for the human race if He had not faith in the souls for whom He died. He knew that a large number would respond to the love He had expressed for humanity. It is not every heart that responds, but every heart may, and can if it will, respond to that love that is without parallel. "My sheep hear my voice," Christ said. A heart yearning for God will recognize the voice of God. God cannot respond to one soul that does not respond to His grace offered, His love bestowed. He is waiting for a response from souls. . . .

The issue rests wholly with themselves. He bids them to the marriage feast; He sets before them the banquet that will satisfy every want. His word is full of marrow and fatness. "And ye shall seek me, and find me, when ye shall search for me with all your heart." . . . Then the Lord will give an outpouring of His Spirit as on the day of Pentecost. . . .

Communion with God is for each one personal and direct. The heart under the guidance of the Holy Spirit will burn within them with the love of God. They are like trustful children. Christ looks not for merit. O if all would come just as they are, and let Him make the preparation in taking them as His. The Lord only wants them to receive Him and learn to wear His yoke, and lift His burdens, that heaven may behold that they are laborers together with God. Why cannot every soul that needs help and rest come to the burden bearer, that he may have light and life.

Christ could not help being bright and shining. His very work was to shine. I am come, He said, "that they might have life, and that they might have it more abundantly." In Me is no darkness at all. . . . Light means revelation, and the light is to shine amid moral darkness. Christ is everything to those who receive Him. He is their Comforter, their safety, their healthfulness. Apart from Christ there is no light at all. There need not be a cloud between the soul and Jesus. . . . His great heart of love is longing to flood the soul with the bright beams of His righteousness (letter 153a, 1897).

July
27

The Shepherd Calls His Sheep by Name

He that entereth in by the door is the shepherd of the sheep. . . . The sheep hear his voice: and he calleth his own sheep by name, and leadeth them out. John 10:2, 3.

The path of the upright is the path of peace. It is so plain that the humble, God-fearing man can walk in it without stumbling and without making crooked paths. It is a narrow path; but men of different temperaments can walk side by side if they but follow the Captain of their salvation. Those who wish to carry along all their evil traits and selfish habits cannot walk in this path, for it is too straight and narrow.

What pains the Great Shepherd takes to call His sheep by name and invite them to follow in His footsteps. He seeks the wandering. He flashes the light from His Word to show them their peril. He speaks to them from heaven in warning and reproofs, and in invitations to return to the right path. He seeks to help the erring by His presence and to lift them when they fall. But many have followed the path of sin so long that they will not hear the voice of Jesus. They leave all that can give them rest and security, yield themselves up to a false guide, and presumptuously hurry on in blind self-confidence, going further and further from light and peace, from happiness and rest. . . .

The cross of Christ is our only hope. It reveals to us the greatness of our Father's love and the fact that the Majesty of heaven submitted to insult, mockery, humiliation, and suffering for the joy of seeing perishing souls saved in His kingdom. If you love your children, let it be your chief study to prepare them for the future, immortal life. . . . Work while it is day; redeem the time, and win the crown of immortal glory. Save yourself and your household, for the salvation of the soul is precious (*Testimonies,* vol. 4, pp. 502, 503).

Many a husband and father might learn a helpful lesson from the carefulness of the faithful shepherd. Jacob, when urged to undertake a rapid and difficult journey, made answer:

"The children are tender, and the flocks and herds with young are with me: and if men should overdrive them one day, all the flock will die. . . . I will lead on softly, according as the cattle that goeth before me and the children be able to endure" (Genesis 33:13, 14).

In life's toilsome way let the husband and father "lead on softly," as the companion of his journey is able to endure. Amidst the world's eager rush for wealth and power, let him learn to stay his steps, to comfort and support the one who is called to walk by his side (*The Ministry of Healing,* p. 374).

July

28

Undershepherds

Feed the flock of God, . . . taking the oversight thereof. 1 Peter 5:2.

The Great Shepherd has undershepherds, to whom He delegates the care of His sheep and lambs. The first work that Christ entrusted to Peter, on restoring him to the ministry, was to feed the lambs. This was a work in which Peter had had little experience. It would require great care and tenderness, much patience and perseverance. It called him to minister to the children and youth, and to those young in the faith, to teach the ignorant, to open the Scriptures to them, and to educate them for usefulness in Christ's service. Heretofore Peter had not been fitted to do this, or even to understand its importance.

The question that Christ put to Peter was significant. He mentioned only one condition of discipleship and service. "Lovest thou me?" He said. This is the essential qualification. Though Peter might possess every other, without the love of Christ he could not be a faithful shepherd over the Lord's flock. Knowledge, benevolence, eloquence, gratitude, and zeal are all aids in the good work; but without the love of Jesus in the heart, the work of the Christian minister will prove a failure.

The lesson which Christ taught him by the Sea of Galilee, Peter carried with him through his life. Writing by the Holy Spirit to the churches, he said:

"The elders which are among you I exhort, who am also an elder, and a witness of the sufferings of Christ, and also a partaker of the glory that shall be revealed: Feed the flock of God which is among you, taking the oversight thereof, not by constraint, but willingly; not for filthy lucre, but of a ready mind; neither as being lords over God's heritage, but being ensamples to the flock. And when the Chief Shepherd shall appear, ye shall receive a crown of glory that fadeth not away" (1 Peter 5:1-4).

The sheep that has strayed from the fold is the most helpless of all creatures. It must be sought for; for it cannot find its way back. So with the soul that has wandered away from God; he is as helpless as the lost sheep; and unless divine love comes to his rescue, he can never find his way to God. Then with what compassion, what sorrow, what persistence, should the undershepherd seek for lost souls! . . . This means the bearing of physical discomfort and the sacrifice of ease. It means a tender solicitude for the erring, a divine compassion and forbearance. It means an ear that can listen with sympathy to heart-breaking recitals of wrong, of degradation, of despair and misery.

The spirit of the true shepherd is one of self-forgetfulness. He loses sight of self (*Gospel Workers,* pp. 182-184).

The Converted Peter, an Undershepherd

"When thou art converted, strengthen thy brethren. Luke 22:32.

Three times Peter had openly denied his Lord, and three times Jesus drew from him the assurance of his love and loyalty, pressing home that pointed question, like a barbed arrow to his wounded heart. Before the assembled disciples Jesus revealed the depth of Peter's repentance, and showed how thoroughly humbled was the once boasting disciple.

Peter was naturally forward and impulsive, and Satan had taken advantage of these characteristics to overthrow him. Just before the fall of Peter, Jesus had said to him, "Satan hath desired to have you, that he may sift you as wheat: but I have prayed for thee, that thy faith fail not: and when thou art converted, strengthen thy brethren" (Luke 22:31, 32). That time had now come, and the transformation in Peter was evident. The close, testing questions of the Lord had not called out one forward, self-sufficient reply; and because of his humiliation and repentance, Peter was better prepared than ever before to act as shepherd to the flock. . . .

Before his fall, Peter was always speaking unadvisedly, from the impulse of the moment. He was always ready to correct others, and to express his mind, before he had a clear comprehension of himself or of what he had to say. But the converted Peter was very different. He retained his former fervor, but the grace of Christ regulated his zeal. He was no longer impetuous, self-confident, and self-exalted, but calm, self-possessed, and teachable. He could then feed the lambs as well as the sheep of Christ's flock.

The Savior's manner of dealing with Peter had a lesson for him and for his brethren. It taught them to meet the transgressor with patience, sympathy, and forgiving love. Although Peter had denied his Lord, the love which Jesus bore him never faltered. Just such love should the undershepherd feel for the sheep and lambs committed to his care. Remembering his own weakness and failure, Peter was to deal with his flock as tenderly as Christ had dealt with him. . . .

Jesus walked alone with Peter, for there was something which He wished to communicate to him only. Before His death, Jesus had said to him, "Whither I go, thou canst not follow me now; but thou shalt follow me afterwards." To this Peter had replied, "Lord, why cannot I follow thee now? I will lay down my life for thy sake" (John 13:36, 37). . . . Peter had failed when the test came, but again he was to have opportunity to prove his love for Christ. . . . Jesus thus made known to Peter the very manner of his death; He even foretold the stretching forth of his hands upon the cross. . . . He felt willing to suffer any death for his Lord (*The Desire of Ages,* pp. 812-815).

In Meekness Feed the Lambs

And the fruit of righteousness is sown in peace of them that make peace. James 3:18.

The true minister of Christ should be encircled by an atmosphere of spiritual light, because he is connected with the world of light, and walks with Christ, who is the light of the world. Arguments may be resisted, persuasion and entreaty may be scorned, the most eloquent appeals, supported by the rigor of logic, may be disregarded; but a living character of righteousness, a daily piety in the walks of life, an anxiety for the sinner wherever found, the spirit of truth burning in the heart, beaming from the countenance, and breathing from the lips in every word, constitute a sermon which is hard to resist or to set aside, and which makes the strongholds of Satan tremble. Ministers who walk with God are clad with the panoply of heaven, and victory will attend their efforts.

Those who are engaged in the great and solemn work of warning the world should not only have an individual experience in the things of God, but they should cultivate love for one another, and should labor to be of one mind, of one judgment, to see eye-to-eye. The absence of this love greatly pleases our wily foe. He is the author of envy, jealousy, hatred, and dissension; and he rejoices to see these vile weeds choke out love, that tender plant of heavenly growth.

It does not please God to have His servants censure, criticize, and condemn one another. He has given them a special work, that of standing in defense of the truth. They are His workmen; all should respect them, and they should respect one another.

In the army, officers are required to respect their fellow officers, and the privates soon learn the lesson. When the leaders of the people in Christian warfare are kind and forbearing, and manifest a special love and regard for their colaborers, they teach others to do the same.

The reputation of a fellow laborer is to be sacredly guarded. If one sees faults in another, he is not to magnify them before others, and make them grievous sins. They may be errors of judgment, that God will give divine grace to overcome. If He had seen that angels, who are perfect, would have done the work for the fallen race better than men, He would have committed it to them. But instead of this He sent the needed assistance by poor, weak, erring mortals, who, having like infirmities as their fellowmen, are best prepared to help them.

There was Peter, who denied his Lord. . . . Before Peter's feet slipped, he had not the spirit of meekness required to feed the lambs; but after he became sensible of his own weakness . . . he could come close to their side in tender sympathy, and could help them (*Historical Sketches,* pp. 120, 121).

July
31

The Voice of the True Shepherd

Many good works have I shewed you from my Father; for which of those works do ye stone me? John 10:32.

Jesus declared Himself to be the true shepherd, because He gave His life for the sheep. He says: "Therefore doth my Father love me, because I lay down my life, that I might take it again. No man taketh it from me, but I lay it down of myself. I have power to lay it down, and I have power to take it again. This commandment have I received of my Father."

Jesus spoke these words in the hearing of a large concourse of people, and a deep impression was made upon the hearts of many who listened. The scribes and Pharisees were filled with jealousy because He was regarded with favor by many. . . . While He represented Himself as the True Shepherd, the Pharisees said, "He hath a devil, and is mad; why hear ye him?" But others distinguished the voice of the True Shepherd, and said:

"These are not the words of him that hath a devil. Can a devil open the eyes of the blind? . . . And Jesus walked in the temple in Solomon's porch. Then came the Jews round about him, and said unto him, How long dost thou make us to doubt? If thou be the Christ, tell us plainly. Jesus answered them, I told you, and ye believed not. . . . My sheep hear my voice, and I know them, and they follow me. . . . I and my Father are one."

With what firmness and power He uttered these words. The Jews had never before heard such words from human lips, and a convicting influence attended them; for it seemed that divinity flashed through humanity as Jesus said, "I and my Father are one." . . . Jesus looked upon them calmly and unshrinkingly, and said, "Many good works have I shewed you from my Father; for which of those works do you stone me?"

The Majesty of heaven stood, calmly assured, as a god before His adversaries. Their scowling faces, their hands filled with stones, did not intimidate Him. He knew that unseen forces, legions of angels, were round about Him, and at one word from His lips they would strike with dismay the throng, should they offer to cast upon Him a single stone. He stood before them undaunted. Why did not the stones fly to the mark? It was because divinity flashed through humanity, and they received a revelation, and were convicted that His were no common claims. The hands relax and the stones fall to the ground. His words had asserted His divinity, but now His personal presence, the light of His eye, the majesty of His attitude, bore witness to the fact that He was the beloved Son of God (*Signs of the Times,* Nov. 27, 1893).

What Matchless Love!

You have received the spirit of sonship. When we cry, "Abba! Father!" it is the Spirit himself bearing witness with our spirit that we are children of God.
Romans 8:15, 16, RSV.

While the law of God is maintained, and its justice vindicated, the sinner can be pardoned. The dearest gift that heaven itself had to bestow has been poured out that God "might be just, and the justifier of him which believeth in Jesus." By that gift men are uplifted from the ruin and degradation of sin to become children of God. Says Paul: "Ye have received the Spirit of adoption, whereby we cry, Abba, Father." . . .

With the beloved John I call upon you to "behold, what manner of love the Father hath bestowed upon us, that we should be called the sons of God." What love, what matchless love, that, sinners and aliens as we are, we may be brought back to God and adopted into His family! We may address Him by the endearing name, "Our Father," which is a sign of our affection for Him and a pledge of His tender regard and relationship to us. And the Son of God, beholding the heirs of grace, "is not ashamed to call them brethren." They have even a more sacred relationship to God than have the angels who have never fallen.

All the paternal love which has come down from generation to generation through the channel of human hearts, all the springs of tenderness which have opened the souls of men, are but as a tiny rill to the boundless ocean when compared with the infinite, exhaustless love of God. Tongue cannot utter it; pen cannot portray it. You may meditate upon it every day of your life; you may search the Scriptures diligently in order to understand it; you may summon every power and capability that God has given you, in the endeavor to comprehend the love and compassion of the heavenly Father; and yet there is an infinity beyond. You may study that love for ages; yet you can never fully comprehend the length and breadth, the depth and the height, of the love of God in giving His Son to die for the world. Eternity itself can never fully reveal it. Yet as we study the Bible and meditate upon the life of Christ and the plan of redemption, these great themes will open to our understanding more and more. And it will be ours to realize the blessing which Paul desired for the Ephesian church when he prayed "that the God of our Lord Jesus Christ, the Father of glory, may give unto you *the spirit of wisdom and revelation in the knowledge of him:* the eyes of your understanding being enlightened; that ye may know what is the hope of his calling, and what the riches of the glory of his inheritance in the saints, and what is the *exceeding greatness of his power* to us-ward who believe" (Ephesians 1:17-19) (*Testimonies,* vol. 5, pp. 739, 740).

Hope and Salvation to the World

They that trust in the Lord shall be as mount Zion, which cannot be removed, but abideth for ever. As the mountains are round about Jerusalem, so the Lord is round about his people from henceforth even for ever. Psalm 125:1, 2.

It was the cross, that instrument of shame and torture, which brought hope and salvation to the world. The disciples were but humble men, without wealth, and with no weapon but the word of God; yet in Christ's strength they went forth to tell the wonderful story of the manger and the cross, and to triumph over all opposition. Without earthly honor or recognition, they were heroes of faith. From their lips came words of divine eloquence that shook the world.

In Jerusalem, where the deepest prejudice existed, and where the most confused ideas prevailed in regard to Him who had been crucified as a malefactor, the disciples continued to speak with boldness the words of life, setting before the Jews the work and mission of Christ, His crucifixion, resurrection, and ascension. Priests and rulers heard with amazement the clear, bold testimony of the apostles. The power of the risen Savior had indeed fallen on the disciples, and their work was accompanied by signs and miracles that daily increased the number of believers. Along the streets where the disciples were to pass, the people laid their sick "on beds and couches, that at the least the shadow of Peter passing by might overshadow some of them." Here also were brought those vexed with unclean spirits. The crowds gathered round them, and those who were healed shouted the praises of God and glorified the name of the Redeemer. . . .

Hitherto all the efforts made to suppress this new teaching had been in vain; but now both Sadducees and Pharisees determined that the work of the disciples should be stopped, for it was proving them guilty of the death of Jesus. Filled with indignation, the priests laid violent hands on Peter and John, and put them in the common prison. . . .

The disciples were not intimidated or cast down by this treatment. . . . The God of heaven, the mighty Ruler of the universe, took the matter of the imprisonment of the disciples into His own hands. . . . By night the angel of the Lord opened the prison doors and said to the disciples, "Go, stand and speak in the temple to the people all the words of this life" (Acts 5:20) (*The Acts of the Apostles,* pp. 77-80).

Shortly before His crucifixion Christ had bequeathed to His disciples a legacy of peace. "Peace I leave with you," He said, "my peace I give unto you." . . . This peace is not the peace that comes through conformity to the world. Christ never purchased peace by compromise with evil. The peace that Christ left His disciples is internal rather than external and was ever to remain with His witnesses through strife and contention (*ibid.,* p. 84).

The Grand, Central Truth

Forasmuch as ye know that you were not redeemed with corruptible things, as silver and gold, . . . but with the precious blood of Christ, as of a lamb without blemish and without spot. 1 Peter 1:18, 19.

The Word of God is the grand instrument which convicts the unconverted, convincing them of their need of the sin-pardoning Savior.

The plan of salvation combines the holy influences of past and present light. These influences are bound together by the golden chain of loving obedience. Receiving Christ by faith and bowing in submission to God's will constitutes men and women sons and daughters of God. By the power which the Savior alone can give they are made members of the royal family, heirs of God and joint-heirs with Christ. . . .

To love God with all the heart, to be a partaker with Christ in His humiliation and suffering, means more than many understand. The atonement of Christ is the great central truth around which cluster all the truths that pertain to the great work of redemption. The mind of man is to blend with the mind of Christ. This union sanctifies the understanding, giving the thoughts clearness and force. . . .

The world is our field of missionary toil, and we are to go forth to our labor surrounded with the atmosphere of Gethsemane and Calvary. . . .

Even more than God abhors infidelity, He abhors indifference in religious matters, because religious pretention without genuine religion is a continual stumbling block to sinners. The more cold and formal men are in the religious life, the more they are filled with egotism, and egotism always works against Christ. You may have much knowledge, but unless you are the possessor of true, pure religion, your knowledge is worthless to Christ. . . .

God forbid that of you should be spoken the words, "I know thy works, that thou art neither cold nor hot: I would thou wert cold or hot. So then because thou art lukewarm, and neither cold nor hot, I will spue thee out of my mouth. Because thou sayest, I am rich, and increased with goods, and have need of nothing; and knowest not that thou art wretched, and miserable, and poor, and blind, and naked: I counsel thee to buy of me gold tried in the fire, that thou mayest be rich; and white raiment, that thou mayest be clothed, and that the shame of thy nakedness do not appear; and anoint thine eyes with eyesalve, that thou mayest see. As many as I love, I rebuke and chasten: be zealous therefore, and repent" (Revelation 3:15-19).

Every soul may become rich in spiritual treasures. Amid the terrible iniquity of this world men may serve God so faithfully that He can bestow on them eternal riches. He will work for those who serve Him faithfully. He can humble the most bitter persecutors of His people, making them friends through a belief of the truth, or removing their power to harm (letter 122, 1901).

The Cross Is the Center

And I, if I be lifted up . . . , will draw all men unto me. John 12:32.

The cross of Calvary challenges, and will finally vanquish every earthly and hellish power. In the cross all influence centers, and from it all influence goes forth. It is the great center of attraction; for on it Christ gave up His life for the human race. This sacrifice was offered for the purpose of restoring man to his original perfection. Yea, more, it was offered to give him an entire transformation of character, making him more than a conqueror. Those who in the strength of Christ overcome the great enemy of God and man will occupy a position in the heavenly courts above angels who have never fallen.

Christ declares, "I, if I be lifted up . . . , will draw all men unto me." If the cross does not find an influence in its favor, it creates an influence. Through generation succeeding generation, the truth for this time is revealed as present truth. Christ on the cross was the medium whereby mercy and truth met together, and righteousness and peace kissed each other. This is the means that is to move the world.

In the plan of God, all the riches of heaven are to be drawn upon by men. Nothing in the treasury of divine resources is deemed too costly to accompany the great gift of the only begotten Son of God. . . . Christ was empowered to breathe into fallen humanity the breath of life. Those who receive Him will never hunger, never thirst; for greater joy than that found in Christ there cannot be. Study the words spoken by the Savior from the Mount of Blessing. How the divine nature shone through His humanity as His lips uttered the benedictions upon those who were the objects of His mercy and love. He blessed them with a fullness that showed that He was drawing from the inexhaustible store of the richest treasures. The treasures of eternity were at His command. The Father committed the riches of heaven to Him, and in the disposal of them He knew no bound. Those who accept Him as their Savior, their Redeemer, the Prince of life, He acknowledges before the heavenly host, before the worlds unfallen, and before the fallen world, as His peculiar treasure. . . .

What is Christianity? God's instrumentality for the conversion of the sinner. Jesus will call to account everyone who is not brought under His control, who does not demonstrate in his life the influence of the cross of Calvary. Christ should be uplifted by those whom He has redeemed by dying on the cross a death of shame. He who has felt the power of the grace of Christ has a story to tell. He seeks to put in operation methods of work which will diffuse the gospel of Christ. Humanity, drawing its efficiency from the great source of wisdom, is made the instrumentality, the working agency, through which the gospel exercises its transforming power on mind and heart (manuscript 56, 1899).

Lift Him Up, the Man of Calvary

Behold the Lamb of God, which taketh away the sin of the world. John 1:29.

The principles that should actuate us as workers in God's cause are laid down by the apostle Paul. He says: "We are labourers together with God." "Whatsoever ye do, do it heartily, as to the Lord, and not unto men." And Peter exhorts the believers: "As every man hath received the gift, even so minister the same one to another, as good stewards of the manifold grace of God. If any man speak, let him speak as the oracles of God; if any man minister, let him do it as of the ability which God giveth: that God in all things may be glorified through Jesus Christ."

When these principles control our hearts, we shall realize that the work is God's, not ours; that He has the same care for every part of the great whole. When Christ and His glory are made first and love of self is swallowed up in love for souls for whom Christ died, then no worker will be so entirely absorbed in one branch of the cause as to lose sight of the importance of every other. . . .

We are taught in God's Word that this is the time, above all others, when we may look for light from heaven. It is now that we are to expect a refreshing from the presence of the Lord. We should watch for the movings of God's providence as the army of Israel watched for "the sound of a going in the tops of the mulberry trees"—the appointed signal that heaven would work for them.

God cannot glorify His name through His people while they are leaning upon man and making flesh their arm. Their present state of weakness will continue until Christ alone shall be exalted; until, with John the Baptist, they shall say from a humble and reverent heart: "He must increase, but I must decrease." Words have been given me to speak to the people of God: "Lift Him up, the Man of Calvary. Let humanity stand back, that all may behold Him in whom their hopes of eternal life are centered. Says the prophet Isaiah: 'Unto us a child is born, unto us a son is given: and the government shall be upon his shoulder: and his name shall be called Wonderful, Counsellor, The mighty God, The everlasting Father, The Prince of Peace.' Let the church and the world look upon their Redeemer. Let every voice proclaim with John: 'Behold the Lamb of God, which taketh away the sin of the world.'"

It is to the thirsting soul that the fountain of living waters is open. God declares: "I will pour water upon him that is thirsty, and floods upon the dry ground." To souls that are earnestly seeking for light and that accept with gladness every ray of divine illumination from His Holy Word, to such alone light will be given. It is through these souls that God will reveal that light and power which will lighten the whole earth with His glory (*Testimonies*, vol. 5, pp. 726-729).

His Crowning Work

The Lord God, merciful and gracious, longsuffering, and abundant in goodness and truth, keeping mercy for thousands, forgiving iniquity and transgression and sin, and that will by no means clear the guilty. Exodus 34:6, 7.

Those who receive Christ by faith will be looked upon by Heaven as precious pearls for which the merchant man has paid an infinite price, and the human agents who find Christ will realize that they have found a heavenly treasure. They will be anxious to sell all that they have in order to buy the field which contains this treasure. As they contemplate the love of God, as the plan of salvation opens to their view, as the mystery of Christ's condescension becomes plainer to them, as they see the sacrifice that He made for them, they count nothing too dear to give up for His sake. . . .

The Lord God of heaven collected all the riches of the universe, and laid them down in order to purchase the pearl of lost humanity. The Father gave all His divine resources into the hands of Christ in order that the richest blessings of heaven might be poured out upon a fallen race. God could not express greater love than He has expressed in giving the Son of His bosom to this world. This gift was given to man to convince him that God had left nothing undone that He could do, that there is nothing held in reserve, but that all heaven has been poured out in one vast gift. The present and eternal happiness of man consists in receiving God's love, and in keeping God's commandments. Christ is our Redeemer. He is the Word that became flesh and dwelt among us. He is the fountain in which we may be washed and cleansed from all impurity. He is the costly sacrifice that has been given for the reconciliation of man. The universe of heaven, the worlds unfallen, the fallen world, and the confederacy of evil cannot say that God could do more for the salvation of man than He has done. Never can His gift be surpassed, never can He display a richer depth of love. Calvary represents His crowning work. It is man's part to respond to His great love, by appropriating the great salvation the blessing of the Lord has made it possible for man to obtain. We are to show our appreciation of the wonderful gift of God by becoming partakers of the divine nature, having escaped the corruption that is in the world through lust. We are to show our gratitude to God by becoming a coworker with Jesus Christ, by representing His character to the world. . . . The Lord looks upon souls as precious pearls. . . .

As they lift Christ up, their eyes are anointed so that they can distinguish the relationship of Christ to the human family. They become wise, and in meekness and lowliness, as opportunity opens, they present to tried and tempted souls the sublime reality of the saving grace of God (*Youth's Instructor*, Oct. 17, 1895).

Christ Died for Us

For Christ also hath once suffered for sins, the just for the unjust, that he might bring us to God, being put to death in the flesh. 1 Peter 3:18.

The cross of Calvary appeals to us in power, affording a reason why we should love our Savior, and why we should make Him first and last and best in everything. We should take our fitting place in humble penitence at the foot of the cross. Here, as we see our Savior in agony, the Son of God dying, the just for the unjust, we may learn lessons of meekness and lowliness of mind. Behold Him who with one word could summon legions of angels to His assistance, a subject of jest and merriment, of reviling and hatred. He gives Himself a sacrifice for sin. When reviled, He threatens not; when falsely accused, He opens not His mouth. He prays on the cross for His murderers. He is dying for them; He is paying an infinite price for every one of them. He bears the penalty of man's sins without a murmur. And this uncomplaining victim is the Son of God. His throne is from everlasting, and His kingdom shall have no end.

Come, you who are seeking your own pleasure in forbidden joys and sinful indulgences, you who are scattering from Christ, look upon the cross of Calvary; behold the royal victim suffering on your account, and while you have opportunity be wise, and seek the fountain of life and true happiness. Come, you who complain and murmur at the little inconveniences and the few trials you must meet in this life, look on Jesus, the author and finisher of your faith. He turned from His royal throne, His high command, and, laying aside His divinity, clothed Himself with humanity. For our sakes He was rejected and despised; He became poor that we through His poverty might be made rich. Can you, beholding by the eye of faith the sufferings of Christ, tell your trials, your tale of woe? Can you nurse revenge in your heart while you remember the prayer that came from the pale and quivering lips of Christ for His revilers, His murderers: "Father, forgive them; for they know not what they do"?

There is a work before us to subdue the pride and vanity that seek a place in our hearts, and through penitence and faith to bring ourselves into familiar and holy converse with Christ. . . . We must deny self, and fight continually against pride. We must hide self in Jesus, and let Him appear in our character and conversation. While we look constantly to Him whom our sins have pierced and our sorrows have burdened, we shall acquire strength to be like Him. Our lives, our deportment, will testify how highly we prize our Redeemer, and the salvation He has wrought out for us at such a cost to Himself. And our peace will be as a river while we bind ourselves in willing, happy captivity to Jesus (*Signs of the Times*, Mar. 17, 1887).

Souls Rescued From Satan's Power

And the Lord said unto Satan, the Lord rebuke thee, O Satan; even the Lord that hath chosen Jerusalem rebuke thee: is not this a brand plucked out of the fire? Zechariah 3:2.

Through the plan of salvation, Jesus is breaking Satan's hold upon the human family and rescuing souls from his power. All the hatred and malignity of the archrebel is stirred as he beholds the evidence of Christ's supremacy, and with fiendish power and cunning he works to wrest from Him the remnant of the children of men who have accepted His salvation.

He leads men into skepticism, causing them to lose confidence in God and to separate from His love; he tempts them to break His law, and then he claims them as his captives and contests the right of Christ to take them from him. He knows that those who seek God earnestly for pardon and grace will obtain it; therefore he presents their sins before them to discourage them. He is constantly seeking occasion against those who are trying to obey God. Even their best and most acceptable services he seeks to make appear corrupt. By countless devices, the most subtle and the most cruel, he endeavors to secure their condemnation. Man cannot meet these charges himself. In his sin-stained garments, confessing his guilt, he stands before God. But Jesus our Advocate presents an effectual plea in behalf of all who by repentance and faith have committed the keeping of their souls to Him. He pleads their cause and vanquishes their accuser by the mighty arguments of Calvary. His perfect obedience to God's law, even unto the death of the cross, has given Him all power in heaven and in earth, and He claims of His Father mercy and reconciliation for guilty man. To the accuser of His people He declares: "'The Lord rebuke thee, O Satan.' These are the purchase of My blood, brands plucked from the burning." Those who rely upon Him in faith receive the comforting assurance: "Behold, I have caused thine iniquity to pass from thee, and I will clothe thee with change of raiment." All that have put on the robe of Christ's righteousness will stand before Him as chosen and faithful and true. Satan has no power to pluck them out of the hand of Christ. Not one soul that in penitence and faith has claimed His protection will Christ permit to pass under the enemy's power. His word is pledged: "Let him take hold of my strength, that he may make peace with me; and he shall make peace with me." The promise given to Joshua is made to all: "If thou wilt keep my charge, . . . I will give thee places to walk among these that stand by." Angels of God will walk on either side of them, even in this world, and they will stand at last among the angels that surround the throne of God. . . . We cannot answer the charges of Satan against us. Christ alone can make an effectual plea in our behalf. He is able to silence the accuser with arguments founded not upon our merits, but on His own (*Testimonies*, vol. 5, pp. 470-472).

Conqueror Over the Power of Darkness

God forbid that I should glory, save in the cross of our Lord Jesus Christ. Galatians 6:14.

Christ left His position in the heavenly courts, and came to this earth to live the life of human beings. This sacrifice He made in order to show that Satan's charge against God is false—that it is possible for man to obey the laws of God's kingdom. Equal with the Father, honored and adored by the angels, in our behalf Christ humbled Himself, and came to this earth to live a life of lowliness and poverty—to be a man of sorrows and acquainted with grief. Yet the stamp of divinity was upon His humanity. He came as a divine Teacher, to uplift human beings, to increase their physical, mental, and spiritual efficiency.

There is no one who can explain the mystery of the incarnation of Christ. Yet we know that He came to this earth and lived as a man among men. The man Christ Jesus was not the Lord God Almighty, yet Christ and the Father are one. The Deity did not sink under the agonizing torture of Calvary, yet it is nonetheless true that "God so loved the world, that he gave his only begotten Son, that whosoever believeth in him should not perish, but have everlasting life."

In every possible way Satan sought to prevent Jesus from developing a perfect childhood, a faultless manhood, a holy ministry, and an unblemished sacrifice. But he was defeated. He could not lead Jesus into sin. He could not discourage Him, or drive Him from the work He had come to this earth to do. From the desert to Calvary the storm of Satan's wrath beat upon Him, but the more merciless it fell, the more firmly did the Son of God cling to the hand of His Father, and press on in the bloodstained path (*The SDA Bible Commentary*, Ellen G. White Comments, vol. 5, pp. 1129, 1130).

Christ was crucified, and in His death the powers of hell seemed to prevail. But even when on the cross the Savior cried, "My God, my God, why hast thou forsaken me?" He was conqueror over the power of darkness. When the words, "It is finished," came from His pale, trembling lips, darkness like the darkness of midnight hid His dying agony from the eyes of the spectators. Through long hours of agony He had been gazed upon by the jesting multitude. Now He was mercifully hidden by the mantle of God.

At His death, there was a violent earthquake. The people were shaken together in heaps. The wildest confusion and consternation ensued. . . . Creation seemed to be shivering to atoms. It was as if nature itself were protesting against the murder of the Son of God.

Christ's death on the cross paid the ransom for every human being. All may overcome, because Christ has made an atonement for the sins of the whole world. To all He offers the power of redeeming grace (manuscript 140, 1903).

By Faith, Christ Was Victor

Father, into thy hands I commend my spirit. Luke 23:46.

The spotless Son of God hung upon the cross, His flesh lacerated with stripes; those hands so often reached out in blessing, nailed to the wooden bars; those feet so tireless on ministries of love, spiked to the tree; that royal head pierced by the crown of thorns; those quivering lips shaped to the cry of woe. And all that He endured—the blood drops that flowed from His head, His hands, His feet, the agony that racked His frame, and the unutterable anguish that filled His soul at the hiding of His Father's face—speaks to each child of humanity, declaring, It is for thee that the Son of God consents to bear this burden of guilt; for thee He spoils the domain of death, and opens the gates of Paradise. He who stilled the angry waves and walked the foam-capped billows, who made devils tremble and disease flee, who opened blind eyes and called forth the dead to life—offers Himself upon the cross as a sacrifice, and this from love to thee. He, the Sinbearer, endures the wrath of divine justice, and for thy sake becomes sin itself.

In silence the beholders watched for the end of the fearful scene. The sun shone forth; but the cross was still enveloped in darkness. Priests and rulers looked toward Jerusalem; and lo, the dense cloud had settled over the city and the plains of Judea. The Sun of Righteousness, the Light of the world, was withdrawing His beams from the once favored city of Jerusalem. The fierce lightnings of God's wrath were directed against the fated city.

Suddenly the gloom lifted from the cross, and in clear, trumpetlike tones, that seemed to resound throughout creation, Jesus cried, "It is finished." "Father, into thy hands I commend my spirit." A light encircled the cross, and the face of the Savior shone with a glory like the sun. He then bowed His head upon His breast, and died.

Amid the awful darkness, apparently forsaken of God, Christ had drained the last dregs in the cup of human woe. In those dreadful hours He had relied upon the evidence of His Father's acceptance heretofore given Him. He was acquainted with the character of His Father; He understood His justice, His mercy, and His great love. By faith He rested in Him whom it had ever been His joy to obey. And as in submission He committed Himself to God, the sense of the loss of His Father's favor was withdrawn. By faith, Christ was victor (*The Desire of Ages*, pp. 755, 756).

Look, Believe, and Live

[We] are kept by the power of God through faith unto salvation ready to be revealed in the last time. 1 Peter 1:5.

Those who depend upon their own righteousness instead of relying upon the righteousness of Christ will lose the prize; they will be weighed in the balances of the sanctuary and found wanting. Let everyone who is striving for the precious boon of eternal life distrust his own strength, and, in much prayer, cast his helpless soul upon Christ. There is too little searching of the Word of God for definite direction in the way of life. The larger number of those who profess to believe on Christ have only superficial ideas as to what constitutes Christian character. . . . Do not deceive yourself with the idea that your own inherent righteousness will bring you into harmony with God. Do not fail to look upon yourself as a sinner in the sight of God. Do not fail to look upon Jesus lifted up upon the cross; and as you look, believe and live; for by faith in the atoning sacrifice you may be justified through the redemption that is in Christ Jesus. Believe that you are forgiven, that you are justified, not in transgression and disobedience, but in submission to the will of God. If through faith you lay hold of the righteousness of Christ, then be not careless of your thoughts, your words, your works. Study much, and pray that as Christ has shown you the way, He may by His grace keep you in the way. For we are "kept by the power of God through faith"; and even faith is not of ourselves, but it also is the gift of God.

In order to grow in grace and in the knowledge of Christ, it is essential that you meditate much upon the great themes of redemption. You should ask yourself why Christ has taken humanity upon Himself, why He suffered upon the cross, why He bore the sins of men, why He was made sin and righteousness for us. You should study to know why He ascended to heaven in the nature of man, and what is His work for us today. . . .

If thoughts of Christ, His work and character, are cherished, you will be led to sink deep the shaft of truth, and you will be enabled to come into possession of precious jewels of truth. Through an appreciation of the character of Christ, through communion with God, sin will become hateful to you. As you meditate upon heavenly things, and walk with God, as did Enoch, you will lay aside every weight, and the sin that doth so easily beset, and will run with patience the race set before you. . . . Our building must be founded upon the Rock Christ Jesus or it will not stand the test of the tempest (*Signs of the Times,* Dec. 1, 1890).

Transformation Through Christ

Therefore if any man be in Christ, he is a new creature: old things are passed away; behold, all things are become new. 2 Corinthians 5:17.

A great change takes place in the character of him who accepts Christ; for "if any man be in Christ, he is a new creature." When we see those who profess Christianity manifesting the old carnal desires in word and action, we may know that they are not in Christ, that the transforming grace of Christ has not touched the soul, molded the character, and cleansed the defilement of the heart. . . .

Those who have an experimental knowledge of the grace of Christ will feel their obligation to Him to be representatives of His power to the world. They will realize that He who knew no sin was made to be sin for them, that they might be made the righteousness of God in Him. An appreciation of this fact will enable us to get correct views of the work of our Redeemer. True believers will realize that while they were separated from Him through impenitence and sin, He did not forsake them, but rather interceded for them, that they might have the benefits of the salvation which He had purchased for them at an infinite sacrifice. In accepting Christ they know that they must come out from the world, and be separate, and touch not the unclean, that they may be the children of God. They must love Christ supremely.

It is impossible for finite minds to make a just estimate of the love of God toward His fallen creatures. We are ever in danger of forgetting this great love, because we fail to meditate upon it, and allow ourselves to become absorbed in the things of this world. We permit our hearts to be divided by placing our affections on things below, and so separate from the true Source of happiness.

Christ should be the theme of our thoughts, the object of our tenderest affection. We should let our minds dwell upon the precious characteristics of our Lord; we should contemplate the rich promises of His Word; we should meditate upon the glories of heaven. We should not be satisfied with but occasional glimpses of our Redeemer, but our minds should be stayed upon God by continual trust in His Word. We should search the Scriptures diligently in order that we may have an understanding of the claims that Christ has upon us, and that we may have right views of the truth. Our wills must be subdued, and brought into harmony with the will of God.

Precious light has been permitted to shine upon our pathway, and around us are the angels of heaven, who are interested in our welfare. . . . The love of Christ manifested toward us in His life of humiliation and self-denial, in His death on Calvary, should call forth songs of gratitude from our lips. The hope of His soon coming should fill us with sacred joy (*Signs of the Times,* Dec. 8, 1890).

The Graces of His Character

And he saith unto him, Verily, verily, I say unto you, Hereafter ye shall see heaven open, and the angels of God ascending and descending upon the Son of man. John 1:51.

God has given us a perfect standard of character, which we are ever to keep before us. Through the strength that Christ can impart, we may keep the law of God. We should be obedient children, whatever difficulty we may have to encounter. We must not expect to enter heaven without conflict and trial, but we have the assurance that if we will not consult our own pleasure, but the will of God, we shall not be left to fight the battle alone.

There is a great work to be done in the world, and every one of us should let his light shine upon the pathway of others. We need to gather divine rays of light from Christ. We need to search the Scriptures, and dig deep in the mines of truth; for the precious jewels do not always lie on the surface; we should search for them as for hidden treasure. There is a heaven of bliss to gain, for Christ has gone to prepare mansions for us; and now is the time for us to seek a preparation for that which He is preparing for us. In order to do this, we must bring Christ into our life daily; for those who dwell in the abodes of bliss must have hearts free from all envy, jealousy, hatred, malice, and selfishness. Jesus is waiting to do great things for us, to fill us with all the fullness of God. We should believe in His promises, for He "keepeth truth forever," "and there is no unrighteousness in him" (Psalm 146:6; 92:15) (*Signs of the Times,* Dec. 8, 1890).

There is a connection between earth and heaven through Christ, the mystic ladder that Jacob saw in his vision at Bethel. When we were separated from God, Christ came to reconcile us to the Father. In pitying love He placed His human arm about the fallen race, and with His divine arm He grasped the throne of the Infinite, thus connecting finite man with the infinite God; through the plan of salvation we are united with the agencies of heaven. Through the merits of a crucified and risen Redeemer, we may look up and see the glory of God shining from heaven to earth. We should be grateful to God for the plan of salvation. We have been blessed with many blessings, and in return we should give to God our undivided hearts.

How sad it is that through our indifference to our eternal interests we are far from Christ. . . . We do not see the glory of God shining upon every round of the ladder; we do not climb up by Christ, making advancement in the divine life. If we did this, we should reflect the image of Christ, have purity of character, and become like lights in the world. We should constantly behold Him, until we should be charmed with the graces of His character; then we would not fail to talk of Him and His love. We should then be in possession of rich blessings which the world cannot give or take away, and we should lose our relish for sin (*ibid.,* Dec. 15, 1890).

The Spotless Lamb of God

He was numbered with the transgressors; and he bare the sin of many, and made intercession for the transgressors. Isaiah 53:12.

While His disciples were contending as to who should be greatest in the promised kingdom, He girded Himself as a servant and washed the feet of those who called Him Lord and Master.

His ministry was nearly completed; He had only a few more lessons to impart. And that they might never forget the humility of the pure and spotless Lamb of God, the great and efficacious Sacrifice for man humbled Himself to wash the feet of His disciples. It will do you good . . . to frequently review the closing scenes in the life of our Redeemer. Here, beset with temptations as He was, we may all learn lessons of the utmost importance to us. It would be well to spend a thoughtful hour each day reviewing the life of Christ from the manger to Calvary. We should take it point by point and let the imagination vividly grasp each scene, especially the closing ones of His earthly life. By thus contemplating His teachings and sufferings, and the infinite sacrifice made by Him for the redemption of the race, we may strengthen our faith, quicken our love, and become more deeply imbued with the spirit which sustained our Savior.

If we would be saved at last we must all learn the lesson of penitence and faith at the foot of the cross. Christ suffered humiliation to save us from everlasting disgrace. He consented to have scorn, mockery, and abuse fall upon Him in order to shield us. It was our transgression that gathered the veil of darkness about His divine soul and extorted the cry from Him, as of one smitten and forsaken of God. He bore our sorrows; He was put to grief for our sins. He made Himself an offering for sin, that we might be justified before God through Him. Everything noble and generous in man will respond to the contemplation of Christ upon the cross. . . .

The mighty argument of the cross will convict of sin. The divine love of God for sinners, expressed in the gift of His Son to suffer shame and death that they might be ennobled and endowed with everlasting life, is the study of a lifetime. I ask you to study anew the cross of Christ. If all the proud and vainglorious, whose hearts are panting for the applause of men and for distinction above their fellows, could rightly estimate the value of the highest earthly glory in contrast with the value of the Son of God, rejected, despised, spit upon, by the very ones whom He came to redeem, how insignificant would appear all the honor that finite man can bestow. . . .

It requires a constant, earnest, and vigilant effort to watch and control self, to keep Jesus prominent and self out of sight (*Testimonies,* vol. 4, pp. 374-376).

The Value of a Soul

We also joy in God through our Lord Jesus Christ, by whom we have now received the atonement. Romans 5:11.

Those who are finally victorious will have seasons of terrible perplexity and trial in their religious life; but they must not cast away their confidence, for this is a part of their discipline in the school of Christ, and it is essential in order that all dross may be purged away. The servant of God must endure with fortitude the attacks of the enemy, his grievous taunts, and must overcome the obstacles which Satan will place in his way.

Satan will seek to discourage the followers of Christ, so that they may not pray or study the Scriptures, and he will throw his hateful shadow athwart the path to hide Jesus from the view, to shut away the vision of His love, and the glories of the heavenly inheritance. It is his delight to cause the children of God to go shrinkingly, tremblingly, and painfully along, under continual doubt. He seeks to make the pathway as sorrowful as possible; but if you keep looking up, not down at your difficulties, you will not faint in the way, you will soon see Jesus reaching His hand to help you, and you will only have to give Him your hand in simple confidence, and let Him lead you. As you become trustful, you will become hopeful.

Jesus is the light of the world, and you are to fashion your life after His. You will find help in Christ to form a strong, symmetrical, beautiful character. Satan cannot make of none effect the light shining forth from such a character. The Lord has a work for each of us to do. He does not provide that we shall be sustained by the influence of human praise and petting; He means that every soul shall stand in the strength of the Lord. God has given us His best gift, even His only begotten Son, to uplift, ennoble, and fit us, by putting on us His own perfection of character, for a home in His kingdom. Jesus came to our world and lived as He expects His followers to live. . . .

God designs that we shall work, not in a despairing manner, but with strong faith and hope. As we search the Scriptures, and are enlightened to behold the wonderful condescension of the Father in giving Jesus to the world, that all who believe on Him should not perish but have everlasting life, we should rejoice with joy unspeakable and full of glory.

Everything that can be gained by education, God means that we shall use for the advancement of the truth. True, vital godliness must be reflected from the life and character, that the cross of Christ may be lifted up before the world, and the value of the soul be revealed in the light of the cross. Our minds must be opened to understand the Scriptures, that we may gain spiritual power by feeding upon the bread of heaven (*Messages to Young People,* pp. 63, 64).

A Person's True Worth

God shows his love for us in that while we were yet sinners Christ died for us. Since, therefore, we are now justified by his blood, much more shall we be saved by him from the wrath of God. Romans 5:8, 9, RSV.

Christ and Him crucified should become the theme of our thoughts and stir the deepest emotions of our souls. The true followers of Christ will appreciate the great salvation which He has wrought for them; and wherever He leads the way, they will follow. They will consider it a privilege to bear whatever burdens Christ may lay upon them. It is through the cross alone that we can estimate the worth of the human soul. Such is the value of men for whom Christ died that the Father is satisfied with the infinite price which He pays for the salvation of man in yielding up His own Son to die for their redemption. What wisdom, mercy, and love in its fullness are here manifested! The worth of man is known only by going to Calvary. In the mystery of the cross of Christ we can place an estimate upon man.

What a responsible position, to unite with the Redeemer of the world in the salvation of men! This work calls for self-denial, sacrifice, and benevolence, for perseverance, courage, and faith. . . . Persistent, prevailing faith is necessary (*Testimonies,* vol. 2, pp. 634, 635).

Self-denial and the cross lie directly in the pathway of every follower of Christ. The cross is that which crosses the natural affections and the will. If the heart is not wholly sanctified to God, if the will and affections and thoughts are not brought into subjection to the will of God, there will be a failure to carry out the principles of true religion and to exemplify in the life the life of Christ (*ibid.,* p. 651).

The followers of Christ should value souls as He valued them. Their sympathies should be with the work of their dear Redeemer, and they should labor to save the purchase of His blood, at any sacrifice. What are money, houses, and lands in comparison with even one soul?

Christ made a full and complete sacrifice, a sacrifice sufficient to save every son and daughter of Adam who should show repentance toward God for having transgressed His law, and manifest faith in our Lord Jesus Christ. Yet notwithstanding the sacrifice was ample, but few consent to a life of obedience that they may have this great salvation. Few are willing to imitate His amazing privations, to endure His sufferings and persecutions, and to share His exhausting labor to bring others to the light. . . . Christ is the Captain of our salvation, and by His own sufferings and sacrifice He has given an example to all His followers that watchfulness and prayer, and persevering effort, were necessary on their part if they would rightly represent the love which dwelt in His bosom for the fallen race (*ibid.,* p. 664).

Christ Elevates Humanity

Both the one who makes men holy and those who are made holy are of the same family. So Jesus is not ashamed to call them brothers. Hebrews 2:11, NIV.

Jesus is "not ashamed to call them brethren" (Hebrews 2:11); He is our Sacrifice, our Advocate, our Brother, bearing our human form before the Father's throne, and through eternal ages one with the race He has redeemed—the Son of man. And all this that man might be uplifted from the ruin and degradation of sin that he might reflect the love of God and share the joy of holiness.

The price paid for our redemption, the infinite sacrifice of our heavenly Father in giving His Son to die for us, should give us exalted conceptions of what we may become through Christ. As the inspired apostle John beheld the height, the depth, the breadth of the Father's love toward the perishing race, he was filled with adoration and reverence; and, failing to find suitable language in which to express the greatness and tenderness of this love, he called upon the world to behold. "Behold, what manner of love the Father hath bestowed upon us, that we should be called the sons of God" (1 John 3:1). What a value this places upon man! Through transgression the sons of man become subjects of Satan. Through faith in the atoning sacrifice of Christ the sons of Adam may become the sons of God. By assuming human nature, Christ elevates humanity. Fallen men are placed where, through connection with Christ, they may indeed become worthy of the name "sons of God."

Such love is without a parallel. Children of the heavenly King! Precious promise! Theme for the most profound meditation! The matchless love of God for a world that did not love Him! The thought has a subduing power upon the soul and brings the mind into captivity to the will of God. The more we study the divine character in the light of the cross, the more we see mercy, tenderness, and forgiveness blended with equity and justice, and the more clearly we discern innumerable evidences of a love that is infinite and a tender pity surpassing a mother's yearning sympathy for her wayward child (*Steps to Christ*, pp. 14, 15).

The heart of God yearns over His earthly children with a love stronger than death. In giving up His Son, He has poured out to us all heaven in one gift. The Savior's life and death and intercession, the ministry of angels, the pleading of the Spirit, the Father working above and through all, the unceasing interest of heavenly beings—all are enlisted in behalf of man's redemption.

Oh, let us contemplate the amazing sacrifice that has been made for us! Let us try to appreciate the labor and energy that Heaven is expending to reclaim the lost, and bring them back to the Father's house. . . . Let us avail ourselves of the means provided for us that we may be transformed into His likeness (*ibid.*, pp. 21, 22).

An Atmosphere of Hopefulness and Cheer

Rejoice in the Lord alway: and again I say, Rejoice. Philippians 4:4.

To the Christian is granted the joy of gathering rays of eternal light from the throne of glory, and of reflecting these rays not only on his own path, but on the paths of those with whom he associates. By speaking words of hope and encouragement, of grateful praise and kindly cheer, he may strive to make those around him better, to elevate them, to point them to heaven and glory, and to lead them to seek, above all earthly things, the eternal substance, the immortal inheritance, the riches that are imperishable.

"Rejoice in the Lord alway," says the apostle; "and again I say, Rejoice." Wherever we go, we should carry an atmosphere of Christian hopefulness and cheer; then those who are out of Christ will see attractiveness in the religion we profess; unbelievers will see the consistency of our faith. We need to have more distinct glimpses of heaven, the land where all is brightness and joy. We need to know more of the fullness of the blessed hope. If we are constantly "rejoicing in hope," we shall be able to speak words of encouragement to those whom we meet. "A word spoken in due season, how good is it!" Souls are perishing for the lack of personal labor.

Not alone in daily association with believers and unbelievers are we to glorify God by speaking often one to another in words of gratitude and rejoicing. As Christians, we are exhorted not to forsake the assembling of ourselves together, for our own refreshing, and to impart the consolation we have received. In these meetings, held from week to week, we should dwell upon God's goodness and manifold mercies, upon His power to save from sin. In features, in temper, in words, in character, we are to witness that the service of God is good. Thus we proclaim that "the law of the Lord is perfect, converting the soul."

Our prayer and social meetings should be seasons of special help and encouragement. Each one has a work to do to make these gatherings as interesting and profitable as possible. This can best be done by having a fresh experience daily in the things of God, and by not hesitating to speak of His love in the assemblies of His people. If you allow no darkness or unbelief to enter your hearts, they will not be manifest in your meetings. . . .

By the mystery and glory of the cross we can estimate the value of man, and then we shall see and feel the importance of working for our fellow men, that they may be exalted to the throne of God (*Southern Watchman,* Mar. 7, 1905).

Surrender to Christ

If any man will come after me, let him deny himself, and take up his cross daily, and follow me. Luke 9:23.

How often do we come in contact with people who are never happy. They fail of enjoying the contentment and peace that Jesus can give. They profess to be Christians, but they do not comply with the conditions upon which the promise of God is fulfilled. Jesus has said, "Come unto me, all ye that labour and are heavy laden, and I will give you rest. Take my yoke upon you, and learn of me; for I am meek and lowly in heart: and ye shall find rest unto your souls. For my yoke is easy, and my burden is light." The reason why many are in a state of unrest is that they are not learning in the school of the Master. The submissive, self-sacrificing child of God understands by experience what it is to have the peace of Christ. True followers of Christ know that they must take His yoke, share His trials, carry His burdens. But they do not feel like complaining; for the meekness and lowliness of Christ makes the yoke easy and the burden light.

It is love of selfish ease, love of pleasure, your self-esteem, self-exaltation, that prevents you from learning the precious life-lessons in the school of Christ. It is the Christian's duty not to permit surroundings and circumstances to mold him; but to live above surroundings, fashioning his character according to the divine Model. He is to be faithful in whatever place he is found. He is to do his duty with fidelity, improving the opportunities given him of God, making the most of his capabilities. With an eye single to the glory of God, he is to work for Jesus wherever he may be. We are to surrender the will, the heart, to God, and become acquainted with Christ. We must deny self, take up the cross, and follow Jesus. Not one of us can reach heaven, save by the narrow, cross-bearing way. But how many wear the cross as an ornament on the person, but fail to bear the cross in practical, everyday life.

How many profess to be servants of Christ; but how loath are they to bear reproach and shame, for His sake. The cross is not to please self; it lies directly across the path of the pleasure-lover, and cuts through our carnal desires and selfish inclinations. . . .

The thing essential for successful work is a knowledge of Christ; for this knowledge will give sound principles of right, impart a noble, unselfish spirit, like that of our Savior whom we profess to serve. Faithfulness, economy, caretaking, thoroughness, should characterize all our work, wherever we may be, whether in the kitchen, in the workshop, . . . or wherever we may be stationed in the vineyard of the Lord (*Review and Herald,* Sept. 22, 1891).

August
20

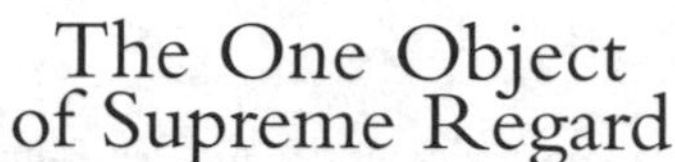

The One Object of Supreme Regard

I determined not to know any thing among you, save Jesus Christ, and him crucified. . . . And my speech and my preaching was not with enticing words of man's wisdom, but in demonstration of the Spirit and of power. 1 Corinthians 2:2-4.

To Paul the cross was the one object of supreme interest. Ever since he had been arrested in his career of persecution against the followers of the crucified Nazarene he had never ceased to glory in the cross. At that time there had been given him a revelation of the infinite love of God, as revealed in the death of Christ; and a marvelous transformation had been wrought in his life, bringing all his plans and purposes into harmony with heaven. From that hour he had been a new man in Christ. He knew by personal experience that when a sinner once beholds the love of the Father, as seen in the sacrifice of His Son, and yields to the divine influence, a change of heart takes place, and henceforth Christ is all and in all.

At the time of his conversion, Paul was inspired with a longing desire to help his fellow men to behold Jesus of Nazareth as the Son of the living God, mighty to transform and to save. Henceforth his life was wholly devoted to an effort to portray the love and power of the Crucified One. His great heart of sympathy took in all classes. "I am debtor," he declared, "both to the Greeks, and to the Barbarians; both to the wise, and to the unwise" (Romans 1:14). Love for the Lord of glory, whom he had so relentlessly persecuted in the person of His saints, was the actuating principle of his conduct, his motive power. If ever his ardor in the path of duty flagged, one glance at the cross and the amazing love there revealed was enough to cause him to gird up the loins of his mind and press forward in the path of self-denial. . . .

In the power of the Spirit, Paul related the story of his own miraculous conversion and of his confidence in the Old Testament Scriptures. . . . His words were spoken with solemn earnestness . . . that he loved with all his heart the crucified and risen Savior. They saw that his mind was centered in Christ, that his whole life was bound up with his Lord. . . .

Paul realized that his sufficiency was not in himself, but in the presence of the Holy Spirit, whose gracious influence filled his heart, bringing every thought into subjection of Christ. He spoke of himself as "always bearing about in the body the dying of the Lord Jesus, that the life also of Jesus might be made manifest in our body" (2 Corinthians 4:10). In the apostle's teachings Christ was the central figure. "I live," he declared; "yet not I, but Christ liveth in me" (Galatians 2:20). Self was hidden; Christ was revealed and exalted (*The Acts of the Apostles,* pp. 245-251).

Glorify the Master

Each of you should look not only to your own interests, but also to the interests of others.
Philippians 2:4, NIV.

How earnest, how touching, [Paul's] appeal: "Ye know the grace of our Lord Jesus Christ, that, though he was rich, yet for your sakes he became poor, that ye through his poverty might be rich." You know the height from which He stooped, the depth of humiliation to which He descended. His feet entered upon the path of sacrifice, and turned not aside until He had given His life. There was no rest for Him between the throne in heaven and the cross. His love for man led Him to welcome every indignity and suffer every abuse.

Paul admonishes us to "look not every man on his own things, but every man also on the things of others." He bids us possess the mind "which was also in Christ Jesus: who, being in the form of God, thought it not robbery to be equal with God: but made himself of no reputation, and took upon him the form of a servant, and was made in the likeness of men: and being found in fashion as a man, he humbled himself, and became obedient unto death, even the death of the cross." . . .

"Ye know," says Peter, "that ye were not redeemed with corruptible things, as silver and gold . . ." (1 Peter 1:18). Oh, had these been sufficient to purchase the salvation of man, how easily it might have been accomplished by Him who says, "The silver is mine, and the gold is mine"! (Haggai 2:8). But the sinner could be redeemed only by the precious blood of the Son of God. Those who, failing to appreciate this wonderful sacrifice, withhold themselves from Christ's service will perish in their selfishness. . . .

Everyone who accepts Christ as his personal Savior will long for the privilege of serving God. Contemplating what heaven has done for him, his heart is moved with boundless love and adoring gratitude. He is eager to signalize his gratitude by devoting his abilities to God's service. He longs to show his love for Christ and for his purchased possession. He covets toil, hardship, sacrifice.

The true worker for God will do his best, because in so doing he can glorify his Master. He will do right in order to regard the requirements of God. He will endeavor to improve all his faculties. He will perform every duty as unto God. His one desire will be that Christ may receive homage and perfect service.

There is a picture representing a bullock standing between a plow and an altar, with the inscription "Ready for either"—ready to toil in the furrow or to be offered on the altar of sacrifice. This is the position of the true child of God—willing to go where duty calls, to deny self, to sacrifice for the Redeemer's cause (*The Ministry of Healing,* pp. 501, 502).

God's Workmen

For our light affliction, which is but for a moment, worketh for us a far more exceeding and eternal weight of glory. 2 Corinthians 4:17.

If Paul, troubled on every side, perplexed, persecuted, could call his trials light afflictions, of what has the Christian of today to complain? How trifling are our trials in comparison with Paul's many afflictions! They are not worthy to be compared with the eternal weight of glory awaiting the overcomer. They are God's workmen, ordained for the perfection of character. However great the deprivation and suffering of the Christian, however dark and inscrutable may seem the way of providence, he is to rejoice in the Lord, knowing that all is working for his good.

How many there are who grieve the Spirit of God by continual repining! This is because they have lost sight of Christ. If we behold Him who bore our sorrows and died as our sacrifice, that we might have an exceeding weight of glory, we shall regard our heaviest sorrows and trials as light afflictions. Think of the Savior upon the cross, bruised, smitten, mocked, yet uncomplaining and unresisting, suffering without a murmur. This is the Lord of heaven, whose throne is from everlasting. All this suffering and shame He endured for the joy that was set before Him—the joy of bringing to men the gift of eternal life.

When the attention is fastened on the cross of Christ, the whole being is ennobled. The knowledge of the Savior's love subdues the soul, and lifts the mind above the things of time and sense. Let us learn to estimate all temporal things in the light that shines from the cross. Let us strive to fathom the depths of humiliation to which our Savior descended in order to make man the possessor of eternal riches. As we study the plan of redemption, the heart will feel the throb of the Savior's love, and will be ravished by the charms of His character.

It is the love of Christ that makes our heaven. But when we seek to tell of this love, language fails us. We think of His life on earth, of His sacrifice for us; we think of His work in heaven as our advocate, of the mansions He is preparing for those who love Him; and we can but exclaim, "O the heights and depths of the love of Christ!" As we linger beneath the cross, we gain a faint conception of the love of God, and we say, "Herein is love, not that we loved God, but that he loved us, and sent his Son to be the propitiation for our sins." But in our contemplation of Christ, we are only lingering round the edge of a love that is measureless. His love is like a vast ocean, without bottom or shore.

In all true disciples this love, like sacred fire, burns on the altar of the heart. It was on the earth that the love of God was revealed through Jesus. It is on the earth that His children are to let this love shine out through blameless lives. Thus sinners will be led to the cross, to behold the Lamb of God (*Review and Herald,* May 6, 1902).

"Live, Sinner, Live!"

Sing praise to the Lord, you saints of His, and give thanks at the remembrance of His holy name. Psalm 30:4, NKJV.

If we thought and talked more of Jesus, and less of ourselves, we should have much more of His presence. If we abide in Him, we shall be so filled with peace, faith, and courage, and shall have so victorious an experience to relate when we come to meeting, that others will be refreshed by our clear, strong testimony for God. These precious acknowledgements to the praise of the glory of His grace, when supported by a Christlike life, have an irresistible power, which works for the salvation of souls.

The bright and cheerful side of religion will be represented by all who are daily consecrated to God. We should not dishonor our Lord by a mournful relation of trials that appear grievous. All trials that are received as educators will produce joy. The whole religious life will be uplifting, elevating, ennobling, fragrant with good words and works. The enemy is well pleased to have souls depressed, downcast; he desires unbelievers to gain wrong impressions regarding the effect of our faith. But God desires the mind to take a higher level. He desires every soul to triumph in the keeping power of the Redeemer. . . .

In the gracious blessings which our heavenly Father has bestowed upon us, we may discern innumerable evidences of a love that is infinite, and a tender pity surpassing a mother's yearning sympathy for her wayward child. When we study the divine character in the light of the cross, we see mercy, tenderness, and forgiveness blended with equity and justice. In the language of John we exclaim, "Behold, what manner of love the Father hath bestowed upon us, that we should be called the sons of God." We see in the midst of the throne One bearing in hands, and feet, and side the marks of the suffering endured to reconcile man to God, and God to man. Matchless mercy reveals to us a Father, infinite, dwelling in light unapproachable, yet receiving us to Himself through the merits of His Son. The cloud of vengeance which threatened only misery and despair in the reflected light from the cross reveals the writing of God: "Live, sinner, live! ye penitent and believing souls, live! I have paid a ransom."

We must gather about the cross. Christ and Him crucified must be the theme of contemplation, of conversation, and of our most joyful emotion. We should have special praise services for the purpose of keeping fresh in our thoughts everything that we receive from God, and of expressing our gratitude for His great love, and our willingness to trust everything to the hand that was nailed to the cross for us. . . . We should learn to talk the language of Canaan, to sing the songs of Zion (*Southern Watchman*, Mar. 7, 1905).

The Eternal Weight of Glory

We fix our eyes not on what is seen, but on what is unseen. For what is seen is temporary, but what is unseen is eternal. 2 Corinthians 4:18, NIV.

The years of self-denial, of privation, of trial, affliction, and persecution that Paul endured, he called a moment. The things of the present time were not considered worth mentioning when compared with the eternal weight of glory that awaited them when the warfare should be over. These very afflictions were God's workmen, ordained for the perfection of Christian character. Whatever may be the circumstances of the Christian, however dark and mysterious may be the ways of Providence, however great his deprivation and suffering, he may look away from them all to the unseen and the eternal. He has the blessed assurance that all things are working for his good. . . .

The Holy Spirit irradiated the soul of Paul with light from heaven, and he was assured that he had an interest in the purchased possession reserved for the faithful. Paul's language was strong. He was not able to find words of sufficient force to express the excellency of that glory, honor, and immortality which believers would receive when Christ should come. Compared with the scene upon which his mind's eye was dwelling, all temporal afflictions were but momentary, light afflictions, unworthy of thought. Viewed in the light of the cross, the things of this life were vanity and emptiness. The glory that attracted him was substantial, weighty, durable, beyond the power of language to describe.

Yet Paul comes as near to expressing it as he can, that the imagination may grasp the reality as far as is possible to finite minds. It was a weight of glory, a fullness of God, knowledge that was measureless. It was an eternal weight of glory. And yet Paul feels that his language is tame. It falls short of expressing the reality. He reaches out for words more expressive. The boldest figures of speech would fall far short of the truth. He seeks the broadest terms which human language can supply, that the imagination may grasp in some degree the superlative excellency of the glory to be given the final overcomer.

Holiness, dignity, honor, and felicity [happiness] in the presence of God are things now unseen except by the eye of faith. But the things which are seen, worldly honor, worldly pleasure, riches, and glory, are eclipsed by the excellency, the beauty, and resplendent glory of the things now unseen. The things of this world are temporal, enduring only for a time, while the things which are not seen are eternal, enduring through endless ages. To secure this infinite treasure is to gain everything and lose nothing (*The SDA Bible Commentary*, Ellen G. White Comments, vol. 6, pp. 1099, 1100).

In the future we shall see how closely all our trials were connected with our salvation, and how these light afflictions worked out for us "a far more exceeding and eternal weight of glory" (2 Corinthians 4:17) (letter 5, 1880).

By Beholding We Become Changed

Behold, what manner of love the Father hath bestowed upon us, that we should be called the sons of God. 1 John 3:1.

Through the merits of Christ, through His righteousness, which by faith is imputed unto us, we are to attain to the perfection of Christian character. Our daily and hourly work is set forth in the words of the apostle: "Looking unto Jesus the author and finisher of our faith." While doing this our minds become clearer and our faith stronger, and our hope is confirmed; we are so engrossed with the view of His purity and loveliness, and the sacrifice He has made to bring us into agreement with God, that we have no disposition to speak of doubts and discouragements.

The manifestation of God's love, His mercy and His goodness, and the work of the Holy Spirit upon the heart to enlighten and renew it, place us, through faith, in so close connection with Christ that, having a clear conception of His character, we are able to discern the masterly deceptions of Satan. Looking unto Jesus and trusting in His merits we appropriate the blessings of light, of peace, of joy in the Holy Ghost. And in view of the great things which Christ has done for us, we are ready to exclaim: "Behold, what manner of love the Father hath bestowed upon us, that we should be called the sons of God."

Brethren and sisters, it is by beholding that we become changed. By dwelling upon the love of God and our Savior, by contemplating the perfection of the divine character and claiming the righteousness of Christ as ours by faith, we are to be transformed into the same image. Then let us not gather together all the unpleasant pictures—the iniquities and corruptions and disappointments, the evidences of Satan's power—to hang in the halls of our memory. . . .

There are, thank God, brighter and more cheering pictures which the Lord has presented to us. Let us group together the blessed assurances of His love as precious treasures, that we may look upon them continually. The Son of God leaving His Father's throne, clothing His divinity with humanity, that He might rescue man from the power of Satan; His triumph in our behalf, opening heaven to man, revealing to human vision the presence chamber where Deity unveils His glory; the fallen race uplifted from the pit of ruin into which sin had plunged them, and brought again into connection with the infinite God, and, having endured the divine test through faith in our Redeemer, clothed in the righteousness of Christ and exalted to His throne—these are the pictures with which God bids us gladden the chambers of the soul.

And "while we look not at the things which are seen, but at the things which are not seen," we shall prove it true that "our light affliction, which is but for a moment, worketh for us a far more exceeding and eternal weight of glory" (2 Corinthians 4:17, 18) (*Testimonies*, vol. 5, pp. 744, 745).

Love and Justice Harmonized

Mercy and truth are met together; righteousness and peace have kissed each other.
Psalm 85:10.

God alone can lead you to so recognize His mercy, love, and forbearance that you will have the faith that works by love and purifies the soul. This is the gift of God. It is the opening of the heart to receive the word which is as the leaves of the tree of life. May God fill your heart with His love, so that it may be said that you . . . have purified your soul by obeying the truth.

Believing in Christ and receiving His transforming grace is not guesswork, but a work which causes Christ's virtues to be reflected in mind and character. When you gain this experience, you will say, "I have tasted and seen that the Lord is good. The Lord Jesus shall be my portion forever." The power of the cross will move in you the mysterious springs of hope and fear, adoration, and love. Angels are watching and waiting, and will witness to the fact that the world has you not. Jesus has found you sitting at His feet to learn from Him, the Way, the Truth, and the Life. Henceforth, surrendering your will to the will of Christ, you are drawn into a region where the cross is the central object. The world fades from your view. The glory shining from the threshold of heaven is the all-attractive influence. The riches of the grace of Christ hold you in willing obedience. . . . You are only too glad to impart to others the gift you have received.

I long to see you improving the capabilities given you by God, so that you can respond to the inquiry, "What must I do to be saved?" Let the words fall from sanctified lips, "Be saved by accepting Christ by faith as your personal Savior." *God is love.* The sinner need not perish if he will exercise faith in the wonderful efficacy of the cross of Christ. The cross is the stupendous expedient by which is harmonized the love and justice of God. It is the sinner's only means of salvation. . . . The image of His love may be so stamped upon the mind that it can never be effaced. Then Jesus Christ will be so evidently set forth crucified before you that you will be a partaker of the dignity of His suffering. I have such an intense longing that you may look into the heart of this great mystery, and find that its interpretation is love. . . .

As you make a full surrender of your will to God's will, your way to God's way, you will learn of Him who is meek and lowly in heart, and will find rest unto your soul. A calm confidence will preside over you. . . . You will experience more and more clearly the sense of an ever-present, all-pervading Savior. This will give the soul power . . . , which the changing circumstances of earth cannot undermine. It plants the feet upon a solid rock (letter 123, 1901).

This World a Battlefield

Let us fix our eyes on Jesus, . . . who for the joy set before him, endured the cross, scorning its shame, and sat down at the right hand of the throne of God. Hebrews 12:2, NIV.

For the joy that was set before Him, Christ endured the cross. . . . He died on the cross as a sacrifice for the world, and through this sacrifice comes the greatest blessing that God could bestow—the gift of the Holy Spirit. This blessing is for all who will receive Christ. The fallen world is the battlefield for the greatest conflict the heavenly universe and earthly powers have ever witnessed. It was appointed as the theater on which would be fought out the grand struggle between good and evil, between heaven and hell. Every human being acts a part in this conflict. No one can stand on neutral ground. Men must either accept or reject the world's Redeemer. All are witnesses, either for or against Christ. Christ calls upon those who stand under His banner to engage in the conflict with Him as faithful soldiers, that they may inherit the crown of life. They have been adopted as sons and daughters of God. . . .

The Lord Jesus has summoned the world to hear. "He that hath ears to hear, let him hear." Let all listen with submissive, reverent attention. He repeats the words given Him by the One who said, "This is my beloved Son. . . . Hear ye him." Who is listening to the words which are light and life to all who receive them? Will men and women consider how God regards the creatures He has made? He formed man's mind. We do not think one noble thought that does not come from Him. He knows all the mysterious workings of the human mind, for did He not make it? God sees that sin has debased and degraded man, but He looks upon him with pity and compassion; for He sees that Satan has him in his power. . . .

Some households have a little church in their home. Mutual love binds heart to heart, and the unity that exists among the members of the family preaches the most effectual sermon that could be preached on practical godliness. As parents faithfully do their duty in the family, restraining, correcting, advising, counseling, guiding, the father as a priest of the household, the mother as a home missionary, they are filling the sphere God would have them fill. By faithfully doing their duty in the home, they are multiplying agencies for doing good outside the home. They are becoming better fitted to labor in the church. By training their little flock discreetly, binding their children to themselves and to God, fathers and mothers become laborers together with God. The cross is erected in their home. The members of the family become members of the royal family above, children of the heavenly King (manuscript 56, 1899).

Gather About the Cross

Ye shall eat before the Lord your God, and ye shall rejoice in all that ye put your hand unto, ye and your households, wherein the Lord thy God hath blessed thee.
Deuteronomy 12:7.

Anciently the Lord bade Israel, when they met together for His service, "Ye shall eat before the Lord your God, and ye shall rejoice in all that ye put your hand unto, ye and your households, wherein the Lord thy God hath blessed thee." That which is done for the glory of God should be done with cheerfulness, with songs of praise and thanksgiving, not with sadness and gloom.

Our God is a tender, merciful Father. His service should not be looked upon as a heart-saddening, distressing exercise. It should be a pleasure to worship the Lord and to take part in His work. God would not have His children, for whom so great salvation has been provided, act as if He were a hard, exacting taskmaster. He is their best friend; and when they worship Him, He expects to be with them, to bless and comfort them, filling their hearts with joy and love. The Lord desires His children to take comfort in His service and to find more pleasure than hardship in His work. He desires that those who come to worship Him shall carry away with them precious thoughts of His care and love, that they may be cheered in all the employments of daily life, that they may have grace to deal honestly and faithfully in all things.

We must gather about the cross. Christ and Him crucified should be the theme of contemplation, of conversation, and of our most joyful emotion. We should keep in our thoughts every blessing we receive from God, and when we realize His great love we should be willing to trust everything to the hand that was nailed to the cross for us.

The soul may ascend nearer heaven on the wings of praise. God is worshiped with song and music in the courts above, and as we express our gratitude we are approximating to the worship of the heavenly hosts. "Whoso offereth praise glorifieth" God (Psalm 50:23). Let us with reverent joy come before our Creator, with "thanksgiving, and the voice of melody" (Isaiah 51:3) (*Steps to Christ*, pp. 103, 104).

If you call God your Father you acknowledge yourselves His children to be guided by His wisdom and to be obedient in all things, knowing that His love is changeless. You will accept His plan for your life. As children of God, you will hold His honor, His character, His family, His work, as the objects of your highest interest. It will be your joy to recognize and honor your relation to your Father and to every member of His family. You will rejoice to do any act, however humble, that will tend to His glory or to the well-being of your kindred (*Thoughts From the Mount of Blessing*, p. 105).

Nature in the Light of Calvary

Sir, didst not thou sow good seed in thy field? from whence then hath it tares? He said unto them, An enemy hath done this. Matthew 13:27, 28.

So far as possible, let the child from his earliest years be placed where this wonderful lesson-book [of nature] shall be open before him. Let him behold the glorious scenes painted by the great Master Artist upon the shifting canvas of the heavens, let him become acquainted with the wonders of earth and sea, let him watch the unfolding mysteries of the changing seasons, and, in all His works, learn of the Creator.

In no other way can the foundation of a true education be so firmly and surely laid. Yet even the child, as he comes in contact with nature, will see cause for perplexity. He can not but recognize the working of antagonistic forces. It is here that nature needs an interpreter. Looking upon the evil manifest even in the natural world, all have the same sorrowful lesson to learn—"an enemy hath done this."

Only in the light that shines from Calvary can nature's teachings be read aright. Through the story of Bethlehem and the cross let it be shown how good is to conquer evil, and how every blessing that comes to us is a gift of redemption.

In brier and thorn, in thistle and tare, is represented the evil that blights and mars. In singing bird and opening blossom, in rain and sunshine, in summer breeze and gentle dew, in ten thousand objects in nature, from the oak of the forest to the violet that blossoms at its root, is seen the love that restores. And nature still speaks to us of God's goodness.

"I know the thoughts that I think toward you, saith the Lord, thoughts of peace, and not of evil." This the message that, in the light from the cross, may be read upon all the face of nature. The heavens declare His glory, and the earth is full of His riches (*Education,* pp. 100, 101).

When Adam and Eve in Eden lost the garments of holiness, they lost the light that had illuminated nature. No longer could they read it aright. But for those who receive the light of the life of Christ, nature is again illuminated. In the light shining from the cross, we can rightly interpret nature's teaching.

He who has a knowledge of God and His Word has a settled faith in the divinity of the Holy Scriptures. He does not test the Bible by man's ideas of science. He brings these ideas to the test of the unerring standard. He knows that God's Word is truth, and truth can never contradict itself. . . . The ways of God as revealed in the natural world and in His dealings with man constitute a treasury from which every student in the school of Christ may draw (*Testimonies*, vol. 8, pp. 324, 325).

Lay Your Guilt at the Foot of the Cross

Cast all your anxiety on him because he cares for you. 1 Peter 5:7, NIV.

Grief, anxiety, discontent, remorse, guilt, distrust, all tend to break down the life forces and to invite decay and death (*The Ministry of Healing,* p. 241).

This feeling of guiltiness must be laid at the foot of the cross of Calvary. The sense of sinfulness has poisoned the springs of life and true happiness. Now Jesus says, Lay it all on Me; I will take your sin. I will give you peace. Destroy no longer your self-respect, for I have bought you with the price of My own blood. You are Mine; your weakened will I will strengthen; your remorse for sin I will remove.

Then turn your grateful heart, trembling with uncertainty, and lay hold upon the hope set before you. God accepts your broken, contrite heart. He offers you free pardon. He offers to adopt you into His family, with His grace to help your weakness, and the dear Jesus will lead you on step by step if you will only put your hand in His and let Him guide you.

Satan seeks to draw our minds away from the mighty Helper, to lead us to ponder over our degeneration of soul. But though Jesus sees the guilt of the past, He speaks pardon; and we should not dishonor Him by doubting His love. . . .

If you feel yourself to be the greatest sinner, Christ is just what you need, the greatest Savior. Lift up your head and look away from yourself, away from your sin, to the uplifted Savior; away from the poisonous, venomous bite of the serpent to the Lamb of God who taketh away the sin of the world.

He has borne the burden of our guilt. He will take the load from our weary shoulders. He will give us rest. The burden of care and sorrow also He will bear. He invites us to cast all our care upon Him, for He carries us upon His heart (*Mind, Character, and Personality,* vol. 2, pp. 451, 452).

When the gospel is received in its purity and power, it is a cure for the maladies that originated in sin. The Sun of Righteousness arises, "with healing in his wings" (Malachi 4:2). . . .

The love which Christ diffuses through the whole being is a vitalizing power. Every vital part—the brain, the heart, the nerves—it touches with healing. By it the highest energies of the being are roused to activity. It frees the soul from the guilt and sorrow, the anxiety and care, that crush the life forces. With it come serenity and composure. It implants in the soul joy that nothing earthly can destroy—joy in the Holy Spirit—health-giving, life-giving joy (*The Ministry of Healing,* p. 115).

A Crucified and Risen Savior

I myself will take a shoot from the very top of a cedar and plant it; I will break off a tender sprig from its topmost shoots and plant it on a high and lofty mountain. On the mountain heights . . . I will plant it; it will produce branches and bear fruit and become a splendid cedar. Ezekiel 17:22, 23, NIV.

It was in order that the heavenly universe might see the conditions of the covenant of redemption that Christ bore the penalty in behalf of the human race. The throne of Justice must be eternally and forever made secure. . . . By the sacrifice Christ was about to make, all doubts would be forever settled, and the human race would be saved if they would return to their allegiance. Christ alone could restore honor to God's government. The cross of Calvary would be looked upon by the unfallen worlds, by the heavenly universe, by Satanic agencies, by the fallen race, and every mouth would be stopped. In making His infinite sacrifice Christ would exalt and honor the law. He would make known the exalted character of God's government, which could not in any way be changed to meet man in his sinful condition.

Who is able to describe the last scenes of Christ's life on earth, His trial in the judgment hall, His crucifixion? Who witnessed these scenes? The heavenly universe, God the Father, Satan and his angels. Wonderful events took place in the betrayal of Christ. At His mock trial, His accusers found nothing by which He could be proved guilty. Three times Pilate declared, "I find no fault in Him at all." Nevertheless he ordered Him to be scourged, and then delivered Him up to suffer the most cruel death that could be devised. . . .

The terrible scenes of the crucifixion revealed what humanity will do when under Satan's control. They revealed what the outcome would be if Satan was to control the world. Those who witnessed these scenes never lost the impressions made upon their minds. Many were converted, and told others of the awful scene they beheld. Many who heard the report of Christ's death were converted, and commenced searching the Scriptures. Thus were fulfilled the words, "So shall he sprinkle many nations."

"Thus saith the Lord God; I will also take of the highest branch of the high cedar, and will set it; I will crop off from the top of his young twigs a tender one, and will plant it upon an high mountain and eminent: in the mountain of the height of Israel will I plant it: and it shall . . . be a goodly cedar; and under it shall dwell all fowl of every wing; in the shadow of the branches thereof shall they dwell."

Christ was this Branch, the highest branch of the highest cedar. He was the plant of the Lord's setting (*Signs of the Times,* July 12, 1899).

Spiritual and Physical Maladies Healed

And Jesus went about all Galilee, teaching in their synagogues, and preaching the gospel of the kingdom, and healing all manner of sickness and all manner of disease among the people. Matthew 4:23.

This world is a vast lazar house, but Christ came to heal the sick, to proclaim deliverance to the captives of Satan. He was in Himself health and strength. He imparted His life to the sick, the afflicted, those possessed of demons. He turned away none who came to receive His healing power. He knew that those who petitioned Him for help had brought disease upon themselves; yet He did not refuse to heal them. And when virtue from Christ entered into these poor souls, they were convicted of sin, and many were healed of their spiritual disease, as well as of their physical maladies. The gospel still possesses the same power, and why should we not today witness the same results?

Christ feels the woes of every sufferer. When evil spirits rend a human frame, Christ feels the curse. When fever is burning up the life current, He feels the agony. And He is just as willing to heal the sick now as when He was personally on earth. Christ's servants are His representatives, the channels for His working. He desires through them to exercise His healing power.

In the Savior's manner of healing there were lessons for His disciples. On one occasion He anointed the eyes of a blind man with clay, and bade him, "Go, wash in the pool of Siloam. . . . He went his way therefore, and washed, and came seeing" (John 9:7). The cure could be wrought only by the power of the Great Healer, yet Christ made use of the simple agencies of nature. . . .

To many of the afflicted ones who received healing, Christ said, "Sin no more, lest a worse thing come unto thee" (John 5:14). Thus He taught that disease is the result of violating God's laws, both natural and spiritual. The great misery in the world would not exist did men but live in harmony with the Creator's plan.

Christ had been the guide and teacher of ancient Israel, and He taught them that health is the reward of obedience to the laws of God. The Great Physician who healed the sick in Palestine had spoken to His people from the pillar of cloud, telling them what they must do, and what God would do for them. "If thou wilt diligently hearken to the voice of the Lord thy God," He said, "and wilt do that which is right in his sight, and wilt give ear to his commandments, and keep all his statutes, I will put none of these diseases upon thee, which I have brought upon the Egyptians: for I am the Lord that healeth thee" (Exodus 15:26). . . . When they fulfilled the conditions, the promise was verified to them. "There was not one feeble person among their tribes" (Psalm 105:37) (*The Desire of Ages,* pp. 823, 824).

Healing for Spiritual Blindness

The Lord is nigh unto all them that call upon him, to all that call upon him in truth.
Psalm 145:18.

In the scribes, Pharisees, and rulers, Jesus found not the bottles for His new wine. He was obliged to turn from them to humble men, whose hearts were not filled with envy, covetousness, and self-righteousness. The lowly fishermen obeyed the call of the divine Teacher, while the scribes and Pharisees refused to become converted.

The disciples that Jesus called were uneducated, and were far from being perfect in character when Jesus united them with Himself; but they were willing to learn from the greatest Teacher the world ever knew. They were truly converted men, and became the new bottles into which Jesus could pour the new wine of His kingdom. But though they were converted to Christ, yet, because of their limited earthly comprehension—the result of the teaching they had had from the Jews—they were unable fully to understand the spiritual nature of the truth He could impart. The burden of His instruction was the necessity of His followers having pure and holy hearts, for holiness alone would fit them to become subjects of His heavenly kingdom.

The divine Sower scattered grains of precious seed, which we cannot see until a skillful laborer, under the guidance of the Holy Spirit, gathers them together and presents them to us as a complete system of truth, unfolding the depths of divine love. For all ages Jesus, the author of truth, through prophets and people, had presented truth upon truth to the Jews, from the pillar of cloud and fire. But the truth He had given had become mingled with error, and it was necessary to separate from the companionship of heresy and evil. It was necessary to readjust it in the framework of the gospel, in order that it might shine forth in its original luster and illuminate the moral darkness of the world. Wherever He found a gem of truth that had been lost from its setting, or had been marred with error, He reset it, and stamped upon it the signature of Jehovah. He proved Himself to be the word and the wisdom of God.

The commonplace matters of time and earth had engrossed the minds of the people at the time of Christ, just as Satan had designed that they should. Sin had expelled from the heart the love of God, and instead of the love of God there was found in the heart the love of the world, the love of sinful indulgence of evil passions. Christ alone could adjust the claims between heaven and earth. Man's vision had become blinded, because he did not keep in view the spiritual and eternal world. . . . In the person and work of Christ the holiness of God is revealed; for Christ came to reveal the Father (*Signs of the Times,* Dec. 11, 1893).

Health to Body and Soul

Beloved, I wish above all things that thou mayest prosper and be in health, even as thy soul prospereth. 3 John 2.

There are conditions to be observed by all who would preserve health. All should learn what these conditions are. The Lord is not pleased with ignorance in regard to His laws, either natural or spiritual. We are to be workers together with God for the restoration of health to the body as well as to the soul.

And we should teach others how to preserve and to recover health. For the sick we should use the remedies which God has provided in nature, and we should point them to Him who alone can restore. It is our work to present the sick and suffering to Christ in the arms of our faith. We should teach them to believe in the Great Healer. We should lay hold on His promise, and pray for the manifestation of His power. The very essence of the gospel is restoration, and the Savior would have us bid the sick, the hopeless, and the afflicted take hold upon His strength.

The power of love was in all Christ's healing, and only by partaking of that love, through faith, can we be instruments for His work. If we neglect to link ourselves in divine connection with Christ, the current of life-giving energy cannot flow in rich streams from us to the people. There were places where the Savior Himself could not do many mighty works because of their unbelief (*The Desire of Ages,* pp. 824, 825).

The body must be kept in a healthy condition in order that the soul may be in health. The condition of the body affects the condition of the soul. He who would have physical and spiritual strength must educate his appetite in right lines. He must be careful not to burden the soul by overtaxing his physical or spiritual powers. Faithful adherence to right principles in eating, drinking, and dressing is a duty that God has laid upon human beings.

The Lord desires us to obey the laws of health and life. He holds each one responsible to care properly for his body, that it may be kept in health (*Evangelism,* p. 261).

The Savior in His miracles revealed the power that is continually at work in man's behalf to sustain and to heal him. Through the agencies of nature, God is working, day by day, hour by hour, moment by moment, to keep us alive, to build up and restore us. . . .

The desire of God for every human being is expressed in the words, "Beloved, I wish above all things that thou mayest prosper and be in health, even as thy soul prospereth." . . .

True religion and the laws of health go hand in hand (*My Life Today,* p. 135).

Strong in the Strength of God

And this is life eternal, that they might know thee the only true God, and Jesus Christ, whom thou hast sent. John 17:3.

There is but little benefit derived from a hasty reading of the Scriptures. One may read the Bible through, and yet fail to see its beauty or to comprehend its deep and hidden meaning. One passage studied until its significance is clear to the mind, and its relation to the plan of salvation is evident, is of more value than the perusal of many chapters with no definite purpose in view, and no positive instruction gained. Keep your Bible with you. As you have opportunity, read it; fix the texts in your memory. Even while you are walking the streets, you may read a passage, and meditate upon it, thus fixing it in the mind.

The life of Christ, that gives life to the world, is in His Word. It was by His word that Jesus healed disease and cast out demons; by His word He stilled the sea, and raised the dead; and the people bore witness that His word was with power. He spoke the word of God, as He had spoken to all the prophets and teachers of the Old Testament. The whole Bible is a manifestation of Christ. It is our source of power.

As our physical life is sustained by food, so our spiritual life is sustained by the Word of God. And every soul is to receive life from God's Word for himself. As we must eat for ourselves in order to receive nourishment, so we must receive the Word for ourselves. We are not to obtain it merely through the medium of another mind.

Yes, the Word of God is the bread of life. Those who eat and digest this Word, making it a part of every action and of every attribute of character, grow strong in the strength of God. It gives immortal vigor to the soul, perfecting the experience and bringing joys that will abide forever (*Signs of the Times,* June 25, 1902).

"In him was life; and the life was the light of men." It is not physical life that is here specified, but eternal life, the life which is exclusively the property of God. The Word, who was with God, and who was God, had this life. Physical life is something which each individual received. It is not eternal or immortal; for God, the Lifegiver, takes it again. . . . But the life of Christ was unborrowed. No one can take this life from Him. "I lay it down of myself," He said. . . . This life is not inherent in man. He can possess it only through Christ. He cannot earn it; it is given him as a free gift if he will believe in Christ as his personal Savior. "This is life eternal, that they might know thee the only true God, and Jesus Christ, whom thou hast sent" (John 17:3). This is the open fountain of life for the world (*The SDA Bible Commentary,* Ellen G. White Comments, vol. 5, p. 1130).

September

5

The Fruits of Self-denial

Whether therefore ye eat, or drink, or whatsoever ye do, do all to the glory of God.
1 Corinthians 10:31.

You do not realize the claims that the Lord has upon you. You have not become acquainted with the sweet results of self-denial. Its fruits are sacred. . . . Instead of purchasing frivolous things, put your little into the bank of heaven, that when the Master comes you may receive both principal and interest. . . .

Religion, pure and undefiled, with its strong principles, would prove to you an anchor. In order to answer life's great ends you must avoid the example of those who are seeking for their own pleasure and enjoyment, and who have not the fear of God before them. God has made provisions for you that are ample. He has provided that if you comply with the conditions laid down in His Word, and separate from the world, you may receive strength from Him to repress every debasing influence and develop that which is noble, good, and elevating. Christ will be in you "a well of water springing up into everlasting life." The will, the intellect, and every emotion, when controlled by religion, have a transforming power.

"Whether therefore ye eat, or drink, or whatsoever ye do, do all to the glory of God." Here is a principle which lies at the foundation of every act, thought, and motive; the consecration of the entire being, both physical and mental, to the control of the Spirit of God. The unsanctified will and passions must be crucified. This may be regarded as a close and severe work. Yet it must be done, or you will hear the terrible sentence from the mouth of Jesus: "Depart." You can do all things through Christ, who strengtheneth you. You are of that age when the will, the appetite, and the passions clamor for indulgence. God has implanted these in your nature for high and holy purposes. It is not necessary that they should become a curse to you by being debased. They will become this only when you refuse to submit to the control of reason and conscience. Restrain, deny, are words and works with which you are not familiar by experience. Temptations have swayed you. Unsanctified minds fail to receive that strength and comfort that God has provided for them. They are restless and possess a strong desire for something new, something to gratify, to please and excite the mind; and this is called pleasure. Satan has alluring charms to engage the interest and excite the imagination of the youth in particular, that he may fasten them to his snare. . . . You need to cry earnestly: "O Lord, my inmost soul convert." You can have an influence for good over other young people. . . . May the God of peace sanctify you wholly, soul, body, and spirit (*Testimonies,* vol. 3, pp. 83, 84).

Wait Upon the Lord for Strength

And . . . [Jesus] said unto them, Come ye yourselves apart into a desert place, and rest a while: for there were many coming and going, and they had no leisure so much as to eat. Mark 6:31.

Those who are connected with the work . . . are to live so near the Lord that light will shine forth from them as from a lamp that burneth. When there is shown a deep, earnest determination to press together, the very oneness of the workers will proclaim the truth with power, making a deep impression on those not of our faith. . . .

Workers for God will meet with turmoil, discomfort, and weariness. At times, uncertain and distracted, the heart is almost in despair. When this restless nervousness comes, the worker should stop and rest. Christ invites him, "Come . . . apart, . . . and rest a while" (Mark 6:31). "He giveth power to the faint; and to them that have no might he increaseth strength. . . . They that wait upon the Lord shall renew their strength; they shall mount up with wings as eagles; they shall run, and not be weary; they shall walk, and not faint" (Isaiah 40:29-31). . . .

A worker cannot gain success while he hurries through his prayers to God, and rushes away to look after something that he fears may be neglected or forgotten. He takes time to give only a few hurried thoughts to God, that is all. He does not give himself time to think, to pray, to wait upon the Lord for a renewal of spiritual and physical strength. He soon becomes jaded. He does not feel the uplifting, inspiring influence of God's Spirit. He is not quickened by fresh life. His jaded frame and tired brain are not soothed by personal contact with Christ.

"Wait on the Lord: be of good courage, and he shall strengthen thine heart: wait, I say, on the Lord" (Psalm 27:14). "It is good that a man should both hope and quietly wait for the salvation of the Lord" (Lamentations 3:26). There are those who work all day and far into the night to do what it seems to them needs to be done. The Lord looks pitifully upon these weary, heavy-laden burden-bearers, and says to them, "Come unto me, . . . and I will give you rest. . . . For my yoke is easy, and my burden is light" (Matthew 11:28-30) (letter 83).

Our life is to be hid with Christ in God; and if it is thus hidden, in His hands it will be converted into a lamp which will shed upon the world a bright and steady light. . . . But though time is short, and there is a great work to be done, the Lord is not pleased to have us so prolong our seasons of activity that there will not be time for periods of rest, for the study of the Bible, and for communion with God. All this is essential to fortify the soul, to place us in a position where we shall receive wisdom from God to employ our talents in the Master's service to the highest account (*Youth's Instructor,* Feb. 3, 1898)

September
7

Moral and Spiritual Perfection Promised

And above all these put on love, which binds everything together in perfect harmony. And let the peace of Christ rule in your hearts, to which indeed you were called in the one body. And be thankful. Colossians 3:14, 15, RSV.

Mortify therefore your members which are upon the earth," Paul wrote to the Colossians; "in the which ye also walked some time, when ye lived in them. But now ye also put off all these; anger, wrath, malice, blasphemy, filthy communication out of your mouth. . . . Put on therefore, as the elect of God, holy and beloved, bowels of mercies, kindness, humbleness of mind, meekness, longsuffering; forbearing one another, and forgiving one another, if any man have a quarrel against any: even as Christ forgave you, so also do ye" (Colossians 3:5, 7-13). . . .

The letter to the Colossians is filled with lessons of highest value to all who are engaged in the service of Christ, lessons that show the singleness of purpose and the loftiness of aim which will be seen in the life of him who rightly represents the Savior. Renouncing all that would hinder him from making progress in the upward way or that would turn the feet of another from the narrow path, the believer will reveal in his daily life mercy, kindness, humility, meekness, forbearance, and the love of Christ. . . .

In his efforts to reach God's ideal for him, the Christian is to despair of nothing. Moral and spiritual perfection, through the grace and power of Christ, is promised to all. Jesus is the source of power, the fountain of life. He brings us to His word, and from the tree of life presents to us leaves for the healing of sin-sick souls. He leads us to the throne of God, and puts into our mouth a prayer through which we are brought into close contact with Himself. In our behalf He set in operation the all-powerful agencies of heaven. At every step we touch His living power.

God fixes no limit to the advancement of those who desire to be "filled with the knowledge of his will in all wisdom and spiritual understanding" (Colossians 1:9). Through prayer, through watchfulness, through growth in knowledge and understanding, they are to be "strengthened with all might, according to his glorious power" (verse 11). Thus they are prepared to work for others. It is the Savior's purpose that human beings, purified and sanctified, shall be His helping hand. For this great privilege let us give thanks to Him who "hath made us meet to be partakers of the inheritance of the saints in light: who hath delivered us from the power of darkness, and hath translated us into the kingdom of his dear Son" (verses 12, 13) (*The Acts of the Apostles,* pp. 477, 478).

Think of God Continually

I bow my knees unto the Father of our Lord Jesus Christ, of whom the whole family in heaven and earth is named, that he would grant you, according to the riches of his glory, to be strengthened with might by his Spirit in the inner man. Ephesians 3:14-16.

The spiritual strength here spoken of is something that we may each obtain; but how shall we get it? Perhaps we are in darkness, feeling weak and discouraged and that God does not love us. If so, we are not to give way to feelings; feeling has nothing whatever to do with the matter. We are to take the Word of God as it reads, the words of Christ as He has spoken them.

Hear these words of our Savior: "Whosoever heareth these sayings of mine, and doeth them, I will liken him unto a wise man, which built his house upon a rock; and the rain descended, and the floods came, and the winds blew, and beat upon that house; and it fell not: for it was founded upon a rock." It is the privilege of every one of us to build upon the Eternal Rock; then we shall not dishonor God, nor by our words and actions scatter away from Christ. . . .

When you have thrown yourself upon the mercy of God, and taken Him at His word, and yet the enemy comes, and suggests your faults and failings, and tells you that you are no better than before you sought the Lord, you can point to Jesus, and repeat His promises, and tell what He has done for you.

The apostle continues: "That Christ may dwell in your hearts by faith; that ye, being rooted and grounded in love, may be able to comprehend with all saints what is the breadth, and length, and depth, and height; and to know the love of Christ, which passeth knowledge, that ye might be filled with all the fullness of God." While this divine fullness has been placed within our reach, how easily we are satisfied. We have accustomed ourselves to think that it is enough to have a knowledge of the truth without its sanctifying power. Just a little sip at the fountain of life quenches our thirst. We do not come again and again to drink. But this is not in accordance with the mind of God. Our souls should be continually athirst for the water of life. Our hearts should ever go out after Christ, longing for communion with Him. It is hungering and thirsting after righteousness that will bring us the full measure of His grace.

Enoch "walked with God"; but how did he gain this sweet intimacy? It was by having thoughts of God continually before him. As he went out and as he came in, his meditations were upon the goodness, the perfection, and the loveliness of the divine character. And as he was thus engaged, he became changed in the glorious image of his Lord; for it is by beholding that we become changed (*Signs of the Times,* Aug. 18, 1887).

Spiritual Power

And I pray that you, being rooted and established in love, may have power together with all the saints. Ephesians 3:17, 18, NIV.

We are to reflect the character of Jesus. Everywhere, whether in the church, at our homes, or in social intercourse with our neighbors, we should let the lovely image of Jesus appear. This we cannot do unless we are filled with His fullness. If we would become better acquainted with Jesus, we should love Him for His goodness and excellence and we should desire to become so assimilated to His divine character that all would know that we had been with Jesus, and learned of Him.

It is by carrying out in our lives the pure principles of the gospel of Christ that we honor and glorify our Father, who is in heaven. When we are doing this, we are reflecting Heaven-given light upon the dark world around us. Sinners will be constrained to confess that we are not the children of darkness, but the children of light. How shall they know this? By the fruits we bear. Men may have their names upon the church book; but that does not make them children of light. They may hold honorable positions and receive the praise of men; but that does not make them children of light. . . . There must be a deep work of grace—the love of God in the heart, and this love is expressed by obedience.

It is Christ dwelling in the soul that gives us spiritual power, and makes us channels of light. The more light we have, the more we can impart to others around us. The more closely we live to Jesus, the clearer views shall we have of His loveliness. As we behold Him in His purity, we discern more clearly our own faults of character. We yearn after Him, and for that fullness that is in Him, and that shines out in the perfection of His heavenly character; and by beholding we become changed into His image. . . .

Everyday we are sowing some kind of seed. If we sow the seeds of unbelief, we shall reap unbelief; if we sow pride, we shall reap pride; if we sow stubbornness, we shall reap stubbornness, "for whatsoever a man soweth, that shall he also reap." . . .

Our hearts may be filled with all the fullness of God; but there is something for us to do. We must not pet our faults and sins, but put them away, and make haste to set our hearts in order. When this is done, let us take the key of faith, and unlock the storehouse of God's rich blessings. . . . There is an infinite fullness to draw from; and we have the promise of our divine Lord, "According to your faith be it unto you." We may win the crown of life, a place at God's right hand, and as we enter the pearly gates, hear the words, sweeter than any music, "Well done, good and faithful servant . . . : enter thou into the joy of thy lord" (Matthew 25:23) (*Signs of the Times,* Aug. 18, 1887).

Be Strong in His Grace

Thou therefore, my son, be strong in the grace that is in Christ Jesus. And the things that thou hast heard of me among many witnesses, the same commit thou to faithful men, who shall be able to teach others also. 2 Timothy 2:1, 2.

The lessons contained in the words of Paul to Timothy are of the greatest importance to us today. He charges him to "be strong"—in his own wisdom? No, but "in the grace that is in Christ Jesus." He who would be a follower of Christ is not to rely upon his own capabilities, or to feel confident in himself. Neither is to be dwarfed in his religious efforts, to shun responsibilities, and remain inefficient in the cause of God. He is to draw strength from a sure and safe source, that never fails those who would have divine power. The exhortation to us is, "Be strong in the grace that is in Christ Jesus." If the Christian feels his weakness, his inability, by putting his trust in God, he will find the grace of Christ sufficient for every emergency.

The soldier of Christ must meet many forms of temptation, and resist and overcome them. The fiercer the conflict, the greater the supply of grace to meet the need of the soul; and the very nature of the grace received will enlarge the capacity of the servant of Christ to know God, and Jesus Christ whom he hath sent. The soul of the believer will go out in intense longing to know and understand more of the truth and righteousness of Christ. All who advance in the divine life will have increased ability to search for truth as for hid treasure, and will appropriate the truth to their own souls. The true Christian will understand what it means to pass through severe conflicts and trying experiences; but he will steadily increase in the grace of Christ to meet successfully the enemy of his soul, who works through human agency to cause the ruin of the servants of Christ. By passing through severe ordeals of trial, the follower of Christ will better understand the ways of God and the plan of redemption, and will not be ignorant of the devices of the enemy. The darkness will press upon his soul at times; but the true light will shine, the bright beams of the Sun of Righteousness will dispel the gloom; and although Satan seeks in every way to discourage him by presenting obstacles before him, through the grace of Christ he will be enabled to be a faithful witness of the things which he has heard from the inspired messenger of God. He does not despise or neglect the message received, but commits his knowledge to faithful men, who in their turn are to be able to teach others also. In communicating the light to others, the Christian proves the truth of the word that "the path of the just is as the shining light, that shineth more and more unto the perfect day" (Proverbs 4:18) (*Review and Herald,* June 16, 1896).

Conformity to the Will of God

A gracious woman retaineth honour. Proverbs 11:16.

You may never be called to do a work which will bring you before the public. But all the work we do that is necessary to be done, be it washing dishes, setting tables, waiting upon the sick, cooking, or washing, is of moral importance; and until you can cheerfully and happily take up these duties you are not fitted for greater and higher duties. The humble tasks before us are to be taken up by someone; and those who do them should feel that they are doing a necessary and honorable work, and that in their mission, humble though it may be, they are doing the work of God just as surely as was Gabriel when sent to the prophets. All are working in their order in their respective spheres. Woman in her home, doing the simple duties of life that must be done, can and should exhibit faithfulness, obedience, and love as sincere as angels in their sphere. Conformity to the will of God makes any work honorable that must be done. . . .

We are not in heaven, but upon the earth. When we are in heaven, then we shall be qualified to do the lofty and elevating work of heaven. It is here in this world that we must be tested and proved. . . .

The highest duty that devolves upon youth is their own homes, blessing father and mother, brothers and sisters, by affection and true interest. Here they can show self-denial and self-forgetfulness in caring and doing for others. Never will women be degraded by this work. It is the most sacred, elevated office that she can fill. What an influence a sister may have over brothers! If she is right she may determine the character of her brothers. Her prayers, her gentleness, and her affection may do much in a household. . . . These noble qualities can never be communicated to other minds unless they first exist in your own. That contentment of mind, that affection, gentleness, and sunniness of temper which will reach every heart, will reflect upon you what your heart gives forth to others. If Christ does not reign in the heart, there will be discontent and moral deformity. Selfishness will require of others that which we are unwilling to give them. If Christ is not in the heart, the character will be unlovely.

It is not the great work and great battles alone which try the soul and demand courage. Everyday life brings its perplexities, trials, and discouragements. It is the humble work which frequently draws upon the patience and the fortitude. Self-reliance and resolution will be necessary to meet and conquer all difficulties. Secure the Lord to stand with you, in every place to be your consolation and comfort (*Testimonies,* vol. 3, pp. 79-81).

Salvation of Children

Even a child makes himself known by his acts, whether what he does is pure and right.
Proverbs 20:11, RSV.

Much study and earnest prayer for heavenly wisdom are needed to know how to deal with youthful minds, for very much depends upon the direction parents give to the minds and wills of their children. To balance their minds in the right direction and at the right time is a most important work, for their eternal destiny may depend on the decisions made at some critical moment. How important, then, that the minds of parents be as free as possible from perplexing, wearing care in temporal things, that they may think and act with calm consideration, wisdom, and love, and make the salvation of the souls of their children the first and highest consideration! The great object which parents should seek to attain for their dear children should be the inward adorning. Parents cannot afford to allow visitors and strangers to claim their attention, and by robbing them of time, which is life's great capital, make it impossible for them to give their children each day that patient instruction which they must have to give right direction to their developing minds.

This lifetime is too short to be squandered in vain and trifling diversion, in unprofitable visiting, in needless dressing for display, or in exciting amusements. We cannot afford to squander the time given us of God in which to bless others and in which to lay up for ourselves a treasure in heaven. We have none too much time for the discharge of necessary duties. We should give time to the culture of our own hearts and minds in order that we may be qualified for our lifework. By neglecting these essential duties and conforming to the habits and customs of fashionable, worldly society, we do ourselves and our children a great wrong. . . .

It is the duty of mothers to cultivate their minds and keep their hearts pure. They should improve every means within their reach for their intellectual and moral improvement, that they may be qualified to improve the minds of their children. Those who indulge their disposition to be in company will soon feel restless unless visiting or entertaining visitors. Such have not the power of adaptation to circumstances. The necessary, sacred home duties seem commonplace and uninteresting to them. They have no love for self-examination or self-discipline. The mind hungers for the varying, exciting scenes of worldly life. . . .

If parents would feel that it is a solemn duty enjoined upon them of God to educate their children for usefulness in this life; if they would adorn the inner temple of the souls of their sons and daughters for the immortal life, we should see a great change in society for the better (*Testimonies,* vol. 3, pp. 146, 147).

Physical, Mental, and Spiritual Development

Train up a child in the way he should go: and when he is old, he will not depart from it.
Proverbs 22:6.

It is the nicest work ever assumed by men and women to deal with youthful minds. The greatest care should be taken in the education of youth to so vary the manner of instruction as to call forth the high and noble powers of the mind. Parents and schoolteachers are certainly disqualified to properly educate children if they have not first learned the lesson of self-control, patience, forbearance, gentleness, and love. What an important position for parents, guardians, and teachers! There are very few who realize the most essential wants of the mind and how to direct the developing intellect, the growing thoughts and feelings of youth. . . .

The early education of youth shapes their characters both in their secular and in their religious life. Solomon says: "Train up a child in the way he should go: and when he is old, he will not depart from it." This language is positive. The training which Solomon enjoins is to direct, educate, and develop. In order for parents and teachers to do this work, they must themselves understand "the way" the child should go. This embraces more than merely having a knowledge of books. It takes in everything that is good, virtuous, righteous, and holy. It comprehends the practice of temperance, godliness, brotherly kindness, and love to God and to one another. In order to attain this object, the physical, mental, moral, and religious education of children must have attention. . . . Children should be taught to respect experienced judgement and be guided by their parents and teachers. They should be so educated that their minds will be united with the minds of their parents and teachers, and so instructed that they can see the propriety of heeding their counsel. Then when they go forth from the guiding hand of their parents and teachers, their characters will not be like the reed trembling in the wind. . . .

Small children should be left as free as lambs to run out of doors, to be free and happy, and should be allowed the most favorable opportunities to lay the foundation for sound constitutions. . . .

The mother should have less love for the artificial in her house . . . and should find time to cultivate, in herself and in her children, a love for the beautiful buds and opening flowers. . . . She can lead their minds up to their Creator and awaken in their young hearts a love for their heavenly Father, who has manifested so great love for them. Parents can associate God with all His created works. . . . These lessons, imprinted upon the minds of young children amid the pleasant, attractive scenes of nature, will not be soon forgotten (*Testimonies,* vol. 3, pp. 131-137).

Moral Powers to Be Tested

Our sons in their youth will be like well-nurtured plants, and our daughters will be like pillars carved to adorn a palace. Psalm 144:12, NIV.

The disposition and habits of youth will be very likely to be manifested in mature manhood. You may bend a young tree into almost any shape that you choose, and if it remains and grows as you have bent it, it will be a deformed tree and will ever tell of the injury and abuse received at your hand. You may, after years of growth, try to straighten the tree, but all your efforts will prove unavailing. It will ever be a crooked tree. This is the case with the minds of youth. They should be carefully and tenderly trained in childhood. They may be trained in the right direction or in the wrong, and in their future lives they will pursue the course in which they were directed in youth. The habits formed in youth will grow with the growth and strengthen with the strength, and will generally be the same in afterlife, only continually growing stronger.

We are living in an age when almost everything is superficial. There is but little stability and firmness of character, because the training and education of children from their cradle is superficial. Their characters are built upon sliding sand. Self-denial and self-control have not been molded into their characters. They have been petted and indulged until they are spoiled for practical life. The love of pleasure controls minds, and children are flattered and indulged to their ruin. Children should be so trained and educated that they will expect temptations and calculate to meet difficulties and dangers. They should be taught to have control over themselves and to nobly overcome difficulties; and if they do not willfully rush into danger and needlessly place themselves in the way of temptation; if they shun evil influences and vicious society, and then are unavoidably compelled to be in dangerous company, they will have strength of character to stand for the right and preserve principle, and will come forth in the strength of God with their morals untainted. If youth who have been properly educated make God their trust, their moral powers will stand the most powerful test. . . .

If parents could be aroused to a sense of the fearful responsibility which rests upon them in the work of educating their children, more of their time would be devoted to prayer and less to needless display. They would reflect and study and pray earnestly to God for wisdom and divine aid to so train their children that they may develop characters that God will approve. Their anxiety would not be to know how they can educate their children so that they will be praised and honored of the world, but how they can educate them to form beautiful characters that God can approve (*Testimonies,* vol. 3, pp. 143-145).

Body and Mind Inseparable

If any man defile the temple of God, him shall God destroy; for the temple of God is holy, which temple ye are. 1 Corinthians 3:17.

One of the strongest temptations that man has to meet is upon the point of appetite. Between the mind and the body there is a mysterious and wonderful relation. They react upon each other. To keep the body in a healthy condition to develop its strength, that every part of the living machinery may act harmoniously, should be the first study of our life. To neglect the body is to neglect the mind. It cannot be to the glory of God for His children to have sickly bodies or dwarfed minds. To indulge the taste at the expense of health is a wicked abuse of the senses. . . .

The Redeemer of the world knew that the indulgence of appetite would bring physical debility, and so deaden the perceptive organs that sacred and eternal things would not be discerned. Christ knew that the world was given up to gluttony and that this indulgence would pervert the moral powers. If the indulgence of appetite was so strong upon the race that, in order to break its power, the divine Son of God, in behalf of man, was required to fast nearly six weeks, what a work is before the Christian in order that he may overcome even as Christ overcame! The strength of the temptation to indulge perverted appetite can be measured only by the inexpressible anguish of Christ in that long fast in the wilderness.

Christ knew that in order to successfully carry forward the plan of salvation He must commence the work of redeeming man just where the ruin began. Adam fell by the indulgence of appetite. In order to impress upon man his obligations to obey the law of God, Christ began His work of redemption by reforming the physical habits of man. . . .

Intemperance in eating, even of food of the right quality, will have a prostrating influence upon the system and will blunt the keener and holier emotions. Strict temperance in eating and drinking is highly essential for the healthy preservation and vigorous exercise of all the functions of the body. . . .

The only safe course is to touch not, taste not, handle not, tea, coffee, wines, tobacco, opium, and alcoholic drinks. The necessity for the men of this generation to call to their aid the power of the will, strengthened by the grace of God, in order to withstand the temptations of Satan and resist the least indulgence of perverted appetite is twice as great as it was several generations ago. . . . The Redeemer of the world came from heaven to help man in his weakness, that, in the power which Jesus came to bring him, he might become strong to overcome appetite and passion, and might be victor on every point (*Testimonies,* vol. 3, pp. 485-488).

Minds Filled With God's Promises

With the heart man believeth unto righteousness; and with the mouth confession is made unto salvation. Romans 10:10.

According to this, there is something to believe, also something to confess. The heart must first accept the truth as it is in Jesus. This is the foundation of true religion. Conviction of sin then begins to be felt; the sin-sick soul, feeling his need of a physician, comes to Jesus of Nazareth for pardon. Taking up the warfare against the enemy, he looks to Jesus for strength to resist temptation. He watches unto prayer, and searches the Scriptures. The truths of the Bible are seen in a new and intensely interesting light, and the Spirit of God opens to him their solemn importance. He studies the life of Christ, and the more clearly he discerns the spotless purity of the Saviour's character, the less confidence he has in his own goodness; the more steadily and closely he views Jesus, the less he discovers of perfection in himself. His self-righteousness disappears, and he falls, all helpless and broken, upon the Rock, Christ Jesus. He will be sorely pressed by the tempter, and at times may have feelings of discouragement, and be tempted to think that God will not accept him; but, taking God at His word, and pleading His sure promises, he presses through the darkness into the clear sunlight of Christ's love.

"And with the mouth confession is made unto salvation." If the heart is indeed the treasure house of grace and the love of Christ, these will be expressed in the words and deportment. There will be a constant attraction to Christ. All will be tested; hence the need of divine grace, and of sound religious faith and principles. The lips should be sanctified, that the words spoken may be few and well chosen.

Oftentimes professed Christians bring upon themselves great spiritual weakness by dwelling upon their trials and grievances. Not only does the matter become magnified by every repetition, but they as surely separate from Jesus as they allow themselves to transgress in this particular. Satan seeks to draw their attention to themselves, and to fasten upon them the idea that they are not appreciated. They begin to pity and sympathize with themselves, and to lose faith and confidence in Jesus; and as the result they walk apart from Him who asks them to cast their burdens upon Him.

To such we would say, Recount what God has done for you. Tell Satan that you do not trust in your own righteousness, but in the righteousness of Christ. Keep the mind filled with the precious promises found in the Bible, and when Satan comes in like a flood to overwhelm you, meet him with the weapon which the Word of God has provided, "It is written." This will break his power and give you the victory (*Historical Sketches,* pp. 129, 130).

Fruit Bearing

For as the rain cometh down, and the snow from heaven, and returneth not thither, but watereth the earth, and maketh it bring forth and bud, that it may give seed to the sower, and bread to the eater. Isaiah 55:10.

Christ is seeking to reproduce Himself in the hearts of men; and He does this through those who believe in Him. The object of the Christian life is fruit bearing—the reproduction of Christ's character in the believer, that it may be reproduced in others.

The plant does not germinate, grow, or bring forth fruit for itself, but to "give seed to the sower, and bread to the eater." So no man is to live unto himself. The Christian is in the world as a representative of Christ, for salvation of other souls.

There can be no growth or fruitfulness in the life that is centered in self. If you have accepted Christ as a personal Savior, you are to forget yourself, and try to help others. Talk of the love of Christ, tell of His goodness. Do every duty that presents itself. Carry the burden of souls upon your heart, and by every means in your power seek to save the lost. As you receive the Spirit of Christ—the Spirit of unselfish love and labor for others—you will grow and bring forth fruit. The graces of the Spirit will ripen in your character. Your faith will increase, your convictions deepen, your love be made perfect. More and more you will reflect the likeness of Christ in all that is pure, noble, and lovely.

"The fruit of the Spirit is love, joy, peace, longsuffering, gentleness, goodness, faith, meekness, temperance" (Galatians 5:22, 23). This fruit can never perish, but will produce after its kind a harvest unto eternal life.

"When the fruit is brought forth, immediately he putteth in the sickle, because the harvest is come." Christ is waiting with longing desire for the manifestation of Himself in His church. When the character of Christ shall be perfectly reproduced in His people, then He will come to claim His own.

It is the privilege of every Christian not only to look for but to hasten the coming of our Lord Jesus Christ. Were all who profess His name bearing fruit to His glory, how quickly the whole world would be sown with the seed of the gospel. Quickly the last great harvest would be ripened, and Christ would come to gather the precious grain (*Christ's Object Lessons,* pp. 67-69).

As the plant takes root in the soil, so we are to take deep root in Christ. As the plant receives the sunshine, the dew, and the rain, we are to open our hearts to the Holy Spirit. The work is to be done "not by might, nor by power, but by my Spirit, saith the Lord of hosts" (Zechariah 4:6) (*ibid.,* p. 67).

Spiritual Development Through Service

Give, and it shall be given unto you; good measure, pressed down, and shaken together, and running over, shall men give into your bosom. For with the same measure that ye mete withal it shall be measured to you again. Luke 6:38.

Those who give their lives to Christlike ministry know the meaning of true happiness. Their interests and their prayers reach far beyond self. They themselves are growing as they try to help others. They become familiar with the largest plans, the most stirring enterprises, and how can they but grow when they place themselves in the divine channel of light and blessing? Such ones receive wisdom from heaven. They become more and more identified with Christ in all His plans. There is no opportunity for spiritual stagnation. Selfish ambition and self-seeking are rebuked by constant contact with the absorbing interests, the elevated aspirations, which belong to high and holy activities (*Testimonies,* vol. 9, p. 42).

Heavenly intelligences are waiting to cooperate with human instrumentalities, that they may reveal to the world what human beings may become and what, through their influence, they may accomplish for the saving of souls that are ready to perish. He who is truly converted will be so filled with the love of God that he will long to impart to others the joy that he himself possesses. The Lord desires His church to show forth to the world the beauty of holiness. She is to demonstrate the power of Christian religion. Heaven is to be reflected in the character of the Christian. The song of gratitude and praise is to be heard by those in darkness. For the good tidings of the gospel, for its promises and assurances, we are to express our gratitude by seeking to do others good. The doing of this work will bring rays of heavenly righteousness to wearied, perplexed, suffering souls. It is as a fountain opened for the wayworn, thirsty traveler. At every work of mercy, every work of love, angels of God are present.

Christ's work is to be our example. Constantly He went about doing good. In the Temple and the synagogues, in the streets of the cities, in the marketplace and the workshop, by the seaside and among the hills, He preached the gospel and healed the sick. His life was one of unselfish service, and it is to be our lesson book. His tender, pitying love rebukes our selfishness and heartlessness.

Wherever Christ went, He scattered blessings in His path. How many who claim to believe on Him have learned His lessons of kindness, of tender pity, of unselfish love? Hear His voice speaking to the weak, the weary, the helpless: "Come unto me, all ye that labour and are heavy laden, and I will give you rest" (Matthew 11:28). There was no wearying of His patience, no repressing of His love (*ibid.,* pp. 30, 31).

Hid With Christ in God

The righteous shall flourish like the palm tree: he shall grow like a cedar in Lebanon.
Psalm 92:12.

See the weary traveler toiling over the hot sand of the desert, with no shelter to protect him from the rays of the tropical sun. His water supply fails, and he has nothing with which to slake his burning thirst. His tongue becomes swollen; he staggers like a drunken man. Visions of home and friends pass before his mind as he believes himself ready to perish. Suddenly he sees in the distance, rising out of the dreary, sandy waste, a palm tree, green and flourishing. Hope quickens his pulses; he presses on, knowing that that which gives vigor and freshness to the palm tree will cool his fevered blood and give him renewed life.

As is the palm tree in the desert—a guide and a consolation to the fainting traveler—so the Christian is to be in the world. He is to guide weary souls, full of unrest, and ready to perish in the desert of sin, to the living water. He is to point his fellowmen to Him who gives to all the invitation, "If any man thirst, let him come unto me, and drink."

The sky may be as brass, the burning sand may beat about the palm tree's roots, and pile itself about its trunk; yet the tree lives on, fresh and vigorous. Remove the sand, and you discover the secret of its life; its roots strike down deep into the waters hidden in the earth.

Thus it is with the Christian. His life is hid with Christ in God. Jesus is to him a well of water, springing up unto everlasting life. His faith, like the rootlets of the palm tree, penetrates beneath the things that are seen, drawing life from the fountain of life. And, amid all the corruption of the world, he is true and loyal to God. The sweet influence of Christ's righteousness surrounds him. His influence elevates and blesses.

The humblest and poorest of the disciples of Jesus can be a blessing to others. They may not realize that they are doing any special good, but by their unconscious influence they may start waves of blessings that will widen and deepen, and the blessed results they may never know till the day of final reward. They are not required to weary themselves with anxiety about success. They have only to go forward quietly, doing faithfully the work God's providence assigns, and their life will not be in vain. Their own souls will be growing more and more into the likeness of Christ; they are workers together with God in this life, and are thus fitting for the higher work and the unshadowed joy of the life to come (*Signs of the Times,* Aug. 6, 1902).

Christ Has Promised Us Rest

Come unto me, all ye that labour and are heavy laden, and I will give you rest. Matthew 11:28.

Jesus invites the weary and care-laden sons and daughters of Adam to come to Him, and lay on Him their heavy burdens. But many who hear this invitation, while sighing for rest, yet press on the rugged path, hugging their burdens close to their heart. Jesus loves them, and longs to bear their burdens and themselves also in His strong arms. He would remove the fears and uncertainties that rob them of peace and rest; but they must first come to Him, and tell Him the secret woes of their heart. He invites the confidence of His people as the proof of their love for Him. The gift of the humble, trusting heart is more precious to Him than all the wealth that riches can bestow. If they would only come to Him in the simplicity and confidence with which a child would come to His parents, the divine touch of His hands would relieve them of their burdens.

Jesus, our compassionate Savior, is the way, the truth, and the life. Why will we not accept His gracious offer of mercy, believe His words of promise, and not make the way of life so hard? . . . The ways of Christ are ways of pleasantness, and all His paths are peace. If we have made rough paths for our feet, and taken heavy burdens of care in laying up for ourselves treasures upon the earth, let us now change, and follow the path Jesus has prepared for us.

We are not always willing to come to Jesus with our trials and difficulties. Sometimes we pour our troubles into human ears, and tell our afflictions to those who cannot help us, and neglect to confide all to Jesus, who is able to change the sorrowful way to paths of joy and peace. . . . Oh, that all, ministers and people, would take their burdens and perplexities to Jesus, who is waiting to receive them, and to give them peace and rest! (*Signs of the Times,* Mar. 17, 1887).

It is a terribly hard struggle to give up your own will and your own way. But this lesson learned, you will find rest and peace. Pride, selfishness, and ambition must be overcome; your will must be swallowed up in the will of Christ. The whole life may become one constant love sacrifice, every action a manifestation, and every word an utterance of love. As the life of the vine circulates through stem and cluster, descends into the lower fibers, and reaches to the topmost leaf, so will the grace and love of Christ burn and abound in the soul, sending its virtues to every part of the being, and pervading every exercise of body and mind (*The SDA Bible Commentary,* Ellen G. White Comments, vol. 5, pp. 1091, 1092).

The Plan of Redemption a Gift

Blessed be the God and Father of our Lord Jesus Christ, who hath blessed us with all spiritual blessings in heavenly places in Christ. Ephesians 1:3.

God, who is rich in mercy, for his great love wherewith he loved us, even when we were dead in sins, hath quickened us together with Christ, . . . and hath raised us up together, and made us sit together in heavenly places in Christ Jesus: that in the ages to come he might show the exceeding riches of his grace in his kindness toward us through Christ Jesus."

Such are the words in which "Paul the aged," "a prisoner of Jesus Christ," writing from his prison house at Rome, endeavored to set before his brethren that which he found language inadequate to express in its fullness—"the unsearchable riches of Christ," the treasure of grace freely offered to the fallen sons of men. The plan of redemption was laid by a sacrifice, a gift. Says the apostle: "Ye know the grace of our Lord Jesus Christ, that, though he was rich, yet for your sakes he became poor, that ye through his poverty might be rich." . . . And as the crowning blessing of redemption, "*the gift of God* is eternal life through Jesus Christ our Lord." . . . Surely there are none that, beholding the riches of grace, can forbear to exclaim with the apostle: "Thanks be unto God for his unspeakable gift."

As the plan of redemption begins and ends with a gift, so it is to be carried forward. The same spirit of sacrifice which purchased salvation for us will dwell in the hearts of all who become partakers of the heavenly gift. Says the apostle Peter: "As every man hath received the gift, even so minister the same one to another, as good stewards of the manifold grace of God." Said Jesus to His disciples as He sent them forth: "Freely ye have received, freely give." In him who is fully in sympathy with Christ there can be nothing selfish or exclusive. He who drinks of the living water will find that it is "in him a well of water springing up into everlasting life." The Spirit of Christ within him is like a spring welling up in the desert, flowing to refresh all, and making those who are ready to perish eager to drink of the water of life. It was the same spirit of love and self-sacrifice which dwelt in Christ that impelled the apostle Paul to his manifold labors. "I am debtor," he says, "both to the Greeks, and to the Barbarians; both to the wise, and to the unwise" (Romans 1:14). "Unto me, who am less than the least of all saints, is this grace given, that I should preach among the Gentiles the unsearchable riches of Christ" (Ephesians 3:8) (*Testimonies,* vol. 5, pp. 730, 731).

The Power of God's Love

Acquaint now thyself with him, and be at peace: thereby good shall come unto thee.
Job 22:21.

Said Jesus: "The Father himself loveth you." If our faith is fixed upon God, through Christ, it will prove "as an anchor of the soul, both sure and steadfast, and which entereth into that within the veil; whither the forerunner is for us entered." It is true that disappointments will come; tribulation we must expect; but we are to commit everything, great and small, to God. He does not become perplexed by the multiplicity of our grievances nor overpowered by the weight of our burdens. His watchcare extends to every household and enriches every individual; He is concerned in all our business and our sorrows. He marks every tear; He is touched with the feeling of our infirmities. All the afflictions and trials that befall us here are permitted, to work out His purposes of love toward us, "that we might be partakers of his holiness," and thus become participants in that fullness of joy which is found in His presence. . . .

The Bible in strongest terms sets before us the importance of obtaining a knowledge of God. Says Peter: "Grace and peace be multiplied unto you through the *knowledge of God,* and of Jesus our Lord." "His divine power hath given unto us *all things* that pertain unto life and godliness, *through the knowledge of him* that hath called us to glory and virtue." And the Scripture bids us: "Acquaint now thyself with him, and be at peace."

God has commanded us, "Ye shall be holy; for I the Lord your God am holy"; and an inspired apostle declares that without holiness "no man shall see the Lord." Holiness is agreement with God. By sin the image of God in man has been marred and well-nigh obliterated; it is the work of the gospel to restore that which has been lost; and we are to cooperate with the divine agency in this work. And how can we come into harmony with God, how shall we receive His likeness, unless we obtain a knowledge of Him? It is this knowledge that Christ came into the world to reveal unto us.

The meager views which so many have had of the exalted character and office of Christ have narrowed their religious experience and have greatly hindered their progress in the divine life. Personal religion among us as a people is at a low ebb. There is much form, much machinery, much tongue religion; but something deeper and more solid must be brought into our religious experience. . . . What we need is to know God and the power of His love, as revealed in Christ, by an experimental knowledge. We must search the Scriptures diligently, prayerfully; our understanding must be quickened by the Holy Spirit, and our hearts must be uplifted to God in faith and hope and continual praise (*Testimonies,* vol. 5, pp. 742-744).

Firm Reliance on Christ

Now the God of hope fill you with all joy and peace in believing, that ye may abound in hope, through the power of the Holy Ghost. Romans 15:13.

At times a deep sense of our unworthiness will send a thrill of terror through the soul; but this is no evidence that God has changed toward us, or we toward God. . . . We should by faith grasp the hand of Christ, and trust Him as fully in the darkness as in the light.

Satan may whisper, "You are too great a sinner for Christ to save." While you acknowledge that you are indeed sinful and unworthy, you may meet the tempter with the cry, "By virtue of the atonement, I claim Christ as my Savior. I trust not to my own merits, but to the precious blood of Jesus, which cleanses me. This moment I hang my helpless soul on Christ." The Christian life must be a life of constant, living faith. An unyielding trust, a firm reliance upon Christ, will bring peace and assurance to the soul. . . .

Every obstacle, every internal foe, only increases your need of Christ. He came to take away the heart of stone, and give you a heart of flesh. Look to Him for special grace to overcome your peculiar faults. When assailed by temptation, steadfastly resist the evil promptings; say to your soul, "How can I dishonor my Redeemer? I have given myself to Christ; I cannot do the works of Satan." Cry to the dear Savior for help to sacrifice every idol, and to put away every darling sin. Let the eye of faith see Jesus standing before the Father's throne, presenting His wounded hands as He pleads for you. Believe that strength comes to you through your precious Savior.

By faith look upon the crowns laid up for those who shall overcome; listen to the exultant song of the redeemed, Worthy, worthy is the Lamb that was slain and hast redeemed us to God! Endeavor to regard these scenes as real. Stephen, the first Christian martyr, in his terrible conflict with principalities and powers, and spiritual wickedness in high places, exclaimed, "Behold, I see the heavens opened, and the Son of man standing on the right hand of God." The Savior of the world was revealed to him as looking down from heaven upon him with the deepest interest; and the glorious light of Christ's countenance shone upon Stephen with such brightness that even his enemies saw his face shine like the face of an angel.

If we would permit our minds to dwell more upon Christ and the heavenly world, we should find a powerful stimulus and support in fighting the battles of the Lord. Pride and love of the world will lose their power as we contemplate the glories of that better land so soon to be our home. Beside the loveliness of Christ, all earthly attractions will seem of little worth (*Review and Herald,* Nov. 15, 1887).

The Sanctifying Power of the Truth

For their sakes I sanctify myself, that they also might be sanctified through the truth.
John 17:19.

Continual application will accomplish for man what nothing else can. Those who are never content without the consciousness that they are growing every day will truly make a success of life. . . .

Do not, then, continually dwell upon . . . one point, concentrating all the energies of the mind upon it, constantly urging it upon the attention of others, but take another subject, and carefully examine that. Thus mystery after mystery will be unfolded to your comprehension. Two valuable victories will be gained by this course. You have not only secured useful knowledge, but the exercise of the mind has increased mental strength and power. The key found to unlock one mystery may develop also other precious gems of knowledge heretofore undiscovered. . . .

The world is teeming with errors and fables. Novelties in the form of sensational dramas are continually arising to engross the mind, and absurd theories abound which are destructive to moral and spiritual advancement. The cause of God needs men of intellect, men of thought, men well versed in the Scriptures, to meet the inflowing tide of opposition. We should give no sanction to arrogance, narrow-mindedness, and inconsistencies, although the garment of professed piety may be thrown over them. Those who have the sanctifying power of the truth upon their hearts will exert a persuasive influence. Knowing that the advocates of error cannot create or destroy truth, they can afford to be calm and considerate. . . .

The satanic delusions of the age must be met clearly and intelligently with the sword of the Spirit, which is the Word of God. The same unseen Hand that guides the planets in their courses, and upholds the worlds by His power, has made provision for man formed in His image, that he may be little less than the angels of God while in the performance of his duties on earth. God's purposes have not been answered by men who have been entrusted with the most solemn truth ever given to man. He designs that we should rise higher and higher toward a state of perfection, seeing and realizing at every step the power and glory of God. Man does not know himself. Our responsibilities are exactly proportioned to our light, opportunities, and privileges. . . .

The precious Book of God contains rules of life for men of every class and every vocation. Examples are here found which it would be well for all to study and imitate. "The Son of God came not to be ministered unto, but to minister." The true honor and glory of the servant of Christ consists, not in the number of sermons preached, nor in the amount of writing accomplished, but in the work of faithfully ministering to the wants of the people (*Testimonies,* vol. 4, pp. 413-416).

September

25

True Humility

God hath chosen the weak things of the world to confound the things which are mighty . . . that no flesh should glory in his presence. 1 Corinthians 1:27-29.

The ascension of Jesus, doctors, lawyers, priests, rulers, scribes, and theologians listened with astonishment to words of wisdom and power from unlearned and humble men. These wise men marveled at the success of the lowly disciples, and finally accounted for it to their own satisfaction from the fact that they had been with Jesus and learned of Him. Their character and the simplicity of their teachings were similar to the character and teachings of Christ. . . .

Those who teach unpopular truth today must have power from on high to combine with their doctrine, or their efforts will be of little account. The precious grace of humility is sadly wanting in the ministry and the church. Men who preach the truth think too highly of their own abilities. True humility will lead a man to exalt Christ and the truth, and to realize his utter dependence upon the God of truth. It is painful to learn lessons of humility, yet nothing is more beneficial in the end. The pain attendant upon learning lessons of humility is in consequence of our being elated by a false estimate of ourselves, so that we are unable to see our great need. Vanity and pride fill the hearts of men. God's grace alone can work a reformation.

It is your work . . . to humble yourself and not wait for God to humble you. God's hand at times bears heavily upon men to humble them and bring them into a proper position before Him; but how much better it is to keep the heart daily humbled before God. We can abase ourselves, or we can build ourselves up in pride and wait till God abases us. . . .

In order to comprehend the truth, you should discipline and train the mind, and seek continually to possess the graces of genuine piety. You scarcely know what this is now. When Christ is in you, you will have something more than a theory of the truth. You will not only be repeating the lessons Christ gave when upon the earth, but you will be educating others by your life of self-denial and devotion to the cause of God. Your life will be a living sermon, possessing greater power than any discourse given in the desk.

You need to cultivate in yourself that unselfish spirit, that self-denying grace and pure devotion, which you wish to see others carry out in their lives. In order to continually increase in spiritual intelligence, and to become more and more efficient, you need to cultivate habits of usefulness in the minor duties lying in your pathway. You must not wait for opportunities to do a great work, but seize the first chance to prove yourself faithful in that which is least, and you may thus work your way up from one position of trust to another (*Testimonies,* vol. 4, pp. 378-380).

In Harmony With Christ

We then, as workers together with him, beseech you also that ye receive not the grace of God in vain. 2 Corinthians 6:1.

All heaven is interested in the work going on in this world, which is to prepare men and women for the future, immortal life. It is God's plan that human agencies shall have the high honor of acting as coworkers with Jesus Christ in the salvation of souls. The Word of God plainly reveals that it is the privilege of the instrument in this great work to realize that there is One at his right hand ready to aid him in every sincere endeavor to reach the highest moral and spiritual excellence in the Master's work. This will be the case with all who feel their need of help. They should look upon the work of God as sacred and holy, and should bring to Him, every day, offerings of joy and gratitude, in return for the power of His grace, by which they are enabled to make advancement in the divine life. The worker should ever take humble views of himself, considering his many lost opportunities for want of diligence and appreciation of the work. He should not become discouraged, but should continually renew his efforts to redeem the time. . . .

It is not necessary that anyone should yield to the temptations of Satan and thus violate his conscience and grieve the Holy Spirit. Every provision has been made in the Word of God whereby all may have divine help in their endeavors to overcome. If they keep Jesus before them they will become changed into His image. All who by faith have Christ abiding in them carry a power into their labor which makes them successful. They will be constantly growing more and more efficient in their work, and the blessing of God, shown in the prosperity of the work, will testify that they are indeed laborers together with Christ. But however much one may advance in spiritual life, he will never come to a point where he will not need diligently to search the Scriptures; for therein are found the evidences of our faith. All points of doctrine, even though they have been accepted as truth, should be brought to the law and to the testimony; if they cannot stand this test, "there is no light in them."

The great plan of redemption, as revealed in the closing work for these last days, should receive close examination. The scenes connected with the sanctuary above should make such an impression upon the minds and hearts of all that they may be able to impress others. All need to become more intelligent in regard to the work of the atonement, which is going on in the sanctuary above. When this grand truth is seen and understood, those who hold it will work in harmony with Christ to prepare a people to stand in the great day of God, and their efforts will be successful (*Testimonies,* vol. 5, pp. 573-575).

September
27

Words Are an Index

A good man out of the good treasure of the heart bringeth forth good things.
Matthew 12:35.

Your words are an index of your character. . . . Here we see the importance of carefulness in the employment of speech. This talent is a great power for good when it is used aright. . . .

It is the privilege of all to fill the chambers of the soul with pure and holy treasures by making themselves thoroughly familiar with the precious words of Christ, spoken for our instruction. . . .

By heeding the reproof and encouragement given in God's Word, we may "walk worthy of the Lord unto all pleasing, being fruitful in every good work, and increasing in the knowledge of God; strengthened with all might, according to his glorious power, unto all patience and longsuffering with joyfulness." Those who are thus strengthened will not walk with head bowed down. . . .

"Giving thanks unto the Father, which hath made us meet to be partakers of the inheritance of the saints in light: who hath delivered us from the power of darkness, and hath translated us into the kingdom of his dear Son: in whom we have redemption through his blood, even the forgiveness of sins." Then shall we not all, old and young, learn to converse in the language that is spoken by those who are translated into God's kingdom? Shall not our words be such as will be heard with pleasure by our heavenly Father?

As those who claim to be Christians, we are under solemn obligations to reveal the truth of our profession by our words. The tongue is a little member; but what an amount of good it can do if the heart is pure! If the heart is stored with good things, if it is stored with Christlike tenderness, sympathy, and politeness, this will be shown by the words spoken and the actions performed. The light shining from the Word of God is our guide. Nothing so weakens a church as a wrong use of the talent of speech. . . .

The quality of our works is shown by our words. When our words and works harmonize in Christ, we show that we are consecrated to God, perfecting holiness in His fear. As we give ourselves, soul, body, and spirit, to Him, He works in us, both to will and to do of His good pleasure.

The love of Christ in the heart is revealed by the expression of praise. Those who are consecrated to God will show this by their sanctified conversation. If their hearts are pure, their words will be pure, showing an elevated principle working in a sanctified direction. The mind will be absorbed in holy contemplation, and there will be a sense of the presence of God (*Review and Herald,* Jan. 18, 1898).

Hezekiah Humbled Himself

Hezekiah humbled himself for the pride of his heart, both he and the inhabitants of Jerusalem, so that the wrath of the Lord came not upon them in the days of Hezekiah.
2 Chronicles 32:26.

Filled with remorse, "Hezekiah humbled himself for the pride of his heart." . . . But the evil seed had been sown and in time was to spring up and yield a harvest of desolation and woe. During his remaining years the king of Judah was to have much prosperity because of his steadfast purpose to redeem the past and to bring honor to the name of the God whom he served; yet his faith was to be severely tried, and he was to learn that only by putting his trust fully in Jehovah could he hope to triumph over the powers of darkness that were plotting his ruin and the utter destruction of his people.

The story of Hezekiah's failure to prove true to his trust at the time of the visit of the ambassadors is fraught with an important lesson for all. Far more than we do, we need to speak of the precious chapters in our experience, of the mercy and loving-kindness of God, of the matchless depths of the Savior's love. When mind and heart are filled with the love of God, it will not be difficult to impart that which enters into the spiritual life. Great thoughts, noble aspirations, clear perceptions of truth, unselfish purposes, yearnings for piety and holiness, will find expression in words that reveal the character of the heart treasure.

Those with whom we associate day by day need our help, our guidance. They may be in such a condition of mind that a word spoken in season will be as a nail in a sure place. Tomorrow some of these souls may be where we can never reach them again. What is our influence over these fellow travelers?

Every day of life is freighted with responsibilities which we must bear. Every day, our words and acts are making impressions upon those with whom we associate. How great the need that we set a watch upon our lips and guard carefully our steps! One reckless movement, one imprudent step, and the surging waves of some strong temptation may sweep a soul into the downward path. We cannot gather up the thoughts we have planted in human minds. . . .

On the other hand, if by our example we aid others in the development of good principles, we give them power to do good. In their turn they exert the same beneficial influence over others. Thus hundreds and thousands are helped by our unconscious influence. The true follower of Christ strengthens the good purposes of all with whom he comes in contact. Before an unbelieving, sin-loving world he reveals the power of God's grace and the perfection of His character (*Prophets and Kings,* pp. 347, 348).

Personal Influence Is a Power

You are a garden fountain, a well of flowing water streaming down from Lebanon.
Song of Solomon 4:15, NIV.

It is through personal contact and association that men are reached by the saving power of the gospel. They are not saved as masses, but as individuals. Personal influence is a power. It is to work with the influence of Christ, to lift where Christ lifts, to impart correct principles, and to stay the progress of the world's corruption. It is to diffuse that grace which Christ alone can impart. It is to uplift, to sweeten the lives and characters of others by the power of a pure example united with earnest faith and love. . . .

Through sin, the whole human organism is deranged, the mind is perverted, the imagination corrupted; the faculties of the soul are degraded. There is an absence of pure religion, of heart holiness. The converting power of God has not wrought in transforming the character. The soul is weak, and for want of moral force to overcome, is polluted and debased.

To the heart that has become purified, all is changed. Transformation of character is the testimony to the world of an indwelling Christ. The Spirit of God produces a new life in the soul, bringing the thoughts and desires into obedience to the will of Christ; and the inward man is renewed in the image of God. Weak and erring men and women show to the world that the redeeming power of grace can cause the faulty character to develop into symmetry and abundant fruitfulness.

The heart that receives the Word of God is not as a pool that evaporates, not like a broken cistern that loses its treasure. It is like the mountain stream, fed by unfailing springs, whose cool, sparkling waters leap from rock to rock, refreshing the weary, the thirsty, the heavy-laden. It is like a river constantly flowing and, as it advances, becoming deeper and wider, until its life-giving waters are spread over all the earth. . . .

So it is with the true child of God. The religion of Christ reveals itself as a vitalizing, pervading principle, a living, working, spiritual energy. When the heart is opened to the heavenly influence of truth and love, these principles will flow forth again like streams in the desert, causing fruitfulness to appear where now are barrenness and dearth.

As those who have been cleansed and sanctified through a knowledge of Bible truth engage heartily in the work of soul saving, they will become indeed a savor of life unto life. And as daily they drink of the inexhaustible fountain of grace and knowledge, they will find that their own hearts are filled to overflowing with the Spirit of their Master, and that through their unselfish ministry many are benefited physically, mentally, and spiritually. The weary are refreshed, the sick restored to health, and the sin-burdened relieved (*Prophets and Kings,* pp. 232-234).

The True, the Frank, the Honest

Be thou faithful unto death, and I will give thee a crown of life. Revelation 2:10.

God's all-seeing eye notes the defects of all and the ruling passion of each, yet He bears with our mistakes and pities our weakness. He bids His people cherish the same spirit of tenderness and forbearance. True Christians will not exult in exposing the faults and deficiencies of others. They will . . . fix the mind upon that which is attractive and lovely. To the Christian every act of faultfinding, every word of censure or condemnation, is painful. . . .

Would all professed Christians use their investigative powers to see what evils needed to be corrected in themselves, instead of talking of others' wrongs, there would be a more healthy condition in the church today. Some will be honest when it costs nothing; but when policy will pay best, honesty is forgotten. Honesty and policy will not work together in the same mind. In time, either policy will be expelled, and truth and honesty reign supreme, or, if policy is cherished, honesty will be forgotten. They are never in agreement; they have nothing in common. One is the prophet of Baal, the other is the true prophet of God. When the Lord makes up His jewels, the true, the frank, the honest, will be looked upon with pleasure. Angels are employed in making crowns for such ones, and upon these star-gemmed crowns will be reflected, with splendor, the light which radiates from the throne of God. . . .

The Lord is testing and proving His people. You may be just as severe and critical with your own defective character as you please; but be kind, pitiful, and courteous toward others. Inquire every day: Am I sound to the core, or am I false-hearted? Entreat the Lord to save you from all deception on this point. Eternal interests are involved. While so many are panting after honor and greedy of gain, do you, my beloved brethren, be eagerly seeking the assurance of the love of God and crying: Who will show me how to make my calling and election sure?

Satan carefully studies the constitutional sins of men, and then he begins his work of alluring and ensnaring them. We are in the thickest of temptations, but there is victory for us if we fight manfully the battles of the Lord. All are in danger. But if you walk humbly and prayerfully you will come forth from the proving process more precious than fine gold, even than the golden wedge of Ophir. If careless and prayerless, you will be as sounding brass and a tinkling cymbal.

Some have become almost lost in the mazes of skepticism. To such I would say: Lift your mind out of that channel. Fasten it upon God. The more closely faith and holiness bind you to the Eternal One, the clearer and brighter will the justice of His dealings appear to you. Make life, eternal life, the object of your pursuit (*Testimonies,* vol. 5, pp. 95-98).

October

1

The Head of the Church

He is the head of the body, the church: who is the beginning, the first born from the dead; that in all things he might have the preeminence. Colossians 1:18.

Since His ascension Christ has carried forward His work on the earth by chosen ambassadors, through whom He speaks to the children of men and ministers to their needs. The great Head of the church superintends His work through the instrumentality of men ordained by God to act as His representatives.

The position of those who have been called of God to labor in word and doctrine for the upbuilding of His church is one of grave responsibility. In Christ's stead they are to beseech men and women to be reconciled to God, and they can fulfill their mission only as they receive wisdom and power from above.

Christ's ministers are the spiritual guardians of the people entrusted to their care. Their work has been likened to that of watchmen. In ancient times sentinels were often stationed on the walls of cities, where, from points of vantage, they could overlook important posts to be guarded, and give warning of the approach of an enemy. Upon their faithfulness depended the safety of all within. At stated intervals they were required to call to one another, to make sure that all were awake and that no harm had befallen any. The cry of good cheer or of warning was borne from one to another, each repeating the call till it echoed round the city. . . .

It is the privilege of the watchmen on the walls of Zion to live so near to God, and to be so susceptible to the impressions of His Spirit, that He can work through them to tell men and women of their peril and point them to the place of safety. Faithfully are they to warn them of the sure result of transgression, and faithfully are they to safeguard the interests of the church. At no time may they relax their vigilance. . . . In trumpet tones their voices are to be lifted, and never are they to sound one wavering, uncertain note. . . .

He who serves under the bloodstained banner of Immanuel will have that to do which will call for heroic effort and patient endurance. But the soldier of the cross stands unshrinkingly in the forefront of the battle. . . . He realizes his need of strength from above. The victories that he gains . . . cause him to lean more and more heavily on the Mighty One. Relying upon that Power, he is enabled to present the message of salvation so forcibly that it vibrates in other minds. . . .

It is by seeing Him who is invisible that strength and vigor of soul are gained and the power of earth over mind and character is broken (*The Acts of the Apostles,* pp. 360-363).

Laborers With Him

Ye are the light of the world. Matthew 5:14.

Our Lord designed that His church should reflect to the world the fullness and sufficiency that we find in Him. We are constantly receiving of God's bounty, and by imparting of the same we are to represent to the world the love and beneficence of Christ. While all heaven is astir, dispatching messengers to every part of the earth to carry forward the work of redemption, the church of the living God are also to be colaborers with Christ. We are members of His mystical body. He is the head, controlling all the members of the body. Jesus Himself, in His infinite mercy, is working on human hearts, effecting spiritual transformations so amazing that angels look on with astonishment and joy. The same unselfish love that characterizes the Master is seen in the character and life of His true followers. Christ expects that men will become partakers of His divine nature while in this world, thus not only reflecting His glory to the praise of God, but illumining the darkness of the world with the radiance of heaven. Thus will be fulfilled the words of Christ: "Ye are the light of the world."

"We are labourers together with God," "stewards of the manifold grace of God." The knowledge of God's grace, the truths of His Word, and temporal gifts as well—time and means, talents and influence—are all a trust from God to be employed to His glory and the salvation of men. Nothing can be more offensive to God, who is constantly bestowing His gifts upon man, than to see him selfishly grasping these gifts and making no returns to the Giver. Jesus is today in heaven preparing mansions for those who love Him; yes, more than mansions, a kingdom which is to be ours. But all who shall inherit these blessings must be partakers of the self-denial and self-sacrifice of Christ for the good of others.

Never was there greater need of earnest, self-sacrificing labor in the cause of Christ than now, when the hours of probation are fast closing and the last message of mercy is to be given to the world. My soul is stirred within me as the Macedonian cry comes from every direction, from the cities and villages of our own land, from across the Atlantic and the broad Pacific, and from the islands of the sea: "Come over . . . , and help us." Brethren and sisters, will you answer the cry? saying: "We will do our best, both in sending you missionaries and money. We will deny ourselves in the embellishment of our houses, in the adornment of our persons, and in the gratification of appetite. We will give the means entrusted to us into the cause of God, and we will devote ourselves also unreservedly to His work." . . . Let every dollar that you can spare be invested in the bank of heaven (*Testimonies,* vol. 5, pp. 731-733).

Christ Glorified in His People

These things I have spoken unto you, that in me ye might have peace. In the world ye shall have tribulation: but be of good cheer; I have overcome the world. John 16:33.

Christ did not fail, neither was He discouraged, and His followers are to manifest a faith of the same enduring nature. They are to live as He lived, and work as He worked, because they depend on Him as the great Master Worker. Courage, energy, and perseverance they must possess. Though apparent impossibilities obstruct their way, by His grace they are to go forward. Instead of deploring difficulties, they are called upon to surmount them. They are to despair of nothing, and to hope for everything. With the golden chain of His matchless love Christ has bound them to the throne of God. It is His purpose that the highest influence in the universe, emanating from the source of all power, shall be theirs. They are to have power to resist evil, power that neither earth, nor death, nor hell can master, power that will enable them to overcome as Christ overcame.

Christ designs that heaven's order, heaven's plan of government, heaven's divine harmony, shall be represented in His church on earth. Thus in His people He is glorified. Through them the Sun of righteousness will shine in undimmed luster to the world. Christ has given to His church ample facilities, that He may receive a large revenue of glory from His redeemed, purchased possession. He has bestowed upon His people capabilities and blessings that they may represent His own sufficiency. The church, endowed with the righteousness of Christ, is His depositary, in which the riches of His mercy, His grace, and His love are to appear in full and final display. Christ looks upon His people in their purity and perfection, as the reward of His humiliation, and the supplement of His glory—Christ, the great Center, from whom radiates all glory. . . .

Christ had finished the work that was given Him to do. He had glorified God on the earth. He had manifested the Father's name. He had gathered out those who were to continue His work among men. And He said, "I am glorified in them. And now I am no more in the world, but these are in the world, and I come to thee. Holy Father, keep through thine own name those whom thou hast given me, that they may be one, as we are." . . .

Thus in the language of one who has divine authority, Christ gives His elect church into the Father's arms. As a consecrated high priest He intercedes for His people. As a faithful shepherd He gathers His flock under the shadow of the Almighty, in the strong and sure refuge. For Him there awaits the last battle with Satan, and He goes forth to meet it (*The Desire of Ages,* pp. 679, 680).

A Royal Name

If any man suffer as a Christian, let him not be ashamed; but let him glorify God on this behalf. 1 Peter 4:16.

God has instructed me to say to His people, ministers and lay members, "Take your stand on higher ground. Move steadily onward and upward in the path that Jesus trod. Do not trust in your own opinions. Sanctification through the truth is your only safety." The Lord God of Israel would have His people stand in His strength, and in His might, receiving to impart. He will uphold and sustain those who serve Him with mind and heart and strength.

We need to understand what it means to put on Christ, what it means to have an experimental knowledge of the grace of Christ, and a continually increasing faith.

Speaking of the mystery "which from the beginning of the world hath been hid in God," Paul says, "Unto me, who am less than the least of all saints, is this grace given, that I should preach among the Gentiles the unsearchable riches of Christ; and to make all men see what is the fellowship of the mystery . . . : to the intent that now unto the principalities and powers in heavenly places might be made known by the church the manifold wisdom of God." Not only to those living in this world, but to the principalities and powers in heavenly places is the church on this earth to reveal the glory of God.

God chose from among the Gentiles a people for Himself, and gave to them the name of Christian. This is a royal name, given to those who join themselves to Christ. . . . Peter says: "If any man suffer as a Christian, let him not be ashamed; but let him glorify God on this behalf." . . .

O that God's people would take Him at His word, and lay hold of the wonderful treasure of knowledge opened to them! . . .

We have before us the highest, holiest example. In thought, word, and deed Jesus was sinless. Perfection marked all that He did. He points us to the path that He trod, saying, "If any man will come after me, let him deny himself, and take up his cross, and follow me."

We have a perfect rule—the Word of the living God. This Word He has given us as our guide and counselor. The psalmist says, "Thy word have I hid in mine heart, that I might not sin against thee." . . .

Christians, those who are to represent God in the world, are not to seek for doctrines that are new and strange. They are not to pry into the mysteries of the future life. Their part is to make their life in this world such as God can approve (*Review and Herald,* Apr. 26, 1906).

October
5

Let the Church Arise and Shine

Arise, shine; for thy light is come, and the glory of the Lord is risen upon thee. For, behold, the darkness shall cover the earth, and gross darkness the people: but the Lord shall arise upon thee, and his glory shall be seen upon thee. Isaiah 60:1, 2.

Jealousy caused the first death in our world. . . . All selfishness comes from Satan. Human beings belong to one great family, the family of God. They are to respect and love one another. They are not to speak words which wound and bruise. No one is to be unfair in his dealings, causing his fellow-beings to lose confidence in him. Selfishness and injustice bring unhappiness. Under their baleful influence men lose the sense of what it means to love one another as Christ loves us.

All are to work in love and unity, looking to God as the great center. Love for Christ is the principle which unites man to his fellowmen. . . .

The opposite of allegiance to God is seen in the world today. Every kingdom, every province, every family, has a desire to make itself a center. Men long to rule over their fellowmen. . . . Self is the mainspring of action. . . .

The Lord calls upon His people to put far from them every stumbling block. Be filled with the Holy Spirit. To unite man with God and with his fellowmen, to restore to human beings the benevolence lost through sin—this is the glory of the gospel. Let the church arise and shine; for her light has come, and the glory of the Lord is risen upon her. Let the members strive earnestly to obtain the victory over self (manuscript 78, 1901).

The religion of Christ means more than the forgiveness of sin; it means taking away our sins, and filling the vacuum with the graces of the Holy Spirit. It means divine illumination, rejoicing in God. It means a heart emptied of self, and blessed with the abiding presence of Christ. When Christ reigns in the soul, there is purity, freedom from sin. The glory, the fullness, the completeness of the gospel plan is fulfilled in the life. The acceptance of the Savior brings a glow of perfect peace, perfect love, perfect assurance. The beauty and fragrance of the character of Christ revealed in the life testifies that God has indeed sent His Son into the world to be its Savior. . . .

The revelation of His own glory in the form of humanity will bring heaven so near to men that the beauty adorning the inner temple will be seen in every soul in whom the Savior dwells. Men will be captivated by the glory of an abiding Christ. And in currents of praise and thanksgiving from the many souls thus won to God, glory will flow back to the great Giver (*Christ's Object Lessons,* pp. 419, 420).

Heaven Waiting to Cooperate

Then shall thy light break forth as the morning . . . and thy righteousness shall go before thee; the glory of the Lord shall be thy rereward. Isaiah 58:8.

It is the constant realization of the preciousness of Christ's atoning sacrifice in our behalf that qualifies us to point others to the Lamb of God that taketh away the sin of the world. We must become exponents of the efficacy of the blood of Christ, by which our own sins have been forgiven. Only thus can we reach the higher class. . . .

Christ has said that it is easier for a camel to go through the eye of a needle than for a rich man to enter the kingdom of God. But all things are possible with God. He can and will work through human agencies upon the minds of rich men whose lives have been devoted to money getting.

The heavenly universe has long been waiting to cooperate with human agents in this work which they have shunned and neglected. Many who have attempted the work have given up in discouragement, when, had they persevered, they would have been largely successful. Those who faithfully do this work will be blessed of God. The righteousness of Christ will go before them, and the glory of the Lord will be their rearward.

There are miracles to be wrought in genuine conversion, miracles that are not now discerned. The greatest men of the earth are not beyond the power of a wonder-working God. If those who are workers together with Him will be men of opportunity, doing their duty bravely and faithfully, God will convert men who occupy responsible places, men of intellect and influence. Through the power of the Holy Spirit, many will accept the divine principles. Beholding Jesus in His loveliness, in His self-denial and self-sacrifice, the self-sufficient rich man will see himself in contrast as wretched, and miserable, and poor, and blind, and naked, and will become so small in his own estimation that he will prefer Christ to himself, and will lay hold on eternal life.

Converted to the truth, he will become an agent in the hand of God to communicate the light. He will have a special burden for other souls of this neglected class. He will feel that a dispensation of the gospel is committed to him for those who have made this world their all. Time and money will be consecrated to God, means will be brought into His treasury, talent and influence will be converted to the truth, and new efficiency and power will be added to the church. . . .

Pure, sanctified love, such love as was expressed in Christ's lifework, is as a sacred perfume. Like Mary's broken box of ointment, it fills the whole house with fragrance. Eloquence, knowledge of truth, rare talents, mingled with love, are all precious endowments . . . Love for God and for those for whom Christ has died will do a work that we can scarcely comprehend (*Testimonies,* vol. 6, pp. 81-84).

Church to Be Added to Church

Seek ye the Lord while he may be found, call ye upon him while he is near. Isaiah 55:6.

Church members are to arise and shine amid the moral darkness of the world. If we are connected with the Light of the world, we shall reflect light to others. If we partake of the Savior's rich grace, we shall be a blessing to those around us. . . .

It is because so many of Christ's professed followers seek to be first that He cannot trust them. Were they humble, willing to be taught by Him, they would be a power in showing to the world the influence of the truth upon human character. Those who work in Christ's lines, never seeking to exalt self, will reveal constant activity and steady progress in missionary enterprises. They will not be satisfied unless church is added to church.

God expects those in His service to contend earnestly for the faith once delivered to the saints. Our aggressive missionary work is to be more abundant than it has been in the past. More territory is to be annexed; the standard of truth is to be planted in new places; churches are to be established; all is to be done that can be done to fulfill the commission, "Go ye therefore, and teach all nations, baptizing them in the name of the Father, and of the Son, and of the Holy Ghost: teaching them to observe all things whatsoever I have commanded you: and, lo, I am with you alway, even unto the end of the world."

The life of a church depends on the interest which its members manifest in those outside the fold. Let the church of God remember that Christ gave Himself as a sacrifice to save a world from destruction. For our sake He became poor, that we through His poverty might come into possession of eternal riches. Shall those whom God has blessed with a knowledge of the truth become narrow in their plans? Let them arouse to a sense of their vast obligations, cutting away every thread of selfishness, that the Lord may pour upon them His Holy Spirit. Let them seek the Lord while He may be found, and call upon Him while He is near. They have no reason for being faithless and complaining. Let them cease all fault-finding and murmuring, and encourage a spirit of gratitude for past mercies and blessings. Let them praise the Lord in unfeigned gratitude for the light of His Word, which shines upon their pathway, to be received into heart and mind, and reflected upon those in darkness. Thus they will be prepared to work to the praise and glory of Christ, and to inscribe upon their banners, "Here are they that keep the commandments of God and the faith of Jesus" (Revelation 14:12) (*Signs of the Times,* Aug. 21, 1901).

The Greatest Object

If we walk in the light, as he is in the light, we have fellowship one with another, and the blood of Jesus Christ his Son cleanseth us from all sin. 1 John 1:7.

Union is strength, and the Lord desires that this truth should be ever revealed in all the members of the body of Christ. All are to be united in love, in meekness, in lowliness of mind. Organized into a society of believers for the purpose of combining and diffusing their influence, they are to work as Christ worked. They are ever to show courtesy and respect for one another. Every talent has its place and is to be kept under the control of the Holy Spirit.

The church is a Christian society formed for the members composing it, that each member may enjoy the assistance of all the graces and talents of the other members, and the working of God upon them, according to their several gifts and abilities. The church is united in the holy bonds of fellowship in order that each member may be benefited by the influence of the other. All are to bind themselves to the covenant of love and harmony. The Christian principles and graces of the whole society of believers are to gather strength and force in harmonious action. Each believer is to be benefited and improved by the refining and transforming influence of the varied capabilities of the other members, that the things lacking in one may be more abundantly displayed in another. All the members are to draw together, that the church may become a spectacle to the world, to angels, and to men.

The covenant of agreement in church membership is that each member would walk in the footsteps of Christ, that all will take His yoke upon them, and learn of Him who is meek and lowly in heart. Doing this, "Ye shall," saith the dear Saviour, "find rest unto your souls. For my yoke is easy, and my burden is light" (Matthew 11:29, 30).

Those who wear Christ's yoke will draw together. They will cultivate sympathy and forbearance, and in holy emulation will strive to show to others the tender sympathy and love of which they feel such great need themselves. He who is weak and inexperienced, although he is weak, may be strengthened by the more hopeful and by those of mature experience. Although the least of all, he is a stone that must shine in the building. He is a vital member of the organized body, united to Christ, the living head, and through Christ identified with all the excellencies of Christ's character so that the Saviour is not ashamed to call him brother. . . . A church, separate and distinct from the world, is in the estimation of heaven the greatest object in all the earth. . . . The church is to be as God designed it should be, a representative of God's family in another world (*Selected Messages,* book 3, pp. 15-17).

Unity in the Church

All the believers were one in heart and mind. Acts 4:32, NIV.

When the Holy Spirit was poured out upon the early church, "the multitude of them that believed were of one heart and of one soul" (Acts 4:32). The Spirit of Christ made them one. This is the fruit of abiding in Christ. . . .

We have need of divine illumination. Every individual is striving to become a center of influence, and until God works for His people, they will not see that subordination to God is the only safety for any soul. His transforming grace upon human hearts will lead to unity that has not yet been realized, for all who are assimilated to Christ will be in harmony with one another. The Holy Spirit will create unity.

The prayer of Christ to His Father, contained in the seventeenth chapter of John, is to be our church creed. It shows us that our difference and disunion are dishonoring to God. . . .

No advice or sanction is given in the Word of God to those who believe the third angel's message to lead them to suppose that they can draw apart. This you may settle with yourselves forever. It is the devising of unsanctified minds that would encourage a state of disunion. The sophistry of men may appear right in their own eyes, but it is not truth and righteousness. "For he is our peace, who hath made both one, and hath broken down the middle wall of partition between us; . . . that he might reconcile both unto God in one body by the cross" (Ephesians 2:14-16).

Christ is the uniting link in the golden chain which binds believers together in God. There must be no separating in this great testing time. . . . The children of God constitute one united whole in Christ, who presents His cross as the center of attraction. All who believe are one in Him.

Human feelings will lead men to take the work into their own hands, and the building thus becomes disproportionate. The Lord therefore employs a variety of gifts to make the building symmetrical. Not one feature of the truth is to be hidden or made of little account. God cannot be glorified unless the building, "fitly framed together groweth unto an holy temple in the Lord." A great subject is here comprehended, and those who understand the truth for this time must take heed how they hear and how they build and educate others to practice. . . .

When every specification which Christ has given has been carried out in the true, Christian spirit, then, and then only, Heaven ratifies the decision of the church, because its members have the mind of Christ, and do as He would do were He upon the earth (*Selected Messages,* book 3, pp. 20-22).

Purity

Don't let anyone look down on you because you are young, but set an example for the believers in speech, in life, in love, in faith and in purity. 1 Timothy 4:12, NIV.

By accepting Christ as His personal Savior, man is brought into the same close relation to God, and enjoys His special favor as does His own beloved Son. He is honored and glorified and intimately associated with God, his life being hid with Christ in God. O what love, what wondrous love!

This is my teaching of moral purity. The opening of the blackness of impurity will not be one half as efficacious in uprooting sin as will the presentation of these grand and ennobling themes. . . . The Bible and the Bible alone has given the true lessons upon purity. Then preach the Word.

Such is the grace of God, such the love wherewith He hath loved us, even when we were dead in trespasses and sins, enemies in our minds by wicked works, serving divers lusts and pleasures, the slaves of debase appetites and passion, servants of sin and Satan. What depth of love is manifested in Christ, as He becomes the propitiation for our sins. Through the ministration of the Holy Spirit souls are led to find forgiveness of sins.

The purity, the holiness, of the life of Jesus as presented from the Word of God possess more power to reform and transform the character than do all the efforts put forth in picturing sins and crimes of men and the sure results. One steadfast look to the Savior uplifted upon the cross will do more to purify the mind and heart from every defilement than will all the scientific explanations by the ablest tongue.

Before the cross the sinner sees his unlikeness of character to Christ. He sees the terrible consequences of transgression; he hates the sin that he has practiced, and he lays hold upon Jesus by living faith. He has judged his position of uncleanness in the light of the presence of God and the heavenly intelligence. He has measured it by the standard of the cross. He has weighed it in the balances of the sanctuary. The purity of Christ has revealed to him his own impurity in its odious colors. He turns from the defiling sin; he looks to Jesus and lives.

He finds an all-absorbing, commanding, attractive character in Jesus Christ, the one who died to deliver him from the deformity of sin, and with quivering lip and tearful eye he declares, "He shall not have died for me in vain." "Thy gentleness hath made me great" (letter 102, 1894).

As a shield from temptation and an inspiration to purity and truth, no other influence can equal the sense of God's presence (*Education,* p. 255).

Love—The Evidence of Discipleship

By this shall all men know that ye are my disciples, if ye have love one to another.
John 13:35.

In this last meeting with His disciples, the great desire which Christ expressed for them was that they might love one another as He had loved them. Again and again He spoke of this. "These things I command you," He said repeatedly, "that ye love one another." His very first injunction when alone with them in the upper chamber was "A new commandment I give unto you, That ye love one another; as I have loved you, that ye also love one another." To the disciples this commandment was new; for they had not loved one another as Christ had loved them. He saw that new ideas and impulses must control them; that new principles must be practiced by them; through His life and death they were to receive a new conception of love. The command to love one another had a new meaning in the light of His self-sacrifice. The whole work of grace is one continual service of love, of self-denying, self-sacrificing effort. During every hour of Christ's sojourn upon the earth, the love of God was flowing from Him in irrepressible streams. All who are imbued with His Spirit will love as He loved. The very principle that actuated Christ will actuate them in all their dealing one with another.

This love is the evidence of their discipleship. "By this shall all men know that ye are my disciples," said Jesus, "if ye have love one to another." When men are bound together, not by force or self-interest, but by love, they show the working of an influence that is above every human influence. Where this oneness exists, it is evidence that the image of God is being restored in humanity, that a new principle of life has been implanted. It shows that there is power in the divine nature to withstand the supernatural agencies of evil, and that the grace of God subdues the selfishness inherent in the natural heart.

This love, manifested in the church, will surely stir the wrath of Satan. Christ did not mark out for His disciples an easy path. "If the world hate you," He said, "ye know that it hated me before it hated you. If ye were of the world, the world would love his own: but because ye are not of the world, but I have chosen you out of the world, therefore the world hateth you. Remember the word that I said unto you, The servant is not greater than his lord. If they have persecuted me, they will also persecute you; if they have kept my saying, they will keep yours also. But all these things will they do unto you for my name's sake, because they know not him that sent me." The gospel is to be carried forward by aggressive warfare, in the midst of opposition, peril, loss, and suffering. But those who do this work are only following in their Master's steps (*The Desire of Ages,* pp. 677, 678).

Secret Prayer and Bible Study

The effectual fervent prayer of a righteous man availeth much. James 5:16.

The church of God is made up of vessels large and small. . . . He does not expect the smaller vessels to hold the contents of the larger ones. He looks for returns according to what a man has, not according to what he has not. Do your best, and God will accept your efforts. Take up the duty lying nearest you, and perform it with fidelity, and your work will be wholly acceptable to the Master. Do not, in your desire to do something great, overlook the smaller tasks awaiting you.

Beware how you neglect secret prayer and a study of God's Word. These are your weapons against him who is striving to hinder your progress heavenward. The first neglect of prayer and Bible study makes easier the second neglect. The first resistance to the Spirit's pleading prepares the way for the second resistance. Thus the heart is hardened, and the conscience seared.

On the other hand, every resistance of temptation makes resistance more easy. Every denial of self makes self-denial easier. Every victory gained prepares the way for a fresh victory. Each resistance of temptation, each self-denial, each triumph over sin, is a seed sown unto eternal life. Every unselfish action gives new strength to spirituality. No one can try to be like Christ without growing more noble and more true.

The Lord will recognize every effort you make to reach His ideal for you. When you make failures, when you are betrayed into sin, do not feel that you cannot pray, that you are not worthy to come before the Lord. "My little children, these things write I unto you, that ye sin not. And if any man sin, we have an advocate with the Father, Jesus Christ the righteous." With outstretched arms He waits to welcome the prodigal. Go to Him, and tell Him about your mistakes and failures. Ask Him to strengthen you for fresh endeavor. He will never disappoint you, never abuse your confidence.

Trial will come to you. Thus the Lord polishes the roughness from your character. Do not murmur. You make the trial harder by repining. Honor God by cheerful submission. Patiently endure the pressure. Even though a wrong is done you, keep the love of God in the heart. . . .

"In quietness and in confidence shall be your strength." Christ knows the strength of your temptations and the strength of your power to resist. His hand is always stretched out in pitying tenderness to every suffering child. To the tempted, discouraged one He says, Child for whom I suffered and died, can not you trust me? "As thy days, so shall thy strength be" (Deuteronomy 33:25) (*Youth's Instructor,* June 26, 1902).

The Truth Will Conquer

The prince of this world cometh, and hath nothing in me. John 14:30.

As the world's Redeemer, Christ was constantly confronted with apparent failure. He, the messenger of mercy to our world, seemed to do little of the work He longed to do in uplifting and saving. Satanic influences were constantly working to oppose His way. But He would not be discouraged. Through the prophecy of Isaiah He declares, "I have laboured in vain, I have spent my strength for nought, and in vain: yet surely my judgment is with the Lord, and my work with my God. . . . Though Israel be not gathered, yet shall I be glorious in the eyes of the Lord, and my God shall be my strength." It is to Christ that the promise is given, "Thus saith the Lord, the Redeemer of Israel, and His Holy One, to him whom man despiseth, to him whom the nation abhorreth; . . . thus saith the Lord: . . . I will preserve thee, and give thee for a covenant of the people, to establish the earth, to cause to inherit the desolate heritages; that thou mayest say to the prisoners, Go forth; to them that are in darkness, Show yourselves. . . . They shall not hunger nor thirst; neither shall the heat nor sun smite them: for he that hath mercy on them shall lead them, even by the springs of water shall he guide them" (Isaiah 49:4, 5, 7-10).

Upon this word Jesus rested, and He gave Satan no advantage. When the last steps of Christ's humiliation were to be taken, when the deepest sorrow was closing about His soul, He said to His disciples, "The prince of this world cometh, and hath nothing in me." "The prince of this world is judged." Now shall he be cast out (John 14:30; 16:11; John 12:31). With prophetic eye Christ traced the scenes to take place in His last great conflict. He knew that when He should exclaim, "It is finished," all heaven would triumph. His ear caught the distant music and the shouts of victory in the heavenly courts. He knew that the knell of Satan's empire would then be sounded, and the name of Christ would be heralded from world to world throughout the universe.

Christ rejoiced that He could do more for His followers than they could ask or think. He spoke with assurance, knowing that an almighty decree had been given before the world was made. He knew that truth, armed with the omnipotence of the Holy Spirit, would conquer in the contest with evil; and that the bloodstained banner would wave triumphantly over His followers. He knew that the life of His trusting disciples would be like His, a series of uninterrupted victories, not seen to be such here, but recognized as such in the great hereafter (*The Desire of Ages,* pp. 678, 679).

October 14

A Decided Reformation Needed

Verily, verily, I say unto you, He that heareth my word, and believeth on him that sent me, hath everlasting life. John 5:24.

Just as long as you allow pride to dwell in your hearts, so long will you lack power in your work. For years a wrong spirit has been cherished, a spirit of pride, a desire for preeminence. In this Satan is served, and God is dishonored. The Lord calls for a decided reformation. . . . Let [a truly reconverted soul] renew his covenant with God, and God will renew His covenant with him. . . . Let angels and men see that there is forgiveness of sin with God. Extraordinary power from God must take hold of Seventh-day Adventist churches. Reconversion must take place among the members, that as God's witnesses they may testify to the authoritative power of the truth that sanctifies the soul. Renewed, purified, sanctified, the church must be, else the wrath of God will fall upon them with much greater power than upon those who have never professed to be saints.

Those who are sanctified through the truth will show that the truth has worked a reformation in their lives, that it is preparing them for translation into the heavenly world. But as long as pride and envy and evil-surmising predominate in the life, Christ does not rule in the heart. His love is not in the soul. In the lives of those who are partakers of the divine nature there is a crucifixion of the haughty, self-sufficient spirit that leads to self-exaltation. In its place the Spirit of Christ abides, and in the life the fruits of the Spirit appear. Having the mind of Christ, His followers reveal the graces of His character.

Nothing short of this will make men acceptable to God. Nothing short of this will give them the pure, holy character that those must have who are admitted to heaven. As soon as a man puts on Christ, an evidence of the change wrought in him is seen in spirit and word and act. A heavenly atmosphere surrounds his soul; for Christ is abiding within.

"Verily, verily, I say unto you," Christ declared, "He that believeth on me hath everlasting life" (John 6:47). Oh, how few there are who reveal in their lives the principles of this life! They profess to believe the most sacred truth ever given to mortals, but in their lives they dishonor God. He that "eateth my flesh, and drinketh my blood, hath eternal life; and I will raise him up at the last day. For my flesh is meat indeed, and my blood is drink indeed. He that eateth my flesh, and drinketh my blood, dwelleth in me, and I in him" (verses 54-56). . . . It behooves us to live in the fear and love of God. God is supreme, and He cooperates with those who represent Christ in life and character, those who are kind, thoughtful, self-denying, and self-sacrificing. Christ says, "If any man will come after me, let him deny himself, and take up his cross, and follow me" (Matthew 16:14) (letter 63, 1903).

The Ordinance of Baptism

Therefore we are buried with him by baptism into death: that like as Christ was raised up from the dead by the glory of the Father, even so we also should walk in newness of life. *Romans 6:4.*

The ordinances of baptism and the Lord's Supper are two monumental pillars. . . . Upon these ordinances Christ has inscribed the name of the true God.

Christ has made baptism the sign of entrance to His spiritual kingdom. He has made this a positive condition with which all must comply who wish to be acknowledged as under the authority of the Father, the Son, and the Holy Spirit. Before man can find a home in the church, before passing the threshold of God's spiritual kingdom, he is to receive the impress of the divine name "The Lord Our Righteousness" (Jeremiah 23:6).

Baptism is a most solemn renunciation of the world. Those who are baptized in the threefold name of the Father, the Son, and the Holy Spirit . . . declare publicly that they have forsaken the service of Satan and have become members of the royal family, children of the heavenly King. They have obeyed the command: "Come out from among them, and be ye separate, . . . and touch not the unclean thing." And to them is fulfilled the promise: "I will receive you, and will be a Father unto you, and ye shall be my sons and daughters, saith the Lord Almighty" (2 Corinthians 6:17, 18). . . .

The principles of the Christian life should be made plain to those who have newly come to the truth. None can depend upon their profession of faith as proof that they have a saving connection with Christ. We are not only to say, "I believe," but to practice the truth. It is by conformity to the will of God in our words, our deportment, our character, that we prove our connection with Him. Whenever one renounces sin, which is the transgression of the law, his life will be brought into conformity to the law, into perfect obedience. This is the work of the Holy Spirit. The light of the Word carefully studied, the voice of conscience, the strivings of the Spirit, produce in the heart genuine love for Christ, who gave Himself a whole sacrifice to redeem the whole person, body, soul, and spirit. And love is manifested in obedience. The line of demarcation will be plain and distinct between those who love God and keep His commandment, and those who love Him not and disregard His precepts.

Faithful Christian men and women should have an intense interest to bring the convicted soul to a correct knowledge of righteousness in Christ Jesus. . . . They must not neglect the faithful, tender, loving instruction so essential to the young converts that there may be no half-hearted work. The very first experience should be right. . . . Through association with those who love and fear God they will receive strength (*Testimonies,* vol. 6, pp. 91-93).

The Blessings of the Sabbath Services

Not forsaking the assembling of ourselves together, as the manner of some is; but exhorting one another: and so much the more, as ye see the day approaching. Hebrews 10:25.

Bring your choicest gifts to God on His holy day. Let the precious life of the soul be given to Him in consecrated service. . . .

Everyone should feel that he has a part to act in making the Sabbath meetings interesting. You are not to come together simply as a matter of form, but for the interchange of thought, for the relation of your daily experiences, for the expression of thanksgiving, for the utterance of your sincere desire for divine enlightenment, that you may know God, and Jesus Christ, whom He has sent. Communing together in regard to Christ will strengthen the soul for life's trials and conflicts. Never think that you can be Christians and yet withdraw yourselves within yourselves. Each one is a part of the great web of humanity, and the experience of each will be largely determined by the experience of his associates.

Why do we not obtain a hundredth part of the blessing we should obtain from assembling together to worship God? Our perceptive faculties need sharpening. Fellowship with one another should make us glad. With such a hope as we have, why are not our hearts all aglow with the love of God?

We must carry to every religious gathering a quickened spiritual consciousness that God and His angels are there, cooperating with all true worshipers. As you enter the place of worship, ask the Lord to remove all evil from your heart. Bring to His house only that which He can bless. Kneel before God in His temple, and consecrate to Him His own, which He has purchased with the blood of Christ. Pray for the speaker or the leader of the meeting. Pray that great blessing may come through the one who is to hold forth the word of life. Strive earnestly to lay hold of a blessing for yourself.

God will bless all who thus prepare themselves for His service. They will understand what it means to have the assurance of the Spirit because they have received Christ by faith.

The place of worship may be very humble, but it is no less acknowledged by God. To those who worship God in spirit and in truth and in the beauty of holiness it will be as the gate of heaven. The company of believers may be few in number, but in God's sight they are very precious. By the cleaver of truth they have been taken as rough stones from the quarry of the world and have been brought into the workshop of God to be hewed and shaped. But even in the rough they are precious in the sight of God. The ax, the hammer, and the chisel of trial are in the hands of One who is skillful; they are used, not to destroy, but to work out the perfection of every soul (*Testimonies,* vol. 6, pp. 361-363).

Recognizing God's Ownership

The law of thy mouth is better unto me than thousands of gold and silver. Psalm 119:72.

The psalmist's words, "The law of thy mouth is better unto me than thousands of gold and silver," state that which is true from other than a religious point of view. They state an absolute truth, and one that is recognized in the business world. Even in this age of passion for money-getting, when competition is so sharp, and methods are so unscrupulous, it is still widely acknowledged that, for a young man starting in life, integrity, diligence, temperance, purity, and thrift constitute a better capital than any amount of mere money. . . .

That which lies at the foundation of business integrity and of true success is the recognition of God's ownership. The Creator of all things, He is the original proprietor. We are His stewards. All that we have is a trust from Him, to be used according to His direction.

This is an obligation that rests upon every human being. It has to do with the whole sphere of human activity. Whether we recognize it or not, we are stewards, supplied from God with talents and facilities, and placed in the world to do a work appointed by Him.

To every man is given "his work" (Mark 13:34)—the work for which his capabilities adapt him—the work which will result in greatest good to himself and to his fellowmen, and in greatest honor to God.

Thus our business or calling is a part of God's great plan, and, so long as it is conducted in accordance with His will, He Himself is responsible for the results. "Labourers together with God" (1 Corinthians 3:9), our part is faithful compliance with His directions. Thus there is no place for anxious care. Diligence, fidelity, care-taking, thrift, and discretion are called for. Every faculty is to be exercised to its highest capacity. But the dependence will be, not on the successful outcome of our efforts, but on the promise of God. The word that fed Israel in the desert, and sustained Elijah through the time of famine, has the same power today. "Be not therefore anxious, saying, What shall we eat? or, What shall we drink?" (Matthew 6:31, RV). . . .

He who gives men power to get wealth has with the gift bound up an obligation. Of all that we acquire He claims a specified portion. The tithe is the Lord's. . . . "Bring ye all the tithes into the storehouse" (Malachi 3:10) is God's command. No appeal is made to gratitude or to generosity. This is a matter of simple honesty. The tithe is the Lord's; and He bids us return to Him that which is His own.

"It is required in stewards, that a man be found faithful" (1 Corinthians 4:2). If honesty is an essential principle of business life, must we not recognize our obligation to God—the obligation that underlies every other? (*Education,* pp. 137-139).

Unfading Beauty

Your beauty should not come from outward adornment, such as braided hair and the wearing of gold jewelry and fine clothes. Instead, it should be that of your inner self, the unfading beauty of a gentle and quiet spirit, which is of great worth in God's sight.
1 Peter 3:3, 4, NIV.

The pure religion of Jesus requires of its followers the simplicity of natural beauty and the polish of natural refinement and elevated purity, rather than the artificial and false. . . .

The religion of the Bible has nothing in it which would jar upon the finest feelings. It is, in all its precepts and requirements, as pure as the character of God and as elevated as His throne.

The Redeemer of the world has warned us against the pride of life, but not against its grace and natural beauty. He pointed to all the glowing beauty of the flowers of the field and to the lily reposing in its spotless purity upon the bosom of the lake. . . .

A disposition in you to dress according to the fashion, and to wear lace and gold and artificials for display, will not recommend to others your religion or the truth that you profess. . . . Simple, plain, unpretending dress will be a recommendation to my youthful sisters. In no better way can you let your light shine to others than in your simplicity of dress and deportment. You may show to all that, in comparison with eternal things, you place a proper estimate upon the things of this life.

Now is your golden opportunity to form pure and holy characters for heaven. You cannot afford to devote these precious moments to . . . beautifying the external to the neglect of the inward adorning. . . .

God, who created everything lovely and beautiful that the eye rests upon, is a lover of the beautiful. He shows you how He estimates true beauty. The ornament of a meek and quiet spirit is in His sight of *great price*. Shall we not seek earnestly to gain that which God estimates as more valuable than costly dress or pearls or gold? The inward adorning, the grace of meekness, a spirit in harmony with the heavenly angels, will not lessen true dignity of character or make us less lovely here in this world.

Religion, pure and undefiled, ennobles its possessor. You will ever find with the true Christian a marked cheerfulness, a holy, happy confidence in God, a submission to His providences, that is refreshing to the soul. By the Christian, God's love and benevolence can be seen in every bounty he receives. The beauties in nature are a theme for contemplation. In studying the natural loveliness surrounding us, the mind is carried up through nature to the Author of all that is lovely. All the works of God are speaking to our senses, magnifying His power, exalting His wisdom. Every created thing has in it charms which interest the child of God and mold his taste to regard these precious evidences of God's love above the work of human skill (*Testimonies,* vol. 3, pp. 375-377).

The Root and Fruit

Had ye believed Moses, ye would have believed me: for he wrote of me. John 5:46.

The Word of God includes the Scriptures of the Old Testament as well as of the New. One is not complete without the other. Christ declared that the truths of the Old Testament are as valuable as those of the New. Christ was as much man's Redeemer in the beginning of the world as He is today. Before He clothed His divinity with humanity and came to our world, the gospel message was given by Adam, Seth, Enoch, Methuselah, and Noah. Abraham in Canaan and Lot in Sodom bore the message, and from generation to generation faithful messengers proclaimed the Coming One. . . .

Of Christ's life and death and intercession, which prophets had foretold, the apostles were to go forth as witnesses. Christ in His humiliation, in His purity and holiness, in His matchless love, was to be their theme. And in order to preach the gospel in its fullness, they must present the Savior not only as revealed in His life and teachings, but as foretold by the prophets of the Old Testament and as symbolized by the sacrificial service. . . .

In every age there is a new development of truth, a message of God to the people of that generation. The old truths are all essential; new truth is not independent of the old, but an unfolding of it. It is only as the old truths are understood that we can comprehend the new. When Christ desired to open to His disciples the truth of His resurrection, He began "at Moses and all the prophets," and "expounded unto them in all the scriptures the things concerning himself" (Luke 24:27). But it is the light which shines in the fresh unfolding of truth that glorifies the old. He who rejects or neglects the new does not really possess the old. For him it loses its vital power and becomes but a lifeless form.

There are those who profess to believe and to teach the truths of the Old Testament, while they reject the New. But in refusing to receive the teachings of Christ, they show that they do not believe that which patriarchs and prophets have spoken. . . .

In rejecting the Old, they virtually reject the New; for both are parts of an inseparable whole. No man can rightly present the law of God without the gospel, or the gospel without the law. The law is the gospel embodied, and the gospel is the law unfolded. The law is the root, the gospel is the fragrant blossom and fruit which it bears.

The Old Testament sheds light upon the New, and the New upon the Old. Each is a revelation of the glory of God in Christ. Both present truths that will continually reveal new depths of meaning to the earnest seeker (*Christ's Object Lessons,* pp. 126-128).

Present Something Better

Behold the Lamb of God! John 1:36.

To reach the people, wherever they are, and whatever their position or condition, and to help them in every way possible—this is true ministry. By such effort you may win hearts and open a door of access to perishing souls.

In all your work remember that you are bound up with Christ, a part of the great plan of redemption. The love of Christ, in a healing, life-giving current, is to flow through your life. As you seek to draw others within the circle of His love, let the purity of your language, the unselfishness of your service, the joyfulness of your demeanor, bear witness to the power of His grace. Give to the world so pure and righteous a representation of Him, that men shall behold Him in His beauty.

It is of little use to try to reform others by attacking what we may regard as wrong habits. Such effort often results in more harm than good. In His talk with the Samaritan woman, instead of disparaging Jacob's well, Christ presented something better. "If thou knewest the gift of God," He said, "and who it is that saith to thee, Give me to drink; thou wouldest have asked of him, and he would have given thee living water" (John 4:10). He turned the conversation to the treasure He had to bestow, offering the woman something better than she possessed, even living water, the joy and hope of the gospel.

This is an illustration of the way in which we are to work. We must offer men something better than that which they possess, even the peace of Christ, which passeth all understanding. We must tell them of God's holy law, the transcript of His character, and an expression of that which He wishes them to become. Show them how infinitely superior to the fleeting joys and pleasures of the world is the imperishable glory of heaven. Tell them of the freedom and rest to be found in the Savior. "Whosoever drinketh of the water that I shall give him shall never thirst," He declared.

Lift up Jesus, crying, "Behold the Lamb of God which taketh away the sin of the world!" (John 1:29). He alone can satisfy the craving of the heart and give peace to the soul.

Of all people in the world, reformers should be the most unselfish, the most kind, the most courteous. In their lives should be seen the true goodness of unselfish deeds. . . .

Christ's disciples are to reveal the spirit that reigns in heaven. . . . The humblest workers, in cooperation with Christ, may touch chords whose vibrations shall ring to the ends of the earth and make melody throughout eternal ages (*The Ministry of Healing,* pp. 156-159).

October
21

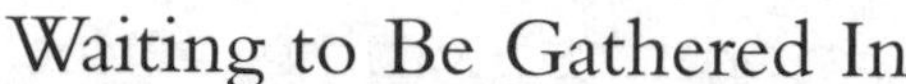

Waiting to Be Gathered In

Stand fast therefore in the liberty wherewith Christ hath made us free. Galatians 5:1.

The Lord has His representatives in all the churches. These persons have not had the special testing truths for these last days presented to them under circumstances that brought conviction to heart and mind; therefore they have not, by rejecting light, severed their connection with God. Many there are who have faithfully walked in the light that has shone upon their pathway. They hunger to know more of the ways and works of God. All over the world men and women are looking wistfully to heaven. Prayers and tears and inquiries go up from souls longing for light, for grace, for the Holy Spirit. Many are on the very verge of the kingdom, waiting only to be gathered in.

As the lessons of Christ, the truths of the Bible in their simplicity, are placed before these souls, they recognize the light and rejoice in it. Their perplexities vanish before the light of truth as dew before the morning sun. Their conceptions of Bible truth are expanded, and the revelation of God in Christ comes to them, showing them the depth, breadth, and height of divine, spiritual mystery that they did not before discern, that cannot be explained, but only exemplified in Christlike character.

Many who are not connected with any church, and who appear wholly unmindful of the claims of God, are not at heart as indifferent as they seem. Even the most irreligious have their hours of conviction, when there comes to them a longing for something they have not. In every town and city there are large numbers who do not attend any place of worship. Many of these are attracted to the camp meeting. Many come who are slaves of sin, the helpless victims of evil habits. Many are convicted and converted. As they by faith grasp the promise of God for the forgiveness of their sins, the bondage of habit is broken. Forsaking their sinful indulgences, they become freemen in Christ Jesus, and rejoice in the liberty of the sons of God (*Testimonies,* vol. 6, pp. 70, 71).

This work requires you to watch for souls as they that must give an account. . . . The fragrance of Christ's love will be revealed in your work. He who gave His own life for the life of the world will cooperate with the unselfish worker to make an impression upon human hearts. . . .

Come close to the people by personal efforts. Teach them that the love of God must come into the sanctuary of the home life. . . . Keep self out of sight. . . . Work as seeing Him who is at your right hand, ready to give you His efficiency and omnipotent power in every emergency. The Lord is your Counselor, your Guide, the Captain of your salvation. He goes before your face, conquering and to conquer (*ibid.,* pp. 75, 76).

Third Angel's Message

But the wisdom that is from above is first pure, then peaceable, gentle, and easy to be intreated, full of mercy and good fruits, without partiality, and without hypocrisy. James 3:17.

The third angel's message is infallible. Upon the grand, ennobling truths connected with that message you can dwell with perfect safety. Labor intelligently to encourage union of faith and union of judgment, that all may be united in the bonds of Christian fellowship and love. . . .

"The wisdom that is from above is first pure, then peaceable, gentle, and easy to be intreated, full of mercy and good fruits, without partiality, and without hypocrisy. And the fruit of righteousness is sown in peace of them that make peace" (James 3:17, 18).

The principle here laid down is the natural outgrowth of the Christian religion. Especially will those who are engaged in proclaiming the last solemn message to a dying world seek to fulfill this scripture. Although possessing different temperaments and dispositions, they will see eye to eye in all matters of religious belief. They will speak the same things; they will have the same judgment; they will be one in Christ Jesus. . . .

No one should feel that his judgment is faultless, that his ideas are above criticism, and that he can pursue a course of his own, regardless of the opinions of others with whom he is united in labor. When we think we know all that is worth knowing, we are in a position where God cannot use us. The third angel's message is not a narrow message. It is worldwide; and we should be united, so far as possible, in the manner of presenting it to the world.

Man is fallible; but the message is infallible. With it all should be in harmony; it is the center of interest, in which all hearts should be united. We may get up points that are of no consequence, and seek to maintain them; but we shall gain no strength by so doing. The message is to prepare a people to stand in the last great day, and to be united in heaven above. None should feel that it is of no special importance whether they are in union with their brethren or not; for those who do not learn to live in harmony here will never be united in heaven. . . .

Some have a natural independence which leads them to think more highly of their own judgment than of that of their brethren. In so doing they place themselves where they fail to obtain much knowledge that God would have them gain. . . . Doctrines and plans should be compared with the law and the testimony. We should never feel too independent to learn of one another (*Historical Sketches,* pp. 122-125).

The great Center of attraction, Jesus Christ, must not be left out of the third angel's message. . . . The sinner must ever look toward Calvary; and with the simple faith of a little child, he must rest in the merits of Christ, accepting His righteousness and believing in His mercy (*Evangelism,* pp. 184, 185).

October
23

Press Together! Press Together!

Because iniquity shall abound, the love of many shall wax cold. But he that shall endure unto the end, the same shall be saved. Matthew 24:12, 13.

God has selected a people in these last days whom He has made the depositaries of His law, and this people will ever have disagreeable tasks to perform. "I know thy works, and thy labour, and thy patience, and how thou canst not bear them which are evil: and thou hast tried them which say they are apostles, and are not, and hast found them liars: and hast borne, and hast patience, and for my name's sake hast laboured, and hast not fainted." It will require much diligence and a continual struggle to keep evil out of our churches. There must be rigid, impartial discipline exercised; for some who have a semblance of religion will seek to undermine the faith of others and will privily work to exalt themselves.

The Lord Jesus, on the Mount of Olives, plainly stated that "because iniquity shall abound, the love of many shall wax cold." He speaks of a class who have fallen from a high state of spirituality. Let such utterances as these come home with solemn, searching power to our hearts. Where is the fervor, the devotion to God, that corresponds to the greatness of the truth which we claim to believe? The love of the world, the love of some darling sin, has weaned the heart from the love of prayer and of meditation on sacred things. A formal round of religious services is kept up; but where is the love of Jesus? Spirituality is dying. Is this torpor, this mournful deterioration, to be perpetuated? Is the lamp of truth to flicker and go out in darkness because it is not replenished by the oil of grace? . . .

Self-esteem and self-sufficiency are killing spiritual life. Self is lifted up; self is talked about. Oh, that self might die! "I die daily," said the apostle Paul. When this proud, boasting self-sufficiency and this complacent self-righteousness permeate the soul, there is no room for Jesus. He is given an inferior place, while self swells into importance and fills the whole temple of the soul. This is the reason why the Lord can do so little for us. Should He work with our efforts, the instrument would appropriate all the glory to his own smartness, his wisdom, his ability, and he would congratulate himself, as did the Pharisee: "I fast twice in the week, I give tithes of all that I possess." When self shall be hidden in Christ, it will not be brought to the surface so frequently. . . .

It is only when we are careful to carry out the Master's orders without leaving our stamp and identity upon the work that we work efficiently and harmoniously. "Press together," said the angel, "press together" (*Testimonies,* vol. 5, pp. 538, 539).

Every Church a Training School

The Spirit of the Lord is upon me, because he hath anointed me to preach the gospel to the poor; he hath sent me to heal the brokenhearted, to preach deliverance to the captives, and recovering of sight to the blind, to set at liberty them that are bruised. Luke 4:18.

In giving light to His people anciently, God did not work exclusively through any one class. Daniel was a prince of Judah. Isaiah also was of the royal line. David was a shepherd boy, Amos a herdsman, Zechariah a captive from Babylon, Elisha a tiller of the soil. The Lord raised up as His representatives prophets and princes, the noble and the lowly, and taught them the truths to be given to the world. . . .

Every church should be a training school for Christian workers. Its members should be taught how to give Bible readings, how to conduct and teach Sabbath school classes, how best to help the poor and to care for the sick, how to work for the unconverted. There should be schools of health, cooking schools, and classes in various lines of Christian help work. There should not only be teaching, but actual work under experienced instructors. Let the teachers lead the way in working among the people, and others, uniting with them, will learn from their example. One example is worth more than many precepts. . . .

If those to whom God has entrusted great talents of intellect put these gifts to a selfish use, they will be left, after a period of trial, to follow their own way. God will take men who do not appear to be so richly endowed, who have not large self-confidence, and He will make the weak strong, because they trust in Him to do for them that which they cannot do for themselves. God will accept the wholehearted service, and will Himself make up the deficiencies. . . .

As His blessing came to the captives in the courts of Babylon, so does He give wisdom and knowledge to His workers today.

Men deficient in school education, lowly in social position, have, through the grace of Christ, sometimes been wonderfully successful in winning souls for Him. The secret of their success was their confidence in God. They learned daily of Him who is wonderful in counsel and mighty in power.

Such workers are to be encouraged. The Lord brings them into connection with those of more marked ability, to fill up the gaps that others leave. Their quickness to see what is to be done, their readiness to help those in need, their kind words and deeds, open doors of usefulness that otherwise would remain closed. They come close to those in trouble, and the persuasive influence of their words has power to draw many trembling souls to God. Their work shows what thousands of others might do (*The Ministry of Healing,* p. 148-151).

A Great Reformatory Movement

He which soweth bountifully shall reap also bountifully. 2 Corinthians 9:6.

When we begin to comprehend what a sacrifice Christ made in order to save a perishing world, there will be seen a mighty wrestling to save souls. Oh, that all our churches might see and realize the infinite sacrifice of Christ!

In visions of the night, representations passed before me of a great reformatory movement among God's people. Many were praising God. The sick were healed, and other miracles were wrought. A spirit of intercession was seen, even as was manifested before the great Day of Pentecost. Hundreds and thousands were seen visiting families and opening before them the Word of God. Hearts were convicted by the power of the Holy Spirit, and a spirit of genuine conversion was manifest. On every side doors were thrown open to the proclamation of the truth. The world seemed to be lightened with the heavenly influence. Great blessings were received by the true and humble people of God. I heard voices of thanksgiving and praise. . . .

The judgments of God are in the earth, and, under the influence of the Holy Spirit, we must give the message of warning that He has entrusted to us. We must give this message quickly, line upon line, precept upon precept. Men will soon be forced to great decisions, and it is our duty to see that they are given an opportunity to understand the truth, that they may take their stand intelligently on the right side. The Lord calls upon His people to labor—labor earnestly and wisely—while probation lingers.

Among the members of our churches there should be more house-to-house labor in giving Bible readings and distributing literature. A Christian character can be symmetrically and completely formed only when the human agent regards it as a privilege to work disinterestedly in the proclamation of the truth and to sustain the cause of God with means. We must sow beside all waters, keeping our souls in the love of God, working while it is day, and using the means the Lord has given us to do whatever duty comes next. Whatever our hands find to do, we are to do with faithfulness; whatever sacrifice we are called upon to make, we are to make it cheerfully. As we sow beside all waters we shall realize that "he which soweth bountifully shall reap also bountifully" (2 Corinthians 9:6). . . .

The Lord has presented before me the work that is to be done in our cities. The believers in these cities are to work for God in the neighborhood of their homes. They are to labor quietly and in humility, carrying with them wherever they go the atmosphere of heaven. If they keep self out of sight, pointing always to Christ, the power of their influence will be felt (*Testimonies,* vol. 9, pp. 125-128).

October
26

God's Chosen People

Therefore, as God's chosen people, holy and dearly loved, clothe yourselves with compassion, kindness, humility, gentleness and patience. Bear with each other and forgive whatever grievances you may have against one another. Colossians 3:12, 13, NIV.

Love "rejoiceth not in iniquity, but rejoiceth in the truth." He whose heart is imbued with love is filled with sorrow at the errors and weaknesses of others; but when truth triumphs, when the cloud that darkened the fair fame of another is removed, or when sins are confessed and wrongs corrected, he rejoices. . . .

Love not only bears with others' faults, but cheerfully submits to whatever suffering or inconvenience such forbearance makes necessary. This love "never faileth." It can never lose its value; it is the attribute of heaven. As a precious treasure it will be carried by its possessor through the portals of the city of God.

The fruit of the Spirit is love, joy, and peace. Discord and strife are the work of Satan and the fruit of sin. If we would as a people enjoy peace and love, we must put away our sins; we must come into harmony with God, and we shall be in harmony with one another. Let each ask himself: Do I possess the grace of love? Have I learned to suffer long and to be kind? Talents, learning, and eloquence, without this heavenly attribute, will be as meaningless as sounding brass or a tinkling cymbal. Alas that this precious treasure is so lightly valued and so little sought by many who profess the faith! . . .

If we would not build our hopes of heaven upon a false foundation we must accept the Bible as it reads and believe that the Lord means what He says. He requires nothing of us that He will not give us grace to perform. We shall have no excuse to offer in the day of God if we fail to reach the standard set before us in His Word.

We are admonished by the apostle: "Let love be without dissimulation. Abhor that which is evil; cleave to that which is good. Be kindly affectioned one to another with brotherly love; in honor preferring one another." Paul would have us distinguish between the pure, unselfish love which is prompted by the spirit of Christ, and the unmeaning, deceitful pretense with which the world abounds. This base counterfeit has misled many souls. It would blot out the distinction between right and wrong, by agreeing with the transgressor instead of faithfully showing him his errors. Such a course never springs from real friendship. The spirit by which it is prompted dwells only in the carnal heart. While the Christian will be ever kind, compassionate, and forgiving, he can feel no harmony with sin. He will abhor evil and cling to that which is good, at the sacrifice of association or friendship with the ungodly. The spirit of Christ will lead us to hate sin, while we are willing to make any sacrifice to save the sinner (*Testimonies,* vol. 5, pp. 169-171).

Always a Witness in the Church

The Lord talked with you face to face in the mount out of the midst of the fire.
Deuteronomy 5:4.

God has never left His church without a witness. In all the scenes of trial and proving, of opposition and persecution amidst moral darkness, through which the church has passed, God has had men of opportunity who have been prepared to take up His work at different stages and carry it forward and upward. Through patriarchs and prophets He revealed His truth to His people. Christ was the teacher of His ancient people as verily as He was when He came to the world clothed in the garments of humanity. Hiding His glory in human form, He often appeared to His people and talked with them "face to face, as a man speaketh unto his friend." He, their invisible Leader, was enshrouded in the pillar of fire and of cloud, and spoke to His people through Moses. The voice of God was heard by the prophets whom He had appointed to a special work and to bear a special message. He sent them to repeat the same words over and over again. He had a message prepared for them that was not after the ways and will of men, and this He put in their mouths and had them proclaim. He assured them the Holy Spirit would give them language and utterance. He who knew the heart would give them words with which to reach the people. . . .

There never will be a time in the history of the church when God's worker can fold his hands and be at ease, saying, "All is peace and safety." Then it is that sudden destruction cometh. Everything may move forward amid apparent prosperity; but Satan is wide awake, and is studying and counseling with his evil angels another mode of attack where he can be successful. The contest will wax more and more fierce on the part of Satan; for he is moved by a power from beneath. As the work of God's people moves forward with sanctified, resistless energy, planting the standard of Christ's righteousness in the church, moved by a power from the throne of God, the great controversy will wax stronger and stronger, and will become more and more determined. Mind will be arrayed against mind, plans against plans, principles of heavenly origin against principles of Satan. Truth in its varied phases will be in conflict with error in its ever-varying, increasing forms, and which, if possible, will deceive the very elect.

Our work must be an earnest one. We are not to fight as those that beat the air. The ministry, the pulpit, and the press demand men like Caleb, who will do and dare, men whose eyes are single to detect the truth from error, whose ears are consecrated to catch the words from the faithful Watcher (*Testimonies to Ministers,* pp. 404-407).

The world needs evidences of sincere Christianity (*ibid.,* p. 416).

The Church Will Triumph

And they sing the song of Moses the servant of God, and the song of the Lamb, saying, Great and marvellous are thy works, Lord God Almighty; just and true are thy ways, thou King of saints. Revelation 15:3.

Christ has given to the church a sacred charge. Every member should be a channel through which God can communicate to the world the treasures of His grace, the unsearchable riches of Christ. There is nothing that the Savior desires so much as agents who will represent to the world His Spirit and His character. There is nothing that the world needs so much as the manifestation through humanity of the Savior's love. All heaven is waiting for men and women through whom God can reveal the power of Christianity.

The church is God's agency for the proclamation of truth, empowered by Him to do a special work; and if she is loyal to Him, obedient to all His commandments, there will dwell within her the excellency of divine grace. If she will be true to her allegiance, if she will honor the Lord God of Israel, there is no power that can stand against her.

Zeal for God and His cause moved the disciples to bear witness to the gospel with mighty power. Should not a like zeal fire our hearts with a determination to tell the story of redeeming love, of Christ and Him crucified? It is the privilege of every Christian, not only to look for, but to hasten the coming of the Savior.

If the church will put on the robe of Christ's righteousness, withdrawing from all allegiance with the world, there is before her the dawn of a bright and glorious day. God's promise to her will stand fast forever. He will make her an eternal excellency, a joy of many generations. Truth, passing by those who despise and reject it, will triumph. Although at times apparently retarded, its progress has never been checked. When the message of God meets with opposition, He gives it additional force, that it may exert greater influence. Endowed with divine energy, it will cut its way through the strongest barriers and triumph over every obstacle.

What sustained the Son of God during His life of toil and sacrifice? He saw the results of the travail of His soul and was satisfied. Looking into eternity, He beheld the happiness of those who through His humiliation had received pardon and everlasting life. His ear caught the shout of the redeemed. He heard the ransomed ones singing the song of Moses and the Lamb. . . .

By faith we may stand on the threshold of the eternal city, and hear the gracious welcome given to those who in this life cooperate with Christ (*The Acts of the Apostles,* pp. 600, 601).

October
29

The Light of Truth

Nevertheless the foundation of God standeth sure, having this seal, The Lord knoweth them that are his. 2 Timothy 2:19.

God Himself will work for Israel. Every lying tongue will be silenced. Angels' hands will overthrow the deceptive schemes that are being formed. The bulwarks of Satan will never triumph. Victory will attend the third angel's message. As the Captain of the Lord's host tore down the walls of Jericho, so will the Lord's commandment-keeping people triumph, and all opposing elements be defeated. Let no soul complain of the servants of God who have come to them with a heaven-sent message. Do not any longer pick flaws in them, saying, "They are too positive; they talk too strongly." They may talk strongly; but is it not needed? God will make the ears of the hearers tingle if they will not heed His voice or His message. He will denounce those who resist the word of God. . . .

The purging and cleansing will surely pass through every church in our land that has had great opportunities and privileges, and has passed them by unheeded. More evidence is not what they want. They need pure and sanctified hearts to gather up and retain all the light that God has given, and then they will walk in that light.

We need not say, "The perils of the last days are soon to come upon us." Already they have come. We need now the sword of the Lord to cut the very soul and marrow of fleshly lusts, appetites, and passions. May it pierce and divide in a far greater degree than it has ever yet done. . . .

I address the people of God who today are holding fast their confidence, who will not depart from the faith once delivered unto the saints, who stand amid the moral darkness of these days of corruption. The word of the Lord to you is: "I will rejoice in Jerusalem, and joy in my people." Can we not here see the paternal love of God expressed to those who hold fast to the faith in righteousness? The closest relationship exists between God and His people. Not only are we objects of His sparing mercy, His pardoning love; we are more than this. The Lord rejoices over His people. He delights in them. He is their surety. He will beautify all who are serving Him with a whole heart with the spirit of holiness. He clothes them with righteousness. He loves those who do His will, who express His image. All who are true and faithful are conformed to the image of His Son. In their mouth is found no guile, for they are without fault before the throne of God (*Testimonies to Ministers,* pp. 410-415).

Power of God, Not Self

I know whom I have believed, and am persuaded that he is able to keep that which I have committed unto him. 2 Timothy 1:12.

To some who witnessed [Paul's] martyrdom, his spirit of forgiveness toward his murderers and his unwavering confidence in Christ till the last, proved a savor of life unto life. . . .

Until his latest hour the life of Paul testified to the truth of his words to the Corinthians: "God, who commanded the light to shine out of darkness, hath shined in our hearts, to give the light of the knowledge of the glory of God in the face of Jesus Christ. But we have this treasure in earthen vessels, that the excellency of the power may be of God, and not of us. We are troubled on every side, yet not distressed; we are perplexed, but not in despair; persecuted, but not forsaken; cast down, but not destroyed; always bearing about in the body the dying of the Lord Jesus, that the life also of Jesus might be made manifest in our body" (2 Corinthians 4:6-10). His sufficiency was not in himself, but in the presence and agency of the divine Spirit that filled his soul and brought every thought into subjection to the will of Christ. The prophet declares, "Thou wilt keep him in perfect peace, whose mind is stayed on thee: because he trusteth in thee" (Isaiah 26:3). The heaven-born peace expressed on Paul's countenance won many a soul to the gospel.

Paul carried with him the atmosphere of heaven. All who associated with him felt the influence of his union with Christ. The fact that his own life exemplified the truth he proclaimed gave convincing power to his preaching. Here lies the power of truth. The unstudied, unconscious influence of a holy life is the most convincing sermon that can be given in favor of Christianity. Argument, even when unanswerable, may provoke only opposition; but a godly example has a power that is impossible wholly to resist. . . . The few Christians who accompanied him to the place of execution he endeavored to strengthen and encourage by repeating the promises given for those who are persecuted for righteousness' sake. He assured them that nothing would fail of all that the Lord had spoken concerning His tried and faithful children. . . . Soon the night of trial and suffering would end, and then would dawn the glad morning of peace and perfect day.

The apostle was looking into the great beyond, not with uncertainty or dread, but with joyous hope and longing expectation. . . .

Ransomed by the sacrifice of Christ, washed from sin in His blood, and clothed in His righteousness, Paul has the witness in himself that his soul is precious in the sight of his Redeemer (*The Acts of the Apostles,* pp. 510-512).

Christ's Eternal Vigilance

Unto the angel of the church of Ephesus write; These things saith he that holdeth the seven stars in his right hand, who walketh in the midst of the seven golden candlesticks; I know thy works, and thy labour, and thy patience. Revelation 2:1, 2.

The picture reveals eternal vigilance. Christ is in the midst of the seven golden candlesticks, walking from church to church, from congregation to congregation, from heart to heart. He that keepeth Israel neither slumbers nor sleeps. If the candlesticks were left to the care of human beings, how often the light would flicker and go out! But God has not given His church into the hands of men. Christ, the One who gave His life for the world, that all who believe in Him may not perish but have everlasting life, is the Watchman of the house. He is the Warder, faithful and true, of the temple courts of the Lord.

"These things saith he that holdeth the seven stars in his right hand." The words are spoken to the teachers in the church—those entrusted by God with weighty responsibilities. The sweet influences that are to be abundant in the church are bound up with God's ministers, who are to reveal the precious love of Christ. The stars of heaven are under His control. He fills them with light. He guides and directs their movements. If He did not do this, they would become fallen stars. So with His ministers. They are but instruments in His hands, and all the good they accomplish is done through His power. Through them His light is to shine forth. The Savior is to be their efficiency. If they will look to Him as He looked to His Father, they will do His work. As they make God their dependence, He will give them His brightness to reflect to the world.

Christ walks in the midst of His churches through the length and breadth of the earth. He looks with intense interest to see whether His people are in such a condition spiritually that they can advance His kingdom. He is present in every assembly of the church. He knows those whose hearts He can fill with the holy oil, that they may impart it to others. Those who faithfully carry forward the work of Christ, representing in word and deed the character of God, fulfill the Lord's purpose for them, and Christ takes pleasure in them.

"I know thy works, and thy labour, and thy patience." Christ is acquainted with the history and experience of every one who has accepted Him. To His people He says, "I have graven thee upon the palms of my hands." He cherishes carefully every act of love and endurance performed by them. . . . Christ holds the stars in His right hand, and it is His purpose to let His light shine forth through them to the world. Thus He desires to prepare His people for higher service in the church above. . . . Let us show forth in our lives what divine grace can do for humanity (*Review and Herald,* May 26, 1903).

Jesus Our Advocate

And if any man sin, we have an advocate with the Father, Jesus Christ the righteous.
1 John 2:1.

Jesus is our Advocate, our High Priest, our Intercessor. Our position is like that of the Israelites on the Day of Atonement. When the high priest entered the Most Holy Place, representing the place where our High Priest is now pleading, and sprinkled the atoning blood upon the mercy seat, no propitiatory sacrifices were offered without. While the priest was interceding with God, every heart was to be bowed in contrition, pleading for the pardon of transgression.

Type met antitype in the death of Christ, the Lamb slain for the sins of the world. Our great High Priest has made the only sacrifice that is of any value in our salvation. When He offered Himself on the cross, a perfect atonement was made for the sins of the people. We are now standing in the outer court, waiting and looking for that blessed hope, the glorious appearing of our Lord and Savior Jesus Christ. No sacrifices are to be offered without, for the great High Priest is performing His work in the Most Holy Place. In His intercession as our advocate, Christ needs no man's virtue, no man's intercession. He is the only sin-bearer, the only sin-offering. Prayer and confession are to be offered only to Him who has entered once for all into the Most Holy Place. He will save to the uttermost all who come to Him in faith. He ever liveth to make intercession for us. . . .

The mightiest created intellect cannot comprehend God; words from the most eloquent tongue fail to describe Him. . . . Men have only one Advocate, one Intercessor, who is able to pardon transgression. Shall not our hearts swell with gratitude to Him who gave Jesus to be the propitiation for our sins? Think deeply upon the love that the Father has manifested in our behalf, the love that He has expressed for us. We can not measure this love; for measurement there is none. Can we measure infinity? We can only point to Calvary, to the Lamb slain from the foundation of the world. . . .

No middleman comes between the sinner and Christ. . . . Christ Himself is our Advocate. All that the Father is to His Son He is to those whom His Son in humanity represented. In every line of His work Christ acted as a representative of the Father. He lived as our substitute and surety. He labored as He would have His followers labor, unselfishly, appreciating the value of every human being for whom He suffered and died (*Signs of the Times,* June 28, 1899).

In the Heavenly Courts

Wherefore he is able also to save them to the uttermost that come unto God by him, seeing he ever liveth to make intercession for them. Hebrews 7:25.

The world's Redeemer possessed the power to draw men to Himself, to quiet their fears, to dispel their gloom, to inspire them with hope and courage, to enable them to believe in the willingness of God to receive them through the merits of the divine Substitute. As subjects of the love of God we ever should be grateful that we have a mediator, an advocate, an intercessor in the heavenly courts, who pleads in our behalf before the Father.

We have everything we could ask to inspire us with faith and trust in God. In earthly courts, when a king would make his greatest pledge to assure men of his truth, he gives his child as a hostage, to be redeemed on the fulfillment of his promise; and behold what a pledge of the Father's faithfulness, for when He would assure men of the immutability of His council, He gave His only-begotten Son to come to earth, to take the nature of man, not only for the brief years of life, but to retain his nature in the heavenly courts, an everlasting pledge of the faithfulness of God. O the depth of the riches both of the wisdom and love of God! . . .

Through faith in Christ we become members of the royal family, heirs of God, and joint heirs with Jesus Christ. In Christ we are one. As we come in sight of Calvary, and view the royal Sufferer who in man's nature bore the curse of the law in his behalf, all national distinctions, all sectarian differences are obliterated; all honor of rank, all pride of caste is lost.

The light shining from the throne of God upon the cross of Calvary forever puts an end to man-made separations between class and race. Men of every class become members of one family, children of the heavenly King, not through earthly power, but through the love of God who gave Jesus to a life of poverty, affliction, and humiliation, to a death of shame and agony, that He might bring many sons and daughters unto glory.

It is not the position, not the finite wisdom, not the qualifications, not the endowments of any person that makes him rank high in the esteem of God. The intellect, the reason, the talents of men, are the gifts of God to be employed to His glory, for the upbuilding of His eternal kingdom. It is the spiritual and moral character that is of value in the sight of Heaven, and that will survive the grave and be made glorious with immortality for the endless ages of eternity. . . . Only those who have appreciated the grace of Christ, which has made them heirs of God and joint heirs with Jesus, will rise from the grave bearing the image of their Redeemer (*Selected Messages,* book 1, pp. 258, 259).

An Intercessor

Seeing then that we have a great high priest, that is passed into the heavens, Jesus the Son of God, let us hold fast our profession. Hebrews 4:14.

We are to fit ourselves with the self-same spirit that was in Christ Jesus. Christ is working for us; will we work for Christ in His lines? Children, cultivate patience and faith and hope. May the Lord increase our joy of faith in this ever-living Intercessor. Try to let no day pass in which you fail to realize your accountability to God through the sacrifice of His only begotten Son. Jesus does not receive glory from any one who is an accuser of the brethren. Let not a day pass that we are not healing and restoring old wounds. Cultivate love, and let no words of evil surmising escape our lips. Close this door quickly, and keep it closed; open the door where Christ presides, and keep it open, because we know the value of Christ's sacrifice and His unchangeable love. Drink in the ever-refreshing waters of life from the wells of Lebanon, but refuse the murky waters from the valley—the dark, suspicious feelings. There is much truthfulness in the cause, but shall we spoil our fragrance of spirit because others clothe themselves with bitterness? God forbid. There is not one tithe of the imaginings of evil that is worth the time we give to consider it and repeat it. Cut away from our speech all severity; talk sweetly; and hold our confidence in Jesus firmly.

We have an ever-living Advocate who is making intercession for us. Then let us become advocates in principle in behalf of those who err. "And having an high priest over the house of God [here is His intercession in our behalf]; let us draw near with a true heart in full assurance of faith, having our hearts sprinkled from an evil conscience; and our bodies washed with pure water. Let us hold fast the profession of our faith without wavering." He is a "faithful high priest in things pertaining to God."

Then as He is working for us, let us work just as earnestly and interestedly to promote union with one another. Christ prayed that we might be of that same nature and oneness as that existing between Himself and His Father. Try in everything we do to secure confidence and love one for another, and thus we will answer the prayer of Christ Jesus. . . . Not all your suppositions and your ideas of your brethren are correct. . . . Let us put away these ugly supposings and imaginings; keep close on the side of Christ, and think of the rich encouragement He has given us, that we may in our turn give to others. . . . Let envy and jealousy be quenched in the flow of love from the fountain of God's love. The cry of them that are ready to perish finds swift entrance into His ear. "He shall deliver the needy when he crieth, the poor also and him that hath no helper" (manuscript 129, 1901).

The Present Mediatorial Work of Christ

And Jesus came and spake unto them, saying,
All power is given unto me in heaven and earth. Matthew 28:18.

At the meeting on a mountain in Galilee, all the believers who could be called together were assembled. Of this meeting Christ Himself, before His death, had designed the time and place. . . .

At the time appointed, about five hundred believers were collected in little knots on the mountainside, eager to learn all that could be learned from those who had seen Christ since His resurrection. From group to group the disciples passed, telling all they had seen and heard of Jesus, and reasoning from the Scriptures as He had done with them. Thomas recounted the story of his unbelief, and told how his doubts had been swept away. Suddenly Jesus stood among them. No one could tell whence or how He came. Many who were present had never before seen Him; but in His hands and feet they beheld the marks of the crucifixion; His countenance was as the face of God, and when they saw Him, they worshiped Him.

But some doubted. So it will always be. There are those who find it hard to exercise faith, and they place themselves on the doubting side. These lose much because of their unbelief.

This was the only interview that Jesus had with many of the believers after His resurrection. He came and spoke to them saying, "All power is given unto me in heaven and in earth." The disciples had worshiped Him before He spoke, but His words, falling from lips that had been closed in death, thrilled them with peculiar power. He was now the risen Savior. Many of them had seen Him exercise His power in healing the sick and controlling satanic agencies. They believed that He possessed power to set up His kingdom at Jerusalem, power to quell all opposition, power over the elements of nature. He had stilled the angry waters; He had walked upon the white-crested billows; He had raised the dead to life. Now He declared that "all power" was given to Him. His words carried the minds of His hearers above earthly and temporal things to the heavenly and eternal. They were lifted to the highest conception of His dignity and glory.

Christ's words on the mountainside were the announcement that His sacrifice in behalf of man was full and complete. The conditions of the atonement had been fulfilled; the work for which He came to this world had been accomplished. He was on His way to the throne of God, to be honored by angels, principalities, and powers. He had entered upon His mediatorial work. Clothed with boundless authority, He gave His commission to the disciples: "Go ye therefore, and teach all nations" (*The Desire of Ages,* pp. 818, 819).

Our Infallible Judge

Know the God of your father, and serve him with a loyal heart and with a willing mind; for the Lord searches all hearts and understands all the intent of the thoughts.
1 Chronicles 28:9, NKJV.

The Lord is exact and infallible in His comprehension. He understands the working of the human mind, the active principles of the human agents He has formed, just how they will be moved upon by the objects that come before them, and in what manner they will act under every temptation that can try them and in every circumstance in which they are placed. "The ways of man are before the eyes of the Lord, and He pondereth all his goings" (Proverbs 5:21). "The eyes of the Lord are in every place" (Proverbs 15:3). "He looketh to the ends of the earth, and seeth under the whole heaven" (Job 28:24). "The Lord searcheth all hearts, and understandeth all the imaginations of the thoughts" (1 Chronicles 28:9). He knows the things that come into our minds, every one of them. . . . God pities the poor, self-deceived souls who are trampling upon His truth. Let the wheat and the tares grow together until the harvest. Pity and deplore the blindness of the minds that are under the dominion of Satan, but restrain your own wrath and passion, and do not pass your judgment upon them. Leave in God's hands the despisers of His truth. The right and liberty of passing judgment upon others is not given to you. It was not given to Moses to pronounce judgment against rebellious Israel. The glaring weakness of His agents, as displayed by Moses, will bring its reward. . . .

God's workmen must continue to bear the blame of being troublers of Israel, but they are not at liberty to make such assertions true. Go not into the assembly of scoffers, sit not in the seat of the scorners, keep away from the gatherings of those who will make your presence an occasion to speak to you humiliating things, and will pour contempt upon your faith. Have no controversy with these men. You have not to do with men only, but with Satan and his synagogue. When compelled to meet them, remember the Savior's words, "I send you forth as lambs among wolves." The Lord must be your dependence; He will clothe you with a divine panoply, and His Holy Spirit will influence your mind and heart so that your voice shall not catch the notes of the baying of the wolves.

We are never to forget that we are representatives of Christ. We are to use no carnal weapons when unbelieving and deluded souls come among us. . . . Not an unkind or discourteous word, defensive or offensive, should escape our lips or be traced by our pen. When reviled, we are not to revile again. "This is the victory that overcometh the world, even our faith" (1 John 5:4) (letter 18, 1895).

The Great Atonement

Neither is there salvation in any other: for there is none other name under heaven given among men, whereby we must be saved. Acts 4:12.

Adam, in his innocence, had enjoyed open communion with his Maker; but sin brought separation between God and man, and the atonement of Christ alone could span the abyss and make possible the communication of blessing or salvation from heaven to earth. Man was still cut off from direct approach to his Creator, but God would communicate with him through Christ and angels.

Thus were revealed to Adam important events in the history of mankind, from the time when the divine sentence was pronounced in Eden, to the Flood, and onward to the first advent of the Son of God. He was shown that while the sacrifice of Christ would be of sufficient value to save the whole world, many would choose a life of sin rather than of repentance and obedience. Crime would increase through successive generations, and the curse of sin would rest more and more heavily upon the human race, upon the beasts, and upon the earth. The days of man would be shortened by his own course of sin; he would deteriorate in physical stature and endurance and in moral and intellectual power, until the world would be filled with misery of every type. Through the indulgence of appetite and passion men would become incapable of appreciating the great truths of the plan of redemption. Yet Christ, true to the purpose for which He left heaven, would continue His interest in men, and still invite them to hide their weakness and deficiencies in Him. He would supply the needs of all who would come unto Him in faith. And there would ever be a few who would preserve the knowledge of God and would remain unsullied amid the prevailing iniquity.

The sacrificial offerings were ordained by God to be to man a perpetual reminder and a penitential acknowledgment of his sin and a confession of his faith in the promised Redeemer. They were intended to impress upon the fallen race the solemn truth that it was sin that caused death. To Adam, the offering of the first sacrifice was a most painful ceremony. His hand must be raised to take life, which only God could give. It was the first time he had ever witnessed death, and he knew that had he been obedient to God, there would have been no death of man or beast. As he slew the innocent victim, he trembled at the thought that his sin must shed the blood of the spotless Lamb of God. . . . And he marveled at the infinite goodness that would give such a ransom to save the guilty. A star of hope illumined the dark and terrible future and relieved it of its utter desolation. . . .

The act of Christ in dying for the salvation of man would not only make heaven accessible to men, but before all the universe it would justify God and His Son in their dealing with the rebellion of Satan (*Patriarchs and Prophets,* pp. 57-69).

The Record Books in Heaven

For God shall bring every work into judgment, with every secret thing, whether it be good, or whether it be evil. Ecclesiastes 12:14.

Let us individually consider what is the record made in the books of heaven concerning our life and character, and our attitude toward God. Has our love for God been increasing during the past year? If Christ is indeed abiding in our hearts, we shall love God, we shall love to obey all His commandments, and this love will continually deepen and strengthen. If we represent Christ to the world, we shall be pure in heart, in life, in character; we shall be holy in conversation; there will be no guile in our hearts or upon our lips. Let us examine our past life and see if we have given evidence of our love for Jesus by seeking to be like Him, and by working, as He worked, to save those for whom He died.

Of the zealous, self-sacrificing disciples of Christ, it is written that Jesus was not ashamed to call them brethren, so fully did they manifest His Spirit, and bear His likeness. By their works they constantly testified that this world was not their home; their citizenship was above; they were seeking a better country, even a heavenly. Their conversation and affections were on heavenly things. They were in the world, but not of the world; in spirit and practice they were separate from its maxims and customs. Their daily example testified that they were living for the glory of God. Their great interest, like that of their Master, was for the salvation of souls. For this they toiled and sacrificed, counting not their lives dear unto themselves. By their life and character they made a bright track heavenward. Upon such disciples, Jesus can look with satisfaction as His representatives. His character will not be misrepresented through them. . . .

God has made the advancement of His cause in the world dependent upon the labors and sacrifices of His followers. The salvation of our souls was purchased by the infinite gift of the Son of God. Jesus left heaven, laid aside His glory, left the communion and adoration of the sinless angels, and for our sake humbled Himself, even to the death of the cross. And now we, who have become partakers of His great gift, are to be partakers also of His sacrifice, extending to others the blessings of salvation.

There was not one trace of selfishness in the life of Christ. All who are laborers together with God will have the same spirit as their Master had. They will be continually growing away from selfishness, and renouncing self-indulgence, even in things that had once appeared innocent to them. . . . And when His glory shall be revealed, they will be glad also "with exceeding joy" (*Signs of the Times,* Dec. 22, 1890).

The Book of Life

He that overcometh, the same shall be clothed in white raiment; and I will not blot out his name out of the book of life, but I will confess his name before my Father, and before his angels. Revelation 3:5.

If we would be overcomers, we must search our hearts to be sure that we are not cherishing anything that is offensive to God. If we are, we cannot wear the white raiment that is here promised. If we would stand before God in the white linen, which is the righteousness of the saints, we must now do the work of overcoming.

Christ says of the overcomer, "I will not blot out his name out of the book of life." The names of all those who have once given themselves to God are written in the book of life, and their characters are now passing in review before him. Angels of God are weighing moral worth. They are watching the development of character in those now living, to see if their names can be retained in the book of life. A probation is granted us in which to wash our robes of character and make them white in the blood of the Lamb. Who is doing this work? Who is separating from himself sin and selfishness? "Ye are dead," says the apostle Paul of the true followers of Christ, "and your life is hid with Christ in God." When we are alive to God, we are dead to self. May God help us to die to self. Whose names will not be blotted out of the book of life? Only the names of those who have loved God with all the powers of their being, and their neighbors as themselves.

There is a great work to be done for many of us. Our minds and characters must become as the mind and character of Christ. Selfishness is inwrought in our very being. It has come to us as an inheritance, and has been cherished by many as a precious treasure. No special work for God can be accomplished until self and selfishness are overcome. To many everything connected with themselves is of great importance. Self is a center, around which everything seems to revolve. Were Christ on the earth now, He would say to such, "Launch out into the deep." Be not so self-caring. There are thousands whose lives are just as precious as yours. Then why do you wrap your coat about you, and hug the shore? Awake to duty and to usefulness! If you will launch out into the deep and let down your nets, the Master will gather in the fishes, and you will see of the mighty working of God (*Historical Sketches,* pp. 138, 139).

When our hearts are all aglow with love for Jesus and the souls for whom He died, success will attend our labors. . . . Let each one inquire, . . . Can I not be the means of saving some soul in the kingdom of God? We want the deep movings of the Spirit of God in our hearts, that we may not only be able to secure for ourselves the white raiment, but that we may so influence others that their names may be entered in the book of life, never to be blotted out (*ibid.,* p. 140).

The Judgment Set—The Books Opened

A stream of fire issued and came forth from before him; a thousand thousands served him, and ten thousand times ten thousand stood before him; the court sat in judgment, and the books were opened. Daniel 7:10, RSV.

The books of record in heaven, in which the names and the deeds of men are registered, are to determine the decisions of the judgment. Says the prophet Daniel: "The judgment was set, and the books were opened." The revelator, describing the same scene, adds: "Another book was opened, which is the book of life: and the dead were judged out of those things which were written in the books, according to their works."

The book of life contains the names of all who have ever entered the service of God. Jesus bade His disciples: "Rejoice, because your names are written in heaven" (Luke 10:20). Paul speaks of his faithful fellow workers, "whose names are in the book of life" (Philippians 4:3). Daniel, looking down to "a time of trouble, such as never was," declares that God's people shall be delivered, "every one that shall be found written in the book." And the revelator says that those only shall enter the city of God whose names "are written in the Lamb's book of life" (Daniel 12:1; Revelation 21:27).

"A book of remembrance" is written before God, in which are recorded the good deeds of "them that feared the Lord, and that thought upon his name" (Malachi 3:16). Their words of faith, their acts of love, are registered in heaven. Nehemiah refers to this when he says: "Remember me, O my God, . . . and wipe not out my good deeds that I have done for the house of my God" (Nehemiah 13:14). In the book of God's remembrance every deed of righteousness is immortalized. There every temptation resisted, every evil overcome, every word of tender pity expressed, is faithfully chronicled. And every act of sacrifice, every suffering and sorrow endured for Christ's sake, is recorded. Says the psalmist: "Thou tellest my wanderings: put thou my tears into thy bottle: are they not in thy book?" (Psalm 56:8). . . .

Every man's work passes in review before God and is registered for faithfulness or unfaithfulness. Opposite each name in the books of heaven is entered with terrible exactness every wrong word, every selfish act, every unfulfilled duty, and every secret sin. . . .

The deepest interest manifested among men in the decisions of earthly tribunals but faintly represents the interest evinced in the heavenly courts when the names entered in the book of life come up in review before the Judge of all the earth. The divine Intercessor presents the plea that all who have overcome through faith in His blood be forgiven their transgressions, that they be restored to their Eden home, and crowned as joint heirs with Himself to "the first dominion" (Micah 4:8) (*The Great Controversy,* pp. 480-484).

Enrolled in the Record Books of Heaven

Now therefore ye are no more strangers and foreigners, but fellow-citizens with the saints.
Ephesians 2:19.

Those who closely connect with God may not be prosperous in the things of this life; they may often be sorely tried and afflicted. Joseph was maligned and persecuted because he preserved his virtue and integrity. David, that chosen messenger of God, was hunted like a beast of prey by his wicked enemies. Daniel was cast into a den of lions because he was true and unyielding in his allegiance to God. Job was deprived of his worldly possessions and so afflicted in body that he was abhorred by his relatives and friends, yet he preserved his integrity and faithfulness to God. Jeremiah would speak the words which God had put into his mouth, and his plain testimony so enraged the king and princes that he was cast into a loathsome pit. Stephen was stoned because he would preach Christ and Him crucified. Paul was imprisoned, beaten with rods, stoned, and finally put to death because he was a faithful messenger to carry the gospel to the Gentiles. The beloved John was banished to the Isle of Patmos "for the word of God, and for the testimony of Jesus Christ."

These examples of human steadfastness, in the might of divine power, are a witness to the world of the faithfulness of God's promises—of His abiding presence and sustaining grace. As the world looks upon these humble men, it cannot discern their moral value with God. It is a work of faith to calmly repose in God in the darkest hour—however severely tried and tempest-tossed, to feel that our Father is at the helm. The eye of faith alone can look beyond the things of time and sense to estimate the worth of eternal riches.

The great military commander conquers nations and shakes the armies of half the world, but he dies of disappointment and in exile. The philosopher who ranges through the universe, everywhere tracing the manifestations of God's power and delighting in their harmony, often fails to behold in these marvelous wonders the Hand that formed them all. "Man that is in honour, and understandeth not, is like the beasts that perish." No hope of glorious immortality lights up the future of the enemies of God. But those heroes of faith have the promise of an inheritance of greater value than any earthly riches—an inheritance that will satisfy the longings of the soul. They may be unknown and unacknowledged of the world, but they are enrolled as citizens in the record books of heaven. An exalted greatness, an enduring, eternal weight of glory, will be the final reward of those whom God has made heirs of all things (*Testimonies,* vol. 4, pp. 525, 526).

The Sanctuary in Heaven

We do have such a high priest, who sat down at the right hand of the throne of the Majesty in heaven, and who serves in the sanctuary, the true tabernacle set up by the Lord, not by man. Hebrews 8:1, 2, NIV.

The subject of the sanctuary and the investigative judgment should be clearly understood by the people of God. All need a knowledge for themselves of the position and work of their great High Priest. Otherwise it will be impossible for them to exercise the faith which is essential at this time or to occupy the position which God designs them to fill. Every individual has a soul to save or to lose. Each has a case pending at the bar of God. Each must meet the great Judge face-to-face. . . .

The sanctuary in heaven is the very center of Christ's work in behalf of men. It concerns every soul living upon the earth. It opens to view the plan of redemption, bringing us down to the very close of time and revealing the triumphant issue of the contest between righteousness and sin. It is of the utmost importance that all should thoroughly investigate these subjects and be able to give an answer to everyone that asketh them a reason of the hope that is in them.

The intercession of Christ in man's behalf in the sanctuary above is as essential to the plan of salvation as was His death upon the cross. By His death He began that work which after His resurrection He ascended to complete in heaven. We must by faith enter within the veil, "whither the forerunner is for us entered" (Hebrews 6:20). There the light from the cross of Calvary is reflected. There we may gain a clearer insight into the mysteries of redemption. The salvation of man is accomplished at an infinite expense to heaven; the sacrifice made is equal to the broadest demands of the broken law of God. Jesus has opened the way to the Father's throne, and through His mediation the sincere desire of all who come to Him in faith may be presented before God.

"He that covereth his sins shall not prosper: but whoso confesseth and forsaketh them shall have mercy" (Proverbs 28:13). If those who hide and excuse their faults could see how Satan exults over them, how he taunts Christ and holy angels with their course, they would make haste to confess their sins and to put them away. Through defects in the character, Satan works to gain control of the whole mind, and he knows that if these defects are cherished, he will succeed. Therefore he is constantly seeking to deceive the followers of Christ with his fatal sophistry that it is impossible for them to overcome. But Jesus pleads in their behalf His wounded hands, His bruised body. . . . Let none, then, regard their defects as incurable. God will give faith and grace to overcome them (*The Great Controversy,* pp. 488, 489).

November
12

Living in the Great Day of Atonement

On the tenth day of this seventh month there shall be a day of atonement: it shall be an holy convocation unto you; and ye shall afflict your souls, and offer an offering made by fire unto the Lord. Leviticus 23:27.

We are now living in the great day of atonement. In the typical service, while the high priest was making the atonement for Israel, all were required to afflict their souls by repentance of sin and humiliation before the Lord, lest they be cut off from among the people. In like manner, all who would have their names retained in the book of life should now, in the few remaining days of their probation, afflict their souls before God by sorrow for sin and true repentance. There must be deep, faithful searching of heart. The light, frivolous spirit indulged by so many professed Christians must be put away. There is earnest warfare before all who would subdue the evil tendencies that strive for the mastery. The work of preparation is an individual work. We are not saved in groups. The purity and devotion of one will not offset the want of these qualities in another. Though all nations are to pass in judgment before God, yet He will examine the case of each individual with as close and searching scrutiny as if there were not another being upon the earth. Everyone must be tested and found without spot or wrinkle or any such thing.

Solemn are the scenes connected with the closing work of the atonement. Momentous are the interests involved therein. The judgment is now passing in the sanctuary above. For many years this work has been in progress. Soon—none know how soon—it will pass to the cases of the living. In the awful presence of God our lives are to come up in review. At this time above all others it behooves every soul to heed the Savior's admonition: "Watch and pray: for ye know not when the time is" (Mark 13:33). "If therefore thou shalt not watch, I will come on thee as a thief, and thou shalt not know what hour I will come upon thee" (Revelation 3:3).

When the work of the investigative judgment closes, the destiny of all will have been decided for life or death. Probation is ended a short time before the appearing of the Lord in the clouds of heaven. Christ in the Revelation, looking forward to that time, declares: "He that is unjust, let him be unjust still: and he which is filthy, let him be filthy still: and he that is righteous, let him be righteous still: and he that is holy, let him be holy still. And, behold, I come quickly; and my reward is with me, to give every man according as his work shall be" (Revelation 22:11, 12) (*The Great Controversy,* pp. 489-491).

In the typical service the high priest, having made the atonement for Israel, came forth and blessed the congregation. So Christ, at the close of His work as mediator, will appear, "without sin unto salvation" (Hebrews 9:28), to bless His waiting people with eternal life (*ibid.,* p. 485).

Faith in the Atonement

We have this hope as an anchor for the soul, firm and secure. It enters the inner sanctuary behind the curtain. Hebrews 6:19, NIV.

When you begin to feel despondent, look unto Jesus, and commune with Him. When you think your brethren misunderstand you, remember that Jesus, your Elder Brother, never makes a mistake. He will judge righteously. The words of Christ uttered in the great day of the feast have a wonderful meaning and power. He lifted up His voice and said, "If any man thirst, let him come unto me, and drink." We are not to be driven to Christ. It is our part to come—to make our own choice, and come to the fountain of life. Why should we not come to Christ? for in Him our hope of eternal life is centered. The lessons that have come to us through Christ are not oft-repeated maxims; they are full of vital thought. But it is our part to appropriate divine truth. The apostle Paul exhorts us to lay hold on the hope set before us in the gospel. By faith we are to appropriate the promises of God, and to provide ourselves with the abundant blessings which have been secured for us through Christ Jesus. Hope has been set before us, even the hope of eternal life. Nothing short of this blessing for us will satisfy our Redeemer; but it is our part to lay hold upon this hope by faith in Him who has promised. We may expect to suffer; for it is those who are partakers with Him in His sufferings who shall be partakers with Him in His glory. He has purchased forgiveness and immortality for the sinful, perishing souls of men; but it is our part to receive these gifts by faith. Believing in Him, we have this hope as an anchor of the soul, sure and steadfast. We are to understand that we may confidently expect God's favor not only in this world, but in the heavenly world, since He paid such a price for our salvation. Faith in the atonement and intercession of Christ will keep us steadfast and immovable amid the temptations that press upon us in the church militant. Let us contemplate the glorious hope that is set before us, and by faith lay hold upon it. . . .

We cannot find salvation in our own individual selves; we are to look unto Jesus, who is the author and finisher of our faith and as we look, we live. . . . How hard poor mortals strive to be sin-bearers for themselves and for others! but the only sin-bearer is Jesus Christ. He alone can be my substitute and sin-bearer. The forerunner of Christ exclaimed, "Behold the Lamb of God, which taketh away the sin of the world." . . . Then take your eyes off yourself, and encourage hope and confidence in Christ. Let your hope not be centered in yourself, but in Him who has entered within the veil. Talk of the blessed hope, and the glorious appearing of our Lord Jesus Christ (*Review and Herald,* June 9, 1896).

November
14

The Atonement—Our Foundation of Peace

Peace I leave with you, my peace I give unto you: not as the world giveth, give I unto you. Let not your heart be troubled, neither let it be afraid. John 14:27.

Jesus says, "My peace I give unto you: not as the world giveth, give I unto you. Let not your heart be troubled, neither let it be afraid." The peace spoken of by the great Teacher is larger and fuller than we have imagined. Christ is ready to do large things for us, to restore our natures by making us partakers of His divine nature. He waits to link our hearts with His heart of infinite love, in order that we may be fully reconciled to God; but it is our privilege to understand that God loves us as He loves His Son. When we believe in Christ as our personal Savior, the peace of Christ is ours. The reconciliation provided for us in the atonement of Christ is the foundation of our peace; but gloomy feelings are no evidence that the promises of God are of no effect. You look at your feelings, and because your outlook is not all brightness, you begin to draw more closely the garment of heaviness about your soul. You look within yourself, and think that God is forsaking you. You are to look to Christ. In me, Christ says, ye shall have peace. Entering into communion with our Savior, we enter the region of peace.

Satan is our destroyer, but Christ is our restorer. We must put faith into constant exercise, and trust in God, whatever our feelings may be. Isaiah says: "Who is among you that feareth the Lord, that obeyeth the voice of his servant, that walketh in darkness, and hath no light? let him trust in the name of the Lord, and stay upon his God." You can say with the psalmist, "Yea, though I walk through the valley of the shadow of death, I will fear no evil: for thou art with me; thy rod and thy staff they comfort me. Thou preparest a table before me in the presence of mine enemies: thou anointest my head with oil; my cup runneth over. Surely goodness and mercy shall follow me all the days of my life: and I will dwell in the house of the Lord for ever." "Believe in the Lord your God, so shall ye be established; believe his prophets, so shall ye prosper. And when he had consulted with the people, he appointed singers unto the Lord, and that should praise the beauty of holiness, as they went out before the army, and to say, Praise the Lord; for his mercy endureth forever. And when they began to sing and to praise, the Lord sent ambushments against the children of Ammon, Moab, and mount Seir, which were come against Judah; and they were smitten." "Unto you therefore which believe He is precious." Consider the fact that the Lord has given His only begotten Son, "that whosoever believeth in him should not perish, but have everlasting life" (*Review and Herald,* May 19, 1896).

Cling Closely to Jesus

If we follow on to know the Lord: his going forth is prepared as the morning. Hosea 6:3.

When Satan tells you that your sins are such that you need not expect any great victories in God, tell him the Bible teaches that those who love most are those who have been forgiven most. Do not try to lessen your guilt by excusing sin. You cannot come near to God by faith unless you realize your sinfulness. Then you can place yourselves right on the promises, and with unwavering faith can claim a share in the infinite sacrifice that has been made for the human race. Cling closely to Jesus, and His great heart of love will draw you unto Himself.

I cannot bear the thought that any should go away . . . without having their faith greatly strengthened. . . . Every advance step they take must be a step of faith. If they have a religious experience that is rich in faith, one can chase a thousand, and two can put ten thousand to flight. But all the talents that they may possess, all the skill and eloquence that they may acquire, will effect nothing unless they are consecrated to God. . . .

The apostle Paul desired that his brethren should be comforted with "the consolation wherewith he was comforted." The Christian finds constant comfort and strength in Jesus. . . .

Let us have an eye single to the glory of God. Let us not allow anything to interpose between us and Him. "If we follow on to know the Lord," we shall know that "his going forth is prepared as the morning; and he shall come unto us as the rain, as the latter and former rain unto the earth." If we are partakers of the divine nature, we shall reflect in life and character the image of our divine Lord. We cannot be indolent in seeking this perfection of character. We cannot yield passively to our surroundings, and think that others will do the work for us. "Every man that hath this hope in him purifieth himself, even as he is pure." We must be workers together with God. Life must become to us a humble, earnest working out of salvation with fear and trembling; and then faith, hope, and love will abide in our hearts, giving us an earnest of the reward that awaits the overcomer.

A relentless and determined foe has prepared his wiles for every soul that is not braced for trial, and guarded by constant prayer and living faith. We cannot individually, or as a body, secure ourselves from his constant assaults; but in the strength of Jesus every temptation, every opposing influence, whether open or secret, may be successfully resisted. Remember that "your adversary the devil, as a roaring lion, walketh about, seeking whom he may devour." Therefore "be sober, be vigilant" (*Historical Sketches,* pp. 135, 136).

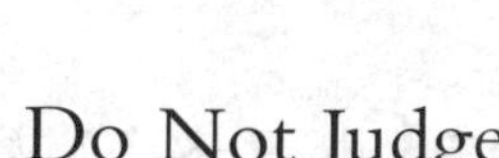

November
16

Do Not Judge

Judge not, that you be not judged. For with what judgment you judge, you will be judged; and with the same measure you use, it will be measured back to you. Matthew 7:1, 2, NKJV.

I understand how the enemy is working, and I wish to say to every soul, "Judge not, that ye be not judged. For with what judgment ye judge, ye shall be judged; and with what measure ye mete, it shall be measured to you again." There are times when we have to take a decided stand, but in magnifying the Lord be sure that you do not condemn and make charges against others. It would cause all the powers of hell to rejoice if our people were to become divided.

The way has been preparing for contention and division. Some are in great danger of drifting into infidelity. Now let your study be to save these imperiled souls. I have sorrow, great sorrow, of heart, that they do not understand their bearings. . . .

There is one thing you can do. You can see that you yourselves are in a condition of repentance. Your hearts need to be converted. The end is near; the time is short. Plead with God; clear the King's highway; and lift up the trailing standard on which is inscribed, "The commandments of God and the faith of Jesus." As you advance step by step, proclaim, "Here are they that keep the commandments of God, and the faith of Jesus."

Moses declared, "Behold, I have taught you statutes and judgments, even as the Lord my God commanded me, that ye should do so in the land whither ye go to possess it. Keep therefore and do them; for this is your wisdom and your understanding in the sight of the nations, which shall hear all these statutes, and say, Sure this great nation is a wise and understanding people. . . . Only take heed to thyself, and keep thy soul diligently, lest thou forget the things which thine eyes have seen, and lest they depart from thy heart all the days of thy life: but teach them thy sons and thy son's sons" (Deuteronomy 4:5-9) (letter 30, 1906).

And the Savior has plainly said, "With what judgment ye judge, ye shall be judged." . . . Who can stand before God and plead a faultless character, a blameless life? And how, then, dare any criticize and condemn their brethren? Those who themselves can hope for salvation only through the merits of Christ, who must seek forgiveness by virtue of His blood, are under the strongest obligation to exercise love, pity, and forgiveness toward their fellow sinners. . . .

While you condemn others, the Lord condemns you. . . . May the Lord move upon the hearts of the individual members of the church, until His transforming grace shall be revealed in life and character. Then when you assemble together it will not be to criticize one another, but to talk of Jesus and His love (*Review and Herald,* Nov. 30, 1886).

The Only True Standard of Character

Why beholdest thou the mote that is in thy brother's eye? Matthew 7:3.

Even the sentence, "Thou that judgest does the same things," does not reach the magnitude of his sin who presumes to criticize and condemn his brother. Jesus said, "Why beholdest thou the mote that is in thy brother's eye, but considerest not the beam that is in thine own eye?"

His words describe one who is swift to discern a defect in others. When he thinks he has detected a flaw in the character of the life he is exceedingly zealous in trying to point it out; but Jesus declares that the very trait of character developed in doing this un-Christlike work is, in comparison with the fault criticized, as a beam in proportion to a mote. It is one's own lack of the spirit of forbearance and love that leads him to make a world of an atom. Those who have never experienced the contrition of an entire surrender to Christ do not in their life make manifest the softening influence of the Savior's love. They misrepresent the gentle, courteous spirit of the gospel and wound precious souls, for whom Christ died. . . .

Christ is the only true standard of character, and he who sets himself up as a standard for others is putting himself in the place of Christ. And since the Father "hath committed all judgment unto the Son" whoever presumes to judge the motives of others is again usurping the prerogative of the Son of God. These would-be judges and critics are placing themselves on the side of antichrist, "who opposeth and exalteth himself above all that is called God, or that is worshipped; so that he as God sitteth in the temple of God, shewing himself that he is God."

The sin that leads to the most unhappy results is the cold, critical, unforgiving spirit that characterizes Pharisaism. When the religious experience is devoid of love, Jesus is not there; the sunshine of His presence is not there. . . . There may be a wonderful keenness of perception to discover the defects of others; but to everyone who indulges this spirit, Jesus says, "Thou hypocrite, first cast out the beam out of thine own eye" (*Thoughts From the Mount of Blessing,* pp. 125, 126).

Not until you feel that you could sacrifice your own self-dignity, and even lay down your life in order to save an erring brother, have you cast the beam out of your own eye so that you are prepared to help your brother. Then you can approach him and touch his heart. . . . A tender spirit, a gentle, winning deportment, may save the erring and hide a multitude of sins. The revelation of Christ in your own character will have a transforming power upon all with whom you come in contact. Let Christ be daily made manifest in you, and He will reveal through you the creative energy of His word—a gentle, persuasive, yet mighty influence to re-create other souls in the beauty of the Lord our God (*ibid.,* pp. 128, 129).

Truth the Basis of Character

Thy word have I hid in mine heart, that I might not sin against thee. Psalm 119:11.

Those who study the Bible, counsel with God, and rely upon Christ will be enabled to act wisely at all times and under all circumstances. Good principles will be illustrated in actual life. Only let the truth for this time be cordially received and become the basis of character, and it will produce steadfastness of purpose, which the allurements of pleasure, the fickleness of custom, the contempt of the world-loving, and the heart's own clamors for self-indulgence are powerless to influence. Conscience must be first enlightened, the will must be brought into subjection. The love of truth and righteousness must reign in the soul, and a character will appear which heaven can approve.

We have marked illustrations of the sustaining power of firm, religious principle. Even the fear of death could not make the fainting David drink of the water of Bethlehem, to obtain which, valiant men had risked their lives. The gaping lions' den could not keep Daniel from his daily prayers, nor could the fiery furnace induce Shadrach and his companions to fall down before the idol which Nebuchadnezzar set up. Young men who have firm principles will eschew [shun] pleasure, defy pain, and brave even the lions' den and the heated fiery furnace rather than be found untrue to God. Mark the character of Joseph. Virtue was severely tested, but its triumph was complete. . . . The same lofty, unbending principle appeared at every trial. The Lord was with him, and His word was law.

Such firmness and untarnished principle shines brightest in contrast with the feebleness and inefficiency of the youth of this age. . . .

The idea that we must submit to ways of perverse children is a mistake. Elisha, at the very commencement of his work, was mocked and derided by the youth of Bethel. He was a man of great mildness, but the Spirit of God impelled him to pronounce a curse upon those railers. They had heard of Elijah's ascension, and they made this solemn event the subject of jeers. Elisha evinced that he was not to be trifled with, by old or young, in his sacred calling. When they told him he had better go up, as Elijah had done before him, he cursed them in the name of the Lord. The awful judgment that came upon them was of God. After this, Elisha had no further trouble in his mission. For 50 years he passed in and out of the gate of Bethel, and went to and from city to city, passing through crowds of the worst and rudest of idle, dissolute youth, but no one ever mocked him or made light of his qualifications as the prophet of the Most High. This one instance of terrible severity in the commencement of his career was sufficient to command respect through his whole life (*Testimonies,* vol. 5, pp. 43, 44).

Christ Spoke as a Judge

O Jerusalem, Jerusalem, thou that killest the prophets, and stonest them which are sent unto thee, how often would I have gathered thy children together even as a hen gathereth her chickens under her wings, and ye would not! Matthew 23:37.

Christ spoke as a judge to those before Him. His voice, that had so often been heard in gentleness and entreaty, was now heard in rebuke and condemnation. The listeners shuddered. Never was the impression made by His words and His look to be effaced.

Christ's indignation was directed against the hypocrisy, the gross sins, by which men were destroying their own souls, deceiving the people and dishonoring God. In the specious deceptive reasoning of the priests and rulers He discerned the working of satanic agencies. Keen and searching had been His denunciation of sin; but He spoke no words of retaliation. He had a holy wrath against the prince of darkness; but He manifested no irritated temper. So the Christian who lives in harmony with God, possessing the sweet attributes of love and mercy, will feel a righteous indignation against sin; but he will not be roused by passion to revile those who revile him. Even in meeting those who are moved by a power from beneath to maintain falsehood, in Christ he will still preserve calmness and self-possession.

Divine pity marked the countenance of the Son of God as He cast one lingering look upon the Temple and then upon His hearers. In a voice choked by deep anguish of heart and bitter tears He exclaimed, "O Jerusalem, Jerusalem, thou that killest the prophets, and stonest them which are sent unto thee, how often would I have gathered thy children together, even as a hen gathereth her chickens under her wings, and ye would not!" This is the separation struggle. In the lamentation of Christ the very heart of God is pouring itself forth. . . .

Pharisees and Sadducees were alike silenced. Jesus summoned His disciples, and prepared to leave the Temple, not as one defeated and forced from the presence of His adversaries, but as one whose work was accomplished. He retired a victor from the contest.

The gems of truth that fell from Christ's lips on that eventful day were treasured in many hearts. For them new thoughts started into life, new aspirations were awakened, and a new history began. After the crucifixion and resurrection of Christ, these persons came to the front, and fulfilled their divine commission with a wisdom and zeal corresponding to the greatness of the work. They bore a message that appealed to the hearts of men, weakening the old superstitions that had long dwarfed the lives of thousands. Before their testimony human theories and philosophies became as idle fables. Mighty were the results flowing from the words of the Savior to that wondering, awestruck crowd in the Temple at Jerusalem (*The Desire of Ages,* pp. 619, 620).

All Must Appear in the Judgment

But why do you judge your brother? Or why do you show contempt for your brother? For we shall all stand before the judgment seat of Christ. Romans 14:10, NKJV.

We are nearing the end of time. Trials will be abundant from without, but let them not come from within the church. Let God's professed people deny self for the truth's sake, for Christ's sake. "For we must all appear before the judgment seat of Christ." . . . Everyone who truly loves God will have the spirit of Christ and a fervent love for his brethren. The more a person's heart is in communion with God, and the more his affections are centered in Christ, the less will he be disturbed by the roughness and hardships he meets in this life. Those who are growing up to the full stature of men and women in Christ Jesus will become more and more like Christ in character, rising above the disposition to murmur and be discontented. They will despise to be faultfinders.

The church at this time should have the faith once delivered to the saints, which will enable them to say boldly: "God is mine helper"; "I can do all things through Christ which strengtheneth me." The Lord bids us arise and go forward. Whenever the church at any period have forsaken their sins, and believed and walked in the truth, they have been honored of God. There is in faith and humble obedience a power that the world cannot withstand. The order of God's providence in relation to His people is progression—continual advancement in the perfection of Christian character, in the way of holiness, rising higher and higher in the clear light and knowledge and love of God, to the very close of time. Oh! why are we ever learning only the first principles of the doctrine of Christ?

The Lord has rich blessings for the church if its members will seek earnestly to arouse from this perilous lukewarmness. A religion of vanity, words devoid of vitality, a character destitute of moral strength—these are pointed out in the solemn message addressed by the True Witness to the churches, warning them against pride, worldliness, formalism, and self-sufficiency. . . . But to the lowly, the suffering, the faithful, the patient, who are alive to their weakness and insufficiency, are given words of encouragement: "Behold, I stand at the door, and knock: if any man hear my voice, and open the door, I will come in to him, and will sup with him, and he with me." . . .

Our Lord delays because of His "longsuffering to us-ward, not willing that any should perish, but that all should come to repentance." But when we, with all the redeemed, shall stand upon the sea of glass, with harps of gold and crowns of glory, and before us the immensity of eternity, then we shall see how short was the waiting period of probation. "Blessed are those servants, whom the lord when he cometh shall find watching" (Luke 12:37) (*Testimonies,* vol. 5, pp. 483-485).

Faithful Mothers Honored in the Judgment

I prayed for this child, and the Lord has granted me what I asked of him. So now I give him to the Lord. For his whole life he will be given over to the Lord.
1 Samuel 1:27, 28, NIV.

The fulfillment of Hannah's vow to dedicate her child to the Lord was not deferred until he could be presented at the tabernacle. From the earliest dawn of intellect she trained his infant mind to love and reverence God, and to regard himself as the Lord's. By every familiar object surrounding him she sought to lead his thoughts up to the Creator.

When separated from her child, the faithful mother's solicitude did not cease. He was the subject of her prayers. . . .

Would that every mother could realize how great are her duties and her responsibilities, and how great will be the reward of faithfulness. The mother's daily influence upon her children is preparing them for everlasting life or eternal death. She exercises in her home a power more decisive than the minister in the desk, or even the king upon his throne. The day of God will reveal how much the world owes to godly mothers for men who have been unflinching advocates of truth and reform—men who have been bold to do and dare, who have stood unshaken amid trials and temptations; men who chose the high and holy interests of truth and the glory of God, before worldly honor or life itself.

When the judgment shall sit, and the books shall be opened; when the "well done" of the great Judge is pronounced, and the crown of immortal glory is placed upon the brow of the victor, many will raise their crowns in sight of the assembled universe, and pointing to their mother say, "She made me all I am through the grace of God. Her instruction, her prayers, have been blessed to my eternal salvation." . . .

God has ordained that with families and nations or with individuals, virtue is the basis of happiness. . . .

By the thoughts and feelings cherished in early years, every youth is determining his own life history. Correct, virtuous, manly habits formed in youth will become a part of the character, and will usually mark the course of the individual through life. The youth may become vicious or virtuous, as they choose. . . .

Young men of today may become as precious in the sight of the Lord as was Samuel. They may have their names enrolled in the book of life, to be looked upon with pleasure by the Monarch of the Universe and the angelic host. By faithfully maintaining their Christian integrity, the young may, like the noble Luther, exert a mighty influence in the work of reform. Such men are needed at this time. God has a position and a work for every one of them (*Signs of the Times,* Nov. 3, 1881).

Choose Christ for Yourself

Choose for yourselves this day whom you will serve. Joshua 24:15, NIV.

To effect the salvation of men, God employs various agencies. He speaks to them by His Word and by His ministers, and He sends by the Holy Spirit messages of warning, reproof, and instruction. These means are designed to enlighten the understanding of the people, to reveal to them their duty and their sins, and the blessings which they may receive; to awaken in them a sense of spiritual want, that they may go to Christ and find in Him the grace they need. But many choose to follow their own way instead of God's way. They are not reconciled to God, neither can be, until self is crucified and Christ lives in the heart by faith.

Every individual, by his own act, either puts Christ from him by refusing to cherish His spirit and follow His example, or he enters into a personal union with Christ by self-renunciation, faith, and obedience. We must, each for himself, choose Christ, because He has first chosen us. This union with Christ is to be formed by those who are naturally at enmity with Him. It is a relation of utter dependence, to be entered into by a proud heart. This is close work, and many who profess to be followers of Christ know nothing of it. They nominally accept the Savior, but not as the sole ruler of their hearts.

Some feel their need of the atonement, and with the recognition of this need, and the desire for a change of heart, a struggle begins. To renounce their own will, perhaps their chosen objects of affection or pursuit, requires an effort, at which many hesitate and falter and turn back. Yet this battle must be fought by every heart that is truly converted. We must war against temptations without and within. We must gain the victory over self, crucify the affections and lusts; and then begins the union of the soul with Christ. As the dry and apparently lifeless branch is grafted into the living tree, so may we become living branches of the True Vine. And the fruit which was borne by Christ will be borne by all His followers. After this union is formed, it can be preserved only by continual, earnest, painstaking effort. Christ exercises His power to preserve and guard this sacred tie, and the dependent, helpless sinner must act his part with untiring energy. . . .

Every Christian must stand on guard continually, watching every avenue of the soul where Satan might find access. He must pray for divine help and at the same time resolutely resist every inclination to sin. By courage, by faith, by persevering toil, he can conquer. But let him remember that to gain the victory Christ must abide in him and he in Christ. . . . It is only by personal union with Christ, by communion with Him daily, hourly, that we can bear the fruits of the Holy Spirit (*Testimonies,* vol. 5, pp. 46-48).

To Be a Christian Is to Be Christlike

Who shall ascend into the hill of the Lord? or who shall stand in his holy place? He that hath clean hands, and a pure heart; he who hath not lifted up his soul unto vanity, nor sworn deceitfully. Psalm 24:3, 4.

What is it to be a Christian? It is to be Christlike; it is to do the works of Christ. Some fail on one point, some on another. Some are naturally impatient. Satan understands their weakness, and manages to overcome them again and again. But let none be discouraged by this. Whenever little annoyances and trials arise, ask God in silent prayer to give you strength and grace to bear them patiently. There is a power in silence; do not speak a word until you have sent up your petition to the God of heaven. If you will always do this, you will soon overcome your hasty temper, and you will have a little heaven here to go to heaven in.

God wants His people to cleanse their hands and purify their hearts. Will it make them unhappy to do this? Will it bring unhappiness into their families if they are kind and patient, courteous and forbearing? Far from it. The kindness they manifest toward their families will be reflected upon themselves. This is the work that should be carried forward in the home. If the members of the family are not prepared to dwell in peace here, they are not prepared to dwell in the family that shall gather around the great white throne. Sin always brings darkness and bondage; but right-doing will bring peace and holy joy. . . .

In the day of affliction, when the enemy presses us, we shall walk among the angels. They will be like a wall of fire about us; and we shall one day walk with them in the city of God. . . .

There has never been a time when the people of God have had greater need to claim His promises than now. Let the hand of faith pass through the darkness, and grasp the arm of infinite power. While we speak of the necessity of separating from sin, remember that Christ came to our world to save sinners, and that "he is able to also save them to the uttermost that come unto God by him." It is our privilege to believe that His blood is able to cleanse us from every spot and stain of sin. We must not limit the power of the Holy One of Israel. He wants us to come to Him just as we are, sinful and polluted. His blood is efficacious. I entreat you not to grieve His Spirit by continuing in sin. If you fall under temptation, do not become discouraged. This promise comes ringing down along the line to our time: "If any man sin, we have an advocate with the Father, Jesus Christ the righteous." I feel that for this one promise a continual song of thanksgiving ought to go forth from the lips of mortals. Let us gather up these precious jewels of promise, and when Satan accuses us of our great sinfulness, and tempts us to doubt the power of God to save, let us repeat the words of Christ, "Him that cometh to me I will in no wise cast out" (*Historical Sketches,* pp. 157, 158).

November
24

The Standard of Character in the Judgment

As many as have sinned in the law shall be judged by the law; (for not the hearers of the law are just before God, but the doers of the law shall be justified).
Romans 2:12, 13.

Those who had accepted the light concerning the mediation of Christ and the perpetuity of the law of God found that these were the truths presented in Revelation 14. The messages of this chapter constitute a threefold warning which is to prepare the inhabitants of the earth for the Lord's second coming. The announcement, "The hour of his judgment is come," points to the closing work of Christ's ministration for the salvation of men. It heralds a truth which must be proclaimed until the Savior's intercession shall cease and He shall return to the earth to take His people to Himself. The work of judgment which began in 1844 must continue until the cases of all are decided, both of the living and the dead; hence it will extend to the close of human probation. That men may be prepared to stand in the judgment, the message commands them to "fear God, and give glory to him," "and worship him that made heaven, and earth, and the sea, and the fountains of waters." The result of an acceptance of these messages is given in the Word: "Here are they that keep the commandments of God, and the faith of Jesus." In order to be prepared for the judgment, it is necessary that men should keep the law of God. That law will be the standard of character in the judgment. The apostle Paul declares: "As many as have sinned in the law shall be judged by the law, . . . in the day when God shall judge the secrets of men by Jesus Christ." And he says that "the doers of the law shall be justified" (Romans 2:12-16). Faith is essential in order to the keeping of the law of God; for "without faith it is impossible to please him." And "whatsoever is not of faith is sin" (Hebrews 11:6; Romans 14:23).

By the first angel, men are called upon to "fear God, and give glory to him" and to worship Him as the Creator of the heavens and the earth. In order to do this, they must obey His law. Says the wise man: "Fear God, and keep his commandments: for this is the whole duty of man" (Ecclesiastes 12:13). Without obedience to His commandments no worship can be pleasing to God. "This is the love of God, that we keep his commandments." "He that turneth away his ear from hearing the law, even his prayer shall be abomination" (*The Great Controversy,* pp. 435, 436).

The question of deepest interest to each one should be, Am I meeting the requirements of the law of God? . . . Only by a close examination of self in the light of God's Word can we discover our deviations from His holy rule of right. . . . In Him we may have pardon for past failures, and in His strength grow up to be perfect men and women in Christ Jesus (*Youth's Instructor,* June 10, 1897).

The Crown of Life

There is laid up for me a crown of righteousness, which the Lord, the righteous judge, shall give me at that day: and not to me only, but unto all them also that love his appearing.
2 Timothy 4:8.

Paul kept ever in view the crown of life which was to be given to him, and not to him only, but also to all those who love Christ's appearing. But it was victory through Jesus Christ that made the crown of life so desirable to him. Jesus would not have us ambitious to obtain reward, but ambitious to do God's will because it is His will, irrespective of the reward we are to receive.

The gift of God is eternal life. The Lord desires all who receive His grace to trust entirely in Him. He calls upon us to exercise pure, simple faith, trusting in Him, without a question as to what recompense we shall receive. We are to work heartily in His service, showing that we have perfect confidence that He will judge righteously.

In the account of the judgment scene, when the reward is given to the righteous, and sentence is passed on the wicked, the righteous are represented as wondering what they have done that they should receive such reward. But they cherished an abiding faith in Christ. They were imbued with His Spirit, and, without conscious effort, they performed for Christ, in the person of His saints, those services that bring a sure reward. But their motive in working was not to receive compensation. They regarded it as the highest honor to be allowed to work as Christ worked. What they did was done from love to Christ and to their fellowmen, and He who has identified Himself with suffering humanity accredited these acts of compassion and love as though done to Himself. . . .

Our every endowment, our every talent, we owe to the Lord. Every victory gained is gained through His grace. Therefore, it is entirely out of place for us to boast. . . .

If we would remember that we are on test and trial before the heavenly universe, that God is proving us, to see what spirit we are of, there would be more serious contemplation, more earnest prayer. Those who work in simplicity realize that of himself man can do no good thing. They are full of gratitude and thanksgiving for the privilege of holding communion with God. Interwoven with their service is a principle that makes their gifts and offerings wholly fragrant. They have the same confidence and trust in God that a child has in its earthly father.

It is not so much for our activity and zeal that we are rewarded, but for the tenderness, the graciousness, the love that we have mingled with our work for the sick, the oppressed, the afflicted (*Signs of the Times,* Aug. 9, 1899).

When Christ Comes His Reward Is With Him

Judge me, O Lord my God, according to thy righteousness. Psalm 35:24.

When the king came in to view the guests, the real character of all was revealed. For every guest at the feast there had been provided a wedding garment. This garment was a gift from the king. By wearing it the guests showed their respect for the giver of the feast. But one man was clothed in his common citizen dress. He had refused to make the preparation required by the king. The garment provided for him at great cost he disdained to wear. Thus he insulted his lord. To the king's demand, "How camest thou in hither not having a wedding garment?" he could answer nothing. He was self-condemned. Then the king said, "Bind him hand and foot, and take him away, and cast him into outer darkness."

By the king's examination of the guests at the feast is represented a work of judgment. The guests at the gospel feast are those who profess to serve God, those whose names are written in the book of life. But not all who profess to be Christians are true disciples. Before the final reward is given, it must be decided who are fitted to share the inheritance of the righteous. This decision must be made prior to the second coming of Christ in the clouds of heaven; for when He comes, His reward is with Him, "to give every man according as his work shall be." Before His coming, then, the character of every man's work will have been determined, and to every one of Christ's followers the reward will have been apportioned according to his deeds.

It is while men are still dwelling upon the earth that the work of investigative judgment takes place in the courts of heaven. The lives of all His professed followers pass in review before God. All are examined according to the record of the books of heaven, and according to his deeds the destiny of each is forever fixed.

By the wedding garment in the parable is represented the pure, spotless character which Christ's true followers will possess. To the church it is given "that she should be arrayed in fine linen, clean and white," "not having spot, or wrinkle, or any such thing." The fine linen, says the Scripture, "is the righteousness of saints." It is the righteousness of Christ, His own unblemished character, that through faith is imparted to all who receive Him as their personal Savior. . . . This covering, the robe of His own righteousness, Christ will put upon every repenting, believing soul (*Christ's Object Lessons,* pp. 309-311).

Our Merciful and Faithful High Priest

Neither by the blood of goats and calves, but by his own blood he entered in once into the holy place, having obtained eternal redemption for us. Hebrews 9:12, KJV.

As the sin bearer, and priest and representative of man before God, He entered into the life of humanity, bearing our flesh and blood. The life is in the living, vital current of blood, which blood was given for the life of the world. Christ made a full atonement, giving His life as a ransom for us. He was born without a taint of sin, but came into the world in like manner as the human family. He did not have a mere semblance of a body, but He took human nature, participating in the life of humanity. . . .

Jesus Christ laid off His royal robe, His kingly crown, and clothed His divinity with humanity, in order to become a substitute and surety for humanity, that dying in humanity He might by his death destroy him who had the power of death. He could not have done this as God, but by coming as man Christ could die. By death He overcame death. The death of Christ bore to the death him who had the power of death, and opened the gates of the tomb for all who receive Him as their personal Savior.

Christ proclaimed over the rent sepulcher of Joseph, "I am the resurrection, and the life." He, the world's Redeemer, has bruised the serpent's head, depriving him of all power ever to make men feel his scorpion sting; for He has brought life and immortality to light. The gates of eternal life are thrown open to all who believe on Jesus Christ. . . . In dying, Jesus has made it impossible for those who believe on Him to die eternally. . . .

Christ lived and died as a man, that He might be God both of the living and of the dead. It was to make it impossible for men to lose eternal life if they believe on Him. The life of men and women is precious in the sight of God; for Christ has purchased that life by being executed in their stead. Thus He made it possible for us to attain to immortality.

In Christ were united the divine and the human—the Creator and the creature. The nature of God, whose law had been transgressed, and the nature of Adam, the transgressor, meet in Jesus—the Son of God, and the Son of man. And having with His own blood paid the price of redemption, having passed through man's experience, having in man's behalf met and conquered temptation, having, though Himself sinless, borne the shame and guilt and burden of sin, He becomes man's Advocate and Intercessor. What an assurance here to the tempted and struggling soul, what an assurance to the witnessing universe, that Christ will be "a merciful and faithful high priest"! (*The SDA Bible Commentary,* Ellen G. White Comments, vol. 7, pp. 925, 926).

At the Day of Judgment

He that is faithful in that which is least is faithful also in much. Luke 16:10.

It is conscientious attention to what the world terms "little things" that makes life a success. Little deeds of charity, little acts of self-denial, speaking simple words of helpfulness, watching against little sins—this is Christianity. A grateful acknowledgment of daily blessings, a wise improvement of daily opportunities, a diligent cultivation of intrusted talents—this is what the Master calls for.

He who faithfully performs small duties will be prepared to answer the demands of larger responsibilities. The man who is kind and courteous in the daily life, who is generous and forbearing in his family, whose constant aim it is to make home happy, will be the first to deny self and make sacrifices when the Master calls. . . .

The longest journey is performed by taking one step at a time. A succession of steps brings us to the end of the road. The longest chain is composed of separate links. If one of these links is faulty, the chain is worthless. Thus it is with character. A well-balanced character is formed by single acts well performed. One defect, cultivated instead of being overcome, makes the man imperfect, and closes against him the gate of the Holy City. He who enters heaven must have a character that is without spot or wrinkle or any such thing. Naught that defileth can ever enter there. In all the redeemed host not one defect will be seen.

God's work is perfect as a whole because it is perfect in every part, however minute. He fashions the tiny spear of grass with as much care as He would exercise in making a world. . . .

That which is worth doing at all is worth doing well. Whatever your work may be, do it faithfully. Speak the truth in regard to the smallest matters. Each day do loving deeds and speak cheerful words. Scatter smiles along the pathway of life. As you work in this way, God will place His approval on you, and Christ will one day say to you, "Well done, thou good and faithful servant."

At the day of judgment, those who have been faithful in their everyday life, who have been quick to see their work and do it, not thinking of praise or profit, will hear the words, "Come, ye blessed of my Father, inherit the kingdom prepared for you from the foundation of the world." Christ does not commend them for the eloquent orations they have made, the intellectual power they have displayed, or the liberal donations they have given. It is for doing little things which are generally overlooked that they are rewarded. "I was an hungered, and ye gave me meat," He says. "Inasmuch as ye have done it unto one of the least of these my brethren, ye have done it unto me" (*Youth's Instructor,* Jan. 17, 1901).

Those Written in the Book of Life

There shall be a time of trouble, such as never was since there was a nation even to that same time: and at that time thy people shall be delivered, every one that shall be found written in the book. Daniel 12:1.

As we approach the perils of the last days, the temptations of the enemy become stronger and more determined. Satan has come down in great power, knowing that his time is short; and he is working "with all deceivableness of unrighteousness in them that perish." The warning comes to us through God's Word, that, if it were possible, he would deceive the very elect.

Wonderful events are soon to open before the world. The end of all things is at hand. The time of trouble is about to come upon the people of God. Then it is that the decree will go forth forbidding those who keep the Sabbath of the Lord to buy or sell, and threatening them with punishment, and even death, if they do not observe the first day of the week as the Sabbath.

"And at that time shall Michael stand up, the great prince which standeth for the children of thy people: and there shall be a time of trouble, such as never was since there was a nation even to that same time: and at that time thy people shall be delivered, every one that shall be found written in the book." By this we see the importance of having our names written in the book of life. All whose names are registered there will be delivered from Satan's power, and Christ will command that their filthy garments be removed, and that they be clothed with His righteousness. "And they shall be mine, saith the Lord of hosts, in that day when I make up my jewels; and I will spare them, as a man spareth his own son that serveth him."

In the time of trouble, Satan stirs up the wicked, and they encircle the people of God to destroy them. But he does not know that "pardon" has been written opposite their names in the books of heaven. He does not know that the command has been given, "Take away the filthy garments" from them, clothe them with "change of raiment," and set "a fair mitre" upon their heads.

The promise made to Joshua is made to all the remnant people of God: "if thou wilt walk in my ways [not in your own ways], and if thou wilt keep my charge, then thou shalt also judge my house, and shalt also keep my courts, and I will give thee places to walk among these that stand by." Who are these that stand by? They are the angels of God. Could our eyes be opened, as were those of the servant of Elisha at Dothan, we should see evil angels all around us, urging their presence upon us, and watching for an opportunity to tempt and overthrow us; we should also see holy angels guarding us, and with their light and power pressing back the evil angels (*Historical Sketches,* pp. 155, 156).

All Judgment to the Son

For as the Father hath life in himself; so hath he given to the Son to have life in himself; and hath given him authority to execute judgment also, because he is the Son of man.
John 5:26, 27.

To His Son the Father has committed all judgment. Christ will declare the reward of loyalty. "The Father judgeth no man, but hath committed all judgment unto the Son. . . . And hath given him authority to execute judgment also, because he is the Son of man." Christ accepted humanity and lived on this earth a pure, sanctified life. For this reason He has received the appointment of judge. He who occupies the position of judge is God manifest in the flesh. What a joy it will be to recognize in Him our Teacher and Redeemer, bearing still the marks of the crucifixion, from which shine beams of glory, giving additional value to the crowns which the redeemed receive from His hands, the very hands outstretched in blessing over His disciples as He ascended. The very voice which said, "Lo, I am with you alway, even unto the end of the world," bids His ransomed ones welcome to His presence. The very One who gave His precious life for them, who by His grace moved their hearts to repentance, who awakened them to their need of repentance, receives them now into His joy. Oh, how they love Him! The realization of their hope is infinitely greater than their expectation. Their joy is complete, and they take their glittering crowns and cast them at their Redeemer's feet. . . .

The judgment will be conducted in accordance with the rules God has laid down. By the law which men are now called upon to obey, but which many refuse to accept, all will be judged. As by it character is tested, every man will find his proper place in one of two classes. He will either be holy to the Lord through obedience to His law, or be stained with sin through transgression. . . . He will place the sheep on His right hand, and the goats on His left. Then men and women will see that their course of action has decided their destiny (*Review and Herald,* June 18, 1901).

To Christ has been committed all judgment, because He is the Son of man. Nothing escapes His knowledge. However high the rank and great the power of spiritual apostates, One higher and greater has borne the sin of the whole world. He is infinite in righteousness, in goodness, and in truth. He has power to withstand principalities and powers and spiritual wickedness in high places. Armed and equipped as the Captain of the Lord's host, He comes to the front in defense of His people. His righteousness covers all who love and trust Him. The General of armies, He leads out the heavenly host to stand as a wall of fire about His people. He alone is the judge of their righteousness, for He created them, and at infinite cost to Himself redeemed them. He will see that obedience to God's commandments is rewarded (*The SDA Bible Commentary,* Ellen G. White Comments, vol. 5, p. 1134).

The King Is Coming

And when these things begin to come to pass, then look up, and lift up your heads; for your redemption draweth nigh. Luke 21:28.

Christ had bidden His people watch for the signs of His advent and rejoice as they should behold the tokens of their coming King. "When these things begin to come to pass," He said, "then look up, and lift up your heads; for your redemption draweth nigh." He pointed His followers to the budding trees of spring, and said: "When they now shoot forth, ye see and know of your own selves that summer is now nigh at hand. So likewise ye, when ye see these things come to pass, know ye that the kingdom of God is nigh at hand" (Luke 21:28, 30, 31).

But as the spirit of humility and devotion in the church had given place to pride and formalism, love for Christ and faith in His coming had grown cold. Absorbed in worldliness and pleasure seeking, the professed people of God were blinded to the Savior's instructions concerning the signs of His appearing. The doctrine of the Second Advent had been neglected; the scriptures relating to it were obscured by misinterpretation, until it was, to a great extent, ignored and forgotten. Especially was this the case in the churches of America. The freedom and comfort enjoyed by all classes of society, the ambitious desire for wealth and luxury, begetting an absorbing devotion to money-making, the eager rush for popularity and power, which seemed to be within the reach of all, led men to center their interests and hopes on the things of this life, and to put far in the future that solemn day when the present order of things should pass away.

When the Savior pointed out to His followers the signs of His return, He foretold the state of backsliding that would exist just prior to His second advent. There would be, as in the days of Noah, the activity and stir of worldly business and pleasure seeking—buying, selling, planting, building, marrying, and giving in marriage—with forgetfulness of God and the future life. For those living at this time, Christ's admonition is: "Take heed to yourselves, lest at any time your hearts be overcharged with surfeiting, and drunkenness, and cares of this life, and so that day come upon you unawares." "Watch ye therefore, and pray always, that ye may be accounted worthy to escape all these things that shall come to pass, and to stand before the Son of man" (Luke 21:34, 36) (*The Great Controversy,* pp. 308, 309).

We are to contend most earnestly for the faith once delivered to the saints. . . . We are now to unify, and . . . prepare the way for our coming King. Let us increase in a knowledge of the truth, and render all excellence and glory due to Him who is one with the Father. Let us seek most earnestly for the heavenly anointing, the Holy Spirit (*Medical Ministry,* p. 22).

Enoch and the Second Coming of Christ

And Enoch also, the seventh from Adam, prophesied . . . saying, Behold, the Lord cometh with ten thousands of his saints, to execute judgment upon all. Jude 14, 15.

The pure and lovely Garden of Eden, from which our first parents were driven, remained until God purposed to destroy the earth by a flood. God had planted that garden and specially blessed it, and in His wonderful providence He withdrew it from the earth, and will return it to the earth again more gloriously adorned than before it was removed from the earth. God purposed to preserve a specimen of His perfect work of creation free from the curse wherewith He had cursed the earth.

The Lord opened more fully to Enoch the plan of salvation, and by the Spirit of prophecy carried him down through the generations which should live after the Flood, and showed him the great events connected with the second coming of Christ and the end of the world (Jude 14).

Enoch was troubled in regard to the dead. It seemed to him that the righteous and the wicked would go to the dust together, and that would be their end. He could not clearly see the life of the just beyond the grave. In prophetic vision he was instructed in regard to the Son of God, who was to die man's sacrifice, and was shown the coming of Christ in the clouds of heaven, attended by the angelic host, to give life to the righteous dead and ransom them from their graves. He also saw the corrupt state of the world at the time when Christ should appear the second time—that there would be a boastful, presumptuous, self-willed generation arrayed in rebellion against the law of God and denying the only Lord God and our Lord Jesus Christ, and trampling upon His blood and despising His atonement. He saw the righteous crowned with glory and honor while the wicked were separated from the presence of the Lord and consumed with fire. . . .

Enoch continued to grow more heavenly while communing with God. His face was radiant with a holy light which would remain upon his countenance while instructing those who would hear his words of wisdom. His heavenly and dignified appearance struck the people with awe. The Lord loved Enoch because he steadfastly followed Him and abhorred iniquity and earnestly sought heavenly knowledge, that he might do His will perfectly. He yearned to unite himself still more closely to God, whom he feared, reverenced, and adored. God would not permit Enoch to die as other men, but sent His angels to take him to heaven without seeing death. In the presence of the righteous and the wicked, Enoch was removed from them. Those who loved him thought that God might have left him in some of his places of retirement, but after seeking him diligently, and being unable to find him, reported that he was not, for God took him (*The Story of Redemption,* pp. 58, 59).

Arouse to Action

Watch ye therefore, and pray always, that ye may be accounted worthy to escape all these things that shall come to pass, and to stand before the Son of man. Luke 21:36.

I was shown our danger, as a people, of becoming assimilated to the world rather than to the image of Christ. We are now upon the very borders of the eternal world, but it is the purpose of the adversary of souls to lead us to put far off the close of time. Satan will in every conceivable manner assail those who profess to be the commandment-keeping people of God and to be waiting for the second appearing of our Savior in the clouds of heaven with power and great glory. He will lead as many as possible to put off the evil day and become in spirit like the world, imitating its customs. I felt alarmed as I saw that the spirit of the world was controlling the hearts and minds of many who make a high profession of the truth. Selfishness and self-indulgence are cherished by them, but true godliness and sterling integrity are not cultivated.

The angel of God pointed to those who profess the truth, and in a solemn voice repeated these words: "And take heed to yourselves, lest at any time your hearts be overcharged with surfeiting, and drunkenness, and cares of this life, and so that day come upon you unawares. For as a snare shall it come on all them that dwell on the face of the whole earth. Watch ye therefore, and pray always, that ye may be accounted worthy to escape all these things that shall come to pass, and to stand before the Son of man."

In consideration of the shortness of time we as a people should watch and pray, and in no case allow ourselves to be diverted from the solemn work of preparation for the great event before us. Because the time is apparently extended, many have become careless and indifferent in regard to their words and actions. They do not realize their danger and do not see and understand the mercy of our God in lengthening their probation, that they may have time to form characters for the future, immortal life. Every moment is of the highest value. Time is granted them, not to be employed in studying their own ease and becoming dwellers on the earth, but to be used in the work of overcoming every defect in their own characters and in helping others, by example and personal effort, to see the beauty of holiness. God has a people upon the earth who in faith and holy hope are tracing down the roll of fast-fulfilling prophecy and are seeking to purify their souls by obeying the truth, that they may not be found without the wedding garment when Christ shall appear. . . . The signs foretold in prophecy are fast fulfilling around us. This should arouse every true follower of Christ to zealous action (*Testimonies,* vol. 4, pp. 306, 307).

To All the World

And he said unto them, Go ye into all the world, and preach the gospel to every creature. Mark 16:15.

The light that God has given His people is not to be shut up within the churches that already know the truth. It is to be shed abroad into the dark places of the earth. Those who walk in the light as Christ is in the light will cooperate with the Savior by revealing to others what He has revealed to them. It is God's purpose that the truth for this time shall be made known to every kindred and nation and tongue and people. In the world today men and women are absorbed in the search for worldly gain and worldly pleasure. There are thousands upon thousands who give no time or thought to the salvation of the soul. The time has come when the message of Christ's soon coming is to sound throughout the world.

Unmistakable evidences point to the nearness of the end. The warning is to be given in certain tones. The way must be prepared for the coming of the Prince of Peace in the clouds of heaven. There is much to be done in the cities that have not yet heard the truth for this time. We are not to establish institutions to rival in size and splendor the institutions of the world; but in the name of the Lord, with the untiring perseverance and unflagging zeal that Christ brought into His labors, we are to carry forward the work of the Lord.

As a people we greatly need to humble our hearts before God, pleading His forgiveness for our neglect to fulfill the gospel commission. We have made large centers in a few places, leaving unworked many important cities. Let us now take up the work appointed us and proclaim the message that is to arouse men and women to a sense of their danger. . . .

Everything in the universe calls upon those who know the truth to consecrate themselves unreservedly to the proclamation of the truth as it has been made known to them in the third angel's message. That which we see and hear calls us to our duty. The working of satanic agencies calls every Christian to stand in his lot. . . .

Men and women are needed whose hearts are touched with human suffering and whose lives give evidence that they are receiving and imparting light and life and grace.

The people of God are to come close to Christ in self-denial and sacrifice, their one aim being to give the message of mercy to all the world. Some will work in one way and some in another, as the Lord shall call and lead them. But they are all to strive together, seeking to make the work a perfect whole. With pen and voice they are to labor for Him. The printed word of truth is to be translated into different languages and carried to the ends of the earth. . . . Every believer, educated or uneducated, can bear the message (*Testimonies,* vol. 9, pp. 24-26).

We Are Capable of Better Things

For when we were yet without strength, in due time Christ died for the ungodly.
Romans 5:6.

Society today is fast approaching the condition of the world before the Flood. As children grow up to youth, and youth to manhood and womanhood, they are becoming full of self-sufficiency, maturing rapidly in the knowledge of evil. . . . The youth of today are educated in crime by reading the stories which fill the popular publications. Having no regard for the right because it is right, as they read stories of theft, murder, and every other species of crime, they are led to devise means by which they could improve upon the criminals' methods, and escape detection. Foul publications assist in perfecting the education of the youth in the way that leads to perdition. The youth of our cities breathe in the tainted, polluted atmosphere of crime; the evil influence is then communicated to the country, and the whole community becomes contaminated. Some of the rulers of the earth are not men of moral worth. They have no desire to check the publication of this foul literature which is increasing year by year, and which feeds the passion for crime and evil. Stories of criminal life such as are found in the papers of the day, and so-called revelations of the future, are treated as realities. . . . Christ saw the conflict that is approaching, and has sent us word to watch and pray, lest we enter into temptation. He has warned us that "as it was in the days of Noe, so shall it be also in the days of the Son of man. . . . Even thus shall it be in the day when the Son of man is revealed."

We are not warned against properly participating in business transactions, but against carrying to excess that which is lawful in itself, against allowing our minds to be so absorbed in earthly things that we shall not discern the important things that concern our eternal interest. We are warned against indulging perverted appetite, against surfeiting and drunkenness. . . .

But even in the corrupt condition in which the society of today is, there are souls capable of better things—souls represented by Christ under the symbol of "the lost pearl." Christ gave up everything, that He might seek and save that which was lost, that He might recover the pearl that He valued at infinite cost. What are we ready to do to cooperate with Him in this work? What sacrifice are we ready to make? . . .

When we consider that Christ died for the ungodly while they were yet sinners, we are led to realize how willing and even anxious He is to bless us, that we may be a blessing to others (*Review and Herald,* Apr. 21, 1896).

Redeeming the Time

Awake thou that sleepest, and arise from the dead, and Christ shall give thee light. See then that ye walk circumspectly, . . . redeeming the time, because the days are evil. Ephesians 5:14-16.

We are living in the most solemn period of this world's history. The destiny of earth's teeming multitudes is about to be decided. . . . We need to be guided by the Spirit of truth. . . .

Many are deceived as to their true condition before God. They congratulate themselves upon the wrong acts which they do not commit, and forget to enumerate the good and noble deeds which God requires of them, but which they have neglected to perform. It is not enough that they are trees in the garden of God. They are to answer His expectation by bearing fruit. He holds them accountable for their failure to accomplish all the good which they could have done, through His grace strengthening them. In the books of heaven they are registered as cumberers of the ground. Yet the case of even this class is not utterly hopeless. With those who have slighted God's mercy and abused His grace, the heart of long-suffering love yet pleads. "Wherefore . . . awake thou that sleepest, and arise from the dead, and Christ shall give thee light. See then that ye walk circumspectly, . . . redeeming the time, because the days are evil" (Ephesians 5:14-16).

When the testing time shall come, those who have made God's Word their rule of life will be revealed. In summer there is no noticeable difference between evergreens and other trees; but when the blasts of winter come, the evergreens remain unchanged, while other trees are stripped of their foliage. So the falsehearted professor may not now be distinguished from the real Christian, but the time is just upon us when the difference will be apparent. Let opposition arise, let bigotry and intolerance again bear sway, let persecution be kindled, and the halfhearted and hypocritical will waver and yield the faith; but the true Christian will stand firm as a rock, his faith stronger, his hope brighter, than in days of prosperity.

Says the psalmist: "Thy testimonies are my meditation." "Through thy precepts I get understanding: therefore I hate every false way" (Psalm 119:99, 104).

"Happy is the man that findeth wisdom." "He shall be as a tree planted by the waters, and that spreadeth out her roots by the river, and shall not see when heat cometh, but her leaf shall be green; and shall not be careful in the year of drought, neither shall cease from yielding fruit" (Proverbs 3:13; Jeremiah 17:8) (*The Great Controversy,* pp. 601, 602).

Not by its name, but by its fruit, is the value of a tree determined (*The Desire of Ages,* p. 107).

Steadfast Unto the End

Wherefore, beloved, seeing that ye look for such things, be diligent that ye may be found of him in peace, without spot, and blameless. 2 Peter 3:14.

Looking down through the ages to the close of time, Peter was inspired to outline conditions that would exist in the world just prior to the second coming of Christ. "There shall come in the last days scoffers," he wrote, "walking after their own lusts, and saying, Where is the promise of his coming? for since the fathers fell asleep, all things continue as they were from the beginning of the creation." But "when they shall say, Peace and safety; then sudden destruction cometh upon them" (1 Thessalonians 5:3). Not all, however, would be ensnared by the enemy's devices. As the end of all things earthly should approach, there would be faithful ones able to discern the signs of the times. . . . There would be a remnant who would endure to the end.

Peter kept alive in his heart the hope of Christ's return, and he assured the church of the certain fulfillment of the Savior's promise, "If I go and prepare a place for you, I will come again, and receive you unto myself" (John 14:3). To the tried and faithful ones the coming might seem long delayed, but the apostle assured them: "The Lord is not slack concerning his promise, as some men count slackness; but is longsuffering to us-ward, not willing that any should perish, but that all should come to repentance. But the day of the Lord will come as a thief in the night; in the which the heavens shall pass away with a great noise, and the elements shall melt with fervent heat, the earth also and the works that are therein shall be burned up.

"Seeing then that all these things shall be dissolved, what manner of persons ought ye to be in all holy conversation and godliness, looking for and hasting unto the coming of the day of God, wherein the heavens being on fire shall be dissolved, and the elements shall melt with fervent heat? Nevertheless we, according to his promise, look for new heavens and a new earth, wherein dwelleth righteousness.

"Wherefore, beloved, seeing that ye look for such things, be diligent that ye may be found of him in peace, without spot, and blameless. And account that the longsuffering of our Lord is salvation; even as our beloved brother Paul also according to the wisdom given unto him hath written unto you. . . . Ye therefore, beloved, seeing ye know these things before, beware lest ye also, being led away with the error of the wicked, fall from your own steadfastness. But grow in grace, and in the knowledge of our Lord and Savior Jesus Christ" (2 Peter 3:9-18) (*The Acts of the Apostles,* pp. 535-537).

The Last Crisis

Justice standeth afar off: for truth is fallen in the street, and equity cannot enter. Isaiah 59:14.

We are living in the time of the end. The fast-fulfilling signs of the times declare that the coming of Christ is near at hand. The days in which we live are solemn and important. The Spirit of God is gradually but surely being withdrawn from the earth. Plagues and judgments are already falling upon the despisers of the grace of God. The calamities by land and sea, the unsettled state of society, the alarms of war, are portentous. They forecast approaching events of the greatest magnitude.

The agencies of evil are combining their forces and consolidating. They are strengthening for the last great crisis. Great changes are soon to take place in our world, and the final movements will be rapid ones.

The condition of things in the world shows that troublous times are right upon us. The daily papers are full of indications of a terrible conflict in the near future. Bold robberies are of frequent occurrence. Strikes are common. Thefts and murders are committed on every hand. Men possessed of demons are taking the lives of men, women, and little children. Men have become infatuated with vice, and every species of evil prevails.

The enemy has succeeded in perverting justice and in filling men's hearts with the desire for selfish gain. "Justice standeth afar off: for truth is fallen in the street, and equity cannot enter." In the great cities there are multitudes living in poverty and wretchedness, well-nigh destitute of food, shelter, and clothing; while in the same cities are those who have more than heart could wish, who live luxuriously, spending their money on richly furnished houses, on personal adornment, or worse still, upon the gratification of sensual appetites, upon liquor, tobacco, and other things that destroy the powers of the brain, unbalance the mind, and debase the soul. The cries of starving humanity are coming up before God, while by every species of oppression and extortion men are piling up colossal fortunes (*Testimonies,* vol. 9, pp. 11, 12).

The Scriptures describe the condition of the world just before Christ's second coming (*ibid.,* p. 13).

Fearful tests and trials await the people of God. The spirit of war is stirring the nations from one end of the earth to the other. But in the midst of the time of trouble that is coming—a time of trouble such as has not been since there was a nation—God's chosen people will stand unmoved. Satan and his host cannot destroy them, for angels that excel in strength will protect them (*ibid.,* p. 17).

Called to Be Witnesses

Let your light so shine before men, that they may see your good works, and glorify your Father which is in heaven. Matthew 5:16.

In a special sense Seventh-day Adventists have been set in the world as watchmen and light bearers. To them has been entrusted the last warning for a perishing world. On them is shining wonderful light from the Word of God. They have been given a work of the most solemn import—the proclamation of the first, second, and third angels' messages. There is no other work of so great importance. They are to allow nothing else to absorb their attention.

The most solemn truths ever entrusted to mortals have been given us to proclaim to the world. The proclamation of these truths is to be our work. The world is to be warned, and God's people are to be true to the trust committed to them. They are not to engage in speculation, neither are they to enter into business enterprises with unbelievers; for this would hinder them in their God-given work.

Christ says of His people: "Ye are the light of the world" (Matthew 5:14). It is not a small matter that the counsels and plans of God have been so clearly opened to us. It is a wonderful privilege to be able to understand the will of God as revealed in the sure word of prophecy. This places on us a heavy responsibility. God expects us to impart to others the knowledge that He has given us. It is His purpose that divine and human instrumentalities shall unite in the proclamation of the warning message.

So far as his opportunities extend, everyone who has received the light of truth is under the same responsibility as was the prophet of Israel to whom came the word: "Son of man, I have set thee a watchman unto the house of Israel; therefore thou shalt hear the word of my mouth, and warn them from me" (Ezekiel 33:7). . . .

In clear, distinct rays light has come to us, showing us that the great day of the Lord is near at hand, "even at the doors." Let us read and understand before it is too late.

We are to be consecrated channels, through which the heavenly life is to flow to others. The Holy Spirit is to animate and pervade the whole church, purifying and cementing hearts. Those who have been buried with Christ in baptism are to rise to newness of life. . . . Upon us is laid a sacred charge. The commission has been given us: "Go therefore and make disciples of all nations" (Matthew 28:19, RSV). . . . You are dedicated to the work of making known the gospel of salvation. Heaven's perfection is to be your power (*Testimonies,* vol. 9, pp. 19-21).

December
10

Seek to Save the Lost

Ye have not chosen me, but I have chosen you, and ordained you, that ye should go and bring forth fruit, and that your fruit should remain. John 15:16.

This commission rests upon everyone who claim to believe in Jesus Christ. We are to seek to save those that are lost. . . .

The true worker for God wrestles with God in prayer, and puts intense earnestness into the work of saving lost souls. He does not seek to exalt self by word or deed, but simply seeks to win souls. God pronounces the purest, the meekest, the most childlike Christian, the best worker for Him, the mightiest in labor for souls. Heavenly intelligences can work with the man or woman who will not absorb the glory to himself, but who will be willing that all the glory shall redound to the honor of God. It is the man who most feels his need of divine wisdom, the man who pleads for heavenly power, that will go forth from communion with Christ, to hold converse with souls perishing in their sins; and because he is anointed with the Spirit of the Lord, he will be successful where the learned minister may have failed. God has given lessons that are all-important in regard to the duty of every disciple. Not one need be in darkness; for it is evident that every Christian is to be a living epistle, known and read of all men.

Everyone who believes in Christ as a personal Savior is under bonds to God to be pure and holy, to be a spiritual worker, seeking to save the lost, whether they are great or small, rich or poor, bond or free. The greatest work on earth is to seek and to save those who are lost, for whom Christ has paid the infinite price of His own blood. Everyone is to do active service. . . . The sheep unsought is not brought back to the fold.

God depends upon you, the human agent, to fulfill your duty to the best of your ability, and He Himself will give the increase. If human agents would but cooperate with the divine intelligences, thousands of souls would be rescued. The Holy Spirit would give devoted workers glimpses of Jesus that would brace them for every conflict, that would elevate and strengthen them, and make them more than conquerors. . . . The Lord has promised that where two or three are met together in His name, there will He be in the midst. Those who meet together for prayer will receive an unction from the Holy One. There is great need of secret prayer, but there is also need that several Christians meet together, and unite with earnestness their petitions to God. In these small companies Jesus is present, the love of souls is deepened in the heart, and the Spirit puts forth its mighty energies, that human agents may be exercised in regard to saving those who are lost. Jesus ever . . . strove to impress upon His disciples that the Holy Spirit must enlighten, renew, and sanctify the soul (*Review and Herald,* June 30, 1896).

Radical Changes Are to Be Made

That ye may be blameless and harmless, the sons of God, without rebuke, in the midst of a crooked and perverse nation, among whom ye shine as lights in the world. Philippians 2:15.

The inhabitants of the heavenly universe expect the followers of Christ to shine as lights in the world. They are to show forth the power of the grace that Christ died to give men. God expects those who profess to be Christians to reveal in their lives the highest development of Christianity. They are recognized representatives of Christ, and they are to show that Christianity is a reality. They are to be men of faith, men of courage, whole-souled men, who, without questioning, trust in God and His promises.

All who would enter the city of God must during their earthly life set forth Christ in their dealings. It is this that constitutes them the messengers of Christ, His witnesses. They are to bear a plain, decided testimony against all evil practices, pointing sinners to the Lamb of God, who taketh away the sin of the world. He gives to all who receive Him, power to become the sons of God. Regeneration is the only path by which we can enter the city of God. It is narrow, and the gate by which we enter is strait; but along it we are to lead men and women and children, teaching them that, in order to be saved, they must have a new heart and a new spirit. The old, hereditary traits of character must be overcome. The natural desires of the soul must be changed. All deception, all falsifying, all evilspeaking, must be put away. The new life, which makes men and women Christlike, is to be lived.

There must be no pretense in the lives of those who have so sacred and solemn a message as we have been called to bear. . . .

Those who love Jesus will bring all in their lives into harmony with His will. They have chosen to be on the Lord's side, and their lives are to stand out in vivid contrast with the lives of worldlings. The tempter will come to them with his blandishments and bribes, saying: "All these things will I give thee if thou wilt . . . worship me." But they know that he has nothing worth receiving, and they refuse to yield to his temptations. Through the grace of God they are enabled to keep their purity of principle unsullied. Holy angels are close beside them, and Christ is revealed in their steadfast adherence to the truth. They are Christ's minutemen, bearing, as true witnesses, a decided testimony in favor of the truth. They show that there is a spiritual power that can enable men and women not to swerve an inch from truth and justice for all the gifts that men can bestow. Such ones, wherever they may be, will be honored of heaven because they have conformed their lives to the will of God, caring not what sacrifices they are called upon to make (*Testimonies,* vol. 9, pp. 22-24).

Nothing Between Us and God

In this you greatly rejoice, though now for a little while you may have had to suffer . . . all kinds of trials. These have come so that your faith . . . worth more than gold, . . . may be proved genuine and may result in praise, glory and honor when Jesus Christ is revealed.
1 Peter 1:6, 7, NIV.

When we are tempted to place our affections on any earthly object that has a tendency to absorb our love, we must seek grace to turn from it, and not allow it to come between us and our God. We want to keep before the mind's eye the mansions which Jesus has gone to prepare for us. We must not allow our houses and lands, our business transactions and worldly enterprises, to come between us and our God. We should keep before us the rich promises that He has left on record. We should study the great waymarks that point out the times in which we are living. We know that we are very near the close of this earth's history, and everything of a worldly nature should be secondary to the service of God. We should now pray most earnestly that we may be prepared for the struggles of the great day of God's preparation. We should rejoice in the prospect of soon being with Jesus in the mansions He has gone to prepare for us. Jesus can supply your every need, if you will look to Him and trust in Him. As you behold Him, you will be charmed with the riches of the glory of His divine love. The idolatrous love of things that are seen will be superseded by a higher and better love for things that are imperishable and precious. You may contemplate eternal riches until your affections are bound to things above, and you may be an instrument in directing others to set their affections on heavenly treasures. You can help them to see that money spent needlessly is wasted, and worse than wasted; for it might have been used in presenting the truth to souls who are ready to perish. If the spendthrift is redeemed, it will be by having an object placed before him that will show him the sin of wasting his Lord's goods. The Lord requires His servants to trade upon the goods that He has put in their charge. The talents which He has given to them are to be improved by exercise. The money placed in their hands is to be put out to the exchangers. . . . Those who rightly value money are those who see its availability in bringing the truth before those who have never heard it, and by this means rescuing them from the power of the enemy. The soul who accepts the truth will find his love for earthly things dislodged. He sees the surpassing glory of heavenly things, and appreciates the excellency of that which relates to everlasting life. He is charmed with the unseen and eternal. His grasp loosens from earthly things; he fastens his eye with admiration upon the invisible glories of the heavenly world. He realizes that his trials are working out for him a far more exceeding and eternal weight of glory, and in comparison to the riches that are his to enjoy, he counts them light afflictions which are but for a moment (*Review and Herald*, June 23, 1896).

Then We Shall Know

O the depths of the riches both of the wisdom and knowledge of God! how unsearchable are his judgments, and his ways past finding out! Romans 11:33.

It is Satan's settled purpose to cut off all communications between God and His people, that he may practice his deceptive wiles with no voice to warn them of their danger. If he can lead men to distrust the messenger, or to attach no sacredness to the message, he knows that they will feel under no obligation to heed the word of God to them. And when light is set aside as darkness, Satan has things his own way.

Our God is a jealous God; He is not to be trifled with. He who does all things according to the counsel of His own will has been pleased to place men under various circumstances, and to enjoin upon them duties and observances peculiar to the times in which they live and the conditions under which they are placed. If they would prize the light given them, their faculties would be greatly enlarged and ennobled, and broader views of truth would be opened before them. The mystery of eternal things, and especially the wonderful grace of God as manifested in the plan of redemption, would be unfolded to their minds; for spiritual things are spiritually discerned. . . .

Jesus is waiting with longing desire to open before His people the glory that will attend His second advent, and to carry them forward to a contemplation of the landscape of bliss. There are wonders to be revealed. A long lifetime of prayer and research will leave much unexplored and unexplained. But what we know not now will be revealed hereafter. The work of instruction begun here will be carried on to all eternity. The Lamb, as He leads the hosts of the redeemed to the fountain of living waters, will impart rich stores of knowledge; He will unravel mysteries in the works and providence of God that have never before been understood.

We can never by searching find out God. He does not lay open His plans to prying, inquisitive minds. We must not attempt to lift with presumptuous hand the curtain behind which He veils His majesty. The apostle exclaims, "How unsearchable are his judgments, and his ways past finding out!" It is a proof of His mercy that there is the hiding of His power, that He is enshrouded in the awful clouds of mystery and obscurity; for to lift the curtain that conceals the Divine Presence is death. No mortal mind can penetrate the secrecy in which the Mighty One dwells and works. We can comprehend no more of His dealings with us and the motives that actuate Him than He sees fit to reveal. He orders everything in righteousness, and we are not to be dissatisfied and distrustful, but to bow in reverent submission. He will reveal to us as much of His purposes as it is for our good to know; and beyond that we must trust the hand that is omnipotent, the heart that is full of love (*Review and Herald,* Apr. 7, 1885).

The Lord Will Come More Quickly Than Many Expect

And will not God bring about justice for his chosen ones, who cry out to him day and night? Will he keep putting them off? I tell you, he will see that they get justice, and quickly. Luke 18:7, 8, NIV.

Could men see with heavenly vision, they would behold companies of angels that excel in strength stationed about those who have kept the word of Christ's patience. With sympathizing tenderness, angels have witnessed their distress and have heard their prayers. They are waiting the word of their Commander to snatch them from their peril. But they must wait yet a little longer. The people of God must drink of the cup and be baptized with the baptism. The very delay, so painful to them, is the best answer to their petitions. As they endeavor to wait trustingly for the Lord to work they are led to exercise faith, hope, and patience, which have been too little exercised during their religious experience. Yet for the elect's sake the time of trouble will be shortened. . . .

Though a general decree has fixed the time when commandment keepers may be put to death, their enemies will in some cases anticipate the decree, and before the time specified, will endeavor to take their lives. But none can pass the mighty guardians stationed about every faithful soul. Some are assailed in their flight from the cities and villages; but the swords raised against them break and fall powerless as a straw. Others are defended by angels in the form of men of war.

In all ages, God has wrought through holy angels for the succor and deliverance of His people. Celestial beings have taken an active part in the affairs of men. They have appeared clothed in garments that shone as the lightning; they have come as men in the garb of wayfarers. Angels have appeared in human form to men of God. They have rested, as if weary, under the oaks at noon. They have accepted the hospitalities of human homes. They have acted as guides to benighted travelers. They have, with their own hands, kindled the fires at the altar. They have opened prison doors and set free the servants of the Lord. Clothed with the panoply of heaven, they came to roll away the stone from the Savior's tomb.

In the form of men, angels are often in the assemblies of the righteous; and they visit the assemblies of the wicked, as they went to Sodom, to make a record of their deeds, to determine whether they have passed the boundary of God's forbearance. The Lord delights in mercy; and for the sake of a few who really serve Him, He restrains calamities and prolongs the tranquility of multitudes. Little do sinners against God realize that they are indebted for their own lives to the faithful few whom they delight to ridicule and oppress (*The Great Controversy,* pp. 630-632).

A Lesson in Temperance

He shall be great in the sight of the Lord, and shall drink neither wine nor strong drink; and he shall be filled with the Holy Ghost. Luke 1:15.

God had called the son of Zacharias to a great work, the greatest ever committed to men. In order to accomplish this work, he must have the Lord to work with him. And the Spirit of God would be with him if he heeded the instruction of the angel.

John was to go forth as Jehovah's messenger, to bring to men the light of God. He must give a new direction to their thoughts. He must impress them with the holiness of God's requirements, and their need of His perfect righteousness. Such a messenger must be holy. He must be a temple for the indwelling Spirit of God. In order to fulfill his mission, he must have a sound physical constitution, and mental and spiritual strength. Therefore it would be necessary for him to control the appetites and passions. He must be able so to control all his powers that he could stand among men as unmoved by surrounding circumstances as the rocks and mountains of the wilderness.

In the time of John the Baptist, greed for riches, and the love of luxury and display had become widespread. Sensuous pleasures, feasting and drinking, were causing physical disease and degeneracy, benumbing the spiritual perceptions, and lessening the sensibility to sin. John was to stand as a reformer. By his abstemious life and plain dress he was to rebuke the excesses of his time. Hence the directions given to the parents of John—a lesson of temperance by an angel from the throne of heaven.

In childhood and youth the character is most impressible. The power of self-control should then be acquired. By the fireside and at the family board influences are exerted whose results are as enduring as eternity. . . . The habits established in early years decide whether a man will be victorious or vanquished. . . .

As a prophet, John was "to turn the hearts of the fathers to the children, and the disobedient to the wisdom of the just; to make ready a people prepared for the Lord." In preparing the way for Christ's first advent, he was a representative of those who are to prepare a people for our Lord's second coming. The world is given to self-indulgence. Errors and fables abound. Satan's snares for destroying souls are multiplied. All who would perfect holiness in the fear of God must learn the lessons of temperance and self-control. The appetites and passions must be held in subjection to the higher powers of the mind. This self-discipline is essential to that mental strength and spiritual insight which will enable us to understand and to practice the sacred truths of God's Word. For this reason temperance finds its place in the work of preparation for Christ's second coming (*The Desire of Ages,* pp. 100, 101).

On the Edge of a Stupendous Crisis

Alas for the day! for the day of the Lord is at hand, and as a destruction from the Almighty shall it come. Joel 1:15.

Today the signs of the times declare that we are standing on the threshold of great and solemn events. Everything in our world is in agitation. Before our eyes is fulfilling the Savior's prophecy of the events to precede His coming: "Ye shall hear of wars and rumours of wars. . . . Nation shall rise against nation, and kingdom against kingdom: and there shall be famines, and pestilences, and earthquakes, in divers places" (Matthew 24:6, 7).

The present is a time of overwhelming interest to all living. Rulers and statesmen, men who occupy positions of trust and authority, thinking men and women of all classes, have their attention fixed upon the events taking place about us. They are watching the relations that exist among the nations. They observe the intensity that is taking possession of every earthly element, and they recognize that something great and decisive is about to take place—that the world is on the verge of a stupendous crisis.

The Bible, and the Bible only, gives a correct view of these things. Here are revealed the great final scenes in the history of our world, events that already are casting their shadows before, the sound of their approach causing the earth to tremble and men's hearts to fail them for fear.

"Behold, the Lord maketh the earth empty. . . . The earth . . . is defiled under the inhabitants thereof; because they have transgressed the laws, changed the ordinance, broken the everlasting covenant" (Isaiah 24:1-5). . . .

"I am pained at my very heart; . . . I cannot hold my peace, because thou hast heard, O my soul, the sound of the trumpet, the alarm of war. Destruction upon destruction is cried; for the whole land is spoiled" (Jeremiah 4:19, 20). . . .

"Because thou hast made the Lord, which is my refuge
Even the most High, thy habitation
There shall no evil befall thee
Neither shall any plague come nigh thy dwelling" (Psalm 91:9, 10). . . .

God will not fail His church in the hour of her greatest peril. He has promised deliverance. "I will bring again the captivity of Jacob's tents," He has declared, "and have mercy on his dwelling places" (Jeremiah 30:18).

Then will the purpose of God be fulfilled; the principles of His kingdom will be honored by all beneath the sun (*Prophets and Kings,* pp. 536-538).

Preparation for Christ's Coming

As the days of Noe were, so shall also the coming of the Son of man be. Matthew 24:37.

Noah preached to the people of his time that God would give them one hundred and twenty years in which to repent of their sins and find refuge in the ark, but they refused the gracious invitation. Abundant time was given them to turn from their sins, overcome their bad habits, and develop righteous characters. But inclination to sin, though weak at first with many, strengthened through repeated indulgence and hurried them on to irretrievable ruin. The merciful warning of God was rejected with sneers, with mockery and derision; and they were left in darkness to follow the course that their sinful hearts had chosen. But their unbelief did not hinder the predicted event. It came, and great was the wrath of God which was seen in the general ruin.

These words of Christ should sink into the hearts of all who believe present truth: "And take heed to yourselves, lest at any time your hearts be overcharged with surfeiting, and drunkenness, and cares of this life, and so that day come upon you unawares." Our danger is presented before us by Christ Himself. He knew the perils we should meet in these last days, and would have us prepare for them. . . .

Belief in the near coming of the Son of man in the clouds of heaven will not cause the true Christian to become neglectful and careless of the ordinary business of life. The waiting ones who look for the soon appearing of Christ will not be idle, but diligent in business. Their work will not be done carelessly and dishonestly, but with fidelity, promptness, and thoroughness. Those who flatter themselves that careless inattention to the things of this life is an evidence of their spirituality and of their separation from the world are under a great deception. Their veracity, faithfulness, and integrity are tested and proved in temporal things. If they are faithful in that which is least they will be faithful in much.

I have been shown that here is where many will fail to bear the test. They develop their true character in the management of temporal concerns. They manifest unfaithfulness, scheming, dishonesty, in dealing with their fellowmen. They do not consider that their hold upon the future, immortal life depends upon how they conduct themselves in the concerns of this life, and that the strictest integrity is indispensable to the formation of a righteous character (*Testimonies,* vol. 4, pp. 308-310).

Those who believe present truth should show their faith by their works. They should be sanctified through the truth which they profess to believe, for they are a savor of life unto life or of death unto death (*ibid.,* p. 308).

To Glorify God—Our Great Motive

Give unto the Lord the glory due unto his name. Psalm 29:2.

We are all living on probation. Those who have passed into their graves have been tested and tried, to see if they would realize their responsibility to serve God. A desire to glorify God should be to us the most powerful of all motives. It should lead us to make every exertion to improve the privileges and opportunities provided for us, to use wisely the Lord's goods. It should lead us to keep brain, bone, and muscle in the most healthful condition, that our physical strength and mental clearness may help us to be faithful stewards. Selfish interest must ever be held subordinate; for if given room to act, it contracts the intellect, hardens the heart, and weakens moral power. . . .

Daniel was regarded by the Lord as *a man,* because he was a steward who traded faithfully on his Lord's goods. He did not forget God, but placed himself in the channel of light, where he could commune with God in prayer. And we read that God gave Daniel and his fellows knowledge and skill in all learning and wisdom. . . .

In every place let those around you see that you give God the glory. Let man be put in the shade; let God appear as the only hope of the human race. Every man must rivet his character-building to the eternal Rock, Christ Jesus; then it will stand amid storm and tempest.

God will prepare the mind to recognize Him who alone can help the striving, struggling soul. All who stand under His banner He will educate to be faithful stewards of His grace. God has given man immortal principles, to which every human power must one day bow. He has given us truth in trust. The precious beams of this light are not to be hidden under a bushel, but are to give light to all that are in the house. Truth, imperishable truth, is to be made prominent. Show those with whom you come in contact that the truth is of consequence to you. It means much to you to stand by the principles that will live through the eternal ages.

God has given every man talents, that His name may be exalted, not that man may be lauded and praised, honored and glorified, while the Giver is forgotten. All have been entrusted with God's gifts, from the lowest and most poverty stricken to the highest and wealthiest. . . . Let none waste their God-given time in regrets that they have only one talent. Spend every moment in using the talents that you have. They are the Lord's, to be returned to Him. It is not your own property you are handling, but the Lord's. One day He will come to receive His own with usury. Faithfully fulfill your appointed stewardship, that you may meet Him in peace (*Review and Herald,* Sept. 12, 1899).

The Transformation of Grace

The end of all things is at hand: be ye therefore sober, and watch unto prayer. 1 Peter 4:7.

Christ] is pleased when His people manifest solidity, strength, and firmness of character, and when they have cheerful, happy, hopeful dispositions.

Says Peter, "Gird up the loins of your mind, be sober, and hope to the end for the grace that is to be brought unto you at the revelation of Jesus Christ." Here is a lesson for us to learn; here is a work for us to do to control the mind, not letting it drift on forbidden themes, or spend its energies on trifling subjects. "The end of all things is at hand: be ye therefore sober, and watch unto prayer." We are not only required to pray, but to guard the words and actions, and even the thoughts—to "watch unto prayer." If the mind is centered upon heavenly things, the conversation will run in the same channel. The heart will overflow at the contemplation of the Christian's hope, the exceeding great and precious promises left on record for our encouragement; and our rejoicing in view of the mercy and goodness of God need not be repressed; it is a joy that no man can take from us.

During the waking hours, the mind will be constantly employed. . . . There may be some spasmodic flashes of thought; but the mind is not disciplined to steady, sober reflection. There are themes that demand serious consideration. They are those connected with the great plan of redemption, which is soon to be finished. Jesus is about to be revealed in the clouds of heaven, and what manner of characters must we have to enable us to stand in that day? By dwelling upon these themes of eternal interest, the mind is strengthened, and the character developed. Here lies the foundation of that firm, unswerving principle which Joseph possessed. Here is the secret of growth in grace and in the knowledge of the truth.

The religion of Christ is not what many think it is, nor what their lives represent it to be. The love of God in the soul will have a direct influence upon the life, and will call the intellect and the affections into active, healthful exercise. The child of God will not rest satisfied until he is clothed with the righteousness of Christ, and sustained by His life-giving power. When he sees a weakness in his character, it is not enough to confess it again and again; he must go to work with determination and energy to overcome his defects by building up opposite traits of character. He will not shun this work because it is difficult. Untiring energy is required of the Christian; but he is not obliged to work in his own strength; divine power awaits his demand. Everyone who is sincerely striving for the victory over self will appropriate the promise, "My grace is sufficient for thee" (*Review and Herald,* June 10, 1884).

Watch and Pray

Take ye heed, watch and pray: for ye know not when the time is. Mark 13:33.

"Take ye heed, watch and pray" were the words of our Savior spoken in reference to the time of the end, and His second coming to take His faithful children home.

First, you are to watch. Watch, lest you should speak hastily, fretfully and impatiently. Watch, lest pride should find a place in your heart. Watch, lest evil passions should overcome you, instead of your subduing them. Watch, lest a careless, indifferent spirit comes upon you, and you neglect your duty and become light and trifling, and your influence savor of death, rather than life.

Second, you are to pray. Jesus would not have enjoined this upon you, unless there was actual necessity for it. It is well known to Him that of yourself you cannot overcome the many temptations of the enemy, and the many snares laid for your feet. He has not left you alone to do this; but has provided a way that you can obtain help. Therefore He has bid you to pray.

To pray aright is to ask God in faith for the very things you need. Go to your chamber, or in some retired place, and ask your Father for Jesus' sake to help you. There is power in that prayer that is sent up from a heart convinced of its own weakness, yet earnestly longing for that strength that comes from God. The earnest, fervent prayer will be heard and answered. Go to your God who is strong, and who loves to hear children pray, and, although you may feel very weak, and find yourself at times overcome by the enemy, because you have neglected the first command of our Savior, to watch, yet do not give up the struggle. Make stronger efforts yourself than before. Faint not. Cast yourself at the feet of Jesus, who has been tempted, and knows how to help such as are tempted. Confess your faults, your weakness, and that you must have help to overcome, or you perish. And as you ask, you must believe that God hears you. . . . God will help you. Angels will watch over you.

But before you can expect this help, you must do what you can on your part. Watch and pray. Let your prayers be fervent. Let this be the language of your heart, "I will not let thee go, except thou bless me." Have a set time, a special season for prayer at least three times a day. Morning, noon, and at night Daniel prayed to his God, notwithstanding the king's decree, and the fearful den of lions. He was not ashamed or afraid to pray, but with his windows opened he prayed three times a day. Did God forget His faithful servant when he was cast into the lions' den? O, No. He was with him there all night. He closed the mouths of these hungry lions, and they could not hurt the praying man of God (*Youth's Instructor,* October 1855).

Simple Faith Unites Us to God

Count yourselves dead to sin but alive to God in Christ Jesus. Romans 6:11, NIV.

We are living in a most solemn period of this earth's history. There is never time to sin; it is always perilous to continue in transgression; but in a special sense is this true at the present time. We are now upon the very borders of the eternal world and stand in a more solemn relation to time and to eternity than ever before. Now let every person search his own heart, and plead for the bright beams of the Sun of Righteousness to expel all spiritual darkness and cleanse from defilement. "If we confess our sins, he is faithful and just to forgive us our sins, and to cleanse us from all unrighteousness." Through faith, irrespective of feeling, Jesus, the Author of our salvation, the Finisher of our faith, will, by His precious grace, strengthen the moral powers, and the sinner may reckon himself "to be dead indeed unto sin, but alive unto God through Jesus Christ." Simple faith, with the love of Christ in the soul, unites the believer to God. While toiling in battle as a faithful soldier of Christ, he has the sympathy of the whole loyal universe. The ministering angels are round about him to aid in the conflict, so that he may boldly say, "The Lord is my helper," "the Lord is my strength and my shield"; I shall not be overcome. "By grace are ye saved through faith; and that not of yourselves: it is the gift of God."

The infinite wisdom and power of God are exerted in our behalf. The heavenly host are surely fighting our battles for us. They are always looking with intense interest upon the souls purchased by the Savior's blood. They see, through the sacrifice of Christ, the value of the human soul. It is always safe to be on the Lord's side, not halfheartedly, but wholly. It is this half-hearted, indifferent, careless work that separates your souls from Jesus, the source of your strength. Let this be your prayer: "Take everything from me, let me lose property, worldly honor, everything, but let Thy presence be with me." It is safe to commit the keeping of the soul to God, who reigns over all heaven and earth (*Testimonies to Ministers,* pp. 147, 148).

There must be thorough repentance, faith in our Savior Jesus Christ, vigilant watchfulness, unceasing prayer, and diligent searching of the Scriptures. God holds us responsible for all that we might be if we would improve our talents. . . . All our influence belongs to God. All that we acquire is to be used to His glory. All the property that the Lord has entrusted to us is to be held on the altar of God, to be returned to Him again. We are working out our own destiny. May God help us all to be wise for eternity (*ibid.,* p. 147).

An Invisible Struggle

Do not be afraid, Daniel. Since the first day that you set your mind to gain understanding and to humble yourself before your God, your words were heard, and I have come in response to them. But the prince of the Persian kingdom resisted me twenty-one days. Then Michael, one of the chief princes, came to help me, because I was detained there with the king of Persia. Daniel 10:12, 13, NIV.

We have before us in the Word of God instances of heavenly agencies working on the minds of kings and rulers, while at the same time satanic agencies were also at work on their minds. No human eloquence, in strongly set forth human opinions, can change the working of satanic agencies. Satan seeks continually to block the way, so that the truth shall be bound about by human devising; and those who have light and knowledge are in the greatest danger unless they constantly consecrate themselves to God, humiliating self, and realizing the peril of the times.

Heavenly beings are appointed to answer the prayers of those who are working unselfishly for the interests of the cause of God. The very highest angels in the heavenly courts are appointed to work out the prayers which ascend to God for the advancement of the cause of God. Each angel has his particular post of duty, which he is not permitted to leave for any other place. If he should leave, the powers of darkness would gain an advantage. . . .

Day by day the conflict between good and evil is going on. Why is it that those who have had many opportunities and advantages do not realize the intensity of this work? They should be intelligent in regard to this. God is the Ruler. By His supreme power He holds in check and controls earthly potentates. Through His agencies He does the work which was ordained before the foundation of the world.

As a people we do not understand as we should the great conflict going on between invisible agencies, the controversy between loyal and disloyal angels. Evil angels are constantly at work, planning their line of attack, controlling as commanders, kings, and rulers, the disloyal human forces. . . . I call upon the ministers of Christ to press home upon the understanding of all who come within the reach of their voice, the truth of the ministration of angels. Do not indulge in fanciful speculations. The Written Word is our only safety. We must pray as did Daniel, that we may be guarded by heavenly intelligences. As ministering spirits angels are sent forth to minister to those who shall be heirs of salvation. Pray, my brethren, pray as you have never prayed before. We are not prepared for the Lord's coming. We need to make thorough work for eternity (*The SDA Bible Commentary,* Ellen G. White Comments, vol. 4, p. 1173).

Lessons From the Antediluvians

Dear friends, build yourselves up in your most holy faith and pray in the Holy Spirit. Keep yourselves in God's love as you wait for the mercy of our Lord Jesus Christ to bring you to eternal life. Jude 20, 21, NIV.

Look at the picture which the world presents today. Dishonesty, fraud, and bankruptcies, violence and bloodshed, exist on every hand. The widows and the fatherless are robbed of their all. Plays, horse races, and amusements of every kind occupy the mind. In the church, sins have become fashionable. They are glossed over and excused. The right hand of fellowship is given to the very men who bring in false theories and sentiments. Thus the discernment and sensibilities have become deadened as to what constitutes right principles. Conscience has become insensible to the counsel and reproofs which have been given. The light given, calling to repentance, has been shut out by the thick cloud of unbelief and opposition brought in by human plans and human inventions.

The inhabitants of the antediluvian world had the warning given them prior to their overthrow; but the warning was not heeded. They refused to listen to the words of Noah; they mocked at his message. Righteous men lived in that generation. Before the destruction of the antediluvian world, Enoch bore his testimony unflinchingly. And in prophetic vision he saw the condition of the world at the present time. He said, "Behold, the Lord cometh with ten thousands of his saints, to execute judgment upon all, and to convince all that are ungodly among them of all their ungodly deeds which they have ungodly committed, and of all their hard speeches which ungodly sinners have spoken against him. These are murmurers, complainers, walking after their own lust; and their mouth speaketh great swelling words, having men's persons in admiration because of advantage." Jude leaves the testimony for the believers: "But, beloved, remember ye the words which were spoken before of the apostles of our Lord Jesus Christ; how that they told you there should be mockers in the last time, who should walk after their own ungodly lusts. These be they who separate themselves, sensual, having not the Spirit" (Jude 15-19) (*Review and Herald,* Nov. 1, 1906).

God determined to purify the world by a flood; but in mercy and love He gave the antediluvians a probation of one hundred and twenty years. During this time, while the ark was building, the voices of Noah, Methuselah, and many others were heard in warning and entreaty, and every blow struck on the ark was a warning message. . . .

The sermon preached by Enoch, and his translation to heaven was a convincing argument to all living in Enoch's time. It was an argument that Methuselah and Noah could use with power to show that the righteous could be translated (*The SDA Bible Commentary,* Ellen G. White Comments, vol. 1, p. 1088).

Waiting and Watching

Cast not away therefore your confidence, which hath great recompence of reward.
Hebrews 10:35.

Jesus is soon coming, and our position should be that of waiting and watching for His appearing. We should not allow anything to come in between us and Jesus. We must learn here to sing the song of heaven, so that when our warfare is over we can join in the song of the heavenly angels in the city of God. What is that song? It is praise, and honor, and glory unto Him that sitteth upon the throne, and unto the Lamb for ever and ever. We shall meet opposition; we shall be hated of all men for Christ's sake, and by Satan, because he knows that there is with the followers of Christ a divine power, which will undermine his influence. We cannot escape reproach. . . .

We should not allow our time to be so occupied with things of a temporal nature, or even with matters pertaining to the cause of God, that we shall pass on day after day without pressing close to the bleeding side of Jesus. We want to commune with Him daily. We are exhorted to fight the good fight of faith. It will be a hard battle to maintain a life of earnest faith; but if we cast ourselves wholly upon Christ, with a settled determination to cleave only to Him, we shall be able to repulse the enemy, and gain a glorious victory. The apostle Paul exhorts us, "Cast not away therefore your confidence, which hath great recompence of reward." Again he says, "Now the just shall live by faith." . . .

When we feel the least inclined to commune with Jesus, let us pray the most. By so doing we shall break Satan's snare, the clouds of darkness will disappear, and we shall realize the sweet presence of Jesus (*Historical Sketches,* pp. 145, 146).

Christians may have the joy of communion with Christ; they may have the light of His love, the perpetual comfort of His presence. Every step in life may bring us closer to Jesus, may give us a deeper experience of His love, and may bring us one step nearer to the blessed home of peace. Then let us not cast away our confidence, but have firm assurance, firmer than ever before. "Hitherto hath the Lord helped us," and He will help us to the end. Let us look to the monumental pillars, reminders of what the Lord has done to comfort us and save us from the hand of the destroyer. Let us keep fresh in our memory all the tender mercies that God has shown us—the tears He has wiped away, the pains He has soothed, the anxieties removed, the fears dispelled, the wants supplied, the blessings bestowed—thus strengthening ourselves for all that is before us (*Steps to Christ,* p. 125).

So surely as there never was a time when God was not, so surely there never was a moment when it was not the delight of the eternal mind to manifest His grace to humanity (*The SDA Bible Commentary,* Ellen G. White Comments, vol. 7, p. 934).

The First and Second Advent

So Christ was sacrificed once to take away the sins of many people; and he will appear a second time, not to bear sin, but to bring salvation to those who are waiting for him.
Hebrews 9:28, NIV.

At the first advent of Christ . . . the angels of heaven could scarcely be restrained from pouring forth their glories to grace the birth of the Son of God. . . . That birth, so little prepared for on earth, was celebrated in the heavenly courts with praise and thanksgiving in behalf of man.

While the shepherds on the hills of Bethlehem watched their flocks by night, "the angel of the Lord came upon them, and the glory of the Lord shone round about them." . . .

The leaders in Israel professed to understand the prophecies, but they had received false ideas in regard to the manner of Christ's coming. Satan had deceived them; and all the glories of Christ's second advent they applied to His first appearing. All the wonderful events clustering around His second coming, they looked for at His first. Therefore, when He came, they were not prepared to receive Him. . . .

Between the first and the second advent of Christ a wonderful contrast will be seen. No human language can portray the scenes of the second coming of the Son of man in the clouds of heaven. He is to come with His own glory, and with the glory of the Father and of the holy angels. He will come clad in the robe of light, which He has worn from the days of eternity. Angels will accompany Him. Ten thousand times ten thousand will escort Him on His way. The sound of the trumpet will be heard, calling the sleeping dead from the grave. The voice of Christ will penetrate the tomb, and pierce the ears of the dead, and "all that are in the graves . . . shall come forth." . . .

We are now amid the perils of the last days. The scenes of conflict are hastening on, and the day of days is just upon us. Are we prepared for the issue? Every deed, small and great, is to be brought into recognition. That which has been considered trivial here will then appear as it is. The two mites of the widow will be recognized. The cup of cold water offered, the prison visited, the hungry fed—each will bring its own reward. . . .

The serpent's head will soon be bruised and crushed. The glorious memorial of God's wonderful power is soon to be restored to its rightful place. Then paradise lost will be paradise restored. God's plan for the redemption of man will be complete. The Son of man will bestow upon the righteous the crown of everlasting life, and they shall "serve him day and night in his temple: and he that sitteth on the throne shall dwell among them" (Revelation 7:15) (*Review and Herald,* Sept. 5, 1899).

December
26

God Will Not Forget His Children

He that toucheth you toucheth the apple of his eye. Zechariah 2:8.

As the decree issued by the various rulers of Christendom against commandment keepers shall withdraw the protection of government and abandon them to those who desire their destruction, the people of God will flee from the cities and villages and associate together in companies, dwelling in the most desolate and solitary places. Many will find refuge in the strongholds of the mountains. Like the Christians of the Piedmont valleys, they will make the high places of the earth their sanctuaries and will thank God for "the munitions of rocks" (Isaiah 33:16). But many of all nations and of all classes, high and low, rich and poor, black and white, will be cast into the most unjust and cruel bondage. The beloved of God pass weary days, bound in chains, shut in by prison bars, sentenced to be slain, some apparently left to die of starvation in dark and loathsome dungeons. No human ear is open to hear their moans; no human hand is ready to lend them help.

Will the Lord forget His people in this trying hour? Did He forget faithful Noah when judgments were visited upon the antediluvian world? Did He forget Lot when the fire came down from heaven to consume the cities of the plain? Did He forget Joseph surrounded by idolaters in Egypt? Did He forget Elijah when the oath of Jezebel threatened him with the fate of the prophets of Baal? Did He forget Jeremiah in the dark and dismal pit of his prison house? Did He forget the three worthies in the fiery furnace? or Daniel in the den of lions? . . .

Though enemies may thrust them into prison, yet dungeon walls cannot cut off the communication between their souls and Christ. One who sees their every weakness, who is acquainted with every trial, is above all earthly powers; and angels will come to them in lonely cells, bringing light and peace from heaven. The prison will be as a palace; for the rich in faith dwell there, and the gloomy walls will be lighted up with heavenly light as when Paul and Silas prayed and sang praises at midnight in the Philippian dungeon (*The Great Controversy,* pp. 626, 627).

With earnest longing, God's people await the tokens of their coming King. . . . Light is gleaming upon the clouds above the mountaintops. Soon there will be a revealing of His glory. . . . The heavens glow with the dawning of eternal day, and like the melody of angel songs the words fall upon the ear; "Stand fast to your allegiance. Help is coming." Christ, the almighty Victor, holds out to His weary soldiers a crown of immortal glory; and His voice comes from the gates ajar: ". . . You are not warring against untried enemies. I have fought the battle in your behalf, and in My name you are more than conquerors" (*ibid.,* pp. 632, 633).

Fitted for Translation

For whatsoever is born of God overcometh the world: and this is the victory that overcometh the world, even our faith. 1 John 5:4.

God leads His people on, step by step. He brings them up to different points calculated to manifest what is in the heart. Some endure at one point, but fall off at the next. At every advanced point the heart is tested and tried a little closer. If the professed people of God find their hearts opposed to this straight work, it should convince them that they have a work to do to overcome, if they would not be spewed out of the mouth of the Lord. Said the angel: "God will bring His work closer and closer to test and prove every one of His people." Some are willing to receive one point; but when God brings them to another testing point, they shrink from it and stand back, because they find that it strikes directly at some cherished idol. Here they have opportunity to see what is in their hearts that shuts out Jesus. They prize something higher than the truth, and their hearts are not prepared to receive Jesus. Individuals are tested and proved a length of time to see if they will sacrifice their idols and heed the counsel of the True Witness. . . . Those who come up to every point, and stand every test, and overcome, be the price what it may, have heeded the counsel of the True Witness, and they will receive the latter rain, and thus be fitted for translation.

God proves His people in this world. This is the fitting-up place to appear in His presence. Here, in this world, in these last days, persons will show what power affects their hearts and controls their actions. If it is the power of divine truth, it will lead to good works. It will elevate the receiver, and make him noblehearted and generous, like His divine Lord. But if evil angels control the heart, it will be seen in various ways. The fruit will be selfishness, covetousness, pride, and evil passions.

The heart is deceitful above all things, and desperately wicked. Professors of religion are not willing to closely examine themselves to see whether they are in the faith; and it is a fearful fact that many are leaning on a false hope. . . . They seem to think that a profession of the truth will save them. When they subdue those sins which God hates, Jesus will come in and sup with them and they with Him. They will then draw divine strength from Jesus, and will grow up in Him, and be able with holy triumph to say: "Thanks be to God, which giveth us the victory through our Lord Jesus Christ" (*Testimonies,* vol. 1, pp. 187, 188).

The third angel is leading up a people, step by step, higher and higher. At every step they will be tested (*ibid.,* p. 190).

The Finishing Touch of Immortality

Beloved, now are we the sons of God, and it doth not yet appear what we shall be: but we know that, when he shall appear, we shall be like him; for we shall see him as he is. And every man that hath this hope in him purifieth himself, even as he is pure.
1 John 3:2, 3.

Through personal effort joined with the prayer of faith, the soul is trained. Day by day the character grows into the likeness of Christ; and finally, instead of being the sport of circumstances, instead of indulging selfishness and being carried away by light and trifling conversation, the man is master of his thoughts and words. It may cost a severe conflict to overcome habits which have been long indulged, but we may triumph through the grace of Christ. He invites us to learn of Him. He would have us practice self-control, and be perfect in character, working that which is well pleasing in His sight. "By their fruits ye shall know them" is His own standard of judging character.

If we are true to the promptings of the Spirit of God, we shall go on from grace to grace, and from glory to glory, until we shall receive the finishing touch of immortality.

"Beloved, now are we the sons of God, and it doth not yet appear what we shall be: but we know that, when he shall appear, we shall be like him; for we shall see him as he is." . . . Can any earthly promotion confer honor equal to this—to be sons of God, children of the heavenly King, members of the royal family? Man may be ambitious of the honor that his finite fellowman can bestow; but what will it avail? The nobility of earth are but men; they die, and return to dust; and there is no lasting satisfaction in their praise and honor. But the honor that comes from God is lasting. To be heirs of God and joint-heirs with Christ, is to be entitled to unsearchable riches—treasures of such value that in comparison with them the gold and silver, the gems and precious stones of earth, sink into insignificance. Through Christ we are offered joy unspeakable, an eternal weight of glory. "Eye hath not seen, nor ear heard, neither have entered into the heart of man, the things which God hath prepared for them that love him."

We are wanting in simple faith; we need to learn the art of trusting our very best friend. Although we see Him not, Jesus is watching over us with tender compassion; and He is touched with the feelings of our infirmities. No one in his great need ever looked to Him by faith, and was disappointed. . . . The Christian is . . . the happiest man in the world. He feels secure; for he trusts in Jesus, and enjoys His presence. His defense is "of God, which saveth the upright in heart." Do not defer this matter, but begin . . . to fix your minds more firmly upon Jesus and heavenly things, remembering that by beholding we become changed into the same image. Have courage in God (*Review and Herald,* June 10, 1884).

The Robe of Christ's Righteousness

And to her was granted that she should be arrayed in fine linen, clean and white: for the fine linen is the righteousness of saints. Revelation 19:8.

The faithful, praying ones are, as it were, shut in with God. They themselves know not how securely they are shielded. . . . But could their eyes be opened, . . . they would see the angels of God encamped about them, by their brightness and glory holding in check the hosts of darkness.

As the people of God afflict their souls before Him, pleading for purity of heart, the command is given, "Take away the filthy garments" from them, and the encouraging words are spoken, "Behold, I have caused thine iniquity to pass from thee, and I will clothe thee with change of raiment" (Zechariah 3:4). The spotless robe of Christ's righteousness is placed upon the tried, tempted, yet faithful children of God. The despised remnant are clothed in glorious apparel, nevermore to be defiled by the corruptions of the world. Their names are retained in the Lamb's book of life, enrolled among the faithful of all ages. They have resisted the wiles of the deceiver; they have not been turned from their loyalty by the dragon's roar. Now they are eternally secure from the tempter's devices. Their sins are transferred to the originator of sin. And the remnant are not only pardoned and accepted, but honored. "A fair miter" is set upon their heads. They are to be as kings and priests unto God. While Satan was urging his accusations and seeking to destroy this company, holy angels, unseen, were passing to and fro, placing upon them the seal of the living God. These are they that stand upon Mount Zion with the Lamb, having the Father's name written in their foreheads. They sing the new song before the throne, that song which no man can learn save the hundred and forty and four thousand, which were redeemed from the earth. "These are they which follow the Lamb whithersoever he goeth. These were redeemed from among men, being the firstfruits unto God and to the Lamb. And in their mouth was found no guile: for they are without fault before the throne of God" (Revelation 14:4, 5).

Now is reached the complete fulfillment of those words of the Angel: "Hear now, O Joshua the high priest, thou, and thy fellows that sit before thee: for they are men wondered at: for, behold, I will bring forth my servant the Branch" (Zechariah 3:8). Christ is revealed as the Redeemer and Deliverer of His people. Now indeed are the remnant "men wondered at," as the tears and humiliation of their pilgrimage give place to joy and honor in the presence of God and the Lamb. "In that day shall the branch of the Lord be beautiful and glorious, and the fruit of the earth shall be excellent and comely. . . . And it shall come to pass, that he that is left in Zion, and he that remaineth in Jerusalem, shall be called holy" (Isaiah 4:2, 3) (*Testimonies,* vol. 5, pp. 475, 476).

December

30

Learning for Eternity

And he made known to us the mystery of his will according to his good pleasure, which he purposed in Christ, to be put into effect when the times will have reached their fulfillment—to bring all things in heaven and on earth together under one head, even Christ. Ephesians 1:9, 10, NIV.

As we near the close of this world's history, the prophecies relating to the last days especially demand our study. The last book of the New Testament scriptures is full of truth that we need to understand. Satan has blinded the minds of many, so that they have been glad of any excuse for not making the Revelation their study. But Christ through His servant John has here declared what shall be in the last days, and He says, "Blessed is he that readeth, and they that hear the words of this prophecy, and keep those things which are written therein."

"This is life eternal," Christ said, "that they might know thee the only true God, and Jesus Christ, whom thou hast sent." Why is it that we do not realize the value of this knowledge? Why are not these glorious truths glowing in our hearts, trembling upon our lips, and pervading our whole being?

In giving us His Word, God has put us in possession of every truth essential for our salvation. Thousands have drawn water from these wells of life, yet there is no diminishing of the supply. Thousands have set the Lord before them, and by beholding have been changed into the same image. Their spirit burns within them as they speak of His character, telling what Christ is to them, and what they are to Christ. But these searchers have not exhausted these grand and holy themes. Thousands more may engage in the work of searching out the mysteries of salvation. As the life of Christ and the character of His mission are dwelt upon, rays of light will shine forth more distinctly at every attempt to discover truth. Each fresh search will reveal something more deeply interesting than has yet been unfolded. The subject is inexhaustible. The study of the incarnation of Christ, His atoning sacrifice and mediatorial work, will employ the mind of the diligent student as long as time shall last; and looking to heaven with its unnumbered years he will exclaim, "Great is the mystery of godliness."

In eternity we shall learn that which, had we received the enlightenment it was possible to obtain here, would have opened our understanding. The themes of redemption will employ the hearts and minds and tongues of the redeemed through the everlasting ages. They will understand the truths which Christ longed to open to His disciples, but which they did not have faith to grasp. Forever and forever new views of the perfection and glory of Christ will appear. Through endless ages will the faithful Householder bring forth from His treasure things new and old (*Christ's Object Lessons,* pp. 133, 134).

Partakers With Christ of His Glory

Lo, this is our God; we have waited for him, and he will save us. . . .
We will be glad and rejoice in his salvation. Isaiah 25:9.

Jesus is coming! But not to listen to the woes of mankind, and to hear the guilty sinner confess his sins, and to speak pardon to Him; for everyone's case will then be decided for life or death. Those who have lived in sin will remain sinners forever. Those who have confessed their sins to Jesus in the sanctuary, have made Him their friend, and have loved His appearing will have pardon written for all their sins, and they, having purified their souls "in obeying the truth," will remain pure and holy forever.

Jesus is coming as He ascended into heaven, only with additional splendor. He is coming with the glory of His Father, and all the holy angels with Him, to escort Him on His way. Instead of the cruel crown of thorns to pierce His holy temples, a crown of dazzling glory will deck His sacred brow. He will not then appear, the man of sorrows and acquainted with grief; but His countenance will shine brighter than the noonday sun. He will not wear a plain seamless coat, but a garment whiter than snow—of dazzling brightness.

Jesus is coming! But not to reign as a temporal prince. He will raise the righteous dead, change the living saints to a glorious immortality, and, with the saints, take the kingdom under the whole heaven. This kingdom will never end. Then those who have patiently waited for Jesus will be made like Him.

If one angel from heaven caused the Roman guard to fall as dead men, how can those who are unprepared, unholy, bear the sight and live, of seeing Jesus in the glory of His Father and ten thousand angels accompanying Him. O how can sinners bear this sight! They will cry for rocks and mountains to fall on them, and hide them from the face of Him that sitteth on the throne, and from the wrath of the Lamb. . . .

Seek a thorough preparation to meet Jesus, that when He appears you may exclaim with joy, "Lo, this is our God; we have waited for him, and he will save us." Eternal life will then be yours, and you will be a partaker with Christ of His glory, ever to hear His glorious approving voice, and behold His lovely person (*Youth's Instructor,* April 1854).

None who truly love Jesus will be sorry that He is coming again. And as they approach nearer to the coming of the Son of man, the true lovers of Jesus will look forward with joyous hope, and will seek to get all ready to behold Him whom their souls loveth, who died to redeem them (*ibid.*).

Scripture Index